Racism in the Irish Experience

# Racism in the
# Irish Experience

Steve Garner

Pluto Press

LONDON • DUBLIN • STERLING, VIRGINIA

First published 2004 by Pluto Press
345 Archway Road, London N6 5AA
and 22883 Quicksilver Drive, Sterling, VA 20166–2012, USA

Distributed in the Republic of Ireland and Northern Ireland by
Columba Mercier Distribution, 55A Spruce Avenue, Stillorgan
Industrial Park, Blackrock, Co. Dublin, Ireland.
Tel: + 353 1 294 2556. Fax: + 353 1 294 2564

www.plutobooks.com

British Library Cataloguing in Publication Data
A catalogue record for this book is available from the British Library

ISBN    0 7453 1997 1 hardback
ISBN    0 7453 1996 3 paperback

Library of Congress Cataloging in Publication Data
Garner, Steve.
    Racism in the Irish experience / Steve Garner.
        p. cm.
Includes bibliographical references (p.    ).
    ISBN 0–7453–1997–1 — ISBN 0–7453–1996–3 (pbk.)
    1. Racism—Ireland. 2. Ireland—Race relations. I. Title.
    DA927 .G37 2004
    305.8'009417—dc22
                                                            2003019286

10   9   8   7   6   5   4   3   2   1

Designed and produced for Pluto Press by
Chase Publishing Services, Fortescue, Sidmouth, EX10 9QG, England
Typeset from disk by Stanford DTP Services, Northampton, England
Printed and bound in the European Union by
Antony Rowe Ltd, Chippenham and Eastbourne, England

# Contents

*Acknowledgements*                                                    viii

Introduction                                                            1

1   Sociological Frameworks for Understanding Racism                    4

2   Money, Migrations and Attitudes                                    35

3   Racing the Irish in the Sixteenth and Seventeenth
    Centuries                                                          69

4   The 'Filthy Aristocracy of Skin': Becoming White in
    the USA                                                            91

5   In the Belly of the Beast: Nineteenth-Century Britain,
    Empire and the Role of 'Race' in Home Rule                        114

6   Other People's Diasporas: The 'Racialisation' of the
    Asylum Issue                                                       140

7   'New Racism', Old Racisms and the Role of Migratory
    Experience                                                         168

8   'Remember Blanqui?': Nation State, Community and
    Some Paradoxes of Irish Anti-Racism                               198

9   Beyond the New Socio-Economic 'Pale': Racialisation
    and belonging in Contemporary Ireland                             225

10  Conclusions                                                       247

Glossary                                                              254
Appendices                                                            256
    Appendix 1 Surveys on Attitudes Towards Minorities and
    Minorities' Experiences of Racism–Discrimination in the
    Republic of Ireland, 1972–2001                                    256
    Appendix 2 Address from the People of Ireland to their
    Countrymen and Countrywomen in America, 1842                      257
Notes                                                                 259
Bibliography                                                          274
Index                                                                 298

TABLES

Table 1    Suggested Specific Characteristics of Irish Racism        28
Table 2    Proportion Employed in each NACE Economic Sector,
1994 and 2002 (%)                                                     38
Table 3    Overall Growth in Terms of Gross Employment for
each NACE Economic Sector, 1994 and 2002 (000s)    38
Table 4    Distributive Impact of Irish Budgets During Low-
and High-Growth Periods                                               43
Table 5    Proportion of Profits, and Wages in Non-Agricultural
Income (as Net Value Added at Factor Cost and at
Market Prices), for Selected Years 1987–2001         46
Table 6    Breakdown of Population by Nationality                     50
Table 7    Immigration and Emigration into and from Ireland,
Selected Years, 1987–2002                                             51
Table 8    Work Permits Granted to Non-EU Nationals in
Ireland, 1996–2002                                                    53
Table 9    Work Permits Granted to Non-EU Nationals in
Ireland, by Sector, 1996 and 2002                                     53
Table 10   Top Five Nationalities Issued with Work Permits,
1996 and 2002                                                         54
Table 11   Proportion of Work Permits Issued, 1996 and 2002,
by Region                                                             54
Table 12   Numbers of Asylum Applications Lodged in Ireland
1996–2002                                                             56
Table 13   Top Five Countries of Origin of Asylum-Seeker
Applications, 2001 and 2002                                           57
Table 14   'Disturbing Difference' in the *Star* Poll                61
Table 15   Top Five Groups Felt to be 'Disturbing', the *Star*
Poll, 2000                                                            61
Table 16   Top 5 Groups Felt to be 'Disturbing',
Eurobarometer 1997                                                    61
Table 17   Comparison of Responses to Identical Questions in
Eurobarometer 1997, 2000 and the *Star* Poll, 2000    62
Table 18   Comparison of Two Sets of Attitudes Toward
Travellers                                                            63
Table 19   Italian Attitudes Towards Immigrants and
Southerners                                                           191
Table 20   Representations of Irish Society by the State             209

# FIGURES

Figure 1   Indicators of Potential Labour Supply,
           1997–2002 (%)                                        37
Figure 2   'Outward Bound', T.H. Maguire, 1854                 96
Figure 3   'Inward Bound', T.H. Maguire, 1854                  97
Figure 4   'The English Labourer's Burden', Archibald Leech,
           1849                                                121
Figure 5   'Parasites', Dog Sharkey, 1997                      162
Figure 6   'Everyone Go Home', Martyn Turner, 2000             195

# Acknowledgements

This book was conceived at the end of the twentieth century and born in the twenty-first. Its labour, while protracted and painful for some of those involved, was relatively uncomplicated. I would like to thank all those who have encouraged and/or assisted me with this project (even if they were unaware of doing so); Paulina Chiwangu, Alistair Christie, Breda Gray, Ronit Lentin, Piaras Mac Einri, Margaret O'Keeffe, Pat O'Mahony, Fred Powell and Allen White spring to mind. Thanks also to Phil and Ashok for printing the manuscript. At Pluto, a big thank you to Roger for having faith in a good idea, Julie for being patient, Robert for guidance and Laura for eagle-eyed editing.

Thanks to anyone on the H-Net email lists (Ethnic and Caribbean) as well as on the Irish Diaspora list who gave me pointers on information relating to the Irish in the Caribbean.

My family bear the brunt of the donkey work involved, by not having that time spent with them. They may or may not think that's a good thing, but I'm thanking them for their support anyway. Annie: what the hell would I do without you? This would not have happened without your support and nurture. Thanks also to my parents, Chris and Chris, whose encouragement has enabled me to pursue what I think is important.

This book is dedicated to my Cork children: Dani, Gabriel and Morganne, who are implicated in this process, whether they like it or not. I hope by the time they can understand the book, it will be primarily of historical interest.

# Introduction

This book is an attempt to put forward a set of arguments on the forms and dynamics of the idea of 'race' in the Irish experience. It is therefore more a group of connecting interpretive and critical essays than a detailed narration. In this it will disappoint historians, and I apologise to them in advance. The text supposes acquaintance with the broad lines of Irish history and attempts to look more closely at less exposed areas rather than those that are adequately covered elsewhere. In this exploratory analysis, there is far too little on the North and the role of Unionism, for example, just as there is inadequate integration of gender relations. Hopefully, these lacunae will be addressed by others. Moreover, racism directed against the Irish in Britain from the twentieth century onwards is expressly not covered here as it adds little to my core argument. That relationship is dealt with *inter alia* by Hickman (1995a), Hickman and Walter (2002) and Douglas (2002). In none of these cases does absence from this study mean that the subjects are not important: merely that my priority has been to cover what has been less effectively tackled so far, within an overall argument. The object is not to reproduce data *per se* (notes will direct interested readers to fuller treatments) but to understand it in a different light, by constructing a new argument founded on the following principle: 'The question is not whether men-in-general [sic] make perceptual distinctions between groups with different racial or ethnic characteristics, but rather *what are the specific conditions which make this form of distinction socially pertinent, historically alive?*' (Hall, 1980:338)

This book hopes to stimulate thought on an area that is beginning to come into the line of fire of academics working in the social policy arena. Yet there has been relatively little sociological work on theorising the place and significance of Irish racism, the relationship between that and anti-Irish racism and the lessons to be drawn thereof. In the following chapters, an attempt is made to elucidate these through a combination of critical and interpretive studies of existing material. Key themes are complexity, the contradictory nature of the location of the Irish, racisms and their link with economic and political change. Overall, I have endeavoured to find appropriate questions to ask, always the most difficult element of a research project, and the answers supplied should be seen for what they are: work in

1

progress. This is a long way from being the first or the last word on racism in the Irish experience, but it does constitute a set of questions and a perspective that have not been placed together before: *súil eile*, as TG4's promotional slogan has it.[1]

Chapter 1 summarises the evolution of the idea of 'race' and introduces some theoretical perspectives on 'race' and racism developed principally by sociologists. There is a focus on the paradigms particularly relevant to Ireland. I then identify some specific contextual characteristics of Irish racism.

Chapter 2 sketches some economic background to the 1990s, to provide contextual information on the arrival of greater numbers of migrants of all kinds witnessed in the second half of that decade. I seek to indicate some of the trends emerging from beneath the 'boom' description in order to suggest likely sources of instability for sections of the Irish population that might account in part for the rise of racism. The figures on migration and asylum are provided for reference and also to indicate trends within them.

Chapters 3–5 attempt to pick out some crucial historical instances in the process of the construction of the 'Irish race'. The list is not exhaustive nor is it meant to be. The principal objective is to use these examples as bases for arguments about the factors influencing racialisation, and to suggest that racism is a constantly changing con-figuration of social relations rather than a narrowly-defined and stable set of criteria. The racialisation of Irish people has been a historical phenomenon, assuming different forms at different times. These are explained by precise economic and political factors. Chapter 3 focuses on the latter part of the sixteenth century in Ireland, and the seventeenth-century Caribbean.

The process of becoming white in America is central to contem-porary views of Irishness, and this is looked at in Chapter 4 as the narrative of transition from marginalised minority (Catholic immigrants in a Protestant state) to a mainstream ethnic group (whites in a racialised hierarchy).

In Chapter 5, the place of Britain and the experience of empire are evaluated. The racialisation of the Catholic Irish in the middle decades of the nineteenth century again demonstrates that the way ideas combine is dependent upon particular socio-historical and political contexts. There is no anti-Irish racism in the singular in nineteenth-century Britain, but a number of climaxes in which specific configurations come to the fore, around the Irish as underclass, as Catholics in a Protestant state, and as racialised Celts in an Anglo-Saxon dominated polity. The Irish contribution to empire throws up a great deal of ambivalence around the colonised in the position of coloniser, and this has fed into contemporary attitudes. Indeed, I demonstrate that 'race' ended up restricting the ideological options of various elements of Irish nationalism by forcing them to conceive their identities in closed racialised terms, as 'white' in the case of the Home Rulers and 'Catholic-Gaelic-Irish' in the case of the separatists.

The context shifts forward to contemporary Ireland in Chapter 6, where the meeting of other peoples' diasporas with the Irish one is the focus. An outline of anti-Semitism and anti-Traveller racism is sketched as a precursor to the intensification of the colour line in the 1990s and the way the issue of asylum has been racialised. This is followed by a discussion on Brah's (1996) concept of diaspora space, as it might be applied to Ireland.

In Chapter 7, I examine the concept of 'new racism' critically in the light of the Irish experience looked at so far, and then draw out one strand of it, the concentration on post-war migration, as a phenomenon that may have ambiguous effects on the formation of racist ideas, particularly in countries with experience of mass emigration. I look at the possibility that in Italy and Ireland, this collective experience of emigration may structure responses to migration in specific ways.

Many studies of anti-racism detail initiatives, or explore the themes emerging from anti-racist practice. The approach chosen in Chapter 8 is to highlight particular structural obstacles to anti-racist work and the development of anti-racist culture, both at national and European level. This draws on work critiquing nationalism and community. Above all, the necessity of constructing an indigenous anti-racist tradition, while balancing this against the need to avoid parochialism, is stressed.

Chapter 9 moves on from that discussion, taking up key issues raised and trying to formulate some broader points about the racialisation of the Irish and the relationship these have had with the specifics of the contemporary situation. The emphasis lies on the complexity and contradictory nature of the way ideas about 'race' are interwoven with other areas such as economics and history, and emerge from writing on Irish identity.

The concluding chapter, rather than summarising the book's arguments in detail, seeks to make links between the argument presented and the wider historical conjuncture, and on the other contends that there is a site for resistance to the neo-liberal 'imperialism of the universal' in civil society that remains unexploited.

# 1
# Sociological Frameworks for Understanding Racism

'An important subject about which clear thinking is generally avoided.'

(Ashley Montagu, 1954:1)

Ashley Montagu's sardonic comment about 'race' forms part of the introduction to his book *Man's Most Dangerous Myth: The Fallacy of Race*. In the immediate post-war period a number of scholars across the world and operating within a range of disciplines attempted to formulate scientific rebuttals against the view that 'race', in terms of human beings, had the biological–cultural meanings attributed to it by most people. Professor Montagu would certainly be disappointed half a century later to note that the idea that 'race' has no biological legitimacy has not broken through from academia into the world of public debate. This after concerted efforts by UNESCO, in the aftermath of the Holocaust, to abolish it from political and academic discourse. Indeed, its continuing unquestioned status is an anomaly. A person asserting that the world was square would be justifiably laughed out of court in the early twenty-first century. The notion that the world is biologically divided up into discrete races, each with its own properties and attributes, is equally unfounded, yet it still provides the backdrop to the vast majority of debates and is a point of intersection between racists and those who would label themselves anti-racists (Gilroy, 1990; Taguieff, 1990a, 1990b). In Ireland, the venerable *Irish Times* has a correspondent for Social and Racial Affairs, while Trinity College, Dublin runs an MPhil in Race and Ethnic Studies. Yet, while the equality legislation enacted in Ireland over the past few years recognises race (with no inverted commas) as being one of its grounds for discrimination (and therefore protection under the law), the Belgian parliament has moved to withdraw the term 'race' from its legislation and usage on the basis that it is not a scientific concept. Book titles including the term 'race' pour out of academia on a monthly basis. Ideas about the value or usefulness of 'race' as an idea and the practices it gives rise to are contingent. However, we are bombarded with intimations that 'race' is a natural part of our social world, one of the legitimate ways in which we try to make sense of difference. We hold these truths, one might contend, to be self-evident: all people are created racial. If opinion-formers and specialists in the area also use the term, and, by extension, conceptualise in these terms, then why should anyone else choose to critically examine it?

This chapter seeks to provide one path towards understanding how to critically engage in the discourse about 'race' and racism from a sociological viewpoint. It makes no claims whatsoever to exclusivity. I shall first explain some of the terminology before tracing the development of the idea of 'race', and summarising the main approaches to the issues of 'race' and racism, particularly in European literature.

## WHAT DOES 'RACE' MEAN?

Why the inverted commas? They indicate that the concept is a contested one, whose meanings are not what they seem. Indeed Robert Miles, author of a number of influential books and articles (1984, 1989, 1993), has argued consistently that the word 'race' should not be used at all, since it prevents focus on what should be the real area of study, namely the discriminatory processes based on the idea that the human race is divisible into distinct categories called 'races':

> I recognise that people do conceive of themselves and others as belonging to 'races' and do describe certain sorts of situation and relations as being 'race relations', but I am also arguing that these categories of everyday life cannot automatically be taken up and employed analytically by an inquiry which aspires to objective or scientific status. (1984:42)

He challenges anyone to define 'race' unproblematically, and, indeed, critiques of Miles' position do not satisfactorily explain what 'race' means. Those who have argued that 'race' should be retained but within inverted commas, as a compromise position, do not share a vision of its meaning. Paul Gilroy for example argues for the maintenance of 'race' as a concept, without saying what it actually is: '"Race" must be retained as an analytical category not because it corresponds to any biological or epistemological absolutes but because it refers investigation to the power that collective identities acquire by means of their roots in tradition' (1987: 247). The debate bubbles under the surface of writing on 'race', bursting forth here and there. Peter Wade's excellent introduction to his 1997 study of Latin America (1997:1–7) for example sides with Miles, but is criticised by Richard Jenkins (1997) in his own review of contemporary theory on race and ethnicity published in the same year. Gilroy comments in a 1998 paper that 'to renounce race for analytical purposes is not to judge all appeals to it in the profane world of political cultures as formally equivalent. I am not Robert Miles' (1998).

This argument is a circular and irresoluble one, based on principled political choices of the protagonists. It could even be suggested that at its heart is a question of how best to organise to overcome the discrimination, either by recognising that people see themselves and others as members of 'races' (and therefore organising on this basis) or by focussing attention on the set of ideas generating discrimination rather than basing resistance on one of them. In any event, I shall look here at two exemplary definitions of 'race' put forward by writers who do use the term.

Omi and Winant in their study of the role of the US state in creating racial identities define 'race' as 'an unstable and "de-centered" complex of social meanings constantly being transformed by political struggle' (1986:68). Here 'race' is modelled as fluid and subject to change deriving from the political sphere. Since the main thrust of the book is that the political is the most important influence, we might imagine that there are other sources also generating meaning. Matthew Jacobson in his book on the boundaries of whiteness suggests further dimensions:

> Race is a palimpsest, a tablet whose most recent inscriptions only imperfectly cover those that had come before, and whose inscriptions can never be regarded as final. Contradictory racial identities come to coexist at the same moment in the same body in unstable combinations, as the specific histories that generated them linger in various cultural forms or on the social and political relationships that are their legacies. (1998:142)

Jacobson thus identifies the complexity of identities in the way that contradictory meanings exist at the same time within cultures and relationships. Cultural logics therefore continue to produce meanings from the collection of physical (phenotypical) interpretations called 'race', even though these meanings no longer necessarily relate to the material conditions that produced them.

The rationale of Miles' stance is irrefutable. 'Race' is not a biological but a social reality; therefore those analysing social realities should not reproduce or reify such a term. Indeed, a single definition is clearly not shared by academics who reject Miles' stance. However, we might draw out the emerging theme: the instability of 'race' over time and place and its overridingly social nature. It is in sociological terms a constructed identity, built from varying foundations and with varying materials from the cultures in which they are embedded, in different places at different times.

This, we might argue, is where sociological thinking derived from the discipline's founding fathers begins to appear obsolete and even anti-sociological. If we follow the sociologists' mission statement to think the unthinkable and question the unquestionable, we should apply this to theories that tend toward (a) essentialising and reifying identity, and (b) those in which sources of identity are limited to one paramount one. Both neo-Marxist and neo-Weberian paradigms can be seen as falling into these traps in different ways. Marxism's refusal to countenance alternative sources of identity as having equal validity with social class was a cliché until the entry of feminists into the discourse in the 1970s, and since then Marxism has been criticised for its failure to deal adequately in theory with nationalism (Nairn, 1978), 'race' and ethnicity (Gilroy, 1987). Weber (1978:395) does point out that social action taken on an 'ethnic' basis *per se* is an illusion:

> All in all, the notion of 'ethnically' determined social action subsumes phenomena that a rigorous sociological analysis [...] would have to distinguish carefully [...]. It is certain that in this process, the collective term 'ethnic' would be abandoned, for it is unsuitable for a really rigorous analysis.

This message, however, does not seem to have been taken on board by those focussing solely on 'race' or gender (as Weberian 'status groups' and/or the basis of 'parties') as alternative but one-dimensional models of social action.

The reasoning from which the argument in this book is derived is that collective identities are multiple and political. People do not live out their lives within one social location, but at the intersection of several; a white European woman may also be, in different but never totally discrete contexts, a mother, a daughter, a sister, a worker, a linguistic minority, a student, the owner of property, a professional with a vested interest, a decision-maker. Combinations of these identities coalesce at different moments in different contexts and can more usefully be seen as what Anthias (2002:43) terms 'transloca-tion', namely an 'interplay of a range of locations and dislocations in relation to gender, ethnicity, national belonging, class and racial-isation'. Moreover, in relation to 'race', even the binary terms 'white' and 'black' are up for examination (or 'unpacking'). Nobody, after all, is actually physically 'white' or 'black': these terms are a form of political shorthand covering explanations for social hierarchies that change from place to place and over time. Indeed, Mac an Ghaill (2001) argues that historically the Irish have never been 'either' white 'or' black, but 'both' white 'and' black, where these terms refer to status positions.

The working conclusion is that I will use 'race' in inverted commas, as a substantive abstract noun, to draw attention to its contested status. I will not, however, use 'race' to refer to specific groups of people, but rather adopt the term 'racialised group' for this purpose. This latter term indicates that the people described have been both objects of, and active agents in, the process of constructing the identity in question. The important proviso to this is that the parts played are not equal, as racism by definition involves a power relationship. The term 'racialised group' also allows that, like all collective identities, the one described is fluid and dynamic, not essentialised and static. Indeed, a salient point of racist ideologies is that they seek to explain the social by the biological, to encapsulate and negate the dynamic by reference only to the static.

I shall return to this theme after a brief overview of the develop-ment of the idea of 'race'. This will demonstrate some of the historical specificity of 'race', and lead to some conclusions that will enable me to propose a working definition of racism.

### The evolution of 'race' thinking

*Pre-enlightenment*

There were Christians and heathens before there were 'black' and 'white' people. In Christian symbolism 'heathen' had connotations as negative as 'Christian' did positive, yet the evidence suggests that explanations of difference focused on religion and climate, without giving the concept of 'race' the detailed content that it was to receive later. How is this to be reconciled with the fact that the European colonial enterprises (including the conquest of Ireland) and the

Atlantic slave trade had been under way for centuries before the Enlightenment? Surely ideas about superiority and inferiority revolved around physical as well as religious difference. The answer is broadly yes, but physical difference was explained largely with reference to religion. This can be seen as an ideological process most clearly in the 'sons of Ham' argument put forward by the Christian churches to justify the enslavement of Africans. The frame of reference for Europeans until the Enlightenment was one in which signs on the body were read as judgements of God, and the argument ran that the punishment given by God to Canaan in the Book of Genesis (Genesis 9:18–27) involved servitude and blackness (to denote inferiority already present in the nature of servitude). However, nowhere in Genesis does it say that Ham's descendants were to be dark complexioned, nor that the form of their servitude would resemble in any way the bondage of the Israelites in the Old Testament. This gloss was added to the very broad lines sketched in scripture in a teleological manoeuvre by clerical scholars.

Their logic ran: Africans could be enslaved in large numbers; therefore their slavery was natural and permitted by God. This is because they were the 'sons of Ham', designated by God to be servants. Moreover, the critical issue around designating peoples as inferior was the necessity for labour in the labour-intensive enterprise of primary material extraction. The debate between Las Casas and Sepulveda in Valladolid in 1550 was one between early humanist thought and imperial imperatives. If Amerindians in the New World had redeemable souls they could not be used as slave labour; if they hadn't, then their labour could be passed off as penance for sinful paganism.

### The Enlightenment and classification

The basis of the all-encompassing categorisation project in which the Enlightenment thinkers were engaged was that the world could be divided up unproblematically into categories and sub-categories. Bauman (1990) cites the classificatory tendency as one of the principal problems in modern European thought. Linnaeus's epic work, *Systems of Nature* (1735) betrays this urge and its anchoring in the physical:

> Man, the last and best of created works, formed after the image of his Maker, endowed with a portion of intellectual divinity, the governor and subjugator of all other beings, is, by his wisdom alone, able to form just conclusions from such things as present

themselves to his senses, which can only consist of bodies merely natural. Hence, the first step of wisdom is to know these bodies; and be able; by those marks imprinted on them by nature, to distinguish them from one another, and to affix to every object its proper name.

In constructing the 'great chain of being', the fulcrum of Enlightenment reasoning was Linnaeus's 'bodies merely natural': a set of common-sense physical markers. Over the decades now referred to as 'the Enlightenment' (c.1720–1820), a diffuse pattern of ideas expressed in relation to a number of disciplines – biology, philosophy, history, economics, political science, *inter alia* – was transformed into a coherent body of thought on humankind's place in the world, containing an elaborate typology of human beings (Linnaeus's *Homo Sapiens*). A causal link was made by writers such as Hume, the Comte de Buffon and Hegel, between climate, 'phenotype', intellectual ability, and capacity for civilisation. In this view of the world, civilisation in its highest forms emanated from the version of human beings dwelling in the temperate zones: they were pale in complexion as a result, and, as contemporary history showed, were capable of mastering both nature and other species of human, with technology. The differences between the categories of human being were explicable in terms of 'race' and culture: two sides of the same phenomenon. Physical appearance became a marker of cultural development, not just in the present, but also an indicator of the parameters of advancement.

Given that these ideas gained legitimacy and became part of elite ideology in the Atlantic world in the context of the commoditisation of human beings in the Atlantic slave trade, the conclusions arrived at by the Western world's most notable minds acted to justify slavery *post facto*. Moreover, the wavering on issues of morality that had fuelled abolitionist campaigns came into conflict with rational and scientific thought: the Enlightenment was also an attempt to place rationality above religion as the dominant explanatory model. It did indeed achieve predominance, and the classifications proposed were honed in the industrial and scientific nineteenth century.

*The industrial and scientific nineteenth century*

Science began to eclipse religion as the legitimate authority for explaining phenomena in both the natural and social worlds. Nineteenth-century scientists built on the groundwork laid by the

Enlightenment thinkers. As the century progressed, the ideas that had been put forward to link appearance, climate and culture increasingly became the assumptions upon which new work was carried out, rather than the subject of scholarly debate. Race had become what Bourdieu (1977) terms 'doxa', in other words, the idea that the causal link existed and explained behaviour was no longer debatable. Moreover, nineteenth-century science and pseudo-science further developed the central thesis of the Enlightenment, namely that the Body is the key to Culture. Sciences that flowered in the nineteenth century, such as craniology, phrenology and later anthropometry, involved the measurement of various body parts and the construction of classificatory types from the findings. The new 'social' sciences such as sociology, ethnology and anthropology which emerged in the second half of the century were equally influenced by the obsession with physical appearances and the meanings attributed to them by their colleagues in the physical sciences. It is clear from the texts produced by these disciplines that the notion of dispassionate and disinterested scientific endeavour has little hold on those interested in 'race': the logic underlying experiments is erroneous and the interpretations of data so weighed down under the assumption of explicit existing hierarchies based on putative racial difference that the findings are not compelling.

American craniologist Samuel Morton, for example, filled the skulls of various 'racial' types to measure their capacity. He emerged with a league table showing that English skulls had the largest capacity and Native Americans the smallest. His inference was that the English mind was larger, more powerful and superior. However, the skulls had all been taken from the corpses of men hanged for murder (the only way to obtain body parts at that time), and so the conclusion might equally have been 'English murderers have the largest skulls'. Moreover, in addition to the inability of scientists to agree upon how many 'races' there were, and which they were, surely a fundamental issue, the cross-fertilisation of ideas and conclusions meant that the enterprise of racialising the population was carried out on the basis of a relatively small, scarcely challenged and scientifically dubious corpus.

It was in the mid nineteenth century that the crude racial hierarchies became more nuanced. Gobineau's *Essai sur l'inégalité des races humaines* (1853) detailed the divisions within the 'white European' section, dividing it into categories including Aryan and Celtic for example. Although his appraisal of the various groups was not wholly negative, the elaborate nature of Gobineau's treatise made it a work of reference for Social Darwinists later in the century and eugenicists in the next. Indeed he prefigured the latter group's phobia about mixing.

### Social Darwinism

The second half of the century witnessed an escalation of the stakes in the process of racialisation. Already parallels between the language and paradigms used to discuss racial and class differences and hierarchies had become evident. Similar body-focussed theories were deployed to justify control of society by dominant elites in the West, and of colonised territories and people.

In 1851, English sociologist Herbert Spencer had coined the phrase 'the survival of the fittest' to refer to his model of society in which the strongest gained the majority of resources. After the publication of Charles Darwin's work on evolution, *On the Origin of Species* (1859), which categorically argued against the monogenetic position of the churches, ideas on 'race' took a new and more sinister turn. Hitherto used to justify exploitation and make sense of a new (industrial) social world in which resources were clearly unequally shared, 'race' became a means of sorting humankind into two groups. In this discourse (referred to today as 'Social Darwinism') these were the fit and the unfit. The former were the dominant, both at home and internationally, while the unfit, generally colonised peoples, could be eliminated, with the pseudo-biological justification that this was nature's way of maintaining the human race in its strongest form.

The old logic of imperialism, in which indigenous people were used as cheap or free labour, but kept alive, thus came under challenge. Those groups deemed 'unproductive' were targeted for elimination. It is no accident that the Tasmanian aboriginals became extinct during this period, having been hunted to death and chased off their ancestral land. Indeed, Darwin's theories had been taken up and reinterpreted to fit the dominant ideology of competition and power relationships developing between the superpowers: Great Britain, France, Germany, Russia and the USA. Darwin's message, that, within species, adaptation is made through natural selection, was applied erroneously to human societies. One could even argue, as Peter Kropotkin (1902) does, that co-operation is as important in the natural world as competition. Yet Darwin's message fitted more comfortably into already influential frameworks of ideology, which sought to explain socially constructed and maintained hierarchies by reference to the natural world.

'Race' then had gone from a means of situating people in a natural hierarchy with political ramifications, to a way in which particular groups could be legitimately removed by force from land they occupied, once they had been ideologically proven 'unproductive' (e.g. non-farming), and possibly eliminated. This phase, from the 1860s onwards, provided the basis for eugenics. As we shall see in Chapter 3 this conclusion was in the form of a 'second coming' in that it had already been applied during and after the English Plantations of Ireland in the latter half of the sixteenth century.

### Eugenics

Francis Galton coined the term 'eugenics' in 1883, in a project aimed at social engineering by encouraging the 'best' to breed. Galton's original notion underwent slow transformation into American, German and Scandinavian forms that leant towards elimination or at best distancing of so-called 'degenerates' and degenerate groups. Although seen as the particular province of the Nazis, eugenics was in fact a mainstream idea gaining plaudits from both the political Left and Right in the first third of the twentieth century. Its government and foundation-funded think tanks inspired sterilisation programmes, and comprehensively shaped the debates that led to the 1924 US Immigration Act. Influential voices in the drafting of that act were eugenicists', and the vision that emerged from the documents produced during the legislation process was one in which advanced Northern and Western Europeans, already in the majority in the USA, faced a potential threat from 'backward' Southern and Eastern Europeans (let alone Blacks and Hispanics). The resulting legislation drastically reduced quotas for the latter groups. Moreover, compulsory sterilisation became widespread in 1920s and '30s America, with at least half the state governments engaging in it. Davis (2001 [1981]:215–18) claims that evidence given during court cases and Senate hearings in the early to mid 1970s indicates that these programmes may have sterilised more women (disproportionately from ethnic minorities and/or on welfare) than the Nazis' own programmes in the 1930s.[1]

### Nazism

The Holocaust (and the genocides of Roma and Sinti) can be read on one level as a logical conclusion of long-standing ideas: classification into distinct 'races' (following Gobineau), purity, and justified extermination (of people with mental and hereditary diseases as well as the aged). What was new was the state's involvement, and the use of 'race' as an organising principle of policy, a principle which drove the war effort (Burleigh and Wippermann, 1991; Burleigh, 2000). Bauman (1991) interprets the Holocaust as above all an embodiment of modernity, with bureaucratisation and industrial-scale methods used to round up, process and murder millions of people. Indeed, the shock of the Holocaust challenged the validity of 'race' as a concept to be openly used in European politics. 'Race Relations' (see below) became a subject serious enough for social scientists to study and propose solutions to, both in Europe and North America in the 1950s.

### The 'new racism'

The term 'new racism' was coined by Martin Barker in his 1981 book of the same title. He contends that certain characteristics demarcated the expression of racist ideas prevalent from the late 1970s, from the previously dominant forms discussed above. Barker's theory linked developments in natural sciences (particularly sociobiology) and their application to society by conservatives in the 1970s to a re-politicisation of 'race'. However, the term 'race' was used with decreasing frequency while the concept of 'culture' was used as a surrogate for it. The political Right's depiction of struggle, he suggests, was no longer one of 'races' but of broader 'national cultures', yet it contained the old component of civilisation v. barbarity (represented by biologically determined social groups).[2]

Barker's thesis is a compelling one when he talks about contemporary political manifestations: the discourse of far-Right political parties, for example, which frame their appeals to populist nationalism in terms of territory, rights and benefits to be defended from those whose eligibility is less legitimate than that of authentic 'nationals'. The argument is less convincing when addressing the key concept of culture, which has been a central element of racialisation, and its precursors. There is nothing new about sorting people into groups of civilised and uncivilised by reference to culture rather than physical appearance, as the history of anti-Irish racism, anti-Semitism and anti-Traveller racism demonstrates. Moreover, the 'separate cultures' line of reasoning is not confined to the extreme Right. Indeed, the seeping of 'new' racist ideas into mainstream politics that is indicated by the continual reworking of immigration criteria by governing parties of the Left, Right and centre in Europe since the 1940s.

The context for the 'new racism' is that of increasing migration from broader sources (Castles and Miller, 1993): first into the more developed Western economies in the period until the mid–late 1980s, and second into the EU as a whole from that point onward. Preponderant in the first migratory waves were inhabitants of former colonies, and workers from peripheral European economies, recruited to fill labour shortages in the rebuilding of post-war Europe. Characteristic of the later wave are the more diverse chains of migration with people travelling longer distances and filling less permanent positions in a less secure labour market (Castles and Miller, 1993; Brah, 1996).

Typical of 'new' racist expressions are claims that national territories are the monopoly of nationals, and that threats to the well-being of the nation are embodied in the physical presence of minorities, whether black or white, and the idea that these minorities have a number of negative impacts on the host society: competition for diminishing welfare resources, a drop in educational standards, the spread of illness, an increase in trafficking in drugs and prostitution, higher levels of crime and insecurity (particularly in urban centres). These and other problems are commonly attributed to 'cultural' rather than 'racial' differences, whose nature is so colossal that no mutual living space is possible. This is the notion of the inability of migrants to 'assimilate' or 'integrate'. The ideas here are based on static concepts of culture and nation, and ultimately of people: that cultures do not change, that nations are stable and long-lasting, and that people are primarily sedentary. In fact the entire history of humankind has been one of frequent and multiple migrations.

A certain amount of the use of culture can be imputed to the virtual taboo on expressing ideas about racial difference that has become mainstream since the 1950s. In the new language of equality, adopted by the liberal Western democracies, it is considered socially and certainly politically unacceptable to openly express opinions about 'race'. Yet using 'culture' as a coded reference to 'race' has merely enabled extreme nationalistic ideas to become legitimate and popular, as witnessed by the upsurge in support for far-Right parties across Europe at the end of the 1990s and in the early twenty-first century. It is quite clear that while in general there has been a softening of hostility toward minorities as measured by opinion polls over the post-war period, a substantial minority of Europeans feel threatened by difference and are prepared to vote for parties offering solutions involving varying degrees of exclusion – from territory, benefits or the labour market, and above all from citizenship.

## Conclusion: the fluidity of 'race'

Ideas about what 'race' means, which 'races' exist, who belongs to which 'race', and the significance of these questions for social inequalities vary to a great extent over time and place. The context of particular forms of racism (which implicitly contain definitions of 'race') is of vital importance in attempting to understand them. Indeed, it could even be argued that the combinations of factors explaining particular versions of racism are so numerous that the correct term for what is studied should be 'racisms'.

The original linking of physical appearance to culture and the projection of the consequences of this equation onto a social order occurred only from the eighteenth century onwards, yet built upon centuries of accumulation of ideas about difference including the construction of a set of hierarchical distinctions between nomadic and sedentary lifestyles, relationships to Christianity, collective and individual property-owning, and the significance of blackness and whiteness. The contemporary paradigm, where the emphasis is on cultural rather than physical difference, is termed the 'new racism'. Yet the wheel has in some ways turned full circle: the domination of Ireland by the English was justified by the perceived cultural inadequacies of the former in the sixteenth century (Canny, 1976; Quinn, 1966), a period crucial to an understanding of racialisation.

## SOME SOCIOLOGICAL PERSPECTIVES ON 'RACE' AND RACISM

Sociology was relatively slow to theorise 'race' as a distinct field of social phenomena. As late as 1970, John Rex was still pointing to the need to fill this epistemological gap. Rex was one of the principal theorists of 'race relations', the paradigm which dominated Anglo-American studies until the 1980s. Its pioneer, the Chicago School's Robert Park, died in 1944, but much of his work on 'race' was published posthumously. Indeed, there had already been an alarming period of inactivity between the first serious attempts to theorise 'race relations' and Park's work. In the early twentieth century, the English writer James Bryce (1902) had ventured insights that would not have been out of place in Park's work, and were indeed taken up by 'race relations' theorists. For Bryce (1902) races were in competition, and there were four possible outcomes of this:

Either the weaker race dies out before the stronger, or it is absorbed into the stronger, the latter remaining practically unaffected, or the two become commingled into something different from what either was before, or, finally, the two continue to dwell together unmixed, each preserving a character of its own.

Park's major contribution was to legitimise 'race' as a sociological, rather than natural, phenomenon to be studied. 'Race relations ... are not so much the relations that exist between individuals of different races, as between individuals conscious of these differences' (1950:81).

Most British theorists of the late 1960s and early '70s adopted this neo-Weberian stance. It proclaimed, first, that 'race' was a source of social identity autonomous from social class, second, that it should be fitted into the existing structures of society and, third, that it principally formed part of urban sociology. What Rex and his collaborators (1967, 1969, 1970) and Banton (1977) did was to formulate theories about relationships between 'races', as a model of how social relationships functioned within cities in Britain. The Weberian emphasis on 'markets' was expressed by the theorising of a number of these that came within the compass of daily features of life for migrants: housing, education, employment, and so forth. A conclusion was that a system of parallel 'markets' was emerging, with minorities at a disadvantage in the mainstream one creating networks of their own.

Three points should be made about the 'race relations' paradigm: it was, first, a policy-related initiative aimed at producing responses from the British state to deal with problems generated by the exclusion of migrants.[3] Second, its formulation of 'races relating' reified difference and relegated class and gender to positions of lesser influence. It also adopted a trait I have flagged up as potentially racist, that is, imagining groups to be static and homogeneous. When the critiques emerged in the late 1970s and '80s, these flaws were the principal targets.

Projects such as those of Sivanandan (1982), Hall et al. (1978), the Centre for Contemporary Cultural Studies (CCCS) (1982) and Miles (1984) altered the direction of thinking by attempting to refocus on the relationship between the material and the ideological elements of racism expressed in the post-oil crisis Western economy. Hall (1980), for example, termed this relationship the 'articulation' of 'race' and class, that is to say, the way in which racialised minorities live out and experience their status from specific class positions. Coupled with this onslaught on the differentialist perspective of 'race relations' was a series of blows dealt from black feminists on both sides of the Atlantic. Davis (2001 [1981]), Carby (1982), hooks (1982), Parmar (1982) and Giddings (1984) all stressed that the limits of contemporary theorising on race and gender were bound up with dominant white middle-class perspectives. They argued in different ways that gender-blind models of 'race', and 'race'-blind models of gender resulted from the neglect of minority women's experiences and their exclusion from the mainstream of feminism and academia. By the late 1980s it was impossible to argue that the dimensions of and relationships between class, gender and 'race' had not been placed high on the agenda, and the 'race relations' perspective had become obsolete.

In the 1990s and early twenty-first century, the debate appears to have settled into a dialogue between those who emphasise historical trends and the role of a changing economy ('materialists'), and those who focus on cultural difference and the specific forms of resistance thrown up by minority communities ('differentialists'), to use the terms given by Mac an Ghaill (1999:42). There is also an emerging strand of work which attempts to combine the two, by looking beyond the traditional binary black–white dualism inherent in both of these approaches, and focussing on the relational aspects of 'whiteness', at relationships between the dominant majorities and white minorities, such as the Irish in the UK, Travellers and Jews, and at the power discrepancies within previously unproblematised 'white' groups (Back, 1996; Cohen, 1997; Brah et al., 1999). Extending beyond the black–white model is particularly important as it enables long-standing patterns of discrimination to be placed in focus alongside contemporary ones, and also allows 'white' migrant workers to be looked at as constituting racialised subjects, a vital project given the imminent enlargement of Europe and the probable relocation of many thousands of Eastern and Central Europeans into Western European economies in first decade of the twenty-first century.

Despite intelligent and subtle exceptions such as the work of Roediger (1991), orthodox Marxism (as opposed to cultural post-Marxism represented in the Gramscian heritage) cannot fully grasp racism nor deal epistemologically with 'race'. This is not just because it subsumes everything under class, and ignores the cross-class elements upon which national, ethnic and 'racial' solidarities are constructed and operationalised (Gilroy, 1987), but also because it founders on the necessity to see the world of work as the only area in which there is a confrontation between capital and labour (thus neglecting or downgrading other domains of life), and because of the misleadingly clear-cut base-superstructure model.[4]

The relationship between the material and the ideological is dealt with far more convincingly by those owing a greater debt to Gramsci than to Marx, such as Gilroy and Hall. Undoubtedly, the labour market is an intrinsic site of class formation and the location through which people live out their racialised identities, or live out their class identities through their racialised ones. Contributions by black and developing world feminisms to theory have also marshalled arguments based on empirical research and activists' experiences of organisational issues to incorporate the gender dimension inextricably into the heart of any discussion on racialised identity. Yet work produced by Miles, for example, has the merit of not allowing us to forget that the wider economic world is there structuring the playing field on which the actors act, and that oppressed workers can be 'white' as well as 'black'.

In short, identities are best viewed as a multiplicity of combinations, which are articulated in specific temporal and spatial contexts, and with specific degrees of relative weight, but can never wholly extricate themselves from one another. The combination is the thing itself, rather than a number of discrete identities reconfiguring to form a given identity at a given moment. Identity can be referred to, for example, as 'multiaxial' (Brah, 1996), or 'transversal' (Yural-Davis, 1997).

### RACISM(S): SOME ELEMENTS OF A DEFINITION

In some respects it is self-defeating to attempt a definitive description of the multifaceted and fluid pattern of social relations that comprise racism. Castles (2000), for example, lists criteria that should be satisfied, and this is the procedure I will follow here with my own list.

1. Dividing the world's population into 'races', each discrete and having particular combinations of physical and cultural characteristics is the foundation of racist ideas and has been since the Enlightenment. The precondition for racism is *the fundamental belief that the world's population is divided into 'races'*, whether culturally or biologically defined, which enjoy distinctive and unchanging characteristics. The logic of both racist and many anti-racist organisations has been based on this erroneous assumption: the former arguing that each 'race' has a different capacity for various forms of activity, and the latter arguing that the cultural

attributes defining this difference are not indicators of inferiority, but grounds for campaigns for equality. A good deal of well-argued criticism of the nature of anti-racist movements has emerged over the past decade in relation to this standpoint (cf. for example Gilroy, 1990; Taguieff, 1990a, 1990b; Wieviorka, 1995).

2.  Racism is an *unequal power relationship* between two or more groups considering themselves to be 'races'. This encompasses confrontations between individuals who are members of these groups.[5] Like other inter-group social relationships, the context is one of uneven control of, and access to, resources. In other words, a dominant group acts out its control in the form of discriminatory practices which militate against the advancement of (an)other group(s), whether these practices are intentional (for example, apartheid, 'Jim Crow' legislation in the USA, immigration controls in contemporary Europe based, *de facto*, on appearance) or, as is more often the case, unintentional ('indirect' discrimination in service provision, and so on). Therefore, if we talk of measuring the impact racism has on people's lives, it is not only in terms of verbal and physical violence, but also in terms of the denial of access to services and resources, measured inter-generationally.

3.  Although there are undoubtedly psychological elements to explain individuals' phobias and hostilities, the degree of autonomy enjoyed by those factors is, from a sociological perspective, minimal. All identities are collective in the sense that definition of oneself can only take place against others or within systems of meaning that are generated by the collective. As Balibar writes: 'All identity is individual, but there is no individual that is not historical or, in other words, constructed within a field of social values, norms of behaviour and collective symbols' (1991b:94).

    Moreover, racism is not simply collective, in this sense, but also, on another level, structural, that is bound up in the workings of social systems in terms of the assumptions of cultural neutrality and universality under which they operate, which accept the dominant as the norm and construct the subaltern as deviant. The structural is beyond the influence of individuals, comprising as it does the very arena in which the social practices are acted out.[6]

## Two definitions of institutional racism

'Institutional' or 'indirect' racism is a concept created to distinguish forms of discrimination that are based in organisational rather than personal abuse, violence or denial of access to services or goods. While theoretically, there might well be a degree of overlap between institutional and direct forms of racism, the important elements of the former are that the discriminatory outcome does not have to be intentional, either in terms of its scope or its victim(s), and that this discrimination derives from a practice or set of practices in which individual responsibility is relatively limited. In contemporary Europe, the concept of indirect racism is enshrined in Article 13 of the Treaty of Amsterdam, and two EC directives produced in 2000: Council Directive 2000/78/EC of 27 November 2000, which established a general framework for equal treatment in employment and occupation; and Council Directive 2000/43/EC of 29 June 2000, which was designed to combat discrimination based on 'race' or ethnic origin in employment, social protection, education and access to and supply of goods and services.

There are a number of definitions of institutional racism, most of which are legal ones, but the two below, taken from quite different social and historical contexts, suffice to give a flavour of the discrepancy between perspectives on a relatively narrow concept.

*Sir William MacPherson,* Report of the Stephen Lawrence Inquiry, *1999:*

> The collective failure of an organisation to provide an appropriate and professional service to people because of their colour, culture or ethnic origin. It can be seen and detected in processes, attitudes, and behaviour which amount to discrimination through unwitting prejudice, ignorance, thoughtlessness, and racist stereotyping which disadvantage minority ethnic people.

MacPherson's definition emerges from a long report on the mismanaged investigation into the racist murder of a young Londoner and is aimed at improving the UK police force's response to the perception among minorities in Britain that they are not given the same degree of service as white Britons. The report has indeed influenced the way the police do their jobs. A new criterion for recording 'racist crimes' was adopted in the wake of the report's publication, a new Code of Practice was produced in April 2000, and the number of racist incidents reported rocketed from 13,878 in 1997–98, to 23,049 in 1998–99 and 47,814 in 1999–2000 (Home Office, 2000).

*Stokely Carmichael and Charles Hamilton,* Black Power: The Politics of Liberation, *1967:*

> Racism takes two closely related forms; individual whites acting against individual blacks, and acts by the total white community against the black community. We call these individual racism and institutional racism. When white terrorists bomb a black church and kill black children, that is an act of individual racism, widely deplored by most segments of society. But when in that same city – Birmingham, Alabama – 500 black babies die each year because of the lack of proper food, clothing, shelter and proper medical facilities, and thousands more are destroyed or maimed physically, emotionally and intellectually because of conditions of poverty and discrimination in the black community, that is a function of institutional racism.

While MacPherson's definition derived from a bureaucratic, organisational and legalistic context, Carmichael and Hamilton wrote as activists from a minority group whose task it was to contest dominant forms of discourse. They were what Gramsci would have referred to as 'organic intellectuals'[7]. Carmichael and Hamilton described measurable as well as unquantifiable outcomes of discrimination, and situated them as unintended, contrasting them with real and intentional terrorist acts.

I would argue that there is room and need for both types of language and perspective, as the combat against racism is waged on multiple fronts. However, as the history of racism has been one of unequal power relations, in which the voices and needs of minorities have been neglected, even in strategies ostensibly aimed at overcoming discrimination, Carmichael and Hamilton ought to represent the starting point from which positions such as MacPherson's develop. No community-based resistance to racism begins in a courtroom, where the legal concepts are deployed, tested and refined.

## FRUITFUL PERSPECTIVES ON 'RACE' AND RACISM IN THE IRISH CONTEXT

The first attempt to explore the phenomenon of racism within an Irish context was that of Robbie McVeigh (1992). He argued that there was a particular combination of independent factors that created the 'specificity of Irish racism'. These were: the diffusion of UK racism; the active participation of Irish people in colonialism; the racism of the Irish emigrant community; the sectarianism endemic to the north of Ireland; and an endogenous anti-Traveller racism.

As yet there has been no detailed critique of McVeigh's trailblazing analysis, and he has gone on to produce further work (1996, 1998a, 1998b, 2002a, 2002b) fleshing out his initial thesis. The broader lines of analysis locate Ireland at a confluence of forces and representations: emigrant experiences of racialisation, both as subjects and agents of imperial rule, cultural domination stemming from this, systemic indigenous anti-nomadic racism and the complicating local factor of sectarianism. All of this, with the exception of sectarianism, is central to the focus of this book. The critique offered here centres primarily around three aspects: historical vagueness, analytical distinctions and emphasis.

Any theory attempting to explain the development of ideas and practices as complex, contradictory and transversal as those of racism requires sufficient detail to account for changes in trajectory and significance over time. The shifts between 'black', 'off-white' and 'white' identities navigated by Irish people, and the Others they help construct have to be placed in their socio-historical contexts. Failure to address this adequately leaves scope for ahistorical and historicist readings, both of which obscure the social 'embeddedness' of the relationships I am examining here. This critique is not an observation about McVeigh's (1992) work alone but is also a warning to all researchers to explain the timing of social change. In relation to McVeigh the criticism is levelled at the material relating to the Empire and US as origins of racist ideas and their appropriation by the Irish. Moreover, he posits little critical distinction between these phenomena, so that we emerge unsure as to the priority to be given to addressing the various salient features identified and how to approach their articulation.

More importantly, in McVeigh's conceptualisation of Irish racism, there is a significant underdevelopment, or at least serious downplaying, of nationalism as a generator of or vehicle for racist ideas and practices (cf. Balibar, 1991a). Various crucial phases in the nationalist struggle during the last part of the nineteenth century resulted in the closure of dominant discourses of identity, enclosing it around the Catholic, Gaelic, idealised rural west of Ireland ideal-type, a process consolidated by the state and the Church in the early years of the Republic (Hutchinson, 1987; Lee, 1989; Goldring, 1993; O'Mahony and Delanty, 1998). The politicised ideological space around nationalism seems to hamper critical examination of the degree to which strains of Irish nationalist ideology, and some nationalists (as well as Unionists and of course British nationalists) have contributed to the production of a vernacular Irish configuration of racism.

Another key writer in this area, Ronit Lentin, has tackled these issues from a feminist perspective, critiquing the notions of Irish identity laid out in the 1937 constitution (1998, 1999), and the failure to address anti-Semitism (2001, 2002a). She also problematises the state-led promulgation of a 'multicultural' solution to the changing face of Irish society (2001), and looks at the racialised and gendered nature of space in Dublin (2002b). Along with McVeigh she co-edited a full-length examination of *Racism and Anti-racism in Ireland* (2002).

Lentin (2001) places the emphasis on an 'interrogation' of Irishness, referring to the work of Freud ('the return of the repressed') and Hesse's 'transruptions' (2000b). She argues that multiculturalism in the Irish case cannot be an effective strategy because it is a top-down and divisive process, and because the Irish have never successfully dealt with the trauma of emigration: the new migrants to Ireland reactivate the collective agony of the Irish, provoking at best ambivalent, and at worst, very hostile responses. While McVeigh's work is rooted in his nationalist politics, Lentin's contributions focus on her experiences as an Irish and Jewish woman and the centripetal pressures exerted on that combination of identities. Nationalism is thus brought into her work, as are the differential effects of racist practices on women, particularly in terms of the restrictions on their mobility within urban spaces (2001, 2002b).

The third of the principal contributors in this area, Jim Mac Laughlin, is a human geographer, who has written extensively on emigration and particularly on Travellers (1995, 1996, 1998, 1999b). Mac Laughlin has developed a historically-based view in which the creation of exclusionary nineteenth-century nationalist ideologies and the establishment of the nation state signalled decisive changes in the way place and difference were articulated. The anti-nomadic racism specifically targeted at Travellers, he maintains, emerged from particular historical conjunctions of social movements and ideas which vilified mobility and rootlessness, and endorsed rootedness and property-holding as key facets of the modern. He also deals extensively with the theoretical and empirical aspects of migration from Ireland (1995, 1997), investigating this phenomenon within a world-systems approach.

Lastly, Bryan Fanning (2002) incorporates some much-needed overviews of the relationship between dominant ideas, institutional practices and the perpetuation of racism, notably anti-Semitism and anti-Traveller racism. His early work consisted of short social policy critiques in relation to asylum-seeking, and in his collection of essays he draws together loose strands of ideas that had already been put forward into a critique of the ideological bases of the Irish state since its inception. Fanning provides absorbing case studies of the treatment of Hungarian refugees in the 1950s, and of Clare County Council's attempts to address the issue of Traveller accommodation between 1963 and 1999. The latter reveals the complex interplay of constructions of the issues by the various actors, the political stakes and the workings of power relationships between councillors, Travellers, residents and the voluntary sector.

The important themes then for these authors, who are the most prolific on the issue of racism in Ireland, are the following:

## 1. The relationship between minority identities and the dominant one, that is, the role of nationalism in the development of power relations

Mac Laughlin's analysis is the most grounded in economics and the politics of place, focussing particularly on the exclusion of Travellers, while McVeigh's places less emphasis on Irish nationalism and more on imperialism and sectarianism. Lentin's focus is on contemporary forms of exclusion of new minorities, alongside Irish Jews and women. Social class is not foregrounded by the latter two, whilst for Mac Laughlin it is a central element of his work on who migrates from Ireland and why. Fanning's contribution contains a lucid development of the ideas of minority statuses being created in the nation-building project for Protestants (post-1922), Jews, Travellers, and asylum-seekers. He links this to an authoritarian, reactionary and monocultural state apparatus which, in a series of *ad hoc* reactive measures, seeks to control entry to Ireland and movement within it according to the state's construction of external threat.

## 2. The historical effects of colonisation in generating ideas and practices

McVeigh's thesis relies on the notion that Ireland extends both westwards and eastwards as a dispersed community whose lines of communication enable racist ideas and practices to pass. Only Rolston and Shannon (2002) really pick up on this precise issue, although the diaspora is clearly a significant presence in Mac Laughlin's work. Lentin does not explore this aspect, which is in fact the basis of the assumptions of nationalist writers (cf. Gibbons, 1996; Waters, 1999). However, her identification of migration as the 'return of the "national" repressed' (2001) points to her slant on the importance of the Irish diaspora, which still structures the Irish collective self-image. Attitudes towards racialised Others, she argues, highlight the failure of the wounds of mass emigration to heal. Clearly, the British influence in Ireland is a determining one, structuring the political and social relationships in which racist ideas and systems develop. It would be accurate to say that most racism in the Irish context derives from English colonial practice, just as it would be to argue that the Irish have 'appropriated' racism as a postcolonial cultural instrument of domination.

This is not in any way to argue that the contributions of others to this debate are not interesting, but merely to acknowledge that the corpus has been largely dependent on Lentin, McVeigh, Mac Laughlin, and now Fanning. Katrina Goldstone's briefer contributions (2000a, 2000b, 2002) seek to place the position of Jews and black people in comparative scrutiny as well as remind us of the ethics of researching minorities. Fintan O'Toole's journalism (in the *Irish Times*) and occasional collections bear directly on Irish identity, modernity, multiculturalism and diaspora, and particular chapters (1994) are as revealing as anything written elsewhere. Meanwhile, the stringent defence of Traveller ethnicity from pathological narratives of Travellers places Sinéad Ní Shuínéar at the forefront of what Gramsci would have termed an 'organic intelligentsia' of Traveller activists. An excellent brief historical overview of Ireland's links with international anti-racist movements and the way ideas have been generated within the diaspora has also been provided by Rolston and Shannon (2002).

*Racism in the Irish Experience* attempts to build on the work accomplished by these pioneering writers and to point, in particular, to potentially revealing complementary approaches including the problematisation of the 'new racism', comparison with other former countries of emigration, and a development of the concept of 'whiteness' using the Irish context.

Indeed, one important strand of criticism into which this new work fits is, significantly, that produced by researchers working on the Irish in the UK. Both Mac an Ghaill (1999, 2001), and Hickman (1995a, 1995b, 1998) critique the black–white dichotomy and essentialisation of debates and literature on racism there, pointing to the resulting invisibility of the Irish. Their work provides a bridge linking the majority of the research into 'whiteness' (which is US-based within either historical or cultural studies) to a European site of interrogation. The story of how the Irish have shifted positions in the space between 'black' and 'white' identities in colonial and postcolonial Britain, North America and Ireland is incomprehensible without reference to both the historical and sociological, and without taking into account the racialisation of the Irish (cf. McVeigh, 2002a), as the obverse of the Irish racialisation of the Other in Ireland: the focus of this particular book.

Working within the area of tension produced by what Mac an Ghaill (1999) terms the 'materialist' (historical and class-based) and 'differentialist' (cultural difference in the short term) approaches ultimately requires that we focus on what is 'new' in the current circumstances. Mac an Ghaill's 'coming times' are with us, and a role of sociologists should be to decode them. Macro-level European and economic discourses and changes ought to be laid alongside the micro-level regional and local ones mediated by the nation state. This book attempts to begin exploring in this way and to set out an argument that can usefully be critiqued and utilised as a way forward. Materialist approaches also assume responsibility for historical contextualisation, unlike ahistorical differentialist critiques that focus on the present without understanding how we arrived where we are (although they attempt to explain who the 'we' is). Indeed, the final chapter questions the extent to which Ireland can be seen to be experiencing the 'new racism', and argues that what is new is not the presence of the particular forms of expression and representation, but the precise combination of contradictory and overlapping forms.

Moreover, while there are many methodological criticisms that can be levelled at the collection of surveys contained in Mac Lachlan and O'Connell (2000) and the numerous opinion polls and surveys from McGréil onwards (Garner and White, 2002), they provide us with glimpses of the small-scale functioning of ideas about particular types of difference in which we are interested among non-elite groups. Further interview- and focus-group-based surveys are a priority (as long as they contest and do not essentialise identities), and will generate data that is sorely needed.

## THE SPECIFICITY OF TWENTY-FIRST CENTURY IRISH RACISM:
## A WORKING MODEL

Building on the work referred to above, the following is a brief attempt to sketch the 'specificity' of Irish racism, placing its features within a hierarchical schema, with the structural ones at the top, given their role of framing the secondary factors.

*Table 1*   Suggested Specific Characteristics of Irish Racism

| Structural | • History of emigration rather than immigration<br>• Background of political violence and colonisation |
| --- | --- |
| Secondary (i.e. framed and generated by the structural) | • History of anti-Traveller racism, anti-Semitism and publicly sanctioned violence<br>• Sectarian and territorial underpinnings of conflict in the North/Northern Ireland<br>• Conflicting nationalisms: Irish, British, Unionist<br>• Near absence of overtly far-Right political organisations |

### Structural

*History of emigration rather than immigration*

There is little need to labour the substantive point here. It should be remembered that Ireland has now been a country of net immigration since 1996 (see Chapter 2), and as such has joined nations such as Italy, Spain, Portugal and Greece, which were formerly providers of labour to the core European economies, and are now net receivers of labour from outside the EU. The cultural and attitudinal lag is the important element of this equation: although the figures speak for themselves, nobody aged 15 or over (the respondents in opinion polls) has lived in an Ireland where emigration was not the model, and it would be difficult to find individuals with no family member or close friend either resident abroad or having resided abroad for a medium–long period. The Irish diaspora is very much part of the Irish identity, and squaring this shared history with the new reality that other people's diasporas are forming in Ireland, is quite a difficult and maybe even traumatic collective process (cf. Lentin, 2001). Nobody likes having to rethink their identity, and doing so sometimes entails confronting elements that are uncomfortable. Irish people have been categorised both as and 'white' and 'in-between' during their experience of colonisation, emigration and national independence, and this transition between positions of relative power and disempowerment informs the ambivalence toward the Other in contemporary Ireland. On the one hand there is the line of argument that equates today's asylum-seekers with nineteenth-century famine refugees, and, on the other, the drive to criminalise asylum-seekers and cast them as 'spongers' and 'freeloaders'.

*Background of political violence and colonisation*

It could be argued that the first part of the above title is redundant, as colonisation is a fundamentally violent process. However the distinction is placed here to make the point relevant to the spread and form of racisms in Ireland as well as possible future forms. Political violence enacted by armed forces and authorities in Ireland, and the violence used against those forces by various organisations, particularly over the last two centuries, have created an unusual level of normalisation of violence. Political violence is one traceable thread of Irish political culture, and the colonial context in which it developed has led to rationalisations of it which can still be found in those parties that refused to sign up to the 1998 Good Friday/Belfast Agreement. At the time of writing, politically derived violence is ongoing, embracing terrorist bombings, punishment attacks, drug turf wars and internecine Loyalist power struggles. Fanning's description of attacks on Travellers (2002) in Clare and their aftermath is reminiscent of accounts of anti-black violence in the pre-desegregation South of the USA, with the forces of law and order failing to provide security, and treating the victims of attacks as the perpetrators. Anxiety over violence is ever-present among Travellers living on the roadside in Ireland. Citizen Traveller's (2001) poll revealed that 43 per cent of Travellers 'fear attack'.

## Secondary

*History of anti-Traveller racism, anti-Semitism and publicly sanctioned violence*

The racialisation of gypsy and nomad groups in Europe reached its peak in the 'nation-building' nineteenth century (Mac Laughlin, 1995:23; Ní Shuínéar, 1994, 2002). Ideas of prioritising individual over collective rights and thus the elevation of property-owning civilisations over others such as those found in Australia and North America were given fresh impetus at that time. The history of discrimination against Travellers in Ireland is thus part of a much broader picture.

Hostile attitudes towards Travellers appear to be particularly deeply entrenched, as witnessed in the surveys reviewed in Chapter 2, and discrimination against them particularly in the fields of accommodation, health services and education, while slowly being overcome (Kenny, 1997), remains a source of very serious concern (Fanning, 2002). One element of the Traveller experience is the constant threat (particularly for those living by the roadside) of forcible movement (Citizen Traveller, 2000b). Traveller organisations have claimed for a long time that Travellers have been the victims of frequent attacks, and that those attacks remain unpunished. The perception that attacking Travellers somehow does not count as a crime is certainly an unhealthy one, and unsanctioned violence against any group opens the door to more of the same for others. Moreover, the notions contained within assumptions about the right of Travellers to move into and out of particular public spaces, and the national tolerance of catastrophic mortality rates for them are markers of social distance whose logic, as has been remarked (McVeigh, 1998b), verges on the genocidal.

### Conflict in the North has sectarian and territorial underpinnings

McVeigh (1998a) has explored the relationship between sectarianism and racism. One of the fundamental elements of racist thought is the concept that groups of people are eternally and naturally different: so different that they can never live within the same space without conflict. Where they do, this becomes a destabilising threat to the dominant ideas, hence records of attacks on neighbourhoods/institutions, and so on, in which Irish people and their Others co-exist, from the New York Draft Riots of 1863 (Bernstein, 1990), to the problems in contemporary Belfast. This phenomenon appears to be dominant in the relationship between the two larger communities in the North (Brown, 2001). Reports on that society are part of everyday information assimilated by people in the Republic of Ireland, and the central message that emerges is that different people have the right to live in different and socially homogeneous areas, and territory can be justifiably 'defended' against encroachment. All of this is accentuated by the fact that many Irish people see themselves as, if not protagonists in the North, observers sympathetic to one or other community, presumably mostly the 'nationalist', Catholic one.

Messages of fundamental difference granting entitlement to territorial exclusivity sound particularly menacing in an era in which apartheid has only just ceased to be a formal state policy, and in which leaders are facing charges of genocide and mass murder in international courts for the parts they played in recent conflicts based on identical logic. This is not to argue that such events are comparable to the Irish case, but that the basic ideas underpinning them are very similar and thus potential ground for generating and justifying racist attitudes and discriminatory practices.

*Conflicting nationalisms*

Nationalism as such is not automatically a causal factor of racism, but the relationship between the two is a complicated one (Balibar, 1991a). Nationalism posits a national community whose traditions and shared experiences are dependent on having shared the same land through history. It is by nature an exclusive set of ideas, drawing lines around one particular group. Where this ideology feeds into racism is when the group in question is constructed as 'racially pure'/homogeneous. Models of citizenship based on the principle of cultural and ethnic diversity within one nation militate against the type of nationalism identified here becoming dominant. However, the two indigenous nationalist traditions on the island of Ireland, Irish nationalism/republicanism on the one hand and 'Unionism' on the other, have historically been constructed on narrow, religious and racially-homogeneous grounds, mainly in opposition to each other, or to British nationalism, which, with its own set of exclusions, can be seen as structuring the other two. Indeed, for the period 1870 to 1916, for example, one of the recurrent themes in Irish nationalist mobilisation was the racial element of the struggle (Celt–Gael pitted against Anglo-Saxon), a form of retaliation against centuries of racialised discourse placing the Celt on a lower level that the Saxon.

This way of perceiving the social world (that is, divided into racially distinct groups with conflicting interests) is useful nationalist shorthand that has mobilised people in many countries at one time or another, often to resist oppression. However, the pertinent point is that this model of 'racial' thinking underpins the way difference is constructed in contemporary Ireland. The Irish 'race' (see Chapters 3–5) is a frequently used term, and it is worth reflecting upon what it actually refers to in a period when a small but increasing number of Irish people are no longer white, Catholic or in their view Celts or Gaels.

*Near absence of overtly far-Right political organisations*

The domination of the national question over that of class has distinguished Ireland's political landscape. Although Ireland has no far-Right political bodies comparable in size or prominence to some in continental Europe (the French Front national, the Belgian Vlaams Blok, the Danish People's Party, the Austrian OP, Alleanza Nazionale and the Lega Nord), or even the less successful but well-publicised British National Party in the UK, some of the ideological ingredients are indeed present. I argue here that the establishment of far-Right political groupings is not necessarily a direct indicator of a high level of racism in a society. The political development of Ireland has been heavily influenced by nationalisms, and the postcolonial issue of asserting independence from the UK. This is a unique situation in Western Europe. The political emphasis given to nationalism and independence has created a political spectrum wholly different from those of most other European nations, where the classic Left–Right division has been the source of ideological development since the end of the nineteenth century. However, some of the elements of far-Right ideas are present in Ireland: nationalism as a mainstream ideology and vicarious notions of white supremacy. More importantly, the conditions out of which far-Right politics has blossomed since the early 1980s are increasingly present: growing apathy toward politics, the construction of immigration as a problem, rapid socioeconomic changes, and the realisation that important decisions are being made beyond the level of the nation state (with US multinationals closing plants, the EU setting interest rates and deciding on currency, and so forth). While Ireland is so far home to only one far-Right political party, the Immigration Control Platform (ICP), which ran two candidates in the 2002 general election, it is not an ideologically insulated island.[8]

Yet Elchardus (1996) argues forcefully that the term 'far Right' might more accurately be 'popular Right', as 'realignment theory' has suggested support from former left-wing voters as well as right-wing ones for anti-immigration parties. He contends that alongside the classic Right–Left divide in political thinking there is now a parallel one relating to authoritarianism. This means that a sizeable proportion of 'far-Right' voters are economically left wing (in favour of redistribution, welfare extensions, and so on) but authoritarian and excluding (placing emphasis on immigration controls, public order, and so forth). Seen in this light, the more populist Irish political mainstream appears much more vulnerable than with the idea that racist politics is the preserve of the extreme right. There is already a minority tradition of vocal and public opposition to minorities that encompasses deputies and local councillors from Fianna Fáil, Fine Gael and Labour, as well as Independents.

A final distinguishing feature of Irish racism is its reformulation within a context of economic boom rather than recession. Racism in Ireland has intensified since the mid 1990s. It could be argued that France is in the same position, having experienced a rise in anti-Semitism over the 1999–2001 periods (CNCDH, 2001). This is why at first glance the 'new racism' paradigm might seem most appropriate. That interpretation is dealt with critically in Chapter 7. The case of Ireland demonstrates the measurable growth in negative sentiment toward minorities during a period of unparalleled growth in a country's economy. This in itself is an interesting counter-case. Generally, resource–competition-based arguments (Scheepers et al., 2002; Quillian, 1995) state that hostility intensifies in economic downturns. The labour shortage in certain sectors of the Irish economy has been a complicating factor in the process of attitudinal change, as employers have thought with their business heads and got on with recruiting from abroad throughout. Only when the lay-offs in the IT sector began to hit the headlines in July–August 2001 was any link between work permits and unemployment actually expressed at high level,[9] and even this ended up with regulations being tightened in relation to 'non-priority' sectors only: computing and health for example remained unaffected. One modifier would therefore be that it is rapid social change *per se*, rather than boom or bust, that exacerbates feelings of insecurity that are expressed as racist. Further, writers such as Kieran Allen (2000) and Peadar Kirby (2002) posit a polarisation of income parallel to a net increase. This might suggest that those feeling themselves left behind in Irish society's material advances would be most likely to exhibit racist tendencies. However, although the surveys and opinion polls conducted on attitudes to minorities shed some light on this (see Chapter 2), it should not be forgotten that neither institutional racism, more the province of the educated middle classes with access to positions of decision-making power, nor structural factors can be measured in opinion polls.

So the potential explanations of the relationship between boom and racism are themselves interestingly contradictory; while some writers point to the spread of materialist values as making people more reluctant to share resources, others base their explanation on the idea that those left furthest behind in the race for higher-paid jobs and more expensive consumer goods are more jealously guarding their territory, and eye competitors for benefits and accommodation with particular malevolence. The truth is that without researching these hypotheses, no one can really say which, if either, is the most accurate. Each may correspond to attitudes prevalent in a particular group. In any event, the relevant point is that Ireland disproves or at least challenges the theory that a rise in racism is linked exclusively to poor economic conditions.

In this chapter, some of the key emphases in writing on 'race' and racism have been outlined, and the work done specifically in relation to Ireland briefly reviewed. Finally, a draft of the features shaping the specificity of vernacular Irish racism, inspired by McVeigh's (1992) attempt, has been put forward. The dynamic interaction of the ideas evoked here will be referred to throughout the argument developed.

# 2
# Money, Migrations and Attitudes

The objective of this chapter is to sketch an economic context for the new immigration into Ireland beginning in the second half of the 1990s and analyse one set of attitudinal changes in the face of this phenomenon. Three elements – money, migrations and attitudes – are linked to provide overlapping narratives and highlight points of contact between them. It will be argued throughout this book that economics, mobility and racism are fundamentally bound up in one another and to see them as completely distinct is erroneous. Cordoning off bodies of knowledge based in particular disciplines from one another is a function of academic practice that hinders comprehension of social phenomena, and contributes to depoliticised discursive procedures. Moreover, the 'cultural turn' and the declassing of social sciences over the past decade and a half have made it more difficult to see what emerges in the cultural sphere in relation to the material–economic one. There is no attempt made here, however, to sustain the classic Marxist distinction of base–superstructure in what follows (see Chapter 1), merely an effort to place literatures that rarely speak to each other in an elementary form of dialogue.

This chapter examines the contours of the economic transformations experienced by the Irish economy, particularly since the late 1980s, and outlines the context in which the increased numbers of migrants have arrived. Through this relationship I seek to find some answers as to why the country is exhibiting increasing levels of racism (expressed in attitudes and violence, see below) during a period of economic boom. In the second section of the chapter, the various status groups are identified and the available figures presented and contextualised. The final section summarises the attitudinal surveys carried out over the period 1973–2001 and draws some conclusions.

## ECONOMIC CONTEXT

In 1996, Ireland, a long-standing exporter of people, became a net importer of that product. Part of the reason for this was the performance of its economy, which created labour shortage in specific sectors, and attracted foreign nationals as well as returning Irish emigrants, to live and work in the country. Since the early 1990s, employment levels have risen rapidly: by 47.5 per cent in the 1994–2002 period. Employment as of the fourth quarter of 2002 stood at 1.77 million (a 59.7 per cent participation rate, cf. EU 15 average of 56.1 per cent in the fourth quarter of 2001), up from 1.2 million (a 53.3 per cent participation rate) in 1994 (CSO, 2003a). Per capita Gross Domestic Product (GDP) 'at current prices', rose 86.7 per cent (from €14,636 to €27,328) between 1995 and 2000, while per capita Gross National Product (GNP) 'at current prices' (see Glossary) increased by 77.2 per cent (from €12,984 to €23,010) over the same period.[1]

The 1993–2002 period has been characterised by unprecedented and sustained growth, during which time the GDP at constant prices (that is, excluding price changes) has almost doubled. Export-led growth has been particularly high. Indeed, the Central Statistics Office (CSO) states that, over the long term (post-1960), the value of exports 'has increased over forty times in real terms' (CSO, 2002a). The other components of GDP, for instance personal consumption and public expenditure, have each increased roughly by a factor of four, while investment has increasedy approximately ten times.

Within the economy as a whole, particular industries have expanded very quickly relative to others. The CSO's annual yearbook for 2002 states that:

> Between 1995 and 2001, the output of Industry (including Building) rose by about 106%, while the output of the sectors dominated by multi-national companies (Reproduction of recorded media, Chemicals, Computers, and Electrical machinery and equipment) increased almost fourfold. There was also an especially strong increase of 92% in the output of the Distribution, Transport and Communications sector during the same period. By contrast Agriculture, Forestry and Fishing output rose by just 5% in real terms.

These trends have seen the country's economy shift decisively onto a service base reliant on specific industries: chemicals, computers and electrical engineering. These are dominated by US TNCs. In 1997, 47.8 per cent of manufacturing employment was in foreign-owned companies (of which 25.2 per cent were US-owned), and 42.6 per cent of this employment was in hi-tech industry (Barrett, FitzGerald and Nolan, 2000:135–6).

These companies dominate not only employment but also output, with just ten large companies accounting for a third of value added in Irish manufacturing in 1994 (Murphy, 1994). O'Hearn (1997:25) suggests that the expansion of Intel and increased output by Dell, for example, have further concentrated that contribution since 1994. This is a key explanatory factor in terms of labour shortages and the attraction of foreign labour to fill them. Figure 1 and Tables 2 and 3 show the overall trends in labour supply and the shift in employment base in recent years. Labour supply according to all three recognised forms of measurement[2] fell rapidly and progressively between 1997 and 2001 by around 50 per cent, and although it rose again over the year 2002, it was still only to something over half of the levels at which it stood in 1997.[3]

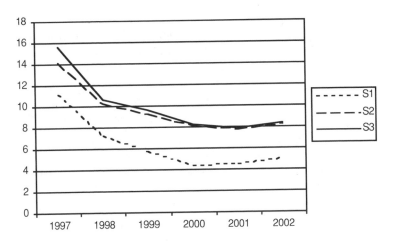

*Figure 1*   Indicators of Potential Labour Supply, 1997–2002 (%)

Source: CSO (2003a).

All figures taken from the third quarter of the relevant year.

The relative growth of the various (NACE) sectors of the economy are presented in Tables 2 and 3. Table 2 shows the percentage of employment accounted for by each sector, and the percentage change over the 1994–2002 period. Production industries, while accounting for one-third of employment in 1994, in 2002 made up less than a quarter, while the biggest growth was in construction and financial–business services.

*Table 2*   Proportion Employed in each NACE Economic Sector, 1994 and 2002 (%)

| NACE economic sector | 1994 | Q3/2002 | Change |
|---|---|---|---|
| Construction | 7.5 | 10.8 | +3.3 |
| Financial and other business services | 9.4 | 12.7 | +3.3 |
| Transport, storage and communication | 4.6 | 6.3 | +1.7 |
| Hotels and restaurants | 5.6 | 6.3 | +0.7 |
| Wholesale and retail trade | 13.8 | 14 | +0.2 |
| Public administration and defence | 5.4 | 4.9 | −0.5 |
| Education and health | 14.9 | 15.4 | +0.5 |
| Other services | 6.1 | 5.5 | −0.6 |
| Other production industries | 20.6 | 17 | −3.6 |
| Agriculture, forestry and fishing | 12 | 6.8 | −5.2 |

Source: CSO (2003a)

Table 3 represents change in gross employment. Construction, transport and communication and financial–business services doubled the size of their workforces, and there was above average expansion in hotels, education–health and wholesale and retail. 'Other services' and 'other production' rose below the average rate, while agriculture and fishing recorded a net fall in employment of nearly one-fifth.

*Table 3*   Overall Growth in Terms of Gross Employment for each NACE Economic Sector, 1994 and 2002 (000s)

| NACE economic sector | 1994 | Q3/2002 | Change (%) |
|---|---|---|---|
| Construction | 91.5 | 190.8 | 108.5 |
| Transport, storage and communication | 55.9 | 112.3 | 100 |
| Financial and other business services | 114.3 | 225.3 | 97 |
| Hotels and restaurants | 68.3 | 112.4 | 65 |
| Education and health | 181.4 | 272.7 | 50 |
| Wholesale and retail trade | 169.1 | 250.3 | 48 |
| Public administration and defence | 66.4 | 87.1 | 31 |
| Other services | 74.8 | 97.7 | 30.6 |
| Other production Industries | 252 | 302.2 | 20 |
| Agriculture, forestry and fishing | 146.9 | 119.8 | −18.5 |
| Irish economy | 1,220.6 | 1,770.7 | 45 |

Source: CSO (2003a)

The Irish economy has therefore undergone radical change since the early 1990s, let alone the early 1960s. This has been documented by a number of authors, including key actors (McSharry and White,

2000), and critiqued by academics (O'Hearn, 1995, 1998; Allen, 2000; Kirby, 2002). As a focus for international capital, particularly American multinationals, the Irish economy has been restructured largely by external sources, and there is nothing exceptional in that. In terms of the 'Tiger' analogy, O'Hearn (1998) sees Ireland closest to Singapore, with foreign direct investment (FDI) having played a dominant driving role. What is exceptional, however, is the rapidity of growth in Ireland (particularly compared to its EU neighbours) and the role occupied by Ireland at a specific moment in the development of global capitalism. O'Hearn (1995, 1997, 1998) argues that the Irish economy has emerged from a colonial phase of dependency on Britain and is now very much dependent on the USA as the principal source of capital, investment and employment. Moreover, unlike McSharry and White, he maintains that there is no causal link between the policies of austerity of the late 1980s and early '90s and the economic growth: the latter is accounted for rather by 'the rapid expansion of exports by transnational corporations, particularly a small number of US computer and pharmaceutical companies who use Ireland as a low-tax and low-cost staging point to get their goods onto continental European markets' (1997:25).

The question arises as to how much of the extra productivity is phantom (O'Hearn 1997, 1998), that is, explicable by transfer-pricing and the discrepancy between GDP and GNP, and how much of it filters through to the workforce. O'Hearn's point is borne out by the relationship between Ireland's GNP and its GDP. The former is a more accurate measure of the value added accruing to residents of the country. Irish GNP has become much lower (roughly 16 per cent in 2001) than GDP because of the profits being exported. This 'outgoing income' consists primarily of the profits and dividends of FDI companies. Before the inflow of foreign investment, in 1960, that relationship was different: GNP was much closer to GDP because of income flows to Irish residents. As a result of the transition described above, GNP growth has been slower than that of GDP, especially in the 1990s: GNP grew by 83 per cent in the 1993–2001 period, but a portion of this resulted from much larger numbers at work. At constant prices, GNP rose 59 per cent (1995–2001), with the increase per person at work accounting for 20 per cent. Overall then, significant amounts of capital leave Ireland every year in the form of price transfers, re-exported profits and dividends to overseas companies and shareholders, a practice made more lucrative by Ireland's exceptionally low corporation tax (on business profits) which stood at 10 per cent until 1 January 2003 (rising to 12.5 per cent as of that date) although there were exemptions for companies that were carrying out 'approved services' before July 1998 (IDA, 2002). The next lowest EU competitor is the UK, with a 30 per cent rate, while Belgium's rate, for example, is 40 per cent.

## Part-time and temporary employment

Within the expansion of employment, which of course can be viewed from a number of perspectives, one noticeable trend is toward greater levels of 'atypical' forms of employment. There has been a growth in the proportion of part-time working that can be broken down into two periods. From 1987 to 1997, the proportion of part-time employment in the Irish economy rose from one-tenth to almost one-fifth (ESRI, 1997). The second period is 1997–2002, when a similar trend emerges from the Labour Force survey and then the Quarterly National Household Survey (QNHS).[4] According to the CSO (2003a), in April 1994, 11.25 per cent of the workforce was working part-time, a figure that had risen to 16.4 per cent by the fourth quarter of 2002. In terms of numbers, the part-time workforce more than doubled over the 1994–2002 period (135,000–290,280). This means that 27 per cent of new jobs (in gross numbers, created since 1994) have been part-time.

O'Connell's statistics (2000) from the 1990–98 period show a growth in the part-time workforce from 8 per cent to 17 per cent, with women constituting 70 per cent of it. This, he argues, accounts for the majority of the growth in the 1983–1993 period. There is also, during this period, a counter-trend in 'underemployment', defined since 1997 as the condition of being in part-time work but stating a desire to work longer hours. The percentage of underemployed fell from 18.3 per cent in 1992 to 12.8 per cent in 1997. This means that the proportion of part-time workers choosing to work part-time has risen. However, men's levels of underemployment for those years were much higher, in the order of 35.9 per cent and 25.6 per cent respectively.

Temporary employment is far harder to assess, and the statistics are far less reliable simply because the CSO, with the vast sample available to it from the QNHS (30,000 households per quarter), does not publish figures on this. The available information is derived from much smaller-scale surveys. The Irish figures appear much lower than the EU 15 average (of 10 per cent) (EIRO, 2002a), rising from 8.5 per cent (1990) to 9.4 per cent (1997). Even taking this to be accurate, it means that the overall numbers of fixed-term contracts have risen much faster, since they constitute a rising percentage of the fastest-growing Labour force in Europe. In all countries, the share of women with a fixed-term contract is higher than the share of men. The 2000 EIRO annual update on gender issues found that, in 1999 across the EU, women were nearly 30 per cent more likely to work on a fixed-term/temporary/casual basis than men. In the Irish case, 6 per cent of women compared to 3.6 per cent of men were on fixed-term contracts in 2000.

By age group, the rate of fixed-term employment is high among the 15–24 and 25–49 cohorts. While the rate for men and women aged 15–24 is the same, the rate is higher for women in the 25–49 age group, perhaps because this is the age when many women have children and may seek more flexible arrangements. The EIRO study cited recent research in Germany which found that the youngest generation of workers was six times more likely to have a fixed-term employment contract than the oldest generation in the workforce. Moreover, non-permanent employment occurs across all levels of qualification. Although the trend has been towards higher levels of non-permanent employment across a variety of sectors in the 1990s, this is particularly evident in the expanding service sector. In the EU, over 66 per cent of all fixed-term employment contracts are in the service sector, covering retail, catering, transport, finance and the public sector, areas in which migrants are particularly represented (see below).

The overall shift towards higher levels of fixed-term contracts as a proportion of all employment between 1983 and 2000 stood at 4.3 per cent for the EU 15 (EIRO, 2002a). This was due in particular to substantial changes in Spain (16.5 per cent) and France (11.7 per cent). Ireland's trend over that period was a negative one (that is, toward permanent contracts) of 1.5 per cent, the third most encouraging in the EU behind Denmark and Greece. As of 2000, Ireland had the lowest proportion of non-permanent contracts (4.6 per cent) in the EU after Luxembourg (3.4 per cent), with the EU average at 13.4 per cent. This means that, as of 2000, there were roughly 80,000 workers in Ireland on fixed-term contracts. However, these apparently positive figures may well conceal less promising ones. They are manifestly not comparable to figures on part-time working derived from much larger samples, and also may exclude *de facto* temporary positions that are outsourced and/or categorised as work done by 'self-employed' workers. Moreover, as the EU data suggests, fixed-term contracts are concentrated in particular sectors, and their impact may well be uneven and thus less likely to show up in small-scale surveys. Lastly, in terms of structural factors affecting employment possibilities, shift work is shown to be quite a substantial element, involving around 200,000 employees (just under one in eight) (CSO, 2001). It is concentrated in the hotels, restaurants and catering sector, a major consumer of foreign (both EU and non-EU) labour. Control over personal schedules is low, and half of that number stated that they did shift work because there were no alternatives.

The figures demonstrate that the economic boom encompassed by the term 'Celtic Tiger' is one whose impact has been uneven, in terms of industry and, therefore, the types of work created. It derives in part from the shift toward services and away from production that has characterised developed economies in the post-war period, and seems to have taken place in an accelerated fashion in Ireland. Moreover, there is a high dependency on external sources of funding which tends to skew the data, artificially raising GDP.

## Booming economy, booming inequalities?

The Industrial Development Agency (IDA) Ireland claims that there are five reasons for locating to Ireland: a developing economy, business-friendly taxation, competitive (that is, low payroll) costs, a growing young population who are well educated for the needs of the economy, and a high-quality infrastructure. The presentation of Ireland as 'flexible' and 'productive' by the IDA is key to understanding something of the dynamic that has propelled the economy forward over the last decade or so. Nobody could argue that, overall, levels of wealth have not risen. What is important to look at, however, in terms of sketching a background against which racism has intensified, is the degree to which increasing wealth has been relative and contingent. There is evidence that the hoped-for trickle-down effect has remained aspirational, and that government policy interventions have helped generate poorer income distribution and exacerbate inter-regional discrepancies in income. The argument that the growth in employment has been as much through poorly-paid and relatively insecure jobs as it has in quality work is not quite supported by figures located in my research. Yet there is a question mark over the scale of temporary work, and the relatively high level of part-time work (over one in six of the 2002 workforce, and more than one in four jobs created since 1994) at least casts doubts on the opposing contention that all new jobs are high-quality, permanent ones. Part-time work is disproportionately affected by changes in policy related to incomes, which then impact on pensions, and it is to incomes that I shall now turn.

One example of the state shaping income distribution is budgetary policy. The Economic and Social Research Institute's (ESRI) 2002 report into the outcomes of budgetary policy over the 1983–2002 period (Callan, Keeney and Walsh: 2002) shows clear patterns of benefit when the population is divided up into quintiles (five bands representing income levels). The authors conclude that the

> distributive shape of budgetary policy varies considerably not just from year to year, but across three- to five-year periods covered by partnership agreements, governments or spells of high and low growth. During Ireland's recent growth spurt, budgetary policy acted to reinforce income gains for the higher income groups, while involving losses for those in the lower income groups.

Table 4 below indicates the distributive impact of Irish budgets during four low- and high-growth periods for each of the five quintiles of income distribution in the population. Revealingly, the gap in income was at its widest during the 1995–2001 boom.

*Table 4*   Distributive Impact of Irish Budgets During Low- and High-Growth Periods

| Average growth (%) | Year of budgets | Change in disposable income (%) by quintile | | | | | |
|---|---|---|---|---|---|---|---|
| | | bottom | 2nd | 3rd | 4th | top | all |
| 0.2 | 1983–86 | −5.8 | −8.5 | −10.4 | −7.2 | −7.1 | −7.7 |
| 2.4 | 1987–89 | 4.2 | −2.5 | −1.9 | −0.2 | 1.0 | 0.1 |
| 2.6 | 1993–94 | −2.1 | −2.4 | −1.0 | 0.6 | 2.0 | 0.5 |
| 8.2 | 1995–2001 | −1.9 | 3.1 | 11.8 | 13.7 | 12.5 | 10.5 |

Source: ESRI, 2002

According to this report:

> During the high growth period (1995–2001), budgetary policy led to gains of 12% or more for the top 60% of tax units, as against a loss of 2% for the bottom 20% of tax units and a small gain for the second quintile.

That finding is echoed by Barret, FitzGerald and Nolan (2000), who stress that it is increased relative growth in the top echelons of income rather than an equivalent drop in the lower and middle ones that accounts for the widening of income discrepancies. Distribution of hourly earnings is greater at the top end, with the bottom end stable: the top decile divided by the bottom decile is 4.16 (1987). In terms of weekly earnings, that figure rose from 3.68 (1987) to 3.93 (1997). When looked at from the perspective of earnings dispersion, Ireland in 1997 was second to the USA in terms of level (3.93 cf. USA 4.61, and Sweden, 2.27 (1996)). More importantly in terms of change over the 1987–97 period, earnings dispersion in the USA increased by 0.37, and in Ireland by 0.25 (cf. Finland –0.18). Dispersion increased particularly for men aged 21 and over: from 2.86 to 3.61 (a rise of 26 per cent). One clue to the insecurity of lower-income workers and households is thus that, while others are benefiting visibly from economic change, they are remaining stable if not going backwards. This perception is all the more acute for those living in particular places, when the overall figures for income are broken down, by region for example.

## Regional variations

The impressive national figures relating to production and income hide large regional discrepancies for which there are figures available. Statistics on disposable income show that, while it rose in absolute terms between 1995 and 1999, it fell, relative to the national average, in 19 of the 26 counties, with a peak in the 1997–98 period. Thus, disposable income rose only in Sligo, Galway, Dublin, Kildare, Wicklow, Clare and Limerick (CSO, 2002a). This should be read against the story of per capita Gross Value Added (GVA) (a measure of output now used in preference to per capita GDP), which fell everywhere except in Dublin and the South West region after its 1996 peak (ibid.).

So while national GVA increased by 60 per cent in the 1995–99 period, this increase was concentrated in the Dublin area and to a lesser extent in the South West (counties Cork and Kerry). The increase in output raises questions, particularly in relation to the South West where it was accompanied by a fall in disposable income: was a rise in prices concurrent with a drop in the standard of living? The inter-regional discrepancies in per capita GVA are relatively large. An index of 100 for the state shows Dublin at 133 and the Midlands at 68.5 for 1999 (i.e. almost double in Dublin). The figures for sectorial output reveal massive increases in the GDP produced by all sectors, but particularly those dominated by multinationals, that is, reproduction of recorded media, computers, chemicals and electrical machinery and equipment. These industries, when taken together, tripled their output. Moreover, there is a relatively high level of spatial concentration of these high-performing industries, which require critical mass: the Greater Dublin and Greater Cork areas. Yet these are also the types of company which, already encouraged by Europe's lowest corporation tax, use transfer pricing to export profits. The 16 per cent discrepancy between GNP and GDP is one indicator of this relationship, which basically means that Irish PAYE workers are to a certain extent subsidising the profits made in those industries, through tax incentives, services consequently not provided (for which they then have to pay private sector rates), and thus overall relative and localised fall-off in incomes.

## Poverty and spending

Ways of defining poverty are numerous and controversial, (see Glossary for the working definitions used here) and here I attempt to provide an illustrative view of change rather than critique the methods. To frame this section, it should be borne in mind that according to the OECD's *Economic Outlook* reports, Ireland in the mid '90s had the equal third highest rate of low-paid workers in the OECD (level with the UK), with 20 per cent of the workforce earning 'low pay' (Barrett et al., 2000:141).[5]

There is no specific definition of the 'working poor' in Ireland, but the commonly accepted definition of 'relative' poverty or the poverty line is income below 50 per cent of average earnings. According to the ESRI, 50 per cent of average income as of 2001 was €150 per week. Of those people earning this figure or below, 70 per cent lived in households where the head of the household did not have a job (EIRO, 2002b). Yet this means that 30 per cent of them were headed by 'poor workers', that is, those whose income did not raise them above the 50 per cent poverty level. The comparative work undertaken by the ESRI for the Combat Poverty Agency in 1994 and 1997 (Callan et al., 1999) demonstrated that 'consistent poverty' (income poverty plus 'basic deprivation') fell during that period, whilst income poverty rose slightly. Again income inequality based on increases at the top and stagnation and regression at the bottom appear as constant themes in work carried out over the last decade. It is explained in part by the fact that benefits have not kept pace with wages. Households headed by home workers, the unemployed, people with disabilities or pensioners are therefore more likely to suffer income poverty, as their principal income is in the form of benefits (or transfers, to use the technical term) (ibid.). One important qualifying factor, as acknowledged by the ESRI research team, is that institutionalised and homeless people are not included in the survey, which leads to the numbers of those experiencing both 'income poverty' and 'consistent poverty' being underestimated.

However, even among those in the workforce there is a differential risk of low pay, with part-timers (usually women), under-25s and women over 25 (vis-à-vis their male counterparts) potentially worse off than others, although this risk diminished slightly between 1994 and 1997. Moreover, the wealth in the economy is being generated to an increasing extent through unearned income. Allen (2000:60) shows that between 1987 and 1997, at factor prices, an increasing proportion of non-agricultural income in the state (from 31 per cent up to 41 per cent) derived from profits, interest, dividends and rent, while this corresponded to a decrease of that acquired through wages, pensions and social security (69 per cent down to 59 per cent). This trend continued over the 1997–2001 period (see Table 5).

*Table 5*   Proportion of Profits, and Wages in Non-Agricultural Income (as Net Value Added at Factor Cost and at Market Prices), for Selected Years 1987–2001

|  | 1987 | 1991 | 1995 | 1999 | 2001 |
|---|---|---|---|---|---|
| Wages, pensions, social security, etc. | 69 | 60.8 | 58 | 49.8 | 49.9 |
| Profits, interest, dividends, rent, etc. | 31 | 39.2 | 42 | 50.2 | 50.1 |

Source: CSO (2002c)

Moreover, the Irish tax system, with its extensive relief provisions including 'double rental' allowance and 'non-quantifiable' allowances such as those for research and development, favours corporate clients. For instance, Elan Ltd., one of the highest performing companies on the Irish stock market, paid only 2.6 per cent tax on its profits for 1998 (Allen, 2000:88). This type of loophole, set alongside the 'bogus non-resident' accounts that had been set up in 1986 by clients seeking to avoid paying DIRT (Deposit Interest Retention Tax), which cost the public purse hundreds of millions of euros in lost revenue, constitute part of the picture that is often left incomplete in discussions of public finances. As Allen argues, money given away in tax breaks to those in upper income brackets together with unpaid taxes mean that the burden on PAYE workers increases disproportionately, and creates a situation in which public services are underfunded and/or of poorer quality than elsewhere. The most glaring example of underfunding is in the public transport system, in which bus companies, for example, are funded at a minute level by international standards: Dublin Bus gets 4.4 per cent public investment compared to the 74.5 per cent and 57.4 per cent enjoyed by its equivalents in Rome and Paris respectively. Even cities in the USA subsidise their transport companies at higher levels. There is manifestly a lack of political will to make fiscal policy equitable. The neo-liberal dominant ideology to which the current government subscribes dictates that the burden of tax falls on consumption rather than income, the effect of which is to further polarise incomes, particularly in periods of rising inflation.

One area which has come to encapsulate the excesses of the economic boom is the housing market. The construction boom has been a double-edged sword. On the one hand construction is a recognised indicator of economic health. English builders are emigrating due to the lure of more secure employment. Yet, while this is good news for that industry, its associated beneficiaries, and those who purchased homes before the mid '90s (who now find themselves sitting on lucrative assets), the post-1996 housing boom has been a major consumer of incomes and has generated debt. Prices of homes more than doubled between 1996 and 2002 (Department of the Environment, 2002). Although there are regional variations, with Dublin prices highest, the national figures give an impression of the magnitude of change. Average new houses rose in price by 128 per cent (from €87,202 to €199,220) while the cost of the average second-hand house increased by 168 per cent (from €85,629 to €229,412). One of the effects of this price hike has been to cut off access to more people at the lower end of the earnings scale, and severely constrain families' options regarding the pace at which there is a return to the workforce after the birth of a child. Figures for the ranges of combined incomes of borrowers (Department of the Environment, 2000:31) show that, in the 1996–2000 period, the profile of borrowers altered substantially. In 1996, 53.1 per cent of borrowers' combined incomes fell within the €25,395–€38,092 range, and 46.8 per cent above that. By 2000, the lower range accounted for only 18.9 per cent of borrowers. Obviously, the national increase in wages and in particular types of employment must account for some of the upward movement between categories, but the skewed graph that emerges from the 2000 figures is still clear enough to convey the message that the purchase of housing became increasingly difficult to finance over that period. In 2000 the proportion of borrowers with a combined income of over €63,487 accounted for 31.1 per cent alone, while those with incomes up to €44,442 made up only 33.2 per cent of borrowers. As Keohane (2001) and Humphreys (2002) note, increasing tension over defending property, which comprises a growing physical stake in territory, is an integral part of the Celtic Tiger phenomenon.

Labelling the economic situation a 'boom', then, distracts attention from other trends, such as income polarisation, regional wealth discrepancies and a changing relationship between income and profits. Moreover, related rising suicide levels among young men[6] and increasing violent crime (including alcohol-related offences) are two 'social facts' of contemporary Irish life (O'Keeffe, 2003).[7] From the Durkheimian perspective, these are indicators of malaise, anomie and alienation, although they may be more indicative of focussed Garda operations and/or record-keeping.[8] In any case, despite a 13 per cent overall increase in per capita spending on food (1995–2000), the Irish spent only 86.5 per cent of the amount spent on tobacco and alcohol on buying food in 2000 (CSO, 2002a). Indeed, since 1999, the amount spent annually on tobacco and alcohol has exceeded that spent on food. It is against centripetal forces, a background of increasing profitability of companies, increasing wealth but also increasing discrepancies of wealth (regional, sectorial and by quintile), and an overall perceived drop in the quality of life (Deegan, 2002), that the resurgence of racist ideas and practices must be read. Instability and rapid social change are inherent to boom periods as they are to bust.

## STATISTICS ON MIGRATION AND MINORITIES

While the justification for the collection of data by the state is to enable more effective planning, it is also clear that this exercise is multifunctional, enabling a degree of social control possible only through the power mobilised by the state. Any study of statistics reveals a number of points about the assumptions of the bodies collecting them, and should lead us to critically appraise the sources. Mac Laughlin (1997) refers to the early days of demographic statistics and charges that they were used to control the poor and served as food for the Malthusian-inspired policy debates, while Allen (2000) notes the near impossibility of obtaining data on the very wealthy *vis-à-vis* the ease with which figures on the least wealthy (through their interaction with the state) are available. Data collection also has consequences for the issue of racialisation, feeding as it does into the methods people use to make sense of difference. Census questions on ethnicity for example classify a population using particular labels, which are then reproduced in monitoring exercises and legislation and finally are accepted by minority groups (as the basis for campaigning or funding applications, as in Omi and Winant's example of the category 'Hispanic' in the USA (1996)[9] or even contested, as happened in the UK in 2000. Religious groups in Asian communities there campaigned for the census to ask questions relating to religion rather than country of origin. The resulting Census Amendment Act introduced categories of Muslim, Hindu and Sikh into the 2001 census. Moreover I contend that the 'EU national'/'non-EU national' boundary is an increasingly racialised and politicised one.

The key questions, then, are who is counted, how and why? In terms of migration figures, these questions enable us to produce a critical survey of the ideological construction of those statistics. Attention to particular groups rather than others, the categories used and the focus given to them by agencies and the media form one of the prisms through which discussion of issues is structured and legitimised. The obvious case is that of asylum-seekers. In Ireland asylum-seekers have been numerically inferior to economic migrants in every year except 1999, yet discussion has been overwhelmingly about legality and threats to the nation that the former pose. Demographic statistics are not only a head count, they are also part of the process of defining, in an ulterior discourse, who is eligible for membership of a national community with access to social resources and who is not.

One look at the CSO's data-collection categories relating to nationality places the framework squarely in the pre-1990 period.[10] In the Quarterly National Household Survey (which replaced the Labour Force Survey in 1997), data is collected using the following categories: Ireland, Northern Ireland, Britain, a number of individual EU countries, 'Other EU', Canada, USA, Australia, New Zealand, and 'Rest of the World'. The sensitive mind might detect a subversive nationalist plot in recording 'Northern Ireland' as separate from 'Britain', while the choice of breakdown reveals traditional sources for sojourn if not lasting migration into Ireland prior to the 1980s. However, when migration estimates are published, the categories are reduced further: UK, Ireland, USA, EU and 'Rest of the World'. This framework was not unreasonable before the second half of the 1990s. Since then though, as asylum-seeking and economic migration have increased, the 'Rest of the World' category has become vague and inadequate. Moreover, estimates of the asylum-seeking population have recently been forced on the CSO because the majority of asylum-seekers are in institutional settings not covered by the QNHS. Figures are therefore approximate and do not reveal the status (asylum-seeker, refugee, migrant worker, student) or the precise nationality (except for Irish, UK or USA) of those counted. The principal demographic data derived from the 2002 census was released in June 2003 (CSO, 2003b).[11] This included statistics on nationality and religion showing the extent to which the experience of net immigration (exactly coterminous with the intercensal period) has impacted in qualitative terms. Table 6 shows the CSO's breakdown of respondents by nationality. The census records an overall population increase of 291,116 (+8 per cent) to 3.917 million (the highest total since 1871).

## Analysis of Irish immigration patterns

In 1996, Ireland became a country of net immigration. Set within a longer-term framework, the majority of immigrants identified by Courtney (2000) in figures up to 1998 had arrived in the country since the 1971 census. Table 7 shows the relationship between

*Table 6*   Breakdown of Population by Nationality

| Nationality | Number (000s) | % |
| --- | --- | --- |
| Irish | 3,535.7 | 91.6 |
| Dual Irish/Other | 49.3 | 1.2 |
| UK | 103.5 | 2.6 |
| Other EU | 30 | 0.7 |
| Rest of Europe | 23.1 | 0.7 |
| Africa | 21 | 0.6 |
| Asia | 21.8 | 0.6 |
| USA | 11.4 | 0.3 |
| Other countries | 11.2 | 0.3 |
| Multiple Nationality | 2.3 | 0.1 |
| No nationality | 0.8 | 0 |
| Not stated | 48.4 | 1.3 |
| Total | 3,858 | 100 |

Source: CSO (2003b)

emigration and immigration for the period 1987–2002. Since 1996, the discrepancy between them has grown, with net immigration standing at 28,700 as of the April 2002 estimate.

These figures indicate that 5.8 per cent of the usually resident population of Ireland (223,7000) are foreign nationals, the highest proportion of whom are UK nationals (103,500, i.e. 2.6 per cent of the total population).

*Table 7*   Immigration and Emigration into and from Ireland, Selected Years, 1987–2002 (000s)

| Year | Emigration | Immigration | Balance |
| --- | --- | --- | --- |
| 1987 | 40.2 | 17.2 | +23 |
| 1990 | 56.3 | 33.3 | +23 |
| 1993 | 35.1 | 34.7 | +0.4 |
| 1996 | 31.2 | 39.2 | –8 |
| 1999 | 29 | 47.5 | –18.5 |
| 2002 | 18.8 | 47.5 | –28.7 |

Source: CSO (2002b)

Moreover, closer inspection of the components of the immigrant body (as revealed in the CSO's *Population and Migration Estimates*) demonstrates five significant trends:

i.   The figure for returning emigrants, who made up over 50 per cent of the increase in the mid '90s, fell for the first time (to 48 per cent) in 2002.

ii.  The 'Rest of the World' category is the fastest-growing source of immigration, rising from 2,400 to 16,400 between 1996 and 2002, and accounting for 17 per cent of immigration over that period.[12] In 2002, returning emigrants accounted for 37.9 per cent, and 'Rest of the World' 34.5 per cent of all immigration respectively, the former comprising 45.4 per cent of 1996–2002 immigration. UK and 'Other EU' have fallen slightly over that period, but still account for 16.7 per cent and 13.5 per cent of immigration respectively.

iii. Between 1994 and 1997, there was still a net outflow among the 15–24 cohort (44,100) and an inflow of the 25–44 cohort (27,400). While this stabilised slightly in the 1998–2002 period (CSO, 2002b), the net outflow stood at 20,700 for 1996–2002 (CSO, 2003b), making a total of 54,000 for 1994–2002. So while the proportion of 15–24-year-olds among those emigrating is decreasing (from 68 per cent in 1996, to 49 per cent in 2002), that cohort is still the most numerically important. The inflow of the 25–44 cohort for that period was 93,200 and the 0–14 cohort saw a massive inflow of 37,100 (1996–2002).

iv.   Among immigrants, overall there were slightly more women (50.9 per cent) over men (49.1 per cent) in the 1996–2002 period, while this was reversed in the 'Rest of the World' category, where the percentages were 56.6 per cent and 43.4 per cent in favour of men.

v.   The educational level of immigrants has been very high. In the 30–39 age group, 28 per cent of returning migrants arriving in the 1994–97 period had a degree, compared with 12.7 per cent of the domestic population, and 43.2 per cent of other immigrants (Barrett and Trace, 1998)

## Work Permits

Work Permits are issued by the Department of Enterprise, Trade and Employment, and all the figures in this section are sourced from that institution. A work permit is the property of the employer rather than the employee, and can be obtained only when the former can prove that 'reasonable efforts' have been made to fill the post from within Ireland or the European Economic Area (EEA). As of March 2003, this meant advertising the job on the FAS (the state training agency) web site and receiving no appropriate applications as a result. The cost of a twelve-month work permit has stood at €500 since 1 January 2003. There is thus no possibility of workers outside the EEA taking jobs from Irish workers using the work permit scheme.

In my review of the statistics, I shall focus on the 1996–2002 period. This has witnessed a rise from 3,778 permits issued in 1996 to 40,321 in 2002 (cf. an increase in employment of around 577,000 jobs over the same period). The statistics are disaggregated by sector and by nationality only, and Tables 8 and 9 present the trends in these.

In 2002 Services, Catering and Agriculture accounted for 78.9 per cent of work permits, whereas they represented 45.7 per cent in 1996. Permits for medical and nursing trades, industry and entertainment fell from the 45.6 per cent they accounted for in 1996, to only 17 per cent in 2002.

A work visa scheme has been in operation since 2000, granting the document to the employee rather than employer (cf. the work permit), and is targeted on skilled professions and trades listed by the

Department of Enterprise (for example, medicine, engineering and computing). The holder of a work visa has the right to family reunification and free school education for dependent children up to the age of 18, but no access to benefits. Compared with the work permit, there are obvious advantages, not least the fact that the document can be obtained in the worker's country of origin and does not tie him/her to one employer within the designated profession. Around 1,200 of these have been delivered.

*Table 8*   Work Permits Granted to Non-EU Nationals in Ireland, 1996–2002

| Year | Total (new permits + renewals) | +/– (%) |
|------|-------------------------------|---------|
| 1996 | 3,778 | |
| 1997 | 4,544 | +20 |
| 1998 | 5,716 | +25.8 |
| 1999 | 6,260 | +9.5 |
| 2000 | 18,006 | +188 |
| 2001 | 36,436 | +102 |
| 2002 | 40,321 | +10.66 |

Source: Department of Enterprise, Trade and Employment

*Table 9*   Work Permits Granted to Non-EU Nationals in Ireland, by Sector, 1996 and 2002 (%)[13]

| Sector | 1996 | 2002 | Change % / factor |
|--------|------|------|-------------------|
| Agriculture and Fisheries | 1.35 | 15.94 | +14.61/ x11.8 |
| Catering | 10.63 | 25.56 | +14.93 / x2.4 |
| Domestic | 0.77 | 1.95 | +1.18 / x2.5 |
| Education | 5.87 | 1.51 | –4.36 /x–3.9 |
| Entertainment | 8.70 | 2.17 | –6.53 / x–4 |
| Exchange Agreements | 0.72 | 0.74 | +0.02 / x +1.02 |
| Industry | 11.32 | 7.67 | –3.65 / x–1.5 |
| Medical and Nursing | 25.58 | 7.15 | –18.43 / x–3.6 |
| Service Industries | 33.78 | 37.37 | +3.59 / x1.1 |
| Sport | 1.24 | 0.38 | –0.86 / x–3.3 |

Source: Department of Enterprise, Trade and Employment

While, overall, the number of permits issued has increased, and quickly, the proportions within this development have substantially changed. US nationals historically accounted for the dominant majority, and this has only altered in very recent times, with former Eastern bloc countries such as Latvia and Lithuania, as well as the Philippines becoming more important sources of labour (see Table 10). Indeed, the approximate regional breakdown (Table 11) clearly demonstrates that the shift has been away from developed economies toward developing ones, with former Communist bloc Europe now the majority labour-provider. This might be viewed as a continuation of a core–periphery process, in which labour transfers from European periphery nations service the economic growth of the larger core economies, as did transfers from the Southern and Western European periphery economies (Spain, Portugal, Italy, Greece, Turkey and Ireland) up until the late 1980s.

*Table 10*   Top Five Nationalities Issued with Work Permits, 1996 and 2002

|   | 1996 Country | No. of permits | 2002 Country | No. of permits |
|---|---|---|---|---|
| 1 | USA | 776 | Latvia | 3,958 |
| 2 | Pakistan | 357 | Lithuania | 3,816 |
| 3 | India | 235 | Philippines | 3,255 |
| 4 | Japan | 212 | Poland | 3,142 |
| 5 | Malaysia | 180 | Romania | 2,459 |
|   | No. of countries | 98 | No. of countries | 130 |

Source: Department of Enterprise, Trade and Employment

*Table 11*   Proportion of Work Permits Issued, 1996 and 2002, by Region[*] (%)

| Region | 1996 | 2002 % | Increase (factor) |
|---|---|---|---|
| Europe (former Communist bloc) | 7 | 55.3 | 48.3 (x7.9) |
| North America and Australasia | 30.8 | 6.9 | –23.9 (x–4.5) |
| Indian sub-continent | 17.5 | 6.4 | –11.1 (x–2.7) |
| Rest of Asia | 17.8 | 16.9 | –0.9 (x–1.05) |
| Latin America | 2.5 | 3.9 | 1.4 (x1.6) |
| North Africa & Middle East | 7.1 | 1.8 | –5.3 (x–3.9) |
| West Indies and Sub-Saharan Africa | 6.5 | 7.2 | 0.7 (x1.1) |
| Other Europe | 3.2 | 0.26 | –2.94 (x–12) |

Source: Department of Enterprise, Trade and Employment
[*]   author's categorisation

Moreover, from 1 January 2004, nationals of the ten 'applicant states' joining the EU[14] will no longer require work permits, and thus around 35 per cent of current economic migration will shift category (to 'Other EU nationals') in the official Irish statistics (O'Brien, 2003). At that point, if current trends continue, it might be Asia that becomes the predominant extra-European Union labour source for Ireland, a fitting tribute to the 'Celtic Tiger' that took its name from Asian models.

Moreover, in addition to work permit recipients, there are also thousands of EU nationals who do not require them. In racialised terms, then, most of the economic migration into Ireland is 'white'. However, this should not lull us into imagining that the patterns witnessed in France and the UK, for example, where 'white' immigration has been conceptualised as virtually unproblematic, in an amnesiac post-war state, will be reproduced in Ireland. Although disproportionate media and political focus on asylum-seekers betrays anxiety over developing world nationals perceived to be sapping the resources of the welfare state, in the newer trends identified in the early twenty-first century, white nationals of underdeveloped European economies are also racialised, in neo-Victorian terms, as the dangerous poor, a form of racism labelled by Sivanandan (2001, 2002; IRR, 2001) as 'xeno-racism'.

## Asylum-seekers and refugees

Whilst obtaining information on overall numbers of asylum-seekers is straightforward, doing so about their nationality is less easy. As for refugees and those with associated status, the trail becomes cool as the individuals leave the Department of Justice's area of responsibility. Moreover, in any given year, the applications dealt with will probably not be those that were lodged, due to the backlog. The figures for those granted refugee status in a particular year are therefore tenuously linked to the number of applications. Added to this there is the further complicating factor that appeals against rejection are mounted, and often successfully. The original appeal decision may be reached some years after the initial application. During the period 1 January 1996–31 December 2002 the total number of people granted refugee status at first instance was 2,101. During this period a further 2,366 people were granted refugee status at appeal,[15] giving a total of 4,467. Added to the 1,816 Programme Refugees arriving since 1973 enumerated by Fanning (2002:96–7),[16] this gives an estimated 6,283. However, this obviously does not include those few hundred given 'humanitarian leave to remain', nor does it take into account anyone from those groups who has died or left the country since being granted refugee status. All in all, the number of refugees in Ireland in early 2003 could not account for much more than 0.15 per cent of the 3.9 million population. Asylum applications (to end 2002) have risen very steeply since 1995 (see Table 12), again from a very low base. Until 1995 there were usually fewer than 50 applications per annum. Yet over the 1996–2002 period, Ireland rose from tenth in Europe in overall numbers of applications to fourth, and in per capita population terms, from 0.33 per 1,000 to almost 3 per 1,000. However, this way of reading the figures conceals Ireland's late arrival among the ranks of refugee-receiving nations. If the clock starts in 1992, for example, Ireland's per capita figure is roughly 1.25 per 1,000 over the 1992–2002 period. Out of 30 industrialised countries in 2001, Ireland ranked tenth in per capita terms (the other nine were all EU) (UNHCR, 2002). In any case, number of applications per capita, despite it being bandied about as the most appropriate indicator, is no less arbitrary than any other. Why not 'number of applications over per capita income'? for example.

In terms of nationalities, 45–50 per cent of applicants in every year since 1996 have been Nigerian and Romanian nationals (principally Roma) combined, although other African states such as Algeria, Somalia, DR Congo, and former Eastern bloc countries have provided hundreds each. Recently Moldova and Ukraine have emerged as asylum-seeking countries (see Table 13).

Current accurate figures on the number of asylum-seekers actually in the country are hard to come by, but there are an estimated 4,600 on direct provision (that is, in collective accommodation paid for by the Department of Justice, and receiving an allowance of €19 per adult per week).

*Table 12*   Numbers of Asylum Applications Lodged in Ireland 1996–2002

| Year | Applications | Increase on Previous Year (%) |
|------|-------------|-------------------------------|
| 1995 | 424 | |
| 1996 | 1,179 | +170 |
| 1997 | 3,883 | +230 |
| 1998 | 4,626 | +20 |
| 1999 | 7,700 | +66 |
| 2000 | 10,938 | +40 |
| 2001 | 10,375 | –0.06 |
| 2002 | 11,634 | +12 |

Source: Office of the Refugee Appeals Commissioner

*Table 13*   Top Five Countries of Origin of Asylum-Seeker Applications, 2001 and 2002

| 2001 (10,325) | | 2002 (11,634) | |
|---|---|---|---|
| Nigeria | 3,461 (33.5%) | Nigeria | 4,050 (34.8%) |
| Romania | 1,348 (13.1%) | Romania | 1,677 (14.4%) |
| Moldova | 549 (5.3%) | Moldova | 536 (4.6%) |
| Ukraine | 376 (3.6%) | Zimbabwe | 357 (3.1%) |
| Croatia | 307 (3%) | Ukraine | 351 (3%) |
| Others | 4,284 (41.5%) | Others | 4,663 (40.1%) |

Source: Office of the Refugee Application Commissioner

### Residence

While work permits and asylum applications enable a rough outline of the national immigrant population to be arrived at, short-term residence permits comprise an essential component. They are granted to those who do not fall into either of the first two categories: students, dependants of those with work permits, and those who do not require work permits in the first place, that is, nationals of other EU states including the UK. Civil servant in the Department of Justice Brian Ingolsby (2002) states that there were around 90,000 non-EEA nationals legally resident in the state as of June 2002 (2.3 per cent of the 3.9 million population) of which the largest number were said to be Chinese. This is an unusual conclusion based on asylum applications and work permits alone, and suggests, by process of elimination, that a very high number of student visas have been granted to Chinese nationals over recent years.

The recent developments in citizenship law and the interpretations of these *vis-à-vis* residency for foreign nationals with Irish-born children are discussed more fully in Chapter 7. Estimates made at the time of the Supreme Court's decision that Irish-born children did not necessarily confer residency rights on foreign parents in January 2003 indicated a figure of around 10,000 parents who had been granted residency on that basis, and a further 7–10,500 in the system having applied for this right (Haughey 2003b).

### Conclusions

Migration patterns have altered in terms of overall direction, as well as source and type. Ireland is now a country of 'new immigration', joining the ranks of Southern and Western Periphery European states in this position. The sources of the various categories of migrants are numerous and diverse, with nationals of 130 countries being granted work permits in 2002 and over 100 countries represented among asylum-seekers. Since the late 1990s, the early trends, with the USA still high on the list of work-permit migrants alongside a few Asian countries providing skilled workers, have given way to a new configuration in which former Eastern bloc nationals dominate, and countries which have been targeted for recruitment such as the Philippines, South Africa and Brazil also provide thousands of workers. On this elementary level, the Irish labour force, as opposed to its economy, is fully globalised, if that is taken to mean open to international labour as much as capital.

Within the new trends of migration are two distinct groups of people, skilled and unskilled, with a targeted work visa scheme recruiting directly into particular sectors, and the work permit scheme filling gaps in the service sector, agriculture and catering. Without a greater level of access to work permit details, further analysis, however, is merely speculative.

Alongside this new immigration sits a continuing emigration. The former has exceeded the latter since 1996, but emigration has not ceased. Indeed, there is still an outflow of the 15–24 age cohort that cannot fully be accounted for by the notion of elite emigration. Moreover, as demonstrated above, economic trends within the boom are strongly suggestive of polarisation: concentration on key industries, discrepancies in income, uneven rates of regional growth, greater levels of temporary and part-time work. All of this corresponds to developments elsewhere in Western Europe, where the three-tier labour market model is emerging (Brah, 1996). In this, a relatively small core of permanent well-paid and highly skilled workers are serviced by lower-paid workers who in turn are supported by casual temporary and part-time workers who may move in and out of the labour market regularly. Brah notes that the last group is dominated by women and migrant workers.

This is of course not to argue that all migrants slot into the foot of the labour hierarchy. Moreover, someone intent on verbal or physical abuse of a racialised group member will not enquire first as to the person's profession. All classes of migrant are equally vulnerable to racist attacks. Yet other restrictions still apply to an Indian computer specialist on a work visa for example: he/she has temporary residence, limited access to state resources and thus to long-term planning.

In this social and economic climate, with other trends showing more intense work, increasing overall wealth and the discrepancies in its distribution between private and public sector, and between the developed south and east and the less-developed west and north (of the Republic), it becomes more important to defend what is earned. The possibility of falling behind, or, worse still, unemployment, means that more is at stake than in the times when unemployment and emigration were more widespread. Defensiveness and its ensuing frustration find targets made available through pre-existing sets of ideas and new numbers of visibly 'different' people: a framework for making sense of uneven, disconcerting and ultimately stressful social change. 'Race' is one readily available tool for trying to understand difference and remain powerful. I shall now turn to the ways in which people have so far utilised 'race' to make sense of this process, by referring to attitudinal surveys.

## ATTITUDINAL SURVEYS (1973–2001)[17]

In Ireland the majority of attitudinal surveys on racism have been carried out since 1997, an indication in itself of the timing of public interest in the topic. However, some pioneering work done in the 1970s and '80s (Mc Gréil, 1996)[18] acts as a point of departure, and a corrective to those arguments that racism was 'born' in the 1990s. Mc Gréil's two sets of fieldwork were done in 1972–73 and 1988, the first in Dublin and the second using a national sample. The two are not then strictly comparable. Moreover, Mc Gréil's methodology uses social distance scales, so it is hard to relate his findings directly to later opinion polls except in the broadest terms.[19] He found widespread levels of prejudice against a very broad palette of 59 target groups ranging from ethnic and racialised minorities to political groups and marginal social groups like alcoholics, the unemployed and drug-users. Racism, anti-Semitism and sectarianism were all present in 1970s Ireland, long before substantial numbers of non-Europeans were resident there. The social distance table containing 59 groups shows the highest ranking group defined as non-white was 'Coloureds' (35) followed by Africans (37), Blacks (39), Indians (43), Nigerians (45) and Black Americans (47). Travellers were 52nd, while Jews came 32nd.

Moreover, in relative terms the greatest hostility toward a racialised minority was expressed in regard to the Travellers, a finding which has been corroborated by more recent research (Citizen Traveller,

2000b; Amnesty International, 2001a; Curry, 2000). The follow-up survey in the 1980s identified generally lower levels of racism than that of the 1970s, except toward Travellers. Hostility towards Travellers, however, was not noticeably affected by the social class variable. Indeed anti-Traveller racism was found to be so great – over 3.5 in the social distance score – as to make them an 'out-group'.

Anti-Semitism was also high and in some cases (for instance, in response to questions on admittance to family and kinship) higher than in 1972–73. The 1988 survey helped produce a rough profile which showed that hostile attitudes were more likely to be held by older people, with less formal education, in lower social classes, living in more rural areas. Hence Connaught/Ulster consistently scored the most negative, since its population most closely fitted that profile. This was, of course, a relative rather than an absolute difference, but one borne out in the more recent work.

## Attitudinal trends, 1997–2001

The trends in opinion in the 1997–2001 period have been identified from sources ranging from the EU Eurobarometers, polls commissioned by Irish newspapers, and those carried out on behalf of organisations with interests in the area such as Amnesty International (see Appendix 1 for presentation of the sources).

The most obvious change is in the intensification of hostile attitudes. Mc Gréil had observed a reduction in racist views between the early 1970s and the late '80s. The material produced in the 1990s gives only a relatively short period for comparison, and sample groups that in general have a –/+3 per cent (that is, 6 per cent) margin of error. Yet, even given these restrictions, there is a noticeable hardening of attitudes between 1997 and 2000. One of the largest changes in all responses in the Eurobarometer 2000 was that given by Irish respondents to the question 'do you find the presence of minorities to be disturbing?' In 1997, 16 per cent had replied in the affirmative, while three years later 42 per cent did so: the highest proportion in the EU 15. An identical question asked in the same period, March–April 2000, and published in the *Star* newspaper (19–20.4.00) produced the results presented in Tables 14 and 15.

The detail of groups felt to be 'disturbing' was not sought in the Eurobarometer 2000, but the responses from the 1997 version (Table 16) are comparable. Romanians have overtaken 'Itinerants/Travellers', presumably as the most high-profile asylum-seeking group, assimilated to Travellers, with similar cultural practices. 'Blacks' and

'Refugees' have also either risen or appeared in the top five. Clearly there is a focus on particular groups identified as comprising a problem by 2000, in a survey period that in addition witnessed the beginning of the government's dispersal programme and the concomitant media coverage received by resistance to the siting of asylum-seekers in provincial centres.

*Table 14*   'Disturbing Difference' in the *Star* Poll

| | |
|---|---|
| Q. Among the groups of people who live in Ireland and are not of the same race, religion or culture as yourself, which one group strikes you as being particularly different from yourself and which a) do you find sometimes disturbing b) Irish people find sometimes disturbing? | |
| Personally find disturbing | 27% |
| *Not* personally but Irish people find disturbing | 10% |
| Not disturbing | 63% |

*Table 15*   Top Five Groups Felt to be 'Disturbing', the *Star* Poll, 2000

| | |
|---|---|
| Romanians | 9% |
| Itinerants/Travellers | 7% |
| Blacks | 5% |
| Refugees | 4% |
| Muslims | 2% |

NB. 4 per cent of responses were 'individual nationalities', and 'Other groups' on 3 per cent.

*Table 16*   Top Five Groups Felt to be 'Disturbing', Eurobarometer 1997

| | |
|---|---|
| Itinerants/Travellers | 6% |
| Muslims | 5% |
| Blacks | 2% |
| Jehovah's Witnesses | 2% |
| New Age Travellers | 2% |

NB. 4 per cent of responses were 'Other groups', with less than 1 per cent each.

Moreover, of the questions asked in opinion poll surveys in the 1997–2001 period, only four are absolutely comparable across more than two studies. The results are tabulated and appear in Table 17. The two 2000 polls show almost identical results, and the comparison with 1997 is also quite conclusive. Sizeable proportions of those who either were positive or non-committal about minorities in 1997 were hostile by 2000.

*Table 17*    Comparison of Responses to Identical Questions in
Eurobarometer (E) 1997, 2000 and the *Star* (Star) Poll, 2000

| Question | | Agree (%) | Disagree (%) | Don't Know (%) |
|---|---|---|---|---|
| 1 The presence of these minority | E 97 | 35 | 37 | 28 |
| groups increases unemployment | E 2000 | 46 | 37 | 18 |
| | Star 2000 | 42 | 44 | 14 |
| 2 People from these minority | E 97 | 33 | 35 | 32 |
| groups abuse the social welfare | E 2000 | 56 | 22 | 22 |
| system | Star 2000 | 56 | 25 | 19 |
| 3 In schools where there are too | E 97 | 30 | 48 | 22 |
| many of these minority children, | E 2000 | 43 | 39 | 18 |
| the quality of education suffers | Star 2000 | 38 | 43 | 19 |
| 4 The presence of people from | E 97 | 16 | 61 | 23 |
| these minority groups is a cause | E 2000 | 42 | 43 | 14 |
| of insecurity | Star 2000 | 43 | 38 | 19 |

## Anti-Traveller attitudes

There were three surveys carried out for the Citizen Traveller project, two of which deal with attitudes towards Travellers, and one with Travellers themselves. The first (Citizen Traveller, 2000a), is a comparative survey placing attitudes toward Travellers held by the settled population in the context of feelings towards other minority groups, similar to Mc Gréil's study. Of 15 groups, Travellers appeared in the top two in measures of exclusion (equal with Hare Krishna but below drug addicts/alcoholics), and the bottom two (above drug addicts/alcoholics) in measures of inclusion. Other minorities relevant to this study fared better in these two scales. 'Black people' came second in inclusion, Africans third, Jews fifth, Indians sixth and Muslims eighth.

The profiles of those with a higher tendency towards unfavourable attitudes to Travellers were found to be in the 45–54 and 55–64 age cohorts, rural dwellers with a farming background, particularly from Munster and Connaught/Ulster. That is to say that all these were over-represented in the group with unfavourable attitudes toward Travellers compared with their proportion of the sample. Men were more likely to be hostile than women. Within the more tolerant groups, there is a pattern of contact echoed in the Amnesty report on minorities (2001a): those with the least amount of contact with Travellers (through school, work, social life or having jobs done by them) were more likely to be hostile. Of these, school was the least decisive in terms of variables.

The *Barometer* replicated a benchmark survey carried out in August 1999 but not made public. One result in the 2000 minorities survey that is very different from the *Barometer Survey* (Citizen Traveller, 2001) is that of general attitudes towards Travellers (see Table 18).

*Table 18*   Comparison of Two Sets of Attitudes Toward Travellers

| Attitude | Attitudes to Minorities (2000) (%) | *Barometer Survey* (2001) (%) |
|---|---|---|
| Favourably disposed | 45 | 25 |
| Neutral | 13 | 52 |
| Unfavourably disposed | 42 | 23 |

The wording in the two surveys is not so different to be obviously less conducive to neutrals, the category which records a difference of 39 per cent. Some of the questions in the 2001 survey related to the campaign's visibility, but the rest were on attitudes towards Travellers. The issue of Travellers was one of those felt by respondents to be less important in 2001 than it had been in the 1999 *Barometer*. However, there was only a minimal change in attitudes over this period, mostly falling within the margin of error for a survey of this size.

The one statistically significant finding was that in the latter survey more people saw Travellers as different *in their own right* from the rest of Irish society (43 per cent felt Travellers were exactly like the rest of the community in 1999, cf. 37 per cent in 2001). Moreover, the basis for holding negative attitudes had become more focussed by 2001, with concerns about rubbish and dirt, coupled with a perception that 'Travellers can be troublesome', particularly prevalent.

There were also slight increases in support for the idea that local and national authorities should act to resolve problems facing Travellers (in 2001 55 per cent agreed that local authorities should prioritise accommodation for Travellers, and 65 per cent felt that the government should provide major investment, compared with 52 per cent and 62 per cent respectively in 1999). However, in 2001 90 per cent said they would oppose Traveller accommodation being sited near their homes, while 61 per cent agreed that 'people rightly blame Travellers for many things'. These levels of antipathy toward Travellers in practice correspond with a legitimisation of difference and point to a worrying intractability in anti-Traveller racism that extends through time and across space. In other words, although the language of equality is now being employed and only wilfully disrespectful commentators now use 'traveller' with a lower-case 't', or even 'itinerant', the actual content of anti-Traveller racism has been markedly unchanged since the beginning of Fanning's case study (2002) of Clare County Council covering the years 1963–99.

## Minority experiences

There is a very small but growing literature on research into minority experiences of racism in Ireland. Here I shall concentrate on the Amnesty International (2001b) report which is based on the largest sample so far, and Citizen Traveller's work on Travellers' experiences. Reference to reports with smaller samples will also be made.

For the respondents in *A Survey of Travellers* (Citizen Traveller, 2000b), the overwhelming majority of experiences of discrimination were encountered when attempting to access services: 71 per cent said they had encountered it from pub owners, 40 per cent from disco and club owners, and 37 per cent from shop owners. Public officials were also represented, with 38 per cent of Travellers claiming to have experienced discrimination from Gardai, 33 per cent from County Councils and 33 per cent from housing authorities. These experiences are mirrored in the rising number of claims under the Equal Status Act 2001–2002, as indicated in the Equality Authority's annual reports (Equality Authority, 2002, 2003), which show the 'Traveller' grounds as the one producing the highest number of claims of discrimination, particularly around licensed premises. Indeed, the thrust of the Vintners' Association campaign in 2002 in response to what they viewed as a 'scam' by Travellers was to argue for disputes involving licensed premises to be withdrawn from the remit of the Office of the Equality Investigator.

Travellers in halting sites have the most direct experience of discrimination, while those living on the roadside are most likely to report experiencing it from councils, housing authorities and schools. Around 50 per cent of all Travellers have reported experiences of being forcibly moved on, frequently more than once, and this is more prevalent among those living in temporary sites or on the roadside. Fear of being moved on is reported as a serious concern for 44 per cent of those polled.

Amnesty International's *Racism in Ireland: The Views of Black and Ethnic Minorities* (2001b) focuses on experiences of minority groups, particularly in terms of discrimination encountered and relationships with the Gardai and the court system. It represents a step forward in capturing the largest sample of ethnic minority people so far, using a model of ethnic categorisation and recording the problems thrown up,[20] and involving minority interviewers, thus granting a degree of ownership of the project to minority groups and securing a remarkably high response rate of 99.5 per cent.[21]

Of those who returned questionnaires, 79 per cent claimed to have experienced racism or discrimination. This figure, obtained from fieldwork completed prior to 11 September 2001, contained a range of scores from 88.6 per cent (Black Irish) to 52 per cent (South Asian). The majority of these experiences were not one-offs, with 32.3 per cent saying they occurred 'occasionally' and 36.2 per cent 'frequently', leading the authors to conclude that: 'racism is becoming a frequent and endemic "structural" feature within Irish society, rather than a mere aberration. Episodes of racist insults or abuse appear to be occurring frequently and on a daily basis in Ireland' (2001a:17). Black Africans and Travellers appear to have had most frequent experiences of racism (43.2 per cent and 41.4 per cent of them respectively stated having these experiences frequently), while only 17 per cent of North Africans reported this.

The overwhelming majority of these incidents occurred in public spaces: 44 per cent on the street, 24 per cent in shops and 23 per cent in pubs. Discrimination 'from neighbours', on buses and in banks were all close behind. Particularly striking in this report is the high level of incidents reported from encounters with Gardai (ranked second). The report's sections on community–police relations (ibid.:30–7, 41–3) paint a bleak picture. The Gardai were viewed as the primary agency responsible for dealing with racist incidents, yet 56 per cent of those polled felt that they were not treated fairly by them (with 27 per cent answering 'don't know'). Four in five had experienced racism at the hands of Gardai, and only 14 per cent thought that reports of racist incidents were taken seriously (against 61 per cent who did not). These results show that 'members of ethnic minorities have a strikingly low level of confidence in the Gardai' (ibid.:34). The conclusions arrived at by most of the respondents are clear. Around 80 per cent believed not enough was being done to protect them, or to stop racism becoming more widespread, and that the state was responsible for leading such initiatives.

The findings of the Amnesty report echo those of much smaller surveys (Pilgrim House Foundation, 1998; African Refugee Network, 1999; Horgan, 2000; Curry, 2000; Boucher, 1998). All of these surveys uncovered experiences of discrimination in public spaces and from actors in 'gatekeeping' roles such as Gardai, shopowners, landlords, bouncers, publicans, and so forth. Levels of verbal abuse outstripped those for physical abuse. Blacks, Travellers and Roma reported the highest and most frequent incidence of abuse, a finding that tallies with the positioning of these three groups as the most 'disturbing' presences in Ireland (Eurobarometer 1997, 2000; *Star*, 2000 – see above).

The strikingly public location of most of the incidents reported indicates a low level of self-censorship among the host population, that is, an atmosphere in which people do not expect any retribution or sanction for their actions (verbal or otherwise) to be administered by those around them. For example, in Casey and O'Connell (2000), Faughnan and Woods (2000), and the Citizen Traveller polls (2000b; 2001), as well as Amnesty's, most respondents who reported discrimination identified service providers, such as publicans, shopkeepers, doormen, Gardai, and so on, as key instigators of racist actions and practices. Clearly, the idea that racism is 'a breach of human rights' or 'unacceptable' is far from having taken root in Ireland.

One worrying feature is the relationship emerging between the minority communities and the Gardai. Despite the progressive work being accomplished in some areas, the overall picture from the minority's perspective appears to be one of suspicion and lack of confidence.

## Conclusions

Coming to any firm conclusions about surveys of racist attitudes in Ireland is difficult. The order, phrasing and tone of questions used in surveys can distort or unduly structure respondents' answers. Equally, important methodological differences and inconsistencies make direct comparisons between different surveys next to impossible. Having said this, however, some broad trends can be unequivocally identified.

There are undoubtedly significant levels of racist hostility expressed in late twentieth- and early twenty-first-century Ireland. However, some evidence suggests that there are possibly important social, cultural and, crucially, geographical differences that underlie this hostility. The most significant change is picked up between 1997 and 2000, although even before this the level of hostility expressed is not negligible.

The findings of those surveys dealing directly with minorities themselves are unambiguous: their experience is of discriminatory practices encountered on a regular basis, in public as well as private spaces. Some groups, namely black people and Travellers/Roma, emerge as the most frequent targets of this discrimination, although this is clearly a relative assessment. Racism emerges as endemic and institutional, with the frequency of incidents in relation to state agencies and public amenities and facilities at a point where minorities have already formed the opinion that the government is failing in its duty to educate the public about racism, and the Gardai is failing in its duty to protect them adequately. Travellers emerge as the most unpopular group across the range of opinion polls and across time. While Citizen Traveller demonstrates that Travellers' claims to be an ethnic majority are recognised as legitimate by a growing proportion of people, it certainly does not appear that antagonism toward Travellers has softened over the last 30 years.

In terms of profiling, hostile attitudes towards Others are more likely to be held by older people, with less formal education, in lower social classes, living in more rural areas. Social and cultural variables (such as income and education) have been used sporadically to distinguish different forms and expressions of racism. However, there have been no large-scale Irish political science-based surveys, such as those carried out in Italy (Sniderman et al., 2000) and Denmark (Andersen, 2000), for example, that attempted to map ideological change among electorates, including attitudes toward minorities, and their affiliation to various parties in the 1990s.

Geographical variables in Irish surveys have often been ignored or meaninglessly categorised following the division into provinces. In many of the smaller surveys, sample populations were simply recruited in Dublin (a large urban area), when very different results may have been available from other types of place in Ireland. It is important to recognise that ideas about 'race', space, and territory compound each other. In short, people emphasise difference between themselves and others by maintaining social as well as spatial boundaries. The regional discrepancies in income and development that articulate with class in Ireland remain to be reviewed in this vein.

The surveys point to respondents' confusion over distinctions between Irish nationals who are members of ethnic minorities, refugees, asylum-seekers and other immigrants. Unfortunately this tendency has also been reproduced by questionnaire design in some of the research reviewed above. The use of problematic categories of 'racial' types, and confusing questions in which refugees/asylum-seekers/migrants/minorities are treated as synonymous actually bolster racist assumptions. The degree of confusion over these terms points to shared collective assumptions about migration, 'race' and Ireland as a culturally homogeneous state. Indeed, high social distance levels between the Irish and the non-Irish and the existence of widely-held assumptions about 'race' and immigration in Ireland indicate the important role the media and political elites play in the struggle against racism in Ireland. While the source of people's opinions has only been asked once, in the Pilgrim House survey (1998), the answer given (61 per cent said 'the media') suggests that, failing direct contact with racialised minorities, newspapers and television provide the raw information upon which opinions are modified, if not created. The idea that opinions are formed on a blank screen with no previous input relating to 'race' does not hold water.

In terms of the mixture between economics, migration and attitudes, a clear set of limited conclusions emerge. The demands of the economy are intimately related to the numbers of migrants who have begun to arrive in Ireland (irrespective of which administrative status they fall into). Since it is impossible for work permits to be obtained without proof being given that no Irish or EEA worker with the appropriate skills has applied for the job, and work visas are targeted specifically on filling shortages in highly-skilled areas of the labour market, the majority of non-EU nationals in Ireland are there to take unfillable positions. Asylum-seekers and refugees may be in Ireland for a variety of reasons such as availability of relatively easy travel from the UK, knowledge of Irish representatives (missionaries and aid workers) in their own country, informal networks transmitting information about regulations. No survey has been carried out that would allow that question to be answered accurately. The response to this phenomenon, however, has been a sharp rise in attitudinal negativity towards minorities, seemingly focussed on new arrivals, plus the indigenous Travellers. Recent patterns of racist attitudes then appear to overlay the longer-standing ones of anti-Semitism and anti-Traveller racism. Yet Mc Gréil's work shows that there was latent racism toward non-whites as long ago as the early 1970s. What has been witnessed in Ireland at the turn of the twenty-first century is a new configuration of the relationship between the economic and the ideological, rather than a vernacular racism born of that period *per se*. This relationship is to be explored in some key exemplary contexts over the next three chapters, while the contemporary configuration is given more reflective coverage in Chapters 6 and 9.

# 3
# Racing the Irish in the Sixteenth and Seventeenth Centuries

'that hackneyed myth the Irish race. There is no Irish race.'
(George Bernard Shaw, in Greene and Lawrence, 1962:294)

Bernard Shaw's dismissive retort to an interviewer's suggestion that he is part of the 'Irish race' is followed by a justification. 'We are a parcel of mongrels' he says, made up of 'Spanish, Scottish, Welsh, English and even a Jew or two'. I have already indicated the fallacy of biological and cultural interpretations of 'race', but also observed the concomitant tenacity of the social practice of imaging oneself and others as members of 'races'. Shaw resists the nationalist interpretation of pure Irish bloodlines, in which none of the last four elements of his list would ever appear, regardless of its accuracy, even to the point of not mentioning Celts and Gaels. His answer provides an interesting counterfoil to the more orthodox version laid out by O'Faoláin (1947), in which the Irish are a composite of Gaelic, Viking, Norman and Saxon lineage. The biological clock stops in the twelfth century. Indeed, as Butler-Cullingford (2001) demonstrates, narratives of 'race' are not marginal to, but constitutive of, political claims to Irish identity. Over the course of the twentieth century, both Unionists and nationalists developed 'race'-based claims to comprise the island's original (that is, authentic) population. These arguments were formulated through geography, anthropology and origin stories involving Milesians and Phoenicians who had moved from the Near East through the Mediterranean into Ireland, thus bringing Catholic and scholarly baggage of advanced civilisations (to counteract the Scythian accusation). The dominant nationalist contention has, since the Book of Invasions, been that the founding group were the Gaels, and that others were absorbed, culturally and racially (with the exception of the British), to produce a homogeneous Irish 'race' by the nineteenth century, in keeping with contemporary European nationalist criteria for a territory to become a self-governing polity.

The work of tracing the development of 'the Irish race' in its entirety remains to be tackled. In this chapter, I confine myself to an attempt to decode the term in contemporary Ireland, before looking at two specific early contexts for the racialisation of Irishness: Ireland in the late sixteenth century, and the Caribbean in the seventeenth century. In those two latter parts of the discussion, the objective is to demonstrate the evolving nature of the idea of 'race', and the political contexts that frame this evolution.

It would be perfectly true to say that until recently the term 'race' was used to refer to groups other than those we now think of erroneously as 'races'. Indeed, usage of the term to denote 'a people' or even 'an occupational or geographical group' continued into the twentieth century. However, with the popularisation of racial ideologies generated in both the natural and social sciences in the nineteenth century, coupled with the use of 'race' as a common political shorthand to express power relations, it cannot be argued that using the term 'the Irish race' in the nineteenth century, and certainly at the end of the twentieth and beginning of the twenty-first centuries, is innocent. What are we to make of a history book entitled *The Story of the Irish Race* (Mac Manus, 1990); a lecture given by one of Ireland's leading poets at Magdalene College, Oxford in 1998 entitled 'Ireland: Race, Nation, State' (Donoghue, 1998); an article by influential journalist Kevin Myers (1997), in which he speaks of 'the genetic truths of traditional Irishness'; or a reference by a leading government minister to Ireland's 'race memory'?[1] Place these references alongside some older ones and note the continuity: Isaac Butt's 1866 pamphlet on landholding, *Land Tenure in Ireland: A Plea for the Celtic Race*; Mary Cusack's polemical nationalist manifesto, *The Present Case of Ireland Plainly Stated: A Plea for My People and My Race*, published in 1881; the series of conferences held in the USA between 1910 and 1916 called the Irish Race Conventions, and W.G. FitzGerald's *The Voice of Ireland: A Survey of the Race and Nation from all Angles by the Foremost Leaders at Home and Abroad*, published in 1923.

There may well be some semantic slippage within the parameters of 'race' as a popular concept, but if close attention is paid to the titles, it becomes evident that the words are carefully chosen. For Butt, the 'race' is Celtic rather than Irish (although the Irish are a major component), while, for Cusack, there is a difference between 'people' and 'race', as there is between 'race' and nation for both FitzGerald and Donoghue.

There is, manifestly, an enduring and well-developed popular notion of the Irish as constituting a 'race'. The idea that there is such a thing is therefore not only the result of the racialisation of the Irish by the British, and later by American WASPs (in other words an ascribed identity), but also the fruit of work by Irish nationalists aiming to construct a positive (that is, self-defined) identity in the face of the negative representations of Irishness around them. In terms of this retaliatory dynamic, the racialisation of the Irish parallels that of twentieth-century African-Americans in their project of infusing the notion of blackness with positivity. This involves ideological labour. The key to positing racialised identities is to link the natural inextricably to the social, as was achieved by Enlightenment thinkers. There must therefore be two dimensions to the idea of 'race': a set of phenotypes that correspond to the cultural and social attributes of the Irish. Myers (1997) stresses this element, contrasting a typical (but unstated) Irish appearance with that of Africans:

> There is nothing wrong with exulting in race, provided it is not done at the expense of another race. We would be importing the banal fallacies of a perverted multiculturalism if we deny *the genetic truths of traditional Irishness*. We will, of course, have to start redefining generous and inclusive Irishness for the incoming races which will lay claim to Irish identity. But that should never prevent us from celebrating *the traditional characteristics of the Irish race*; nor prevent Hiberno-Caribbeans from one day celebrating the dark skin and Bantu noses of their Dahomeyan ancestors. (my emphasis)

This same gene pool is held by columnist Mary Kenny, writing in April 2000, to be homogeneous and relatively untainted: 'Some genetic researchers claim that the Irish are the whitest people in Europe, that is, less mixed with darker-skinned races than any other.'

The qualifying statement is the determining one: 'lighter-skinned races' do not count as different. Definitions of the Irish such as those provided by Sigerson (1868) and O'Faoláin (1947) list assimilable white Europeans – Gaels, Vikings, Normans and Saxons – while Minister Micheál Martin's introductory speech to a conference in 2002 narrated a triumphant stream of multiculturalism in Irish history (St Patrick being the first multiculturalist) that ended in the twelfth century.

These concepts revolve around ideas of purity, whose evolution from the pre-capitalist era is focussed in Christian thought on the idea that whiteness denotes goodness, while blackness indicates evil. Indeed, this has even impacted on the Irish language. The term for Satan in Irish is *an fear dubh* (literally 'the black man'), while that for a man who might be described in English as 'black' is *an fear gorm* ('the blue man'). The etymology of these expressions is traceable to the Viking settlement of Ireland (Rolston and Shannon, 2002: 25–6), as they are taken not from English but directly from Old Norse. Indeed, African prisoners of war were taken by Vikings to Ireland as early as 867 AD. The genealogy of the 'blue man' stresses the long-standing nature of Irish contact with black people, and situates Ireland in the mainstream of international trade, shipping and migration patterns long before colonialism impacted on the country.

The process of racialising the Irish began in the Early Middle Ages and consisted of two inter-related strands. One involved the Irish depicting themselves as a people, or later a 'race', with its own genius, culture, and special place in the world. Boyce (1991:28–9) points to the fact that twelfth- and thirteenth-century Irish historians narrated the story in such a way that the Gaelic conquest was seen in a positive light, and as the starting point for authentic Irishness. According to Boyce, religion does not become the overriding political dividing line in Ireland until the 1640s, a caveat echoed by Coughlan, talking of the seventeenth century, who states: 'But Irish divisions are not readily to be understood as simple ethnic polarities' (1990:205). The second and parallel strand consisted of the colonisers developing a discourse that placed the Irish on an inferior footing, since the former 'insisted that they were there to better the Irish and Ireland, and themselves only incidentally' (Barnard, 1994:281). Hence work such as Cambrensis' *History and Topography of Ireland* (1189), and the array of accounts by colonists such as Moryson, Smith, Campion, Davies and Spenser, appearing in the sixteenth and early seventeenth centuries following on in their detailed and hostile depictions of the Gaelic Irish as uncivilised. Defensive dialogue was used by Irish historians like Keating (*History of Ireland*, 1725),[2] who attempted to correct or counteract what they saw as propaganda casting aspersions on a civilisation they felt had already played a crucial part in the maintenance of scholarship and Christianity by the time the Elizabethan plantations got under way.[3]

Whilst the idea of what constitutes 'looking Irish' is not often made explicit, we can guess that it corresponds to terms such as 'white' and 'European' in popular thought. The 'genetic truths of traditional Irishness' presumably refers to a gene pool in which particular characteristics are typical, as identified even by more sympathetic nineteenth-century commentators such as Engels, who quotes Carlyle's diatribe against the 'Milesians' (1969:122–3) before arguing that: 'Whenever a district is distinguished for especial filth and especial ruinousness, the explorer may safely count upon meeting chiefly those Celtic faces which one recognizes at the first glance as different from the Saxon physiognomy of the native' (ibid.:123). This is certainly the pivotal assumption of a line of discourse embodied by contemporary reviewer Joe Queenan (2002): 'I must confess to a certain confusion as to why actors who do not look even vaguely Celtic are suddenly popping up in movies about Irish-Americans.'[4] On his return from Newfoundland in March 2000, where he had been seeking potential employees, recruitment consultant Denis Moylan proclaimed: 'We are talking about people to fill jobs from management level down. Most are of Irish descent, *look Irish*, and even speak with an Irish accent' (my emphasis, *Irish Examiner* 2000b).

In any case, it can be made clear what does not constitute 'looking Irish'. Irish immigration officials' policy of prioritising black and Asian passengers for questioning when attempting to enter the state since 1997 is looked at in greater detail in Chapter 6, but other clues can be found in unusual places. The 1999 Miss Ireland, Emir Holoran-Doyle, complained that she was barracked by some members of the Irish-American community in Chicago because she looked 'too foreign' (that is, had dark eyes, hair and complexion) (*Examiner*, 2000c).

How then did we reach a point where 'the Irish race' became a reference point for collective identity, with a social and biological strain? Certain periods have been particularly, although not exclusively, formative in this process and I shall briefly examine the way that the creation of 'the Irish race' was shaped by them. Rather than provide a long and detailed narrative of Irish history, I shall focus on the particular contexts that produced definitive changes in the way the term 'Irish race' was constituted and understood by contemporary actors.

'Clear men ... careless and bestial': cultural classification and the importance of being 'civil' in late sixteenth-century Ireland

The racialisation of populations in Ireland, which had begun with the questions of language and religion, reached its most crucial phase in the latter half of the sixteenth and the seventeenth century, with the definitive codifying of the link between land, religion and power. The important three-way split between 'Mere Irish', Catholic 'Old English' and Protestant 'New English' was pertinent prior to 1641. The most salient lines of division in terms of property-holding and access to resources (rather than political factions) become religions from that point on. It is indeed the cultural aspect of difference that would be stressed repeatedly in the dominant English discourse of the period, in which the lines between the political and the cultural were far less restrictive than they are today.

The period from 1550 until the 1600s cannot be read only from an Irish perspective: the broad lines of what happened in Ireland were shaped by and mirrored in the international context. The historical framework is important not solely because of the specifically Irish events that form its parameters, but because it also straddles the beginnings of the expansion of the British Empire into the Americas and the transitional phase of the relationship between the constituent parts of Britain and the United Kingdom (Maley, 1998), and coincides with the process of enclosure, begun in Britain around 1500. This profoundly transformed the links between people and land. Workers and families forced off land were criminalised as vagabonds and those who failed to find work elsewhere were potential colony fodder. Only in the sixteenth century did laws specifically dealing with 'vagabondage', that is, the state of having no immediate and stable link to land, emerge. The removal of both rich and poor Catholics from land in Ireland during the plantations and in the Cromwellian period served at least three purposes: it provided an example of punishment, it freed up territory to be redistributed as military compensation (that is, covering the costs of conquest), and it created a landless class of workers who could be induced to work the newly transferred property, as well as land taken from indigenous peoples in the Americas.

The ensuing justificatory ideology sought to criminalise loose attachment to land and make it a morally justifiable reason for severing the attachment altogether. With the Elizabethan laws on vagrancy, and Cromwellian Council of State orders in the 1650s and 1660s, being exploited and used as a pretext for kidnapping future bonded labourers (Smith, 1947:162–74), the process of freeing up workers for the use of what would today be referred to as global business or capital was under way. It is against this backdrop that the racialisation of the Irish in Ireland, and the Irish and Africans in the Americas, must be read.

### The ideology of British conquest
Quinn (1966:23) notes that the trend for comparing the Irish to Native Americans began with a commentator on Virginia in 1588[5] and

continued throughout the first 40 years of the seventeenth century. These comparisons, he argues, focussed mainly on clothes and culture and were descriptive, generated by the experiences of explorers and soldiers in both Ireland and America. Yet the sanctioning truth of this type of analogy is a comparison of like with like in terms of perceived levels of civilisation. The point is not whether or not the Irish were actually like Native Americans, or Africans, or anybody else, or whether the political contexts were similar. The principal idea is that a technologically and militarily superior culture assumed that it was also morally superior, and looked at others through the prism of its own value system. In the 1600s observers made links between the practices of African tribes with Irish customs (Quinn, 1966:25–7). The idea was that Native Americans, the Irish and Africans were linked by their shared barbarity, or at least incivility (Coughlan, 1989b), a theme common to writers such as Spenser, Smith and Campion. Moreover, the work of these observers was undertaken with political ends in view. The anglicisation of Ireland depended on a shared understanding among those who could influence decision-making that the English were on a civilising mission. Were this not the case, then how could the usurpation of people from land and the brutal treatment meted out to civilians from the 1570s be justified in the dominant discourse of the day? Indeed, there were seventeenth-century voices contesting the new assumptions of innate barbarism and their consequences for political organisation, even among transatlantic colonists such as the Gookin brothers (Coughlan, 2000). Yet the most significant part of the body of ideas whose objective was to transform the Irish into a people fit for a particularly savage form of colonisation is that it did not concentrate on the body, as have later forms of racism, but on culture as the matrix of difference, and, more particularly, the culture's relationship to Protestantism as the benchmark of civilisation.

Canny's convincing exposition of the sources and structure of the 'uncivilising' discourse about the Irish (1976:117–36) merits summarising here, as it clearly lays out an explanation of the timing of ideological shifts that enabled the racialisation of the Irish by the English to attain a more deadly level. Both Canny (1976) and Quinn point out that even by 1560 the Irish had become a metaphor for barbarity, with Bishop Matthew Parker commenting that the process of finding clergy for the North of England should be carried out as quickly as possible in order to avoid the people becoming 'too much Irish and savage'.[6]

Canny concentrates on the 1570s, linking political action and actors to the production of a justificatory ideology based on the right of a superior religion and culture to colonise an inferior one. Massacres committed by Gilbert and Essex (in Ulster in 1574, and Munster in the early 1570s respectively) represented a step beyond the normal way of dealing with foe who lay on an equal footing. Canny's explanation of how this conduct was justified begins with the statement that the Irish had been successfully portrayed as pagans since the fourteenth century (1976:123). In the version of ideas dominant until the mid sixteenth century, this paganism was deemed to stem not from innate incapacity for civilisation, but from features of Gaelic law, government and custom (that is, the realm of the social) that hampered the development of Christian (and civil) behaviour. These elements related to communal rights, kinship-based institutions, marriage practices, and transhumance in particular. The Gaelic Irish were accepted as landholders in the Pale provided that they adhered to English law and customs, and the model of government found there was seen as a potential source for bringing the 'wild' Irish into civilised governance.

The relationship to land ownership and cultivation was to become the justification par excellence of the colonisation, with claims to the concept of *res nullis* (Canny, 2001:133–4) in the 1580s. Failure to adopt sedentary agricultural techniques and display due industriousness was seen as an effect of paganism, with this view being held more deeply the more the observer tended toward Calvinism, as did many of the colonists. Writers such as Johannes Boemus and Olaus Magnus were translated into English in the 1550s, and their depictions of Scythians and Tartars, transhumance farmers, as representing the lowest rung of civilisation, were widely read by the English colonists and referred to in the works of colonial justificatory authors (Canny, 1976). They surfaced in Spenser and particularly Boate's *Ireland's Naturall History*, 1652, where what Coughlan calls 'pathological sloth' (1990:213) was perceived as the reason that locals had not made more effort in extraction of mineral resources, the next step up the ladder after sedentary farming.

In summary, the flaws interpreted as socially rectifiable by Old English settlers prior to the 1570s were re-read as evidence of pathological incorrigibility from then on by the New English. The distinction was not arcane: its ramifications were massacres, mass clearances and transportation.

## Wilderness and wildness

In his analysis of general Renaissance representations of Otherness, Hayden White states that Wild Men were characterised as having particular features: 'mobile, shifting, confused, chaotic incapable of sedentary existence, of self-discipline, and of sustained labour' (1985:165–6). This appears as almost a checklist for the putative Irish traits viewed as irredeemably uncivilised and non-modern by sixteenth- and seventeenth-century writers. What differed among the colonists was the solution proposed: redemption through religion and reform through government, or obliteration. People could be civilised without being Christians (for example the Romans) but 'not Christianised without being made civil' (Canny, 1976:125). If the Irish were to be considered redeemable (as Las Casas had argued of the Amerindians in the Spanish Empire), they had first to be Christianised. This process would initially have to involve civilising them, by instituting forms of government liable to produce civil behaviour. The descriptions of the 'wild Irish' so prevalent in sixteenth- and seventeenth-century accounts served to concretise the incivility of the Irish culture. Hairstyles, clothing, eating habits, agricultural practices, language, legal systems and the condition of churches were all denegrated. The Irish were viewed not as pagan because wild, but wild because pagan. And wild men represented a threat, as White (1985:166) argues, 'both as nemesis and as a possible destiny' for people who might degenerate from civilised values to barbarous ones. Spenser, for example, in *A View of the Present State of Ireland* categorises the Old English as potential degenerates, while the Irish fluctuate between being barbarians and wild men (that is, non-redeemable and redeemable) (Coughlan, 1989b:50).

Moreover, the Irish scarcely differed physically from their colonisers, or at least that is the picture emerging from the type of account that stresses cultural difference. Perhaps the physical similarities being so overpowering (understandably so, since the English and Irish had a similar genetic lineage including Celts, Vikings, Normans and Saxons), the differences in dress and customs had to be exaggerated in order to maintain the distinction between civilised and uncivilised peoples. Edmund Campion's description of the Gaelic Irish encapsulates this duality in the coloniser's eyes: 'Clear men they are of skin and hue, but of themselves careless and bestial' (*History of Ireland*, 1633).

Where Canny's account of the new post-1570 racialisation is most enlightening is in his explanation of timing. There is nothing natural or static about 'race' or racism: they are ideas embedded in the social world. All that is social is transformable, and we need explanations of why particular ideas and practices have developed, emerged or assumed different forms at various moments. The racialisation of the Irish underwent a 'sea change' (Allen, 1994a) in the latter part of the sixteenth century because of the composition of the colonists (mainly what might be labelled in the twenty-first century 'fundamentalist' Protestants). These 'New English' came into direct contact with the Gaelic Irish without passing through the transitional zone of the Pale, where previous English administrators had become acclimatised to difference. The new colonists' objective was to remove the locals from land rather than win them over to new ways, and their ideas on colonial domination were drawn from the Roman colonisation of Britain and the Spanish in the New World, accounts of which were available and circulating among elites. Furthermore, a broad intellectual movement towards the classification of cultures and civilisations into two broad groups, the civilised and the barbaric, characteristic of modernity (Bauman, 1990) was under way, with translated authors cross-fertilising European constructions of difference.

So, from the 1570s, the idea that the Irish were innately pagans, rather than simply at an earlier stage of social evolution toward civilisation, took hold. This was not a one-way debate: there was still support for reform in the Pale in the 1570s, for example, and arguments against colonisation in England into the 1580s. The rationale for these counter-arguments was that the Irish were reasonable and liable to be converted, as demonstrated by those Irish living under English law in the Pale. Nonetheless, the consequence of the ideological shift was that the Irish became barbarians to be conquered, subjugated and civilised – in Sir Thomas Smith's vision expressed in *De Republica Anglorum*, like the Britons under the Romans – rather than heathens to be Christianised. Conversion was a declared intention of the colonisers, but in practice figured very low on their list of priorities.

### Wild place, wild 'race'

An additional dimension of the racialisation of the Irish through the all-encompassing civilised–barbaric binary is the relationship between people and place imposed from as early as the fifteenth century (Cairns and Richards, 1988). The discourses generated linking wild people to wild places have both constructed a particular exclusive and genetic (natural) identity for the Irish, fusing nature (landscape) with the social (cultural characteristics), and generated a series of opposing discourses, marshalled by anti-imperialist campaigners and nationalists (Graham, 1994).[7] Indeed, landscape in Spenser's *View*, for example, actually mirrors and sustains its uncivilised population, conspiring against the forces of colonisation. Coughlan comments that the Irish terrain in Spenser is 'mostly composed of dark and impenetrable forests, mountains and bogs, threatening places among which a savage and implacable enemy fleetingly appears and disappears' (1989b:53). The response to the uncivilised landscape mirrors the solution to the problem of the uncivilised people: obliteration. Irenius in the *View* (1633:64) suggests 'cutting down and opening of all paces through woods, so that a wide space of a hundred yards might be laid open in every of them for the safety of travellers'. The voice of Spenser thus echoes through Hausmann's clearance of mid-nineteenth-century Paris, designed to make barricading narrow streets no longer viable and enabling greater levels of social control and mobility for security forces.

Moreover, Cromwellian initiatives, including the Boates' *Naturall History* and William Petty's *Down Survey*, carried out in the 1650s, involved an ostensibly more rational and scientific approach to Ireland as a 'clean slate' to be worked upon, yet Barnard (1994) and Coughlan (1990) locate them in their contexts and draw out the underlying continuities with the previous centuries' alluvial build-up of stereotypical representations and vilification.

Central to the process of linking people to place was the production of representations of a wild and untamed 'race' and landscape in the west of Ireland, as far from the cityscape of Protestant and Renaissance civilisation as possible. Mac Laughlin (2001) shows how resistance to these negative representations was part of nationalist discourse in nineteenth-century Donegal. On a larger scale, the west was incorporated into a 'Gaelic Revival' form of cultural nationalism which celebrated the symbolic attachment of Irishness to this same rural western landscape, making it a physical source of traditional culture, of authenticity with which to wage war on the inauthentic material, urban and alien culture imposed on Ireland (Graham, 1994, 1998; Gibbons, 1996; Johnson, 1996; Nash, 1993; Proudfoot, 2000). The landscape of western Ireland has been constructed as archetypal and 'national', and held a special place in twentieth-century Irish political discourse through its definition as the authentic and continuous home of a Celtic (and later Catholic) 'race'. Thus the element of the nationalist metanarrative of Ireland which depicts

Irish culture as continuous Celtic, rural and homogeneous is anchored by a symbolic universe in which the 'purity' and exceptional nature of Irish society and culture emerge (Graham, 1994).

This form of place-based nationalism is ideologically capable of incorporating the obvious differences and cultural métissage of Ireland through representations of a uniquely Irish material heritage and landscape (ibid.). Thus, in 1980, Ireland could be described by Charles Haughey (quoted in Morgan, 1991:15) as a 'melting pot' of 'Celts, Danes, Normans, Scots, Huguenots, Palatines and others'. Each group, once assimilated into the Gaelicised mainstream, no longer posed a disruptive cultural threat to the nation-building story. The stress placed on a 'pure' rural western landscape[8] helped define the differences between the Irish Republic and Britain, as well as implicitly show up the 'alien' characteristics of the urbanised and industrialised (and 'Other') north-east of the island of Ireland (Graham and Proudfoot, 1993, Graham, 1998; Nash, 1993, 1996).

Just as imperialist representations imposed on Ireland and the Irish in the sixteenth century were appropriated by nationalists and finally became part of the traditional, conservative nationalist ideology, ideas about rootlessness, mobility and modernity would also undergo the process of appropriation and remodelling. The ease with which they are reworked to exclude Travellers and the 'wandering' Jew suggests that these notions form part of hegemonic discourse available to dominant groups in modernity and on one level cannot be reduced to specific places or times except to explain particular configurations of power.

## Conclusions

We have deliberately focussed here on the period before Catholicism (regardless of language and antecedents) became the primary basis of landholding and the line of discrimination embodied in the Penal Laws, before, that is, the obvious starting point of what Allen (1994a) terms 'religio-racial oppression'. The point in doing so is to highlight the processual nature of ideas about 'race' (Winant's 'narration' (1994), Jacobson's 'palimpsest' (1998)) and stress the historical nature of the forces that propel this process. The argument is not that 1653–54 and the Penal Law period were less important in shaping ideas about difference and institutionalising inequalities. Rather, that they were arrived at via previous and more subtle shifts in the way difference was comprehended and acted upon politically. Moreover, the slide from redeemable pagan to barbaric pagan serves to illustrate that 'race' and racism are always above all political issues: the outcomes of the ideological shift were to justify further colonisation and sub-jugation of people hitherto seen as relatively similar culturally.

Ownership structures and agricultural practices that did not lead to the maximisation of yield or satisfy Baconian notions of mineral resource extraction were prime targets in the ideological offensive aimed at making the Irish fit subjects for colonisation and dispos-session of land. Their 'non-productive' relationship to land was a key element, enabling comparisons of culture and customs with Native Americans from the 1580s onwards, and tying the Irish to an inferior level of civilisation as proposed by Boemus and his readership. As a result this proposition led to the Irish being bracketed with the Tartars and 'Arabians'.[9] This process of transposing the anthropological writings of others and embellishing them to suit one's own purposes prefigures the late-eighteenth- and early-nineteenth-century discourse on phrenology and craniology.

The development of ideas on difference in this period generates a contentious point for historians of racism. The neo-Marxist school sees racism as primarily a functional ideology, enabling greater labour control. Yet, in Ireland during this period, the control of a labour force was a secondary problem until after the land had been appro-priated. In the writings of the time, the principal locus of difference was not the body, key to culture and capacity for civilisation, as it was to become from the late eighteenth-century, but collective rela-tionships to dominant norms and values. People's identities were primarily nationally or religiously defined. The dividing line was Christian/pagan–heathen rather than free/unfree or black/white, as was to develop in the British Americas from the early seventeenth century. If we understand 'race' to involve a notion of (real or imagined) phenotypical similarity between the members of a 'race', then what I have examined above is a form of proto-racism. Yet in it can be perceived the seeds of the later forms, and ironically the dominant element of what has been referred to as the 'new racism' (Barker, 1981), which will be investigated further in Chapter 7.

## THE IRISH IN THE CARIBBEAN:
## FROM SUBALTERN TO ELITE MINORITY

Beginning in the 1630s (Smith, 1947; Dunn, 1972; Silke, 1976), Irish people went to the Caribbean as political prisoners, indentured labourers (either through choice or as a result of illegal round-ups) and occasionally as administrators and priests. Once in the Caribbean, the Irish had a status which was ambiguous, plural and dynamic. By the late seventeenth century they had become part of the dominant group there. That group was referred to in a variety of terms. Although 'black' and 'white' were used (increasingly from the 1700s onwards) to describe the social groups in the Caribbean, so also were nationalities and terms such as 'Christian' and 'heathen'.

The logic of class, status and colour that by and large held true for the colonies in which the Irish lived meant that while there were class distinctions within the white group, these were minimal compared to the gulf in status and power separating white from black until the post-World War II period. While the Irish in the Caribbean have attracted little academic interest since their turbulent introduction to the region, their social ascendancy there is critical in the development of consciousness of racialised differences and the political outcomes of that process.

The existing historiography of the Irish as a distinct group in the Caribbean has concentrated primarily on Barbados, the shipping of indentured labourers that was part of a broader trade (Smith, 1947; Dunn, 1972; Silke, 1976)[10] and the removal of prisoners of war and indentured labour from Ireland to the Caribbean in the decades following Cromwell's campaign. As early as the 1630s, soldiers, wives and children, widows and orphans were being shipped out to Virginia Colony, Barbados and the Leeward Islands. Indeed, the surviving records of one trip in 1636–37 (Smith, 1947:62–6) show that 53 servants (whose names do not appear in the account book) were sold in two days in Barbados in January 1637, at an average price of 522lb of tobacco, transactions that parallel the practice of trading African slaves for raw materials.

Yet, the focus on Barbados (O'Callaghan, 2000) has slightly distorted the image of Irish settlement in the region for three reasons. First, Barbados represented the worst experience by far for the Irish in terms of oppressive practices and regulations. Second, scrutiny ends in the late seventeenth century, just as the Irish began to melt more substantially into the 'white' category that grew specific to the Caribbean. Thirdly, some Irish people were also important actors in the Spanish Caribbean colonies, such as Cuba (Kuethe, 1986) and Puerto Rico (Caro de Delgado, 1969), just as they were later in South America as immigrants (McKenna, 2000)[11] and as missionaries (Silke, 1976).[12]

An approximate idea of the relative numbers involved in the Caribbean can be gauged from the figures accumulated from various primary sources. The only source to count Irish as a separate category was Governor Stapleton's 1678 census of the Leeward Islands (Nevis, Antigua, St Christopher and Montserrat). The Irish made up 18.4 per cent of the overall population, that is, 30 per cent of whites (who in turn comprised 55 per cent of the nearly 19,000 counted). They were most numerous in Montserrat (1,869 out of 3,674, i.e. 51 per cent), where they outnumbered the other white groups as well as the blacks. Overall, men outnumbered women by nearly three to one, although there may be undercounting of women in that respect, as Irish women and children in St Christopher were not counted.[13]

Other figures are more difficult to arrive at because of the lack of detail. Contemporaries other than Stapleton, an Irishman, apparently found the need to distinguish between the Irish, English and even Scots irrelevant. Moreover, the trade in indentured servants extended throughout the British Isles and not only to the Caribbean but also the American colonies, Virginia and Maryland. Add to this the frequent immigration of former indentured Europeans between these places, and the prospects for accurate statistics are diminished further. An increase is reported by Smith (1947) from 1728, but this appears to have focussed on the American colonies. In any case, we can assume that a substantial proportion of the white inhabitants (maybe 30 per cent or more) of the Caribbean colonies *in toto* were Irish in the mid seventeenth century, and that around 20 per cent of the whole population. Yet the last two decades of that century saw the African element of the population overtake and then numerically dominate the European, a point that both relegates the precise proportion of Irish inhabitants to a far lower level and means that this question became increasingly immaterial.

What is important for the current argument is to establish that there were twin social distinctions made in the early period (c. 1650–1700) between the Irish and blacks on the one hand, and between the Irish and the dominant English and, to a lesser extent, Scots on the other. In the eighteenth century, the rising proportion of enslaved Africans to Europeans meant that the latter group could no longer afford to be split nationally in the face of the constant potential for rebellion. The terms English, Scots and Irish thus diminished rapidly in importance to be replaced by 'white' or 'European'.

The Irish occupied a mixture of positions within 25 years of the arrival of the first political prisoners in Barbados: deported indentured labourers, free labourers, property-owners. The range of these positions, in terms of the rights and power inherent in them, should indicate the error of consigning the Irish to a single undifferentiated subordinate slot in the New World hierarchy. A few Africans (particularly children of planters and slave women) may well have become free and owned property up to the last crucial decades of the seventeenth century, but this should not blind us to the principal order of things. Irishmen could own African slaves; Africans could not own Irishmen, bondsmen or not. By the time of Governor Modyford's 1678 survey, the Irish owned 10–20 per cent of the property in Jamaica (Williams, 1932; Silke: 1976) and substantially more on Montserrat (Akenson, 1997). The fact that, compared with their English and Scots counterparts, the Irish owned relatively small holdings and few slaves proves only that there was a status gap between those groups, of a relative not absolute nature. This was not the case of the relationship between the Irish and Africans. The search for parallels between African slaves and Irish indentured labourers on the micro-level obscures the macro-level pattern of inter-group relations. This relationship is portrayed by Europeans as one in which the Africans enjoyed better conditions, a perspective stemming from a seventeenth-century eye-witness account written by French writer Jean Ligon (1673), in which he stated that the Irish bondservants were treated more harshly than the slaves. His comment is taken up by Williams (1932), Silke (1976) and O'Callaghan (2000). Particularly revealing is that they all paraphrase Ligon's assertion that white servants were not physically capable of hard work in the tropics as were Africans. Williams in particular stresses the racial–cultural aspect of punishing field work:

> If this [suffering because of very hard labour and living conditions] was true of the Negro, inured as he was to hardship and privations, what must have been the mortality among the white indentured servants who were frequently of gentle origin and whose lot in bondage was more arduous and exhausting than that of the Negro slaves? (1932:45)

There is an assumption here (more excusable for the seventeenth-century commentator) that racial type indicated suitability for different types of labour.[14] More soberly, Craton (1997) maintains that white servants in Barbados were certainly treated worse than agricultural labourers in Britain, and were less free, in that they could not use labour as a marketable commodity. Yet he points to the fact that although in the mid seventeenth century there were as many laws on the regulation of servants as on that of slaves, this was a transitional phase: ultimately the lower rungs of white society in the Caribbean provided 'managers, voters and militiamen for external and internal defence' (1997:166) and enabled the planters to dominate in societies in which they represented a tiny minority.

Moreover, Beckles (1989:103) argues that, from the outset, white labourers could afford to be more rebellious and less anxious about the consequences of escape and recapture: 'They [white runaway servants] were aware that, in the final analysis, they constituted an important part of white society's anti-slave military vanguard, and they could be more openly aggressive than their slave counterparts.' This was particularly true, he argues, for Irish Catholics.

Irish indentured labourers and African slaves worked side by side in the fields for years in the New World. It is not surprising that planters would be watchful for signs of relationships between them. Yet, ultimately, reports of alliances between Irish indentured labourers and slaves appear to have been mainly expressions of English planters' paranoia. Only a couple of such revolts are supported by documentary evidence: an escape and subsequent attacks in Barbados in 1655 (Beckles, 1990a:513; O'Callaghan, 2000:123–5; Allen, 1994b:230–1); and a more elaborate plot in 1686, which ultimately resulted in no prosecutions of the Irish allegedly involved. In a context in which free Irishmen (who had served out their indentureship) could be whipped, fined and imprisoned for publicly slurring the English Crown (Beckles, 1990a:515), the fact that no charges were pressed against any Irishman in relation to a potentially large-scale revolt points to a total lack of existing evidence that any were involved.[15] Moreover, the planters' strategy of dividing the workforce along national lines 'in order to keep resistance focused on an individual and hence unorganised and at a containable level' (Beckles, 1989:98) bore fruit, remarked upon by nineteenth-century historians such as Dicks[16] (quoted by Beckles, 1989:99) who noted that such a policy 'drew an impassable boundary line between black and white servants' that was so effective that unity became difficult to imagine. Indeed the Irish on English-held islands were actually more likely to side with the French than the slaves. There is evidence of this in St Kitts and Montserrat in the 1660s for example (Beckles, 1990a: 519). The picture emerging from the seventeenth-century texts studied by Beckles is that planters were extremely fearful of Irish–African alliances and Irish allegiance to Catholic European powers, and that this anxiety led them as far as to request the reduction or elimination of the supply of labour from Ireland at a time when such labour was still relatively important (that is, until the 1680s) and a shortfall still existed. Governor Willoughby of Barbados wrote to the Privy Council in 1667:

> There yet remains that I acquainte your Lordships with the great want of servants in this island, which the late war hath occasioned. If labour fayles here, His Majesty's customes will at home; if the supply be not of good and sure men the saifety of this place will always be in question; for though there be noe enemy abroad, the keeping of slaves in subjection must still be provided for. If your Lordship shall offer a trade with Scotland for transporting people of that nation hither and prevent any excess of Irish in the future, it will accommodate all the ends propounded.[17]

The same governor had, a few months earlier, pleaded with the King for servants other than Irish, expressing his preference for the 'downright Scot who, I am certain, will fight without a crucifix round his neck'.[18]

Moreover, this anxiety sometimes led to the implementation of distinct social control systems for the Irish, such as passes (Barbados, 1657) and the withdrawal of the right to bear arms (Antigua, 1689) (Beckles, 1990a: 519–20). The fact that there were so few Irish–African uprisings at least raises the possibility that for those who envisaged leaving indentured labour status the racial status quo was understood as their ticket to relative privilege.

Despite early disparaging references made by planters about the Irish servants' capacity for hard work on plantations and their 'disloyalty' in the period before the 1680s (ibid.:511–12), the crucial point is that when slaves outnumbered whites, as they did by the last quarter of the seventeenth century, the Irish were almost always included in the latter group and armed to police the colour line.

Indeed, many of the Irish originally sent to Barbados migrated to the USA and other Caribbean territories from the end of the seventeenth century. Silke explains, in an unorthodox interpretation, that whites were 'driven away to America by the incoming blacks' in the 1690s (1976:604). In Jamaica, Montserrat, Trinidad and British Guiana, for example, they accessed land more cheaply and were able to rise to intermediate positions in a hierarchy predicated upon black disenfranchisement. Again, after the initial two decades or so of testing living conditions, the Irish melted into the dominant white groups in the anglophone (and some parts of the Spanish-speaking) Caribbean (Beckles, 1990b; Brereton: 1998; Kuethe, 1986; Caro de Delgado, 1969).

## The Irish as members of the Caribbean elites

As a high-ranking Irish servant of the Crown in the West Indies, Governor Stapleton of the Leewards was in an unusual position. That he governed a principally Irish-populated territory, Montserrat, made the situation an anomaly. Many others would have to work their way up through indentureship to land-holding to slave-holding and/or administration. Another route was taken by the lawyer Michael Keane (Quintanilla, 2003), an eighteenth-century 'fixer', who managed businesses for Irish-based clients, dabbled in property, located workers and set up deals across islands and across the Atlantic. Much of Keane's work was based in St Vincent, where he had originally arrived in 1773 to sort out his deceased brother's legal affairs. Keane's facility for making connections, in a colony where prices were lower and the planter class was less well established and exclusive than in older ones, culminated in his rise to the position of Attorney-General (1783) from where he amassed a fortune worth £14,331.

Alejandro O'Reilly left Ireland for Spain and rose through the ranks, beginning in the Infantry Regiment of Hibernia in the War of Jenkins' Ear, then fighting for the Austrian army in the Seven Years' War. O'Reilly's next mission was to reform the Cuban army, which was divided into racially segregated sections: white, *pardo* and *moreno*,[19] as well as infantry, cavalry and dragoons. The reforms he pushed through strengthened the link between the families at the summit of the sugar industry and the militia's officer corps, thus cementing the former's stake in the maintenance of the social status quo (in which there was also a racialised hierarchy). O'Reilly 'proudly reported to Spain that he had recruited the flower of Havana society into the city's two white regiments' (Kuethe, 1986:58–9). One of those planter families, the O'Farrills, was of Irish origin and married into the O'Reillys, a position from which they dominated the colonelships of the Havana militia in the 1780s and '90s.

Trinidad is unusual in that although a British colony, it became one rather late and had previously been dominated by French and Spanish Catholics. The social elites, in the generations after the British takeover in 1797, were dominated by French and Spanish 'creoles' (born in Trinidad), even if the complexion of control began to change. Coogan (2000), in his entry for Trinidad, refers principally to Irish missionaries. Indeed, the Irish began to penetrate the Trinidadian church in the mid nineteenth century (De Verteuil, 1986): four of the seven Catholic bishops of Port-of-Spain between 1820 and 1900 were Irish, as were three co-adjutants. Although there are records showing that one of the *cabildo* (city council) members in 1786 in Trinidad was one John Nihell who had arrived from Antigua, it was later, in the nineteenth century, that, as a consequence of increasing numbers of Irish settlers from other islands relocating to Trinidad, the Irish began to join the island's elite (marrying into French creole society). Moreover, their influence on internal social order was significant, in that they formed a bridge between the conflicting French and English creoles (as bilingual members of the former), and had gained enough clout locally to have Irish Dominicans hired to replace their French counterparts from the 1890s, much to the latter's annoyance (Brereton, 1998).[20] Once the British had taken over the running of the island, English language skills gave the Irish an advantage in areas of professional activity such as the law and the civil service administration, whose ranks they appear to have penetrated successfully by the 1870s (De Verteuil, 1986), although they did not own estates (mainly cocoa and sugar) until the 1880s. The overall picture is of gradual and unhindered integration, principally over the 1830–1900 period, into the governing and business elites of a plantation society whose social system was one in which Europeans exploited the labour of slaves, former slaves and, after 1834, indentured labourers from India recruited to fill the plantation labour force (Tinker, 1974).

## Conclusion

The resurgence of anxieties about colour in contemporary Ireland has a history. The erasure of this element of the story from the meta-narrative in which Irish overcome the odds to triumph abroad enables a discourse of denial to endure into the twenty-first century.

Ideas about whiteness and blackness, providing racialised models of understanding difference and politicising it, have thus circulated in the Irish imaginary since at least the mid seventeenth century, when Irish ex-indentured labourers began to own slaves. Akenson (1997:70) quotes John Blake, a Galway-born planter writing home in 1675 to say that he had just bought a 'neger wench'. Thus the Irish only discovered their 'whiteness' and the privileges flowing from this identity in the Americas, where the social stakes of being 'white' were valuable. It was based on positions in the labour market and group solidarity and not being black. However their exact locations within the white hierarchies of the New World differed over time and place. Irish Americans would have to work harder to become white in the nineteenth century than their compatriots in the seventeenth-century Caribbean.

From this reading of the racialisation of the Irish and of Ireland, three important points suggest themselves:

1.  Racialisation takes place at a different pace in different spaces and takes many forms. However, it is always both an outcome of and justification for political projects. The forced removal of the Irish from land in the sixteenth century was such a project, as was the nationalist one of reclaiming and revalorising identity in the late nineteenth century. The establishment of racial hierarchies in tropical colonies relied upon a minority monopolising legitimate violence, in Weberian terms, and, after two or three generations, that minority included the Irish.

    In the twentieth century another project involved drawing a line around the nation and stating the historical point at which the nation absorbed its perceived core peoples; in France and the UK, this line was drawn by the far-Right in the immediate post-war period (see Chapter 8). In Ireland, that moment is represented as having occurred in the twelfth century. The erasure of eight centuries of métissage with Britain and British people in Ireland and Great Britain is thus a key element of that particular nationalist meta-narrative. Suddenly in the 1990s, the concept of mixing resurfaced. Yet even this ignored internal minorities, particularly Jews and Travellers.

2.  Culture and space are just as important in racialisation as physical appearance. The concept of 'white' and 'black' people does not emerge until the seventeenth century, with the nomenclature used more likely to be 'Christians' and 'heathens', or national groups and 'Africans' in the New World. Even the most disdainful of contemporary colonist commentators in sixteenth-century Ireland could point to no physical difference between the English and Irish. The socially-constructed divergence was grounded in the cultural rather than the physical, although the two were seen as a seamless whole. Statutes forbad mixing between the 'English by blood' and the 'mere Irish' as early as 1297 (Boyce, 1991:30–1), because this mixing was perceived as resulting in a collapse of cultural differences upon which the social order was

premised. If culture was not innate and could be bought into at will, then what genuine basis was there for English rule? This is why punitive laws were placed in the Statutes of Kilkenny in the fourteenth century (the 1297 warnings had obviously not worked!). By adopting Irish language and customs (let alone intermarrying), the English could slide into Irishness in a way that (in the terms of this racist framework) no white European could fully metamorphose culturally into Chineseness or Africanness. The significance of this for Ireland was the forging of the unbreakable link between culture and 'race', which are elements of the same idea. Robert Young (1995:54) affirms this in his thought-provoking account of the genesis of culture in colonialism:

> Culture has always marked difference by producing the other; it has always been comparative, and racism has always been an integral part of it: the two are inextricably clustered together, feeding off and generating each other. Race has always been culturally constructed. Culture has always been racially constructed.

3.  From an Irish perspective, black–white paradigms of 'race' (which neglect the mystification of whiteness and assume power lies unproblematically and equally with all whites) and 'new racism' are hardly new. The experience of the Irish, as a racialised 'white' group *vis-à-vis* other more powerful white groups and less powerful Others, is an ideal-type from which to develop arguments about the contemporary field. The contemporary configuration of racialisation includes 'white' Eastern Europeans and Travellers, as the mobile Others of the twenty-first century EU.

# 4

# The 'Filthy Aristocracy of Skin': Becoming White in the USA

In 1842, a petition (see Appendix 2) sent from 'the people of Ireland' with between 60,000 and 70,000 signatures against slavery[1] calling on Irish Americans to support it met with responses ranging from indifference to hostility. Some of these responses identified their authors in such terms as 'white', as distinguished from the 'Negro', who was 'of a lower order'.[2] In an oral retort to the Cincinnati Repeal Association's letter dated August 1843, the petition's chief instigator, Daniel O'Connell, wondered aloud why his compatriots, addressed as Irishmen, had replied as 'depraved' white Americans. Arguing for equal status for Africans, he argued that the only way to judge people was free of the social shackles restraining them, which he termed 'the filthy aristocracy of skin'.[3] Why and how the experience of nineteenth-century America turned Irish emigrants into White Americans, granting them membership of this filthy aristocracy, and what ramifications the process has had for contemporary society have been the subjects of increasing attention since the early 1990s, particularly among American labour historians. In respect of this book's narrative of racialisation, this formative process is of paramount importance in establishing a racialised (white) identity for the Irish. It draws attention to the fact that even the most naturalised and taken-for-granted elements of our social world (for instance, that there are groups of people who are clearly 'white' and 'black') are temporally and spatially contingent. Lastly, and very importantly, it emphasises the Janus-faced nature of the relationship between Irish racialisation and the racialisation of Others by the Irish.

## THE CATHOLIC IRISH IN
## NINETEENTH-CENTURY RACIAL HIERARCHY

Before embarking on this analysis, it should be made clear that the focus is on Catholic immigrants, rather than Irish immigrants *per se*. The Protestant Irish, who comprised a sizeable proportion of immigrants to North America, have been relatively neglected in Irish

American studies, which posit a numerically dominant Catholic presence. Akenson (2000) is the most stringent critic of this, arguing that from the breakdown of census material carried out by CUNY (Komin et al., 1991) as many as 58.6 per cent of Irish Americans are of Protestant origin (2000:113). This would be the result of extensive immigration in the second half of the nineteenth century building on the 100,000 Protestants who emigrated between 1718 and 1775 (Griffin, 2001), particularly in the slumps of 1718–19 and 1739–40. The debate is clearly of importance in establishing historical patterns and interpreting the degree of representativeness of experiences. In terms of racialisation it does not alter the principal dividing line separating Irish immigrants into two kinds: Protestant and readily assimilable, and Catholic and suspect. The former, Presbyterians, settled overwhelmingly in Pennsylvania and Virginia. Having arrived as 'British', 'Irish' or 'Presbyterian', they shifted to 'Scotch Irish' with the arrival of the Famine Irish in the middle of the century (Miller, 1985). The following argument is not, implicitly, that Protestant Irish immigrants encountered no discrimination, but that the forms directed against Catholic countrymen and women were more durable, made more appeal to racialised difference, and ultimately placed them in symbolic competition for privileged access to resources within the specific social hierarchy of the nineteenth century. Moreover, the geographical focus is the north-eastern urban seaboard, for reasons of availability of material and the importance of New York in the narrative of Irish–Black relations in the 1860s. With these caveats, I will now examine what was at stake for Catholic Irish immigrants entering US society in the middle decades of the nineteenth century.

In 1790, the American constitution had opened citizenship to 'white men', while blacks were defined as 'imports'. The 1870 legislative debates on citizenship defined it as the right of 'civilised whites'. Jacobson's analysis of the debates on citizenship in the US senate in 1870 (1998:73–85) leads him to conclude that 'whiteness' referred to four overlapping factors: colour, degree of freedom, level of civilisation and devotion to Christianity. The period of history between this debate and the eugenics-influenced 1924 Immigration Act demonstrates the way these perceived differences within the part of the population that today would be considered unproblematically 'white', played out into an exclusionary ideology based on relative rather than absolute difference.[4]

The nineteenth century witnessed an extraordinary set of developments in the ways in which 'race' was understood and used as a determining point of social difference. Scientific racism, developing through pseudo-sciences like phrenology and craniology, had in the first few decades attempted to reinforce the more general claims of the Enlightenment thinkers (Eze, 1997) about the links between climate, appearance and collective intellectual capacity. A transatlantic network of writers and scientists sharing the belief that people's physical characteristics determined their ability to reason and achieve civilisation grew up around the 1820s (Horsman, 1981; Fryer, 1984). Europeans and Americans engaged in the enterprise of racialising humanity referred to each other's work, and gradually gained dominance over the monogenesists (who explained the human race as being descended from Adam and Eve) so that 'By the 1850s, the inherent inequality of races was simply accepted as a scientific fact in America' (Horsman, 1981:135).

## CATHOLIC IRISH, BLACK AMERICANS AND THE LOGIC OF WHITENESS

The putative degeneracy of the Celtic 'race', however, had been a minor but pertinent theme in these circles (Morton, 1839). Theorists like Robert Knox (*The Races of Man*, 1850) and Gobineau (*Essai sur l'inégalité des races humaines*, 1853) saw the Celt as a less-developed element of the 'white race'. In America, 'race' commentators in the mid nineteenth century tended to place Celts well below Anglo-Saxons, in a no man's land between Europeans and Africans. The point of difference between the Irish and Americans on which nativist discourse concentrated was religion. The putative backwardness of the former, manifested in tribalism and dogma, was diagnosed as a symptom of popery. Yet the aspects that seemed to matter most were related to incorporation within the political system of the USA: loyalty to a Protestant state, industriousness and readiness for democracy. Irish Catholics, as we have seen, had been viewed as bearers of a non-modern culture and were thus a threat to the republic, with their propensity for idleness and political corruptibility and external allegiances.

Central to the American perception of Irish Catholics was their loyalty to Rome, expressed as supranational and spiritual as opposed to patriotic and material, in an era of nation-building. This also spilled over into tension over the national education system, whose curriculum was based primarily on biblical teachings and which was run by Protestant churches, as it came into conflict with Catholic teachings to which immigrant children were exposed. Moreover, in terms of fitness for democracy, the Catholics' fealty to Rome was constructed as inculcating a slavish, childish and above all pre-modern mentality unsuited to the rigours of one-man-one-vote democracy. Indeed, Morton (1839:16) claimed that the Celts' 'physical traits', 'moral character' and 'peculiar customs' had 'undergone little change since the time of Caesar', before going on to describe the natives of the south-west of Ireland, whose 'wild look and manner, mud cabins and funereal howlings recall the memory of a barbarous age'. Indeed, the incompatibility of the Irish with modernity became a cliché in American commentary. After the Fenian raid in Canada, in 1866, *Atlantic Monthly* stated: 'All the qualities which go to make a republican, in the true sense of the word, are wanting in the Irish nature.'

Yet the Irish in nineteenth-century America were deemed open to improvement by exposure to civilisation. The illustrations 'Inward Bound' and 'Outward Bound' (Figures 2 and 3) demonstrate this in graphic terms. In the first instance a dark-skinned simian Irish emigrant wearing tattered clothes and clutching a shillelagh scours a boat departures notice-board. In the second picture, the noticeably paler man, well dressed and holding no weapon, reads information relating to the return journey. America has thus literally whitened (that is to say, civilised) the Irish Celt.

This construction of the social (developed or undeveloped culture) as manifesting itself in putative physical 'whiteness' is clearly a vital element of the historical context in which the Famine Irish arrived in North America. Attitudes toward the cultural baggage carried by Irish Catholics were to hamper their access to the upper echelons of WASP America until the late nineteenth century. Moreover, it should be reiterated that the arrival of tens of thousands of Catholics altered the profile of the waves of emigrants, the majority of whom in the eighteenth century had been Protestants, and most of whom settled in more rural areas. Irish emigration to the USA peaked in 1851. The principally Catholic Famine Irish remained overwhelmingly in the urban setting (although duties in the army might bring them later to other areas). In the period between 1 May 1847 and 31 December 1860, the Irish comprised 41.4 per cent of immigrants disembarking in New York (that is, over 1 million),[5] and the Irish-born, 53.1 per cent of the city's immigrant population at the 1860 census. Indeed, the increased level of immigration and its focus especially on New York City are of significance in the story.

Linebaugh and Rediker (2000) argue that New York in the 1780s was much more socially fluid, had a higher level of black settlement and more radical and colour-blind political consciousness than in later years. Based on one case study this might be an overstatement, yet there is certainly a qualitative difference between the city they describe and that of the Draft Riots (Bernstein, 1990). The exceptional role of New York City as the town most deeply integrated commercially with the Southern states and therefore in the slave mode of production meant that it had most to lose from abolition. Within the USA as a whole, the number of Irish immigrants had more or less doubled every five years over the 1821–50 period. If New York's business community had a lot to lose, then so did those employed in its factories. The Irish-born comprised around 25 per cent of the city's population in 1860, most of whom were unskilled workers, the most vulnerable to even minor economic deterioration. With profound economic links to the South and staunchly anti-abolitionist local politicians and popular press working hard to attack the Republicans and the war effort (Miller, 1969; Allen, 1994a), New York assumed an exceptional position in the story of Black–Irish relations and thus of the evolution of the Irish 'race'.

The majority of work done on the interface between Irish and black Americans in the nineteenth century has been accomplished by labour historians. It is no surprise that the labour market has become the predominant focus in this small but growing area of study. The forms of hostility between these two groups constitute the point of departure for our knowledge. Some of these forms are described by Allen (1994a, 1994b), Ignatiev (1995), Roediger (1991), Barret and Roediger (1997, 2002) and Jacobson (1995, 1998) and included labour organisation aimed at removing rival black workforces from specific locations and thus competition, political organisation such as Tammany Hall, cultural organisation such as the 1910–16 Irish Race Conventions, violent protests like the 1863 Draft Riots (Bernstein, 1990:27–31), smaller-scale attacks on black homes and places of worship, and public places in which blacks and whites spent time together (Ignatiev, 1995 125–7, 134–9, 151–3) and participation in white supremacist projects such as lynching.[6] This pattern of collective action can also be witnessed in anti-Chinese immigration activity (in the Order of Caucasians) (Saxton, 1995; Almaguer, 1994), and involvement in the army's campaigns to remove and persecute Native Americans.

The geographical concentration of Catholic emigrants in urban areas of the eastern seaboard in particular, but not exclusively, brought them into close contact with another racialised group: free black Americans. The ideological positioning of the two groups who shared

*Figure 2*   The Dark Celt Before Leaving for the USA ... 'Outward Bound – The Quay of Dublin', T.H. Maguire, 1854, after a painting by J. Nicol, printed by M&H Hanhart. Collection of the New-York Historical Society.

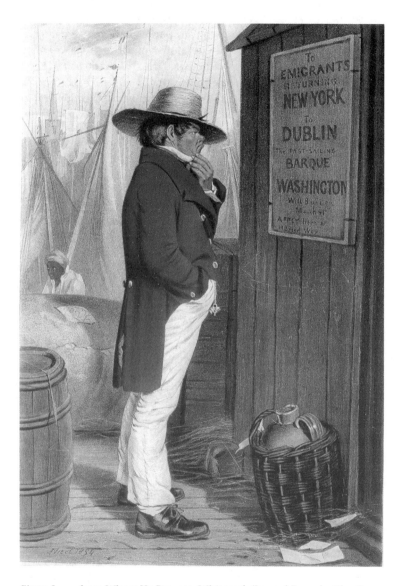

*Figure 3*   ... from Where He Returns, Whitened. 'Inward Bound – The Quay of New York', T.H. Maguire, 1854, after a painting by J. Nicol, printed by M&H Hanhart. Collection of the New-York Historical Society.

a similar social place (concentration in the lower echelons of the workforce) was dialectical. Blacks were abolitionists and Protestant, voted for the Federal and Republican parties and maybe even the nativist (and rabidly anti-Catholic) Know-Nothings. Moreover, they were fans of Britain, which had abolished the slave trade in 1807 and slavery in 1838. The urban Irish were Catholic and anti-abolition (if not pro-slavery), supported the Democratic Party and regarded Britain as the overriding source of Irish suffering (Miller, 1969). Even without the addition of difficult access to resources there was enough to indicate that antipathy would develop.

In the eyes of WASP America, the two groups were perceived in racist discourse as being comparable if not interchangeable, as late as the 1870s. The simianisation of Irish and black characters in later nineteenth-century pictorial representations created equivalence in their positions at the foot of the racial chain, while their juxtaposition in publications such as *Harper's Weekly* (the self-styled 'journal of civilization') indicated the limits of fitness for citizenship.[7] Frequently their attitudes would be compared (and often flatteringly for blacks) in terms of level of civilised behaviour and aptitude for citizenship. The following is an extract from a book review published in *Atlantic Monthly* in 1864:

> The emancipated Negro is at least as industrious and thrifty as the Celt, takes more pride in self-support, is far more eager for education, and has fewer vices. It is impossible to name any standard of requisites for the full rights of citizenship which will give the vote to the Celt and exclude the Negro.[8]

It is in this context then that the Irish drive for whiteness must be interpreted: the attainment of whiteness meant above all the banishment of blackness. Whiteness safeguarded access to the labour market, the vote and a degree of social prestige constituted from its antithesis, and ensured a constant flattering comparison with occupationally and residentially segregated blacks.

The theme of slavery provides an interesting focus for the complexities of the Irish–black relationship. Irish nationalists, particularly in the era of O'Connell, developed the use of the term to refer to Britain's control of Ireland. In America, where slavery had acquired a specific institutional form, the two interpretations co-existed, creating a barrier to solidarity. On the one hand, the Irish claimed to be enslaved, both nationally and as a class of wage slaves in the

American economy, a line pushed hard by anti-abolitionists. There was even an argument that white workers were worse off than the slaves, who were fed and kept by their masters, while the former were left to their own devices. Frederick Douglass (a fan of the Irish in Ireland) took issue with this understanding of slavery:

> there is no analogy between the two cases. The Irishman may be poor, but he is not a slave. He may be in rags but he is not a slave [...] The Irishman has not only the liberty to emigrate from his country, but he has liberty at home. He can write, and speak, and co-operate for the attainment of his rights and the redress of his wrongs. (Foner, 1999:169–70)[9]

Moreover, he often raised the matter in public speaking engagements, stating that he had recently vacated a position of slave that was now available, but to his knowledge there had been no applications from Irishmen to fill it.

Within the logic of anti-abolitionism and Democratic populism from the 1830s onwards, the plight of the white worker in the North and the slave in the South had been bound with a particular message: the end of slavery for blacks would lead to its reinforcement for whites, and then force the latter to compete for low-paid work with an influx of freed slaves. Elements of the Democratic Party and local New York newspapers such as the *New York Weekly Caucasian*, the *New York Day Book*, the *Freeman's Journal*, the *Herald* and the *Metropolitan Record* habitually propounded this message (Miller, 1969). It was the basis of the idea that the abolitionists had fomented the war, which took root prior to the Draft Riots. As a consequence, Irish workers were being recruited to fight for 'negro emancipation'. Slavery then was a relative and contested term, and helped lead Irish immigrants into an ideological cul-de-sac where it appeared to make little sense to show solidarity with slaves.

This background helps us grasp what was at stake for Irish Americans in the 1850s and 1860s. John Mitchel's championing of slavery, from his American publishing base, the *Citizen*, and Arthur Griffith's defence of Mitchel's sentiment, in which he stated that an Irishman should not consider 'the negro his peer',[10] evolved from a context in which Mitchel felt it was essential to distance the Irish from the blacks. Indeed, he wrote in the *Citizen*, in 1856: 'He would be a bad Irishman who voted for the ascendancy of principles which proscribed himself, and which jeopardized the present system of a nation of white men.'[11]

The cultural and employment statuses of a would-be 'white' group and a black one had to be clearly differentiated; the colour line would only work to the advantage of the Irish if every member of the subjugated group had lower status than the lowest member of the dominant one, as Allen (1994a) aptly points out in relation to the case of the Catholic Irish and Protestant English and Scots during the Plantation of Ireland. Too much overlap between Irish and black, both in the occupational and residential spheres, therefore militated against social advance for the former, certainly in America. This is proposed as an explanation for attacks on blacks living in mixed areas or even neighbourhoods next to Irish ones in urban America (Ignatiev, 1995:136–7) while the theme of informal policing of racialised borders is further explored by Barret and Roediger (2002). They observe that broader gate-keeping duties performed by the Irish provided a model for other white and 'off-white' European groups, whose earliest experiences of urban America later in the nineteenth century were of Irish-dominated neighbourhoods and institutions, that is, those in which control of police, political appointments, and some other areas of employment lay in Irish and usually Democratic Party hands. In other words, the new arrivals learnt the codes of racial conduct from their Irish-descended peers. The removal of blacks from areas of proximity to the Irish thus paralleled the usurpation of the former from specific economic niches within the urban setting, and established ground rules for incoming apprentice Caucasians. Indeed, transforming 'nigger work' (that performed exclusively or usually by black Americans) into 'white man's work' (that from which black Americans were excluded) was a project successfully accomplished by urban-based Irish immigrants over the 1830–65 period (Roediger, 1991; Ignatiev, 1995). The 20 per cent drop in the black population of New York City in the 1860–65 period testifies to the unfavourable climate, both residentially and occupationally, generated by events of the time (Man, 1951:371).

## WORK, SOLIDARITY AND THE STAKES OF AMALGAMATION

Socialisation through the workforce was a crucible of Americanisation in the nineteenth century, and for 'immigrant workers, the processes of becoming white and "becoming American" were intertwined at every turn' (Barret and Roediger, 1997:6). The economic relations between immigrant and indigenous groups became a key focus of Democratic Party propaganda under Benton and Douglas in the 1850s.

Moreover, the Democrats' willingness to enlist immigrants into 'white' America through local patronage networks and even institutions such as the New Orleans Choctaw Club saw appeals couched in terms of the 'workingman' slide into those for the 'white workingman' as the century progressed. From the conclusions of Schlesinger (1988), Bridges (1984) and Fox (1917), we might go as far as to say that the Democrats created a white vote over the middle decades of the nineteenth century.

Certainly attempts to scare workers away from sympathising with slaves involved explicit calls for racial solidarity. Allen identifies the pro-active role of the Democrats as one of two strategies (the other being the Catholic Church's official 'neutrality' on slavery and anti-war position) that pushed Irish immigrants to oppose abolition. As we have seen, it was argued that freeing the slave population would create a massive pool of cheap labour, which would then lower wages in the Northern cities in which immigrants were already pitted against each other. Indeed, the success of this strategy is that it managed to construct the debate on competition to cast the free blacks as the potential rivals, whereas the Irish had actually usurped them! Moreover, Allen (1994a:192–8),[12] shows that other white immigrant groups provided by far the stiffer opposition in terms of jobs held in those occupations where the Irish were dominant by 1855, while Ignatiev (1995) concludes that it was not competition but its absence (that is, the protection of jobs from blacks) that generated conflict. Miller (1969:40) lucidly expresses the historical findings:

> One fact which seems abundantly clear from reading the literature of this period is that while there was job competition between Irish and Negroes in New York, the overwhelmingly predominant pattern was not of Negroes taking jobs from the Irish, but rather of the Irish driving the blacks out of their old employments.

Indeed, the free blacks who the Irish encountered in New York and other urban areas had been improving their social standing between 1810 and the 1830s, accessing unskilled and semi-skilled occupations in addition to the domestic service into which, as an extension to the practices of slavery, they were accepted. Albon Man summarises the position:

> Before the spurt in immigration in the decades of the forties and fifties, such occupations in New York as those of longshoremen,

hod-carriers, brickmakers, whitewashers, coachmen, stablemen, porters, bootblacks, barbers, and waiters in hotels and restaurants had been almost wholly in the hands of colored men. Domestic maids, cooks, scullions, laundresses and seamstresses were generally colored women. They were secure in these types of employment and earned relatively good wages. But with the huge influx of white foreigners, particularly after the Irish famine of 1846, their position changed radically. (1951:376)

The timing described by Man underscores the processual nature of the whitening of the Irish. This whitening began prior to the Famine, and was spurred by the arrival of Famine refugees, who pushed Irish immigration to its 1851 peak. The theory of the Irish defending their position from free blacks assumes white solidarity against perceived black threat to employment: the positions of the protagonists in the competition for resources have thus been reversed. The conditions in which expulsions of blacks from workplaces, and attacks on workplaces employing mixed workforces became commonplace (Man, 1951; Ignatiev, 1995; Bernstein, 1990) are therefore the opposite of that which competition theory would suppose.

Lessons learned from the Democrats' ideological labours manifested themselves in the internalisation of the American system of classification. The Irish-dominated unions, such as the longshoremen, for instance, both legitimised the expulsion of black workers and then sought to protect Irish jobs by attempting to ban Germans from the dock under the pretext of safeguarding 'white men's work' (Ignatiev, 1995). Similar tactics were deployed on the west coast later in the century in the campaign against Chinese labour and employers of Chinese immigrants, led by the Order of Caucasians. It is hard to imagine a more forceful expression of assimilation of values. Indeed, Barret and Roediger (1997:31) detect a strategic movement from the terrain in which the Irish were most exposed to one in which power relations could be invoked in their favour: 'Changing the political subject from Americanness and religion to race whenever possible, they challenged anti-Celtic Anglo-Saxonism by becoming leaders in the cause of white supremacy.'

## SOME LIMITS OF LABOUR-DERIVED MATERIAL

The focus on labour market-generated conflicts, of which there is ample evidence, however, should not blind us to other aspects of racialisation. Moreover, there are qualifications to the work done so far that have to be borne in mind. Ignatiev's engrossing contribution, for example, is limited in geographical and temporal scope (to Philadelphia between the 1780s and the 1860s) and by the assumption that all Irish immigrants were Catholics. In the period prior to the 1840s and 1850s, when much of the action he refers to occurred, this is far from true. Allen's paradigm is that of control of labour forces, and while this provides a welcome long-term critical framework, other elements, particularly comparisons between the Irish and other racialised 'white' groups in the USA, are missing. Here, Roediger's insertion of the Irish into a racialised and fragmented working class (1991) is exemplary, and Jacobson (1995, 1998) provides a complementary perspective, linking labour historians, such as Foner, Man and Handlin, to historians of the idea of 'race', such as Saxton, and exposing cultural production to analysis.

Labour historians can tell us much about the context in which identity formation occurred and the specific stages of development of the economy that favoured particular forms of organisation. Ultimately, however, avenues of exploration relating to ideas and practices generated outside the workplace are a vital component of our understanding of the phenomenon of racialisation. Ignatiev's work on prison records and on local disorder in nineteenth-century Philadelphia illuminates a linkage between work and leisure. Bernstein's examination of the 1863 New York Draft Riots (1990) points out the ferocity of Irish antipathy to black people in terms of perceived labour competition, political rivalry and sexual anxieties within a multi-ethnic urban setting (all themes touched on by Miller, 1969).

Allen's strong point is his attempt to provide an explanation of the ideological forces at play in the whitening process: those emanating from the Catholic Church and the Democratic Party. The former, he argues, downplayed the immorality of slavery, remained at best neutral on abolition and focussed on the threat posed to Irish Catholics by zealous evangelical abolitionists and black morals. The Democratic Party emphasised the negative outcomes that abolition would purportedly have for white workers in the north and raised fears of 'amalgamation' (both in the workplace and the bedroom). The protection provided by these two powerful institutions for incoming Catholic migrants meant that the latter were unwilling to denounce the statements of either. Moreover, in simple terms, most Irish immigrants were quick to understand the value of whiteness in America, and this realisation usually overrode any opposition to slavery and similar forms of oppression.

A far less researched area is the contribution of the Irish to the US army and its Indian wars (Finerty, 1961). The Irish and the Germans comprised a disproportionate share of infantrymen in the nineteenth century. There were around 144,000 Irish-born members of the Union army and 30,000 Irishmen among the Confederates during the Civil War.[13] Allegiance to ideas expressed through membership of armed forces is not a straightforward link to make. Indeed, Irishmen fought on both sides during the Civil War, often in Irish-only regiments raised in centres of Irish population. The New York Draft Riots of 1863 (resisting participation in the army) appear to have been unrepresentative in this respect, and a pointer to the special conditions operating in New York City. No argument can thus convincingly be made that Irish soldiers were overwhelmingly pro- or anti-slavery, even if we suspend disbelief enough to contend that the Civil War was primarily about human rights.

A more revealing picture emerges from participation in the Indian Wars of the second half of the century. Neither the Democrats nor the Catholic Church urged people to desist from this type of operation, and even African American ('buffalo') soldiers were involved in these wars. The strategic importance of the Indian Wars was to clear land and secure resources for settlement, and in this the Mexican Wars of the 1840s had been a forerunner. In that situation, one regiment, the 'St Patrick's Brigade' (the San Patricios), most of whose members were of Irish origin, swapped sides in solidarity with the Mexican Catholic forces. They were led by Galway-born John Riley. After the Battle of Churubusco, 85 of them were captured. Fifty were executed for desertion (Miller, 1986; Stevens, 1998). There is an annual day of celebration for the contribution of the San Patricios in Mexico on 12 September.

Yet there are no recorded instances of Irish soldiers siding with the Native Americans. Indeed, certain of them made successful careers out of the execution of campaigns against the latter, most famously General Philip Sheridan. A decorated Civil War officer and a native of County Cavan, Sheridan led US troops in the Sioux–Cheyenne wars of 1865–79. Sheridan is cited as the originator of the phrase 'The only good Indian is a dead Indian.' While this may be apocryphal (based on his actions), Brown (1970:254) quotes him in revealing mode. Texans concerned by the slaughter of buffalo by white hunters (who skinned and left rotting carcasses on the plains) in the early

1870s were told by Sheridan: 'Let them skin, kill and sell until the buffalo is exterminated, as it is the only way to bring lasting peace and allow civilisation to advance.'[14] Sheridan perhaps shared with contemporaries the definition of Native Americans who resisted as 'savages', but his comprehension of genocidal logic marks him out in such an era as remarkable. Young Irelander and Civil War veteran Thomas Meagher became Governor of Montana in 1866 and dealt there with the Blackfoot, Crow, Sioux and Cheyenne nations as they confronted and attacked settlers on their tribal lands. Even the largely sympathetic Keneally argues that 'Irish Americans saw no parallel between dispossession and the crisis for the tribes' of that time (1998:464).

The role of Irish soldiers in removing Native Americans from land and killing them is thus a parallel one to that of the English and Scots in sixteenth- and seventeenth-century Ireland, leading to the ambivalence over identification with 'cowboys' and/or 'Indians' carefully explored by O'Toole (1994) and Butler-Cullingford (2001). It also has echoes in the relations between Europeans and Aboriginal Australians and Maoris, where dispossession was also carried out with Irish involvement.

## ASTRIDE CIVILISATION: THE INVENTION OF THE IRISH RACE

O'Toole (1994:58) argues that the Irish represented the 'the locus of impurity, the dread crossroads at which civilisation and barbarism meet', having occupied a position similar to Native Americans in their relation to nature, and to blacks in their position on the labour market. The celebration of Tammany Day, marking the assertive presence of the Irish in urban American politics and social life, is bursting with ambiguity: Irish Americans dressed as Native Americans celebrate Indians storming the citadel as rebels, a positive and aspirational evaluation. Yet the real 'Indians' were hunted and displaced by, *inter alia*, displaced Irish emigrants.

The use of a putative ideological division between civilised and uncivilised as justification for the collective dispossession of a racialised group then is not a trope limited in its applicability to sixteenth-century Ireland, but a recurring configuration in which the actors on both sides of the line (and in the Irish case, straddling it) may alter, while the political project it protects and propels remains relatively unaltered.

In terms of this binary civilisation/savagery model, in whose clutches the Irish in America remained ensnared for half a century or more, Morrison (1993) provides an illuminating insight. In her essay on early American literature, she argues that a dominant theme in this literature was what she terms 'the highly problematic construction of the American as a new white man' (1993:39). This worked by placing Europeans against a background (both physical and figurative) of barbarity to better highlight their civilised status. Of the new man thus created, she writes: 'The site of his transformation is within rawness: he is backgrounded by savagery' (ibid.:44).

This insight elucidates a further dimension of the identity conflict undergone by Irish immigrants. On arrival in the USA they received treatment similar to that which they had experienced under colonial rule, but with three important differences. First, the combination of the Democratic Party machinery in urban America and the strength of the Catholic Church gave them membership of powerful networks, on the basis of which they could consolidate and then advance their social position. Second, by the nineteenth century, the distinction between 'free' and 'unfree' labour endorsed the natural order of 'white' and 'black' worker, providing a glimpse of the abyss from which Irish labourers had escaped, and permitting the threat of its dissolution to assume an apocalyptic nature. The relationship between ideas about working-class freedoms and those of slaves was a key factor in framing and motivating the frequent outbursts of violence against free blacks in urban America in the mid nineteenth century. Freedom thus depends on the 'unfreedom' of others, a relationship that Morrison (1993:57) terms 'the parasitical nature of white freedom'. Third, there were already uncivilised 'Others' in the American ideological landscape against whom the Irish could aim to whiten themselves; black and Native Americans encapsulated the 'savagery' that would 'background' them. The intertwining of these three factors from the middle of the nineteenth century created an impetus for all European immigrant groups to distance themselves from black Americans. Yet it was the Irish who historically performed this border-policing role to a greater extent because of the timing of their mass arrival, the extent of their implication in Democratic politics and the ideological pressures on them to distinguish themselves from free blacks in the urban areas in which they overwhelmingly settled in the mid nineteenth century.

The role of Irish America in developing the notion of the Irish 'race' lay in the provision of solidarity with Irish nationalism and the creation of an interest group to further Irish causes in the USA. The emphasis on an 'Irish race' rather than the Irish, as a collective identity, tied the diasporic community to the homeland in a relationship that to a degree eliminated time and space, and made the Irish equivalent on the world stage to any other group that had not been colonised. The exact content of the 'race' had, in America, been evacuated of its Protestant component, with the linguistic switch to Scotch-Irish, and this is reflected in the cultural organisations, nationalist activities and newspapers produced. In the post-Civil War period, organisations such as the Fenian Brotherhood, the Ladies Land League, the AOH, Clann na Gael, the Irish National League, and Gaelic Societies (the first of which was set up in Boston in 1873 (Ní Bhroiméil, 2003)) were established, while the community's press was dominated by the *Irish World,* and the *Catholic Citizen.* There was also the Irish-language *An Gaodhal*, which was published in the 1881–98 period.

Moreover, the functional assistance to nationalism provided by Irish America enabled identity to be framed in terms of exile (Jacobson, 1995:14–15), a parallel with Jewish America in the late nineteenth century. The job description of Irish America was to be, in Davitt's words, nationalism's 'avenging wolfhound' (McCaffrey, 1976:130), a view that fostered such expressions of collective expectancy as that of Robert Ellis Thompson's book, *Spirit of the Nation* (1898), serialised in the *Irish World*: 'From every quarter of the inhabited world, the Irish race watch and wait for the hour of deliverance.'[15]

It was with this sense of destiny then, that Catholic Irish America invented itself as a diasporic community bound by bloodlines to its homeland and united against its enemies, be they landlords or Know Nothings. The 'Irish race', in this form, developed in the heart of a society undergoing industrialisation, whose racialisation processes were derived from a different social base to that of Ireland; in a neo-colonial country of mass immigration with indigenous people, and an enslaved population of African origin. I have already noted that the adoption of American racialised norms involved embracing a 'white' social identity, in contradistinction to other non-white ones. The Irish, Celtic and Catholic content of that 'white' identity was a mixture of confidence and victimhood whose significant Other remained Imperial Britain, just as much as it became the free black or the 'Know-Nothing'. These two components can be seen in the triumphant narrative of Irish success in America: on the one hand in the economic and political prominence of Irish America as expressed in its lobby groups, high-profile politicians and business networks, and on the other in the reiteration of discriminatory experience such as the 'No Irish Need Apply' signs allegedly ubiquitous well into the twentieth century, in relation to which Jensen (2002) has recently provoked a small controversy (Lyons, 2003). Jensen claims that these signs and particularly newspaper adverts for domestic help were relatively short-lived, and in any case did not prevent Irish women from dominating the labour market for nannies in the latter half of the nineteenth century. Moreover, they had disappeared well before their claimed sightings in 1920s Boston, for example. In some ways, the notion of continued discrimination is internally crucial to the narrative of success: success against the odds is always sweeter. Nonetheless the absence of that particular form of discrimination does not negate all the other empirically provable obstacles that Irish immigrants and their descendants had to face: from Know Nothings and other nativist political groups, to their structural position at the lower end of the skills range, which doomed them to the poorest employment, housing and health statuses for generations. The 'No Irish Need Apply' signs may well be, as Jensen concludes, 'a leprechaun', but they serve as a symbolic representation encompassing a host of more complex experiences, less-readily compressible into a slogan.

It bears repeating that the project of racialising the Irish involved virtually dialectic confrontation between those seeking to place a generally positive interpretation on Irishness (and by extension give it a constitutive position within Americanness) and those seeking to place a generally negative interpretation on Irishness, and thus excluding it from Americanness. Jacobson's work on popular Irish American culture (1995) shows that within the printed output of diaspora – the autobiographies, political pamphlets and Irish press in the latter part of the nineteenth century and early twentieth century – can be found an attachment to particular notions that can be synthesised to give an impression of the content of the Irish American perception of itself as a 'race'. These include a natural (even genetic) disposition to anti-British feeling; natural abilities in martial capacity; the defence of women (as the embodiment of nation); and an overriding belief in a distinct Catholic, Celtic and Irish value system that is based on the spiritual, the collective and the traditional, and is thus intrinsically superior to materialistic British culture.

What makes this pertinent in a study of racialisation is that reflexive procedures of identity creation, specific to precise conjunctions and understood in specific historical contexts, have by the end of the nineteenth century become the *taken-for-granted* assumptions upon which identity is constructed. In other words, they no longer have to be explained by reference to the social, because they have become innate. This is expressed in the way they are conceptualised as timeless. Two examples are illustrative. In the build-up to the Spanish American (Cuban) War, an editorial in the *Irish World* spoke of Irish Americans' readiness to engage for their country: 'What splendid fighters the Irish have always been, in every cause except their own: unsurpassed by the sons of any age, nation or race.'[16] Compare this with the memoirs of O'Donovan Rossa (Rossa, 1898), the organiser of the first nationalist bombing campaign on the British mainland, arguing that particular responses to enemy deaths are shared by all Irish people: 'That kind of instinct [i.e. relief at the shooting of a landlord] is in the whole Irish race today' (ibid.:77). He goes on to maintain that he did not become anti-English when imprisoned for nationalist activities: 'What I am now, I was, before I ever saw the inside of an English prison. I am so from nature' (ibid.:115). Thus time and space are obliterated in these martial-derived images in which the natural results in the social. Racial memory for the Irish is held up as one of timeless military exertion focussed specifically against the English, but also on behalf of other powers (understood as stemming from the English repression that generated the exile of the Wild Geese).

What is specific to the racialisation of Irish Americans is not only their confrontation with new racialised Others within a particular social context, but also their ambivalent membership of a superpower dominated by Anglo-Saxonism and involvement in that power's imperial project. It was clear to Irish Catholics in mid-nineteenth-century America that the country's dominant groups did not include them in their imagined community. By the 1890s, however, that had changed, as new Southern and Eastern European immigrants filled the subaltern slots in the labour market vacated by the Irish. So the question is, how did Irish Americans see themselves in relation to America's imperial conquests? In that period, the comprehension of social and political differences through the prism of 'race' was the dominant one, and the key theory among the tangled and confusing foliage of racial logics was that of social Darwinism. This stated that the human races were engaged in a struggle for survival, in which the weaker would be eliminated by the stronger. Moreover, this model was used not only to explain social inequalities within the nation state (with regard to class, gender or ethnicity, for example), but increasingly to justify imperial expansion and domination.

What emerges in an admittedly restricted study (Jacobson, 1995) which focuses on the Irish press response to the Cuban and Philippines

Wars in 1898 is a collective worldview marked by the sensibility of colonised people, but which also incorporates that of an interiorised colonialism. The most interesting example of this is an article by Humphrey Desmond, editor of the *Catholic Citizen*, who writes attacking the Cuban war: 'Barbarian dominions can never be amalgamated with the American Republic: and we want no such satrapies.'[17] Thus in an ostensibly anti-imperialist contribution, the framework of discussion is that of civilisation and savagery, an opposition utilised to justify the expansion of colonisation in Ireland three centuries previously, and within North America in relation both to Native Americans and Mexicans over the decades preceding this article. In a later article arguing against the Philippines War,[18] a similar logic is applied. Desmond opposes the colonisation of the Philippines on two principal grounds: first, it would amount to 'playing England's game in the Orient', and second, it would mean that 'American citizenship is to be diluted by Malay citizenship and that America's democracy is to stand the trial of working itself out among inferior people.' This time, there is a combination of anti-imperialism derived from a parallel experience of colonisation and a rehearsal of arguments that could have been put forward by any theorist of Manifest Destiny, or, for that matter, Know Nothing politicians arguing against the vote for Irish immigrants in the middle of the century. The multiple layers of ambivalence in this position should not be minimised by the acknowledgement that other Irish American outlets were more straightforwardly opposed to, or in favour of the expansion of American influence through imperialism. James Roche's *Pilot*, for example, was stringently opposed to imperialism, primarily British, but also American. Yet Roche also drew on contemporary understandings of difference even in his critique of the American ruling elites: 'Let the Anglo-Saxon call the roll of his relations and confess, with shame, that a grand race like that of the Puritan and pilgrim is vanishing [...] The fittest will always survive, when they care to do so.'[19] Roche's application of social Darwinism is subversive, but, as in the best satire, his grasp of his target's logic is faultless.

The integration of ethnic Irish Americans into the mainstream of white America that would become the Caucasian 'race' in the twentieth century was thus far from complete at this time. This incomplete incorporation into hyphenless America entailed ambivalence over its imperial projects, particularly due to recollections of Britain's own role in Ireland, yet integration into the ideology of racialised difference had been accomplished long before. Barret and

Roediger stress the ambivalence in the definition of white and off-white immigrant groups in US society, arguing that for Irish Americans pressure to distance themselves from blacks in order to join 'white' society co-existed with an impulse to show solidarity with other groups discriminated against: 'the exposed position of racial inbetweenness generated both positions at once' (1997:31). Irish Americans, however, crossed a social Rubicon in the twentieth century. The eugenicist-inspired 1924 Immigration Act imposed no quotas on immigration from Ireland, a sign that it was no longer considered a contaminating source of manpower.

Not only had Irish Americans learned the rules of 'this racial thing' (ibid.:3), and what was at stake in being white, but now they saw international conflicts through this same hall of mirrors. The ideological struggle in which they were engaged did not involve throwing the rule book out of the window, but honing skills and playing better than those from whom they had learned the rules in the first place. This meant accepting that there was 'civilisation' and 'barbary', staking out their claim to a position within the former category, and then seeking to reach the upper echelons of it. Parallels with the attitudes of Home Rulers to British imperialism before World War I can be seen in the next chapter.

## CONCLUSION

The Irish in nineteenth-century America could therefore be seen as carriers of an inferior, less-civilised culture, and compared unfavourably to blacks in terms of their readiness for full membership of the republic, whilst forming the core of an army whose principal mission was to dispossess those deemed to have cultures inferior to that of white America, and being in the vanguard of a movement to drive Chinese workers out of California to preserve the labour market for the 'white man'.

The existence of powerful anti-Irish racist ideology throughout the nineteenth and early twentieth centuries does not negate the Irish ascension through the ranks of white America, but bears out Jacobson's image of 'race' as a palimpsest (1998:141), whereby previous meanings accorded to difference are still legible beneath newer ones, creating a multiplicity of ideas in currency at any given moment. Negra for example argues in her essay on 'Irish' actress Colleen Moore (1995) that stereotypical representations (traditional and numerous family, rural-based, over-emotional responses, unthreatening patriarchal values) were a key element of Moore's appeal, and that she was constructed as Irish because of that group's model minority status in the 1920s *vis-à-vis* more 'threatening' Southern and Eastern Europeans. Interestingly, the promotional activities for Moore's films often involved 'blackface'.[20]

In the new context of the New World, new classificatory dichotomies (free/unfree, white/black) cross-cut and reinforced older categories (civilised and barbaric) thus forming unique configurations of power relationships founded on 'race'. The Irish grasped that they were capable of attaining whiteness but would have to argue their case, and that revolved around distancing themselves from Others, especially blacks. Passage through this transitional zone, between blackness and whiteness, was successfully negotiated over the 1830–90 period.

Yet Irish immigrants started off as 'not white' (in terms of culture and religion) and ended the century as white (that is, part of the dominant majority). The argument that they were basically a 'white' race as good as any other, and therefore better than non-white ones was key to their success. John Mitchel's writing displays a complete grasp of this tactical consideration. In his attempt to demonstrate that the Irish were '*plus royalistes que le roi*', his appropriation of racial superiority led him to couch arguments in racial terms.

The specific historical context of the Irish whitening process explains a shift in perceptions of 'race' and of Irish 'race' in particular. The process occurred at the height of a period when the language of 'race' was a dominant discourse, not just in national, but in global politics. The development of an Irish nationalist movement in Ireland relied on its transnational network not just for financial, but also ideological sustenance. Part of the latter involved projecting the Irish as a 'race' like any other element of the dominant 'white race'. McVeigh (1992) and Rolston and Shannon (2002) stress the ideological linkages between diaspora and Ireland as a key mechanism for the import of racist discourse and its appropriation and incorporation into specific contexts. What came out of America is thus a crucial process for the nationalist meta-narrative. The rise of the Irish through the ranks to become powerful and integrated Americans is an example of how well the Irish have done abroad. Indeed, the American setting and the transatlantic network of migration could be argued to comprise part of the collective imaginary, an Irish

'American dream'. However, the glossed-over element of this history is that black and Native Americans, not to mention Asians, lost out to the Irish in this battle for privilege, whose consequences have profoundly shaped the life chances and work opportunities available in America to the present day (Luibhéid 1997a, 1997b; Corcoran, 1997; Lloyd, 1999:10–56).

# 5

# In the Belly of the Beast: Nineteenth-Century Britain, Empire and the Role of 'Race' in Home Rule

## ANTI-CATHOLICISM IN BRITAIN

The nineteenth-century forms of racialisation of the Irish in Britain, whilst contemporaneous and in part overlapping with what occurred in the USA, require a separate overview. The context of nineteenth-century Britain was one from which the black–white binary model of urban America was absent. This is not to say that there were no black people in Britain at that time, or that their presence is necessary for ideas about blackness to exist. Britain's collective Others since the Reformation had primarily been Catholics (Colley, 1992; Paz, 1992). Paz asserts that in Victorian Britain, 'fear and loathing of Roman Catholicism was a major part of nineteenth-century cultural context' (1992:1).

Labour market segmentation, religious identification, the state's attempts to impose law and order, the stage of industrial development attained by the British economy and the spatial and occupational concentration of the Irish in particular parts of urban centres combined to produce new versions of pre-existing anti-Catholicism (Hickman, 1995a). These shared plenty with the sixteenth-century culture-based ideologies, while supplementing them with elements derived from the interplay of the forces of the state and the work of scientists engaged in the classification of human beings into 'races'. However, even within the relatively short period from the increase in Irish settlement[1] observed during the Famine to the end of the century, the political context also changed. This context forms the backdrop of the following argument and is crucial to understanding why anti-Catholicism alone cannot explain the variety of responses to Irish immigrants, for it is a constant factor. Specific social and political processes and events fed on it to trigger anti-Catholic rioting with an anti-Irish flavour, conflict with the police, and conflict with the British working classes. This section, like its predecessor on the USA, is on one level an attempt to bring together two distinct sets of literature: historians' work on Irish migration and sociologists' reflections on collective identities.[2]

The Famine Irish in England, Scotland and Wales stepped into a social context in which their Catholicism marked them as different and potentially dangerous, before their occupational and residential status was even up for analysis. Anti-Irish feeling was not generated solely by labour market competition. As noted in the previous chapter, antipathy towards Catholicism had already provided part of the justification for Britain's first colonial enterprise. The threat of 'papist plots', the domestic ones more apparent than real, studded sixteenth- and seventeenth-century history. Catholicism was generally viewed as a threat to British liberties, based as it was on allegiance to Rome and non-scriptural theology. Although an element of popular culture, anti-Catholicism became more evident at particular moments when the stakes of being a Protestant state seemed higher: in the nineteenth century this meant the Act of Union (1800) that brought Ireland into the Kingdom and the Catholic Emancipation Act (1829), which split the Tory Party. Yet what was witnessed from the 1840s through to the 1890s was a distinct set of socio-political contexts in which the various disparate elements of anti-Irish racist ideas combined in different ways. The racialisation of the Irish in Britain involved focussing on difference in three overlapping arenas: religion, class and 'race'.

## The Irish as Catholics

Notions of Englishness had evolved, since the sixteenth-century break with Rome, around particular attachments (the Crown, land, a parliament) and the distance between Protestantism and Catholicism. The Presbyterian Church in Scotland (Gallagher, 1985; Handley, 1943) was particularly insistent on the ideological, moral and social differences between Protestants and Catholics. English Catholics had been a suspect population since Elizabethan times, and, as noted earlier, the distinction between Protestant rationalism and property-holding, and Irish 'superstition' and collective rights had been used to justify colonisation and appropriation of land in the sixteenth century. The rebellions of the seventeenth and eighteenth centuries in Ireland had created a sense that Ireland was an insurgent nation, and one with far greater allegiance to Rome than to the British monarch. Anti-Catholic demagoguery and riots increased in intensity when the political stakes were raised when, at the end of the eighteenth century, the United Irishmen's short-lived alliance with (paradoxically secular) revolutionary France and Ireland's accession to the Union brought external threats during wartime to the top of the political agenda. A generation later the Catholic Emancipation Act split the Tory Party for over a decade, while the repeal of the Corn Laws in 1846 marked the end of another process of internal dissension again generated partly by the 'Irish question'.[3]

It is against this contextual background that the nature of Irish settlement in Britain altered, particularly from the late 1840s when people fleeing the Famine arrived. The peak in the numbers of Irish-born was identified in the 1861 census, where they accounted for 3.5 per cent of the population. Within a rapidly-growing population overall, the Irish comprised a relatively small segment (an average of 2.3 per cent between 1841 and 1900), but a relatively large one in the areas of greatest concentration. Scotland's proportion of Irish-born was generally higher than that of England and Wales (rising to 7.2 per cent in 1851, but falling to 3.7 per cent in 1921 compared with 1 per cent south of the border).[4] In terms of numbers, the largest Irish-born communities were to be found in London, Liverpool, Glasgow and Manchester in the 1851–71 period. In terms of percentages, Liverpool (22.3 per cent), Dundee (18.9 per cent) and Glasgow (18.2 per cent) had the highest proportion in 1851, while 20 years later it was Greenock (outer Glasgow) (16.6 per cent), then Liverpool (15.6 per cent) and Glasgow (14.3 per cent). The greatest extent of local residential concentration can be shown with reference to Liverpool, where in 1841 the pre-Famine proportion of Irish-born in Vauxhall and Exchange wards was around 33 per cent. Only a decade later the Irish comprised 47 per cent of the population in these wards.

By the middle of the century, therefore, the Catholicism against which the British character had been defined over the previous few centuries, was now within Britain, and viewed as the source of a number of potential threats. Paz argues that anti-Catholicism rested upon three fundamental ideas, relating to 'the Protestant constitution, the Norman Yoke and … Providentialism' (1992:2). These translated as the preference for constitutional rule over that of absolute monarchs, the notion that the Catholic Normans had imposed foreign rule on essentially democratic Anglo-Saxons, and the concept that every event was evidence of God's plan, including Britain's imperial dominance, while disasters were forms of punishment for poor collective behaviour. Best (1967) identifies a combination of doctrinal and moral strands to popular Protestantism in its clash with Catholicism. Many of these revolved around moral panics relating to the celibate priesthood, thought to result in sexual excess, the influence held by priests over families, and the perception that Catholics were not only disloyal but intent on proselytising Protestants. This anxiety cannot have been assuaged by the restoration of the Catholic hierarchy in Britain in 1850, with twelve bishoprics created. The Protestant response was to christen this 'Papal Agression'. A round of small-scale conflicts erupted in a number of towns over the following two or three years, the largest being the Stockport riot of June 1852, in which a man died and hundreds were injured (Milward, 1985). The trigger was the annual Catholic schools' march through the town, yet the analyses of the incident (Milward, 1985; Kirk, 1980; Fielding, 1992) suggest that more complex socio-economic forces underlay the violence. It should be noted that in Stockport, the period was one of relative prosperity after a bad few years, and the local Protestant Association was a key player both in the dissemination of anti-Catholic propaganda and in the minimisation of the rioting's legal consequences (Milward, 1985).

The 'No Popery' movement, involving, *inter alia*, speaking tours given by ardently anti-Catholic clergy and laymen in areas of high Irish concentration, was another catalyst for violent conflict. This also points to the shift in use of the term 'Catholic', from one which required the qualifier 'Irish' in the early part of the century, to one which found that qualifier redundant by the 1850s. The Catholic Church played an organisational role for Irish emigrants and their descendants, particularly in the areas of education – setting up schools – and informal welfare and guidance. The Church's attempts to establish respectability and refute charges of disloyalty were undone by the efforts of speakers from the 'No Popery' movement, such as the Baron de Carmin in 1857–58, and William Murphy in the 1860s, as well as the rise of Fenianism at the end of that decade. Indeed, the most severe conflicts in urban Britain between the Irish and the English, in the late 1850s and 1867–68, coincided with the most intense moments of those campaigns. Local factors such as the extent of economic hardship in relation to local economy, were also relevant. Kirk (1980) points to the severe economic hardship in the winter of 1867, as well as the rise of Fenianism and the 'No Popery' election of 1868 as compounding each other's influence on social relationships in Lancashire for example.

## The Irish as an 'underclass'

The economic strands of racialisation have been alluded to above. They revolve around the threats posed by Irish immigrants in terms of both employment and welfare, in the form of the Poor Law. Contemporary views posited the Irish as simultaneously a substitute workforce capable of cutting wages and strikebreaking, and inveterately indolent claimants of Poor Law funds, whose dip below normal standards of decency was evidenced by their frequent susceptibility to air- and water-borne illnesses prevalent in the period. The way in which these threads could be tied into a neat ideological bow is illustrated in a *Stockport Advertiser* editorial from June 1852, quoted by Milward (1985:210): 'What is it that so often disturbs the peace of the borough, increases our rates and saps the very foundation of all our charitable institutions, but popery embodied in Irish mobs, paupers and fever patients.' While it is clear that Irish immigrants did access Poor Law assistance, this was only available to people with five years' residence in the borough. Newly-arrived immigrants did not qualify. Moreover, the borough had the right to remove those deemed to be vagrants from its jurisdiction. According to the Select Committee on Settlement and Poor Removal (ibid.) this was practised in 1840s Stockport, for example, with 42 people removed in 1846 and 73 in the first quarter of 1847.

The link between poverty and disease made in the nineteenth century was not the one informed by medical knowledge of unsanitary conditions, but a racialised and moralising one that associated 'naturally' depraved lifestyles, as embodied in the despicable living conditions endured by Irish immigrants in their districts (Engels, 1969 [1844]; Swift, 1984; Handley, 1943; Mac Laughlin, 1999a), with a punitive (providential) judgement in the form of diseases such as cholera, typhus or smallpox. Yet this posed public health threats to the wider community, and thus led to anxiety and expenditure on the part of newly-created borough corporations (set up by the 1835 Municipal Corporations Act). Considering that the vast majority of immigrants from the late 1840s were fleeing the Famine, it would not be surprising to observe higher than usual rates of illness among that group, even if they did not then settle in poor housing. The conditions of the crossing alone would have been conducive to the spread of illnesses, particularly as most passengers would have been weakened by malnourishment. In any case, Irish immigrants in mid-nineteenth-century Britain came to be the embodiment of disease, dirtiness and low morals, and were thus viewed as a bas relief to Protestant cleanliness and purity. Moreover, in the aporia of racist ideology that sought to establish the Irish as bearers of anti-Protestant values, not only were they seen as being settled in the most insalubrious conditions, but also as comprising a disproportionate amount of the vagrant (that is, mobile) population, where this represented a different moral menace. Jones (1982:178) comments that the 'vagrant was the epitome of uncivilised self-indulgence, lacking in both "industrious habits" and "independence"'. Moreover, Mac Laughlin (1999a:53) points out that the distinction between '*wandering and migratory* Celts and *settled* Anglo-Saxons was a particularly longstanding one in English political discourses'. The former were perceived as inferior because rootless, especially in the second half of the nineteenth century. Whether mobile or settled then, the Irish could not escape the racialising logics of Victorian Britain.

### The Irish as labour

The role of the Irish labour force has been seen as primarily one of substitute labour, in Engels' terms, the 'reserve at command' (1969 [1844]:122) on which Britain's accelerating industrial development was based. What this meant for employers was access to mobile, flexible and relatively cheap labour at a moment when large-scale infrastructural development and industrial expansion in particular locally-relevant trades (cotton in Lancashire and parts of Scotland, mining and sugar production in Greenock, furnaces in the Black Country, and so on)[5] required such labour. Traditional seasonal migration for work in agriculture (especially harvesting) diminished from the 1840s onwards, falling by around half from 60,000 such migrants per year in the 1830s to 30,000 by the turn of the century (Swift, 2002:51). By 1861, the Irish-born accounted for 8.8 per cent of the workforce (ibid:52) and tended to be involved in unskilled, and gendered (men in heavy industry, women in cotton, laundry, domestic service, and so forth) forms of employment. Yet it would be foolhardy to attempt to generalise. What is important is to note first that the local economy was more determinant than any cultural baggage brought by the migrants, and second, that the crucial paradigm of competition as fuelling conflict should be looked at carefully. As in the USA, this framework should be interrogated for its assumptions and erasures, if only to end up with a more qualified judgement.

Gallagher (1985), for example, contrasts the labour markets of Liverpool and Glasgow in the mid nineteenth century and finds that they presented very different opportunities and obstacles to migrants. Liverpool's, being based on trade rather than industry, gave rise to a fluid situation in which predominantly unskilled and short-term opportunities were available. Here English and Irish, Protestants and Catholics, of both nationalities, were in direct competition. The result was greater conflict around the labour market. Yet in Glasgow, where the labour market was based on industry, a division of skilled and unskilled labour was already well established, and the Irish took the latter, in mining and textiles, while the Scots generally held onto skilled work with their superior skills capital, their control of the unions and due to exclusion enforced by the Orange Order. The result: less direct competition. The 1836 *Report on the State of the Irish Poor in Great Britain* found occupational clustering of Irish immigrants in unskilled labour; generally employed in labouring, crafts and factory work, and within the cotton industry, they were concentrated in the lowest-paid sectors. Between 1841 and 1861 in the north-west of England there was a movement of Irish immigrants out of crafts and into cotton, as operatives: 57 per cent of Stockport's Irish-born were cotton operatives, while this figure was as high as 69 per cent in Stalybridge (Kirk, 1980:84–5).

On this basis, the paradigm of competition fuelling antagonism should not necessarily be taken to apply in every urban centre in which the Irish settled. Overall, it seems likely that with thousands of extra workers flooding a labour market in a relatively short space of time, wages were lowered according to the laws of supply and demand. Yet people do not work in overall economies *per se*; they work in, and perceive themselves as part of, local economies and industries. The picture appears to be more varied and complex than was clear to contemporaries, with direct and indirect forms of competition at play simultaneously. Kirk (1980:86) suggests that there is no evidence that Irish workers in the cotton industry in the north-west, which boomed for most of the mid nineteenth century, actually lowered wages, but they did work in the lowest-paid sections of the industry. Moreover, he argues: 'In periods of rising industrial militancy (in 1853–4, 1859–61, 1866–7 and 1869) Irish and English cotton operatives generally acted together against the forces of capital' (1980:87). Indeed, what may well be the most salient point is not whether wages were lowered, by how much or in which location, but the fact that English workers may generally have perceived Irish workers, *in toto*, to be lowering wages. Figure 4 is a cartoon showing a contemporary view of an Irish worker being carried around on the

# THE ENGLISH LABOURER'S BURDEN;

## Or, THE IRISH OLD MAN OF THE MOUNTAIN.

[See *Sinbad the Sailor.*

*Figure 4*  Free Rides on the Worker's Back? A Nineteenth-Century Representation of the Relationship between Irish and English Labour. 'The English Labourer's Burden', Archibald Leech, 1849. © Punch Ltd.

shoulders of an English counterpart. Local workers would have related the arrival of the Irish with the 'degradation' of their living standards in times of bust and constructed the Irish worker as an instrument of forces beyond their control, an agent of capital rather than labour. Allied to the religious and cultural differences, this made for a potentially explosive cocktail.

Moreover, Belchem (1985) argues that in the 1815–50 period, the popular press associated the loaded term 'Irish' with the feared disorder provoked by trade union activities and protests, raising fears and allowing their legitimacy to be called into question. This allowed the authorities to enact more draconian measures than would otherwise have been acceptable (ibid.: 92–4).

Although there was also residential segregation (Pooley, 1977), this was not generally in the form of ghettoes as we now understand them. The two Liverpool wards referred to above, with the highest concentration of Irish-born residents, still had less than 50 per cent. Swift (1984) suggests that Wolverhampton's Caribee Island and Rock Row Streets were 75 per cent Irish. The practices of socialising and engaging in cultural activities as a group probably compounded residential segregation with cultural segregation. While these areas were conveniently compact for the forces of law and order (Swift, ibid.), they were not walled off, or entirely absent of English inhabitants. In any case, as Hickman (1995a) argues, in England residential segregation *per se* was not unique to the Irish; the Welsh, for example, also lived in relative concentrations and sometimes competed with English workers (Pooley, 1977). Nonetheless, the strident and aggressive response was reserved for the Irish rather than Welsh.

Not only were Irish migrants identified as culturally other, they also fitted into the profile of the 'dangerous classes' that was used by urban police forces in nineteenth-century Britain. Set up from the 1830s onwards, municipal police forces developed patterns of policing that prioritised visible street crime, which meant, *de facto*, a focus on, and large presence in, areas where Irish people congregated. The police's concentration on drunkenness and disorder was bound to come into painful conflict with a working-class way of life which contained a vigorous pub culture, for example. Swift argues forcefully that many small-scale urban disorders were the product of policing tactics. Referring to work on Leeds in 1844 (Storch, 1975) and Birkenhead in 1862 (Neal, 1982), Liverpool (Cockcroft, 1974), Manchester and Merthyr (Jones, 1982), Swift concludes that the Wolverhampton events fit the same pattern: 'these ugly disorders may be explained largely in terms of the ideology, organisation and priorities of a developing police force in Wolverhampton during the period' (Swift, 1984:184).[6]

In a period when the hegemony of 'race' as a way of naturalising the social world had reached a point where it was applied to explain class differences (Lorimer, 1978, 1996; Bonnett, 2000), Irish migrants fell into two complementary categories: one that stressed their dangerous, potentially criminal character as workers, alongside their English, Welsh and Scottish counterparts, and the other that emphasised their religion and nationality. The Irish were thus racialised as one section of a more widely racialised working class, but also with an extra dimension. In the logic of this view, their natural propensity for fighting, drinking and low morals, present to a certain extent among English Protestant workers, was exacerbated by their popish religion and inferior cultural background. They were seen as having brought the slum with them.

In this light, a reasonable question might be, why were there not more 'Stockport-style' riots? Surely if competition was as intense, and hostility so basic an element of culture as might be suggested by the notion that anti-Irish racism grew in the nineteenth century, we would expect to see a far greater number of serious conflicts. It is impossible to explain variables with constants. If it is established that popular Protestantism constructed Catholicism as a threat, that the Irish were seen as an underclass and as economic competitors, there must be extra factors that explain why these ingredients led to only sporadic eruptions and relatively little rioting. These are explained as political and structural factors, such as the relative dynamism of local Protestant associations, elections and 'No Popery' speaking tours, which disturbed partial integration into local working-class life and trade union activities, particularly after the failure of Chartism, which had provided an alternative set of bases for solidarity to those of religion and nationalism (Kirk, 1980).

### The Irish as Celts

The idea that 'race' constituted the primary classification of the social world had been gaining currency since the Enlightenment, and by the middle of the nineteenth century was hegemonic on both sides of the Atlantic. Yet a more esoteric strain of ideology within the broad, sometimes contradictory and often discordant body of thinking that is the Victorians on 'race', argued that there were internal categorisations within the principal categories of white, yellow, red and black.

Gobineau's *Essai sur l'inégalité des races humaines* is a seminal work, yet it had been preceded in its exposé of hierarchical distinctions within the 'white race' by British writers concerned with the problem of explaining the military and political dominance of England over Scotland, Wales and Ireland in racial terms. The notion that the Celt was weaker than the Anglo-Saxon was a nineteenth-century expression of a centuries-old power relationship. The new racialised gloss given to old relationships had the benefit of being backed up by natural science, and comprising the founding principles of the new social sciences, sociology, ethnology and anthropology. Robert Knox had been arguing that 'race' was not just about colour but also about culture since the 1840s. His influential *Races of Man* (1850) represented a powerful statement on the superiority of the Anglo-Saxon, constructed as reflective, reforming and masculine in contrast to the rash, childish, rebellious and feminine Celt and the indolent, feckless and barbarous African. In the introduction to their edited collection, Swift and Gilley (1985:5) argue, however, that the role of Anglo-Saxonism was relatively minor as it lacked a constituency beyond an intellectual elite: 'As a highly sophisticated intellectual prejudice developed by ethnologists, historians and poets, Anglo-Saxonism was restricted by its very nature to literate members of the Victorian middle class and cannot therefore be invoked to explain the attitudes of the anti-Irish mob.' Paz (1992) is equally sceptical about the factors motivating the English working classes in anti-Irish violence and places firmer emphasis on the capacity of middle-class activists to organise and influence them. From available information on some of the activities engaged in by the membership of Protestant Operative Associations and Orange Orders, for example, he concludes that they consisted of principally 'skilled workers, clerks, traders and supervisory workers' (1992:269).[7] Moreover, he argues (ibid.) that the anti-Catholic propaganda disseminated in the form of pamphlets, and so forth, in working-class areas did not reinforce anti-Irish sentiment as it was focussed on Catholics *per se* rather than the Irish. The latter point is open to the response, what if the local Catholics were mainly Irish? However, the idea that particular sections of society were more interested in anti-Irish ideology than others is worth taking further.

It appears incontestable in relation to the disorders of the 1850s and 1860s that the racial taxonomies and literary culture required to fully grasp Anglo-Saxonism were absent. Yet it is probably more difficult to sustain an argument that ideas about Anglo-Saxonism did not reach below an educated middle-class level across the entire century. While readers of specialist journals were obviously from an elite background, the kind of ideas espoused by Knox were reproduced in simplified and popular fashion in the pages of *Punch* for example (just as they were in *Harpers' Weekly* in the USA). Moreover, in the latter half of the century, particularly as political events in Ireland began to spill over into Britain, the frame within which the Anglo-Saxon/Celt binary was constructed was transformed into something more belligerent. Into the intellectual colonial project of classification came Darwin's theory of evolution, and the resulting take on this in terms of how the English and Americans saw the Irish was the simianisation of the Irishman. This element of the relationship has assumed popular status, and served as the basis for resurgent stereotypes in the British press, post 1969 (Curtis, 1984). Yet it should be stressed that the timing of this originally corresponded to the presence of specific historical factors: the revolutionary idea that humankind was related to the ape, the ready identification of Africans with apes in racist thought, the anomalous position of the Irish as a colonised white European 'race', and imperial anxiety over Britain's place in the world (as the distance between its industrial output and that of competitors such as the USA and Germany slowly diminished over the last quarter of the nineteenth century). The status of the colonised fitted only with a 'white' race that could be at least marginally explained as black in ancestry. Lebow's argument (1976) that the Irish held a 'black' colonised status, captures the fusion of colour, culture and status arising from Victorian ideas on 'race' and fitness for government, but pushes the black–Irish analogy too far. John Beddoe's 'Index of Nigrescence'[8] (first put forward in 1868) claimed to prove that the Irish, particularly those from the west and south, were related to 'Negroid' peoples, a strain of argument that had been floating around since the 1840s. This also drew on colonially derived experiences such as those of Richard Tuthill Massy, whose letter to the Editor of the *Medical Times* in November 1848 recounted a letter from a cousin in the Second West India Regiment, who had made these remarks:

> In a mountain district, thirteen miles from Linstead, St. Thomas' Vale, Jamaica, there is not a decent cottage to be had; nothing but a negro hut, quite like an Irish cabin. One might fairly infer, from the similarity between the huts of the Connaught Irish and the African, that either one must have visited the country of the other first.

The letter goes on to refer to the story of the Milesians, who had left their Asian base, mixed with North Africans and ended up in Galway. 'I remember' continued Dr Tuthill:

> when in the County Galway, being very much struck with the *copper-coloured* skins of the inhabitants, especially about the Connemara Mountains. Their long straight hair, the red garment, wove or worked throughout, without the appearance of a seam, the want of energy among them, as likewise the peculiar structure of their houses, which reminded me that they sprung from the black and European, most probably the Spaniards, as they were most likely of all Europeans to sail at that time upon the Atlantic [...] All these are worthy of note.

What happened, from the 1860s, is that these global colonial images became infused with contemporary anxieties. The Irish were a colonised 'race', whose lack of civilisation was expressed, from this perspective, in their resistance: the Fenian outrages of 1867–68, the Home Rule campaigns, the Land League. The parallels with the framing of discourse on the Irish and Native Americans and Africans that developed since the 1580s (Quinn, 1966) are obvious.[9]

Yet, ideas on 'race' were not a one-way street. In relation to the question of Anglo-Saxons and Celts, there were strong arguments that the British were a mixture of the two, rather than pure stocks. Matthew Arnold of course famously argued from this position (while holding anti-Irish opinions) as did anthropologist Thomas Huxley, in an 1870 article in the *Pall Mall Gazette*. In 1880, writer Grant Allen in *Fortnightly Review* claimed that the Celts were 'the strength of British industrialism' and that in reality, due to the level of Irish participation in empire, 'it is the Kelt [sic] who colonises'.[10]

From his studies of the North of England, McCraild suggests that by the 1870s the Orange Order in Britain had already adopted the language of Anglo-Saxonism 'to distance themselves' from the Catholic-Celtic Irish (1996:131). Moreover, the issue of Home Rule reconfigured 'race' as not only the idiom in which to express support or antipathy, but the entire basis on which Home Rule should be resisted. 'Opponents of Home Rule in this period came increasingly to see the Irish question as a racial struggle fought between superior Anglo-Saxons on one hand, and inferior Celts on the other' (ibid.:137). Indeed the 1870s were a watershed, during which the previous elite discourse was popularised and translated into mobilising strategies, both for Tories in England, through the intermediary of the Orange Order, but also the Irish nationalists in the Home Rule campaign. Boyce (1991:197) points to Home Rule as a 'rallying point for those whose motive was hostility to British rule in Ireland'. The language of Celt and Saxon and their connotations of civilisations locked in combat was expressed by a Waterford Home Rule campaigner, who claimed Home Rule was 'a protest by his countrymen against the Saxon laws of England as administered here', and that the nation of Ireland had been 'civilised and highly educated when England was sunk in barbarism'.[11] By the mid 1880s, the struggle had been cast as 'this great racial conflict, which has been going on so long, which began in blood and suffering 700 years ago',[12] and Parnellite *United Ireland*'s Westminster report was entitled 'Among the Saxons' (Boyce, 1991:215).

The issue of Home Rule in 1886 and 1893–94 brought to a head the underlying stakes in the power relationship between Britain and Ireland in racialised terms, and split the Conservative Party's imperialist wing from its less extreme rump. Opponents of Home Rule expressed this opposition in terms of 'extreme anti-Irish prejudice, in which anti-Catholicism, a denial of Irish nationhood and the equation of self-determination with Teutonic rather than Celtic peoples came to the fore time and time again' (McCraild, 1996:137).[13] Fitness for government among peoples not fortunate enough to be included in the Anglo-Saxon family had been an issue on the other side of the Atlantic since the abolition movement had become a force in politics, and in 1870 the debates around citizenship there involved a definition of whiteness that linked racial ancestry to capacity to meet the standards required of members of a democratic polity (Jacobson, 1998). It was not solely Native Americans and former slaves who were excluded on these grounds, but non-Teutonic European immigrants, with the line particularly hazy around the Catholic Irish. Future PM Lord Salisbury drew the 'fitness for government' parallel starkly in May 1886, when he argued that 'you would not confide free representative institutions to the Hottentots for instance'.[14] Salisbury's comments then formed part of an enduring transatlantic discourse on fitness for government that foretold anarchy if particular groups were granted autonomy. Whelan (1996:152) quotes Lord Redesdale making an analogy between Santo Domingo blacks overthrowing the whites, and the potential fate of Ireland if the Catholics were seen on an equal footing to the Protestants.[15]

Moreover, not only was the debate around Home Rule phrased along racial lines by parliamentarians, but also in localised elements of the popular media, where 'the language of Anglo-Saxons versus Celts trickled down all the way to the grass roots, entering the discourse which devoured countless column inches in local newspapers' (McCraild, ibid.:138).

Swift and Gilley's refutation of the influence of Anglo-Saxonism in anti-Irish racism (1985) then does not necessarily hold water after the 1870s, when the political framework had altered. Racist ideas are reconfigured and reappear in different forms at different social and political moments, when they bear specific messages.

## Summary: anti-Irish racism in Victorian Britain

The Catholic Irish in nineteenth-century Britain found themselves at the confluence of a series of hegemonic discourses – on religious affiliation, about social class, dominant values and putative racial ancestry. The dominant ideas regarding their Catholicism, nationality, position in social hierarchy, and frequently antagonistic relationship with English, Scots and Welsh populations meant that they occupied a 'marginal' location (Boyce, 1986). Violent conflict was not a constant but a variable, explained by combinations of local factors, and their articulation with the structural. Paz, whose survey is probably the fullest (1992:225–65), concludes that hostility between the English and the Irish was minor, and argues, as does Jones (1992), that the 1830s and '40s (that is, before the largest wave of Irish migration) witnessed the peak of incidents of drunkenness and offences against the person.

Indeed, the question of anti-Irish racism should be viewed as complex and inherently contradictory. Gilley's (1978) essay on this subject and the retort from Gibbons (1996) which it provoked deserve consideration. Gilley's historical argument on the two-way process of stereotype construction, the positive appraisal of Irish characteristics in Arnold's argument for a plural basis to British cultural production and the anomaly of a 'white' group being treated as a distinct 'race' is well made, but inadequate in two respects. First, as has been noted by Gibbons, it fails to address the power relationship between coloniser and colonised (as collectivities). Gibbons argues that racialisation may well be a two-way process but that it does not involve equal access to representations. Moreover, Arnold's ideas were embedded in the process of cultural othering that I referred to in the previous chapter, whereby particular cultural characteristics are identified, essentialised and fossilised as 'natural' capacities of a particular group.

The second deficiency in Gilley's argument is in his grasp of 'race'. His is a popular understanding of racism uninformed by sociological writing. Gilley principally argues two things. First, that 'race' cannot have been an issue between the English and the Irish since they both belonged to the same (white) 'race'. Second, that among the various views of the Irish in nineteenth-century Britain were positive interpretations that mitigated the wholly negative picture which was the province of racist stereotyping. Starkly put, neither of his arguments means that racism was not the issue. Race theorists from de Gobineau onwards have included positive differential assessments of 'races' categorised as inferior, and the trope of the 'Noble Savage' has been in currency since the seventeenth century. Moreover, 'race' is not solely a question of skin colour in terms of the way that difference is conceptualised. Lastly, the sometimes contradictory and plural understandings of 'race' in nineteenth-century Britain resulted in a situation where at least two 'registers' – as Hall (2000) names them in relation to post-war Europe – the biological and the cultural, were available for discussing 'race'. Lorimer (1996:32) contends that: 'The Victorian language of race may well be ubiquitous within the culture, but its power flowed from its flexibility rather than from its rigidity.' Gilley's definition of racism is simply too narrow and one-dimensional to cope conceptually with its anti-Irish forms.

## EMPIRES

The object of this section is not to detail Irish people's involvement with the British Empire, in all their guises: indentured labourer, missionary, soldier, political activist, administrator. To an extent this process has been started by Beckles (1990a), Jeffery (1996a), Holmes (2000) and Rolston and Shannon (2002). The point that there was a significant Irish contribution to the day-to-day management of the Empire, and of the coercive physical enforcement of its control, has by now surely been made unanswerably. The ambivalence of colonised groups carrying out these functions has also been discussed (McVeigh, 1992, 1996; Kestner, 1996; Rolston and Shannon, 2002; Bielenberg, 2000a; Mac Laughlin, 2001), as have the paradoxes and ironies this entailed in places that were no longer parts of empire such as the USA (cf. Chapter 4).

In specific places and times, Ireland and the Irish experienced empire not solely as victims but also as collaborators and beneficiaries, in terms of trade, employment, and the power to exert authority of various kinds over non-Europeans. At the Battle of Pondichery in 1761, to take one example, Limerick man Eyre Coote led the British forces to victory over the French, led by Galway man Thomas Lally (Kapur, 1997:4). We must surely have progressed beyond denial in these matters. The area that is more open to debate is how did these things function in terms of racialisation and what are their implications?

Involvement in empire and the various strands of diaspora has exposed Irish people to justificatory ideologies of exploitation and placed them in antagonistic relationships with other groups, notably indigenous and enslaved non-whites in the Americas, Australia and Southern Africa. Kestner (1996:127) notes the identity ambivalence of Scots and Irish soldiers fighting colonial wars. Jeffery (1996b) argues that levels of enlistment in the British armed forces always had more to do with economic opportunities than ideological affiliation to empire, or later to Irish nationalism. Casement's failure to turn many prisoners of war in Germany to the cause of Irish nationalism (Rolston and Shannon, 2002) and the 1920 mutiny of the Connaught Rangers in India represent extreme elements of an experience characterised by internalisation of the values and ideas surrounding Britain's presence in colonial countries (Holmes, 2000). The ambivalence of soldiers and administrators was not shared by missionaries, who were given scope to work with a literally captive audience, or landholders and slave-owners in the Americas (Rolston and Shannon, 2002:65–6). Moreover, the popular conceptions of Africans that filtered back into Ireland were of passivity and weakness, encapsulated in the 'Black Babies' collections, remembered vividly by most Irish people over the age of 30.[16]

The racist ideologies used to justify and sustain inequalities (in Ireland also) were engaged with and often absorbed by the Irish abroad. These ideas and experiences, according to McVeigh (1992, 1996) and Rolston and Shannon (2002) fed back into Ireland through the networks of the diaspora, and were reworked into Irish versions. The networks extended beyond the British Empire, to continental Europe (source of the Limerick Redemptorists' 1904 anti-Semitic campaign) and the Hapsburg Spanish Empire, in which Irish and Irish-descended people played important military and administrative roles: both emancipatory (such as O'Higgins in Chile) and reactionary (O'Reilly in Cuba).

Research into these issues has been far from extensive, so the conclusions here are necessarily tentative. Yet they are situated on an ideological fault line in the 'revisionism' debate. The question of the generation of racism within the diaspora is here analysed through the prism of the relationship between structure and agency.

One line of argument raised by Gibbons (1996:174–6) requires serious response, lying as it does at the crux of contemporary treatment of racism in Ireland. He places the origin of racism squarely in the hands of the British Empire, and contends that Irish people 'caught up in this racial thing' (Barret and Roediger, 1997:3) were merely responding to the dominant ideas and social practices of their immediate context:

> This is not to say, of course, that some Catholic or indigenous Irish did not buy into hegemonic forms of racism in the United States and Australia when they themselves managed to throw off the shackles of slavery or subjugation. But it is important to recognise this for what it is, a process of identifying with existing supremacist ideologies, derived mainly from the same legacy of British colonialism from which they were trying to escape. (1996:174–5)

Moreover, Gibbons' footnote (ibid.:208) indicates that 'there may well be some truth in the observation that the only reason the Irish are not racist at home is that there are not enough racial minorities or non-Europeans in the country to make immigration a social problem'.[17] Under this particular post-colonial argument then lurk assumptions of the absence of racism within the Irish camp. Yet McVeigh (1998a), who also writes from a nationalist perspective, draws attention to the erasure and denial entailed in the equation of no blacks in Ireland with no racism in Ireland. He rightly points out that there is an indigenous tradition of racialising Travellers and Jews existing before the 1990s. Lloyd (1999:105–6) equally argues that Irish Americans cannot elide their participation in racist practices,[18] and in any case has also maintained that Irish literary contribution is at its best where it resisted, rather than dovetailed with British colonial values (1993).

I shall use Gibbons' main contention as the basis for exploring the complicated legacy of Empire in respect of Ireland and racism. There are four interlinked points to deal with here: agency, the conceptualisation of racism, nationalism, and 'race' as a colonial construct.

## Agency

The argument that agency (as personal and collective autonomy) is reduced to a debilitating level by the imposition and practice of colonial rule has a beguiling simplicity. Adopting social practices (for example, racism) as survival strategies is also easily comprehensible, and it is a theme that recurs in the narratives of immigrants to America (Barrett and Roediger, 1997; Orsi, 1992) as does resistance to these practices and the complicated ideological outcomes involved in seeing one's individual and collective advancement predicated on the annulment of deeply-held values (Brodkin, 1998). Yet if the term 'hegemonic' is tied in with Gramscian theorising on the relationship between dominant ideas and political action, then what clearly emerges is that ideas and practices are as much sites of conflict as tools that result in the unresisted transmission of values. Dominant ideas are resisted to varying degrees, subverted and appropriated, as the Gaelic revivalists appropriated the idea of the Celtic 'race' and used it as a mobilising idea in a project revalorising Irish identity. It is therefore one thing to argue that most people adopt survival strategies when in positions of relative powerlessness (which is what Gibbons appears to argue), but another to invest the source of the ideas with power that denudes people of their agency to the point where they are incapable of resisting. The historical record shows that the Catholic Irish in urban America did not merely respond to their ideological 'unwhitening' by adopting the language of Anglo-Saxon racism, but overall, after a brief initial period of collecting their bearings, set about physically removing free blacks by violence from the neighbourhoods and occupations where they had moored themselves over the previous generations.

They were not alone in pursuing such practices: other European immigrant groups had to learn this basic lesson of American survival. The idea of only 'some Catholic or indigenous Irish' buying 'into hegemonic forms of racism' is inaccurate: the majority did, at least to the point where their rise was indexed to the domination of other groups. This point is not solely germane to nineteenth-century America, but to other contexts; slaveholding in the Caribbean and southern USA before that period was not boycotted by Irish settlers, while policing subaltern colonised populations such as Aboriginals, and Indians (Holmes, 2000) was engaged in enthusiastically.

The fact that there was also sporadic Irish resistance to these projects, such as that of the San Patricios in the Mexican–American Wars and the mutiny of the Connaught Rangers in 1920, does not render the majority experience invalid, but confirms the possibility of active resistance which is seemingly effaced in the view that the Irish merely acted out the imperatives of British imperialism. Moreover, the American diaspora developed particular ideological resistance to US imperial projects, as witnessed in the press coverage of the Philippines War dealt with by Jacobson (1995), where action was criticised from a framework in which the Filipinos were equated with the Irish and the Americans with the British. Moreover, in a context where the ultimate removal of British rule from most of the island of Ireland depended on the concerted action of thousands of Irish people actively resisting the same imperial ideologies as were prevalent elsewhere in the Empire, it seems a particularly selective argument to minimise agency in one context and allow it in another.

### Racism as a response to the presence of the Other

The levels of denial surrounding Irish racism from the late 1990s onwards unfortunately necessitate a rehearsal of the adequate rebuttals offered by a host of academic writers (McVeigh, Lentin) as well as agencies dealing with this issue in contemporary Ireland. The concept of minorities provoking racism amongst the host nation by their physical presence has also been a cliché in political discourse for decades. There is a distinction to be made between arguing that the late 1990s saw the beginning of a new phase in Irish racism due in part to the increasing number of minorities, and assuming that newcomers have caused racist responses. The first attempts to situate a phenomenon in its history, while the latter attempts the opposite. Several accounts have pointed to the existence of anti-Semitism, and indigenous anti-Traveller racism at least since the nineteenth century, while I have demonstrated that the colonists of the sixteenth century institutionalised the process of racialisation. The line of reasoning entailed in the numbers game being played over immigration (in which only some immigrants are counted as problematic) (Garner, 1998) leads to the logic of the 'threshold of tolerance' that emerged in French discourse in the early 1980s, that is, an unspoken limit to what a host society can reasonably absorb in terms of gross numbers, devoid of qualitative explanation.

Moreover, levels of hostility to Jews identified by Mc Gréil (1996) show that there is anti-Semitism without Jews. The object of discourse does not have to be physically present for the discriminatory discourse to be called into being. An all-male club can be sexist without women entering it, for example. Moreover, it is difficult to imagine such an argument being used to justify anti-Irish racism in the UK or the USA.

## The internalisation of 'race' as a founding principle: 'ties mystic and spiritual'

Gibbons contends that to deploy 'race' as a descriptive concept with which to mobilise cultural nationalist support (as evidenced in Hyde's 'De-anglicisation of Ireland' for example) was to use a colonial construct (of the Celt, with good and bad character traits) which had evolved as much from the English as the Irish nationalists (1996:156). We might usefully take this perceptive comment a stage further. In the use of 'race' to contain the national essence of a colonised people, the colonisers' argument is thus deployed to procure recognition on their terms. The notion of 'race' fits snugly onto that of 'community' and carries with its assumptions of continuity and unity that might dissipate under the scrutiny of other analytical tools. It becomes one of the instruments of a nationalist movement in the phase during which it defines itself against a foreign power. Gibbons is also quite correct to point out that there was no consensus on this issue among nationalists, and cites George Sigerson and Thomas McDonagh (ibid.) as examples of nationalists who contested the validity of 'race' as a weapon of Irish nationalism.[19] He could well have added Eoin Mac Neill and Frederick Ryan. Indeed, within Unionism also there was a distinction between those who saw Ireland as containing two nations and/or two races, and those who viewed it as one nation with cultural diversity under the imperial flag (Hennessey, 1998:8–15).Yet the important point arising from this is not that 'revisionists' picked up 'race' as a way of neutralising anti-colonial resistance, as Gibbons asserts, but that those strands of nationalism that did so confined themselves to imagining the world in terms of a racial hierarchy, a profoundly colonial and reactionary framework. Yet the Irish nationalists were of their time, and this means the majority of them accepted notions such as 'race' as part of the assumptions underlying political arguments.[20] The project of distinguishing Ireland culturally from England was premised on putative differences that became racialised, that is to say, located in nature rather than the social world. Pearse (1916:343) encapsulates the argument for the Irish nation (based on language and shared heritage):

> The nation is a natural division, as natural as the family and inevitable. This is one reason why the nation is holy and an empire

is not holy. A nation is knit together by natural ties, ties mystic and spiritual, and ties human and kindly.

Mystic and spiritual ties remove the concept of the nation from the arena of social analysis. The acquisition of Irishness through residence, cultural exposure, and involvement in the day-to-day contribution to social and economic life, as in the pluralist model of citizenship, has no place in such visions. Indeed, the issue of placing the 'nation' in a 'transcendental' relationship with the *Volk* (Eisenstadt and Giesen, 1995:89) is discussed by Delanty and O'Mahony (1998:82–6). Ultimately it created a view of the Irish nation/people as being 'beyond rational reflection'. Here we have entered into the imaginative landscape of 'race'. Indeed, Pearse's inscription of the nation into a non-social dimension describes aspects of the new racism (see Chapter 7) where difference is not a quality of the social, but of the essence, and therefore static and unmeltable.

The naturalisation of the Irish nation was conferred with the legitimising stamp of continuity through a metanarrative popularised by such works as, *inter alia*, A.M. Sullivan's *Story of Ireland* (1867), the Sullivans' *Speeches from the Dock* (1890) and J.M. O'Brien's *Irish History Reader* (1905).[21] It is historiography functioning from within the shadow of the successful political and cultural manoeuvre executed by the cultural nationalists that has reproduced this racialised distinction. Paradoxically, the notion of unbridgeable cultural (rather than physical) difference promulgated by the English colonists as justificatory ideology was reconstructed by influential Irish nationalists in their efforts to put clear blue water between 'Celt' and 'Anglo-Saxon' at the end of the twentieth century.[22] Moreover, as Ní Shuínéar (1994) remarks, it is a further paradox that the discrimination against a nomadic people that comprised a significant element of sixteenth-century colonial argument (see Chapter 3) has been internalised and focussed on Travellers.

### 'White' nations and democracy

It has been noted that underlying opposition to Home Rule was the belief that, racially, Celts could not be trusted with self-government, like other inferior 'races'. Nationalist campaigners and politicians were of their age and argued within the idioms of their time; their objective was to get the Irish recognised as a white European culture that was the equal of Anglo-Saxons. Home Rulers such as Redmond in the 1910s aimed to incorporate Ireland within the Empire, as the equal of Australia, New Zealand, Canada and South Africa. From the 1870s the language of Celt v. Anglo-Saxon had been a mobilising paradigm for Unionists and Home Rulers, and it is not therefore surprising to find Irish nationalists sometimes following a path blazed by Irish Americans in the generations before, and sidestepping the 'Celtic' for the sake of the 'white'.

As Home Rule became increasingly likely in the years prior to World War I, ideological labour stressing the whiteness of the Irish was particularly important to allay the fears of the Tory Unionists and Ulster Unionists. Yet this ideological and political work assumed the form of arguments around fitness for self-government and loyalty to the Crown rather than the Vatican. In the idiom of the late nineteenth century and early twentieth century, self-government was a principle applicable only to white Europeans, wherever they had settled.

What was at stake was the right to assume nationhood, and the key was whiteness at a political moment in which this term denoted superiority and aptitude for self-rule. As a response to the kind of assertion made by Conservative Unionists that the Celts were not able to govern themselves, John Dillon's argument in 1889 that Ireland deserved self-rule because 'we are white men' (Aniagolu, 1997:48) demonstrates the underlying stakes of debate.

Griffith (2003 [1911]) also propounded the idea that the Empire could be Anglo-Hibernian, in an adaptation of his Dual Monarchy model based on the Austro-Hungarian empire (Davis, 1974). While this coupling appears odd, given Griffith's casting of England as the root of much evil in its economic values and exploitation, it fits perfectly with the logic of asserting Ireland's equality as a white, civilised nation-in-waiting. Indeed, the dynamic was towards avoiding discussion of Ireland in a colonial framework, and being particularly careful not to assert its rights by any reference to parts of the Empire dominated politically by non-Europeans. Childers' *Framework for Home Rule* (1911), for example, denies that Ireland is a colony and prefers to resurrect eighteenth-century constitutional arguments about Ireland's status. It made political sense to couch arguments in these terms because the underlying text read that colonies were for people unfit for self-government, and that more advanced populations (that is, those dominated by European stock) could negotiate greater autonomy. 'The right of the Irish to political independence' then, as Griffith asserted, 'never was, is not, and never can be dependent upon the admission of equal right in all other peoples' (Mitchel, 1982 [1913]:371).

As Rolston and Shannon (2002:44–8) and Howe (2000) have argued, within the Irish nationalist community, support for Third World independence movements (particularly African and black American) has a weak pedigree. The case of India is more interesting, including as it does individual missionaries, philanthropists, and activists like Besant and Cousins (Kapur, 1997).

Irish nationalists had already shown support for the Boers (and thus implicit support for white supremacy), but the difficult trick of squaring armed resistance to the Empire with promises of loyalty to the Empire was accomplishable by reference to inherent rights to liberty, as white colonials fighting to unshackle themselves. Willie Redmond argued in 1913 that Home Rule was a right, a solution to internal strife and a means of harmonising the aspirations of the various components of Empire (Hennessey, 1998:23–4).[23] Indeed, the Home Rulers in 1911–13 had arrived at a point where their eagerness to stake a claim on empire rivalled that of the Unionists, albeit from a different direction. Hennessey (1998:10–11) cites Lord Primate of the Church of Ireland Dr Crozier addressing the 1912 General Synod:

> Wherever the flag of Great Britain and Ireland waves, there Irishmen have won honour and fame for their native land. The mention of India recalls what the Empire owes to Irishmen like Gough [...] Napier [...] Lawrence and Roberts, or to statesmen like Nicolson [...] Montgomery [...] Lord Mayo and Lord Dufferin.[24]

Read this alongside Home Rule MP Sir Thomas Esmonde's contribution to a parliamentary debate in the same week:

> We Irish people have no rooted antipathy to Empire. The Empire is quite as much our Empire as yours. As a matter of history Irish brains [...] valour, and genius have done quite as much to build up this Empire [as] either British genius or [...] intelligence. (ibid.:24)[25]

Nationalism could at this point encompass both a separatist wing that stressed distinct Irish cultural difference as the starting point for independence, and a liberal constitutional one that emphasised a history of shared enterprise in Empire.

## A RACIALISED LEGACY OF EMPIRE?

How can we begin to make sense of 'race', Ireland and Empire in the late nineteenth century and early twentieth century? The experience of Empire and the various forms of cultural and political resistance to it internalised the notion of 'race', so that the assumption of superiority involved in embracing a white identity was combined with a refusal to acknowledge that this assumption existed. A zero-sum argument emerged which stated that because the Irish had been victims of colonial exploitation and racialised in this process, they could not be responsible for perpetrating the same forms of discrimination. As noted in the previous chapter, the ambivalence shown by the Irish toward the British Empire is mirrored by that of Irish Americans in the face of the Spanish–American War in Cuba and the Philippines. The Irish American press expressed the concerns of a community which contained empire builders content to subscribe to the Manifest Destiny project based on European supremacy, as well as critics who viewed the conflict through the lens of the colonising–colonised relationship embodied by the British domination of Ireland.

So whilst framing themselves as victims of colonial exploitation, the Irish also created and sustained social and political distance between themselves and Others. The projects of proto-ethnic cleansing in nineteenth-century urban America (and the Midwest in respect of Native Americans) and that of the quest for political independence share this profoundly ambivalent relationship to others with an oppressed status. The relationship of the Irish to the British was cast in terms of slavery until mass immigration to America enabled contact with a society in which the term 'slavery' linked that status to another racialised population; the independence movement sought to free Ireland from its colonial status yet intentionally avoided situating Ireland in the same position as other colonies. The determining factor in this ambivalence is racism: quite simply, the Irish had to emphasise their whiteness, both as a section of the American working class, and as a nation-in-waiting, by distancing themselves from association with non-white Others. The entire social dynamic of Irish settlement in the New World has been one in which upward mobility involves direct or indirect instrumentalisation of whiteness, both as a means of achieving, and an outcome of, unequal power relations with black and other Third World people.

Cultural and political nationalists then recognised the parameters within which the independence project could be played out at different times, and sometimes based their calls for independence on profoundly reactionary ideas, notably the division of the world hierarchically into 'races'. This alone in no way refutes any nationalist case for a united Ireland, or calls into question the validity of that movement's resistance to colonial domination, but it illustrates to what extent dominant ideas framed the political resistance to this domination, and indicates how embedded they are in the post-1922 identity discourses of the Republic of Ireland and Northern Ireland.[26]

# 6
# Other People's Diasporas: The 'Racialisation' of the Asylum Issue

The popular notion that Ireland's homogeneous population has only started to interact with migrants since the mid 1990s is in contradiction to the element of the nationalist metanarrative in which Ireland absorbs waves of conquerors and fashions a Gaelic culture from them. Moreover, implicit in the various contested ideas about the genesis of the 'Irish race' that I looked at in Chapter 3, the ever-present trope was arrival by sea. Ireland had no land borders before 1921, suggesting on the one hand that it was a sealed insular island to be defended and on the other that its borders were open to the world.[1] The former position appears to have developed in the republican–nationalist domain in relatively recent times, with a symbolic narrative of the pure island defending itself from external moral and political contamination. The second position is inscribed, more or less explicitly, into common-sense Irish history. In the Milesian and Phoenician origin narratives, the migrants are sea-borne, as are the documented invaders – the Danes, the Normans, the English, the Scots and, much earlier, the Gaels themselves. As an information board at Dingle's Oceanworld reads: 'The Irish are of mixed race and origins: all arrived by sea.' Yet even this is not finished business: geographer Estyn Evans' (1992) controversial theory argues that the first Irish people were Upper Paelolithic era Scots who crossed the land bridge existing at that time between Ireland and Scotland.

It is clear that the debates around origins, and about the ways that various invaders have dominated, altered and integrated into the societies which they found on arrival are intensely political. No Irish politician or anti-revisionist writer could publicly state that any positive outcomes had emerged from the long colonial domination of Britain, while the Normans and the Danes are viewed as having made distinctive contributions to Irish culture, which is perceived as indigenously Gaelic. The contours that such debates assume are of importance when attempting to place the history of immigration into Ireland and the state's response into an analytical framework. Simply put, all migrations are viewed either positively or negatively, and contemporary ones are seen as more threatening than others. Leaning on an analysis of the opinion poll and attitudinal surveys conducted in Ireland in the 1972–2001 period (covered in detail in Chapter 2), I will now analyse the key elements of popular reaction to the increases in the numbers of foreign nationals, and expand on the concept of diaspora space developed by Brah (1996), incorporating into it the framing roles of the state, particularly since 1997.

## PRIOR TO THE 1990s: 'THERE'S NO RACISM BECAUSE THERE'S NO BLACK PEOPLE'

This ideological non sequitur[2] on minorities in Northern Ireland is not only historically inaccurate, but occludes forms of racism based on culture rather than colour, and constructs poor planning (in the face of advice to plan ahead) as an understandable failing. This type of reasoning is a convenient get-out clause enabling denial and attributing the failure to deal with the rise in the numbers of migrants from the mid '90s to the surprise of it all happening so fast.

Let's begin with the last part: 'there's no black people'. It is quite clear that in its context, the rise in numbers of migrants and asylum-seekers has been substantial and rapid since the mid 1990s. Yet this is not to say that it was either not predicted or not discussed before then. I noted in Chapter 3 that there had been black people in Ireland as early as the ninth century. This emerges from Irish historical annals relating to Viking trade through Dublin. Prisoners of war were taken from North Africa to Dublin and remained there for some time, and the Irish seafarers also became involved to a certain degree (Sheehan, 1998). The presence of those people and naming of them as different integrates Ireland into the history of international maritime trade, conquest (by proxy), and of Europeans 'othering' those they met. Far from lying pure, unsullied and insular, Ireland then has been part of this process for at least 1,100 years.

Further evidence of black people's presence is provided by Hart (2003) who pieces together a picture of an eighteenth-century Ireland with one of the largest black populations of any European country. Moreover, it appears that Ireland had a relatively hospitable climate in which black people rose to positions of prominence in the arts. In more recent times, students from developing countries, particularly medical students, have been training in Irish hospitals for decades, and a number of such people have married and settled in Ireland to raise families and pursue careers (Valarasan Toomey, 1998). To take two well-known examples, Philip Lynott was a household name in the early 1970s and South African-born politician Moses Bhamjee was a Labour Party deputy in the 1980s. It is ludicrous therefore to contend, even on the most superficial level, that there were no black people in Ireland until the mid 1990s, and such a line of argument points to a willingness to seek face-saving denial strategies.

Another strand of the denial strategy outlined in the above statement is the assumption that racism is only targeted on black people. In the Irish context, this enables an argument to be held that points to the absence of black racialised objects and therefore of racism. Yet even were this absence to be the case, there can be racism without the presence of a racialised minority, 'blackness without blacks' to use Gilman's term (1982) taken up by McMaster (2001) in the context of late-nineteenth-century and pre World War I Europe, and anti-Semitism without Jews (Goldhagen, 1996). McMaster (2001:58–85) contends for example that 'blackness without blacks' was possible during the 1870–1914 period in countries without colonies and for people who had no contact with blacks in their own countries as black people, though rarely represented in elite forms of discourse, featured in popular fiction, education, newspapers, magazines and travelling shows.[3]

In Ireland, however, there has been a process of racialisation whose objects have been the indigenous Catholic population, and at least two others, Jews and Travellers, three nominally 'white' groups whose cultures have been literally 'denigrated' or blackened so that their status lies either between 'black' and 'white', or in both at once.

### Anti-Semitism

Jews arrived in Ireland at the end of the fifteenth century and there was a Jewish mayor of Youghal (Co. Cork) in 1558. In later times, Gerard Goldberg was mayor of Cork in the 1980s. There have been notable Jewish TDs: the Briscoe family, Mervyn Taylor, former Labour minister for equality affairs, and Alan Shatter (Fine Gael), a constitutional expert on family law. The numbers have shrunk from a peak after World War II of only 3,907 (0.13 per cent of the population) recorded in the 1946 census, falling to 1,790 (0.045 per cent) at the 2002 census.

Little examination of anti-Semitism had occurred prior to the 1990s with notable exceptions (Hyman, 1972; Feeley and O'Riordan, 1984), despite high-profile nationalists and a number of small political organisations being involved in the discourse from the 1880s on and off through to the 1950s (Keogh, 1998; Feeley and O'Riordan, 1984).

The Irish state's response to the Holocaust then came under scrutiny, with a 1997 documentary *No More Blooms*[4] focussing on the country's refugee policy in World War II, and Keogh's book. The key Berlin-based Irish diplomat during World War II, Charles Bewley, pursued a *de facto* policy of minimising the number of Jewish refugees allowed into Ireland, basing his argument on their putative cultural inability to assimilate and the threat posed by Jewish values for Catholic Ireland.

The crucial synergy in Irish anti-Semitism appears to derive from the combination of an economic downturn in the last part of the nineteenth century, which placed pressure on shopkeepers and opened a space for itinerant pedlars who introduced hire purchase (Moore, 1981), and the growth of a specific strand in the cultural nationalist discourse. The latter was the result of two sources, the first being Redemptorist priests returning from training in France. These priests attacked international capitalist Jewry and linked this modern discourse with the longer-standing deicide one. Ireland's contribution to the series of pogroms that took place in Europe in the first decade of the twentieth century was triggered by the preachings of Redemptorist Fr. Creagh in Limerick between 1904 and 1906. There the small Jewish population which found itself to be a political football between the Catholic Church (organising a boycott of Jewish-owned businesses) and the local Protestants who conspicuously ignored the boycott, thus bringing tension to a head.

The second source is Arthur Griffith's *United Irishman*, as well as the Jesuit journal *Lyceum* (particularly articles by Fr. Thomas Finlay) and the work of D.P. Moran in the *Leader*. While far from reaching the same pitch and intensity (Moran's being the most vehement) as the anti-Semitism of the Redemptionist priests, *United Irishman* was generated in a project to highlight the distinctiveness of Irish nationalism, and the distinguishing features of Irishness. In these texts, Jews are perceived as cosmopolitan, rootless, disloyal and dishonourable in business, qualities that place them outside the boundaries of anti-capitalist Catholic-Gaelic culture profoundly rooted within its location.

Mc Gréil's findings (1996) from surveys done in 1974 and 1988, demonstrate a significant level of anti-Semitism. Jews appear in 32nd place (out of 59) in the social distance scale he produces (from a number of interviews well in excess of the nationally-agreed minimum sample), behind foreign national groups and other religions. Interestingly he finds that anti-Semitism is at its highest in the Connacht-Ulster region, where the number of Jews is statistically insignificant. There appears therefore to be 'anti-Semitism' without Jews, just as there is 'blackness without blacks'. The areas in which this hostility is expressed are those around deicide, business methods and values. The church's teachings must explain the continued resilience of the deicide theme: Lentin (2002a:156) recounts how she was asked by an RTE co-worker in 1970 why her people crucified 'her Lord'. Indeed, the difficulty of making the two terms Irish–Jew stick together and drawing parallels with other forms of racism is the subject of an embryonic discourse powered by Lentin (2002a) and Goldstone (2002) to which I shall return in Chapter 9.

## Anti-Traveller racism

In the attitudinal survey work done between 1972 and 2001 Travellers are found to be the subject of particularly hostile attitudes when compared with other Irish racialised or ethnic minorities. Despite the presence of refugees and black people in growing numbers, antipathy towards whom is identified in the Eurobarometer 1997 and 2000, and the 2000 *Star* poll, Travellers are identified as the most socially distant ethnic group in Mc Gréil's work (1996), coming 52nd out of 59 groups, and constitute those whose presence is found to be 'most disturbing' in the surveys named above. They record the highest frequency of physical and verbal attacks among the minorities in the (2001b) Amnesty International survey, and experience discrimination principally in the areas of accommodation, leisure, health services and education. Mortality levels are well in excess of those of the settled population and life expectancy far lower (Barry et al., 1989; CSO, 1998). Successive attempts to reassess the nature of the problem and propose action (Commission on Itinerancy, 1963; Travelling People Review Body, 1983; Task Force on the Travelling Community, 1995) have still not brought about either the infrastructure required to provide adequate living conditions or the cultural change required for Travellers to be viewed as equal members of the nation. The Department of Justice's Monitoring Committee on the 1995 Task Force's recommendations even acknowledged in its report (Dept. of Justice, 2000: 13) that the numbers of families on the roadside had increased rather than diminished since the 1995 report, and that one in four Travellers still had no access to toilet facilities or running water.

Mac Laughlin (1995) maintains that anti-nomadism assumed new dimensions in the conservative and aggressive forms of blood and soil nationalism of the nation-building nineteenth century, when attachment to land in the form of individual (not communal) property relations was posited as the keystone of modernity. Ní Shuínéar (1994) notes that the appearance of the 'Irish Traveller' as a distinct grouping in academic circles occurred in the 1890s, although references to Irish tinkers are traceable to the thirteenth century. Moreover, as I noted in Chapter 3, the discourse equating nomadism with barbarity has existed since Giraldus Cambrensis' *History and Topography of Ireland* (1189). It was modified over the following centuries and intensified from the 1570s onwards.

The Irish state's response to the Travellers has wavered between assimilation (the elimination of cultural differences through housing policy), expulsion (the elimination of bodies from territory)[5] and lastly, a recognition of cultural difference. Fanning (2002:112–51) explores the institutionalisation of anti-Traveller racism through the workings of Clare County Council 1963–99. He argues that Councillors prevaricated around the statutory obligation to provide accommodation for Travellers, and finally did so only in relation to a space that Travellers did not want to stay in (close to a cemetery). They used putative distinctions between 'local' and 'outsider' to argue about eligibility for housing, which ran parallel with a *de facto* policy of offering council housing to Travellers only rarely. They helped create a climate of antipathy to Travellers by giving popular leadership to residents' fears of Traveller settlement in their areas; they criticised third sector initiatives aimed at helping Travellers; and they contributed to the focussing of attention on Travellers themselves (and their behavioural norms) rather than on the Council's failure to initiate policy. This despite senior local authority officials' warnings that they risked being overridden by central government in the case of non-compliance with directives. The occasional suggestion that Travellers should not be dealt with by the same criteria as others indicates to what degree they could be successfully excluded. Indeed, popular discourse on Travellers is still saturated with assumptions that they are inherently hooligans, thieves, and out to cheat others,[6] and therefore any claim that they have been discriminated against draws responses that they are actually being given special treatment (Collins, 2002) and/or are engaging in a massive shakedown inspired by equality legislation. The Equality Authority's 2002 Annual Report (Equality Authority, 2003) shows that Travellers are making the largest number of claims. Yet this is interpreted as evidence of bad faith in some powerful quarters. The Vintners' Association has been lobbying the government since 2002 about what its leadership describes as a 'scam' in which Travellers reportedly target pubs and hotels asking for money to stop them filing claims for discrimination under the Equal Status Act.

While since the mid '90s, the official language used has assumed the more moderate and equality-based model (couching references in terms of 'ethnic' difference; using a capital 'T' for Travellers; including a question on 'membership of the Traveller community' in the 2002 census), the policy to support this linguistic gear-shift has remained wedded to a simplistic framework of criminalisation. A failure to translate established and agreed housing, health or education targets into reality is combined with legislation that simultaneously recognises Travellers' citizens' rights to non-discrimination (Equal Employment Act 1998; Equal Status Act 2000) and criminalises and delegitimises their culture (1998 Accommodation Act, Section 32; Amendment to the Criminal Justice Act 2002, making trespass a criminal offence). One of the principal functions of racism, the ordering and government of movement into and within physical and imaginary spaces, is thus starkly apparent. Spaces central to the maintenance of Traveller culture have been made 'unenterable', as a *quid pro quo* for the provision of some accommodation sites. Moreover, the unacceptable behaviour of small groups of Travellers is used as a justification for legislation impinging on the rights of those unrelated to these incidents, and Travellers are treated collectively as potential vandals *per se*.

The ideological bases of twentieth- and twenty-first-century government policy on Travellers are thus consistent with both sixteenth-century thinking on nomadism and the cultural element of discrimination in the eighteenth-century Enlightenment project. Quinn (1966) stresses that analogies between the Irish and Native Americans in Elizabethan times (from the 1580s especially) demonstrated their ideological proximity in the minds of members of the dominant groups in English society. Native Americans and Australian aboriginals were not the only people then to suffer from the fallout of this nation-building process (ironically at the hands of European soldiers and settlers numbering many displaced Irish). In Europe, Travellers, Gypsies, Roma and Sinti have also suffered progressive exclusion from the land and the cultures of the countries they have crossed.

The treatment of Travellers, Native Americans and Australians derives from the common assumption that the irrational, nomadic, non-landowning, non-capitalist organisation of collective life is backward and inferior to rational, modern capitalist society, that the individual members of the groups share a pathology of degeneracy. This assumpton is used as a justification for controlling and decimating these groups through state intervention, whether passive or active (Ní Shuínéar, 2002, 1994). Moreover, as Fanning (2002) points out, there is a link between the state's responses to Travellers, Jews and asylum-seekers in that a mono-cultural set of assumptions given expression by the authoritarian and conservative set of values inherent in the dominant form of Irish nationalism in the Republic has consistently framed these groups as 'different', where this difference is understood as threatening. The aim of policy has therefore been to control movement, exclude and eliminate the Other from national space as they have been excluded from the imagined space of the nation.

## NATIONALISM'S RACIALISING CONTRIBUTION, c.1870–1922

Given that the period c.1870–1922 covered the emergence of Sinn Fein, the Irish Republican Brotherhood, the Land League, the Irish Nationalist Party, the rise and fall of Parnell, the Gaelic League, the Gaelic Revival, Home Rule, the Easter Rising, the Civil War, Partition and the foundation of the Free State, it would be foolish to argue that any monolithic ideology was at play during this time. Yet the period is vital because it is the formative one for the post-1922 state, in which the Catholic-Gaelic and rural norms of Irishness, together with the metanarrative of a nation with a mission, being divided then reunited were placed at the forefront of the independence struggle.

In the previous chapter, Home Rule was identified as a dominant strand of nationalist thought that was seeking to utilise 'race' strategically. Here, I shall examine the way Irish identity was politically racialised in the half century between 1870 and 1922, contributing to the formation of a reactionary state ideology from 1922 onwards. This process involved drawing a line around Irishness, marking out its boundaries, and contrasting its content favourably with that of other identities.

This took place in a context of a racialisation by Protestant institutions – the British State, the Church of England, Protestant Associations (see Chapter 4) – and against an institutional backdrop in which 'race' had become the key organising concept of international politics. It can in no way be viewed as one-way traffic, as if the Irish nationalists were inventing themselves and their constituency in a vacuum.

Self-definition thus came as a response to ascribed difference, but also served political ends, in the form of a hegemonic discourse of ideal-type Irishness that lay at the root of the Free State. Goldring, for example, concludes from the civil service requirements proposed by Sinn Féin in 1917[7] – command of Irish, knowledge of Irish literature and history – that the 'sole function of this elementary culture was ideological: it was the mark of patriotism and of loyalty to the new state' (1993:51). In other words, the functional skills requirements for civil service work were deprioritised in favour of academic nationalist knowledge, and the higher the position within the civil service, the more perfect the language skills and knowledge of culture and so on were required to be.

The Irish had been Catholic politically since the late eighteenth century. Tone's reference to the 'Irish people, properly so called' which follows his more famous anti-sectarian mission statement[8] indicates that even the United Irishmen realised that they were attempting to square some kind of circle in yoking the Catholic masses to the Dissenters' cart. Their failure, together with that of Emmet, in 1803, sounded the death knell of a particular secular revolutionary political project in which religious affiliation was downplayed. According to Whelan, Catholic nationalists after Emmet exploited sectarian tensions

> at the cost of superseding the Enlightenment United Irish project with a Catholic version which stressed confessional allegiance as the prime ingredient in national identity. The United Irishmen's sense of the imperative of a cosmopolitan future was now confronted by a project stressing the primacy and potency of a particularist past, which valorised history, the regional and the customary, at the expense of the new, the cosmopolitan, the universal. (1996:152–3)

Indeed, while the Young Ireland movement had attempted to wrest the leadership from O'Connell on the grounds of methods, the secondary question was the racialised conundrum expressed by Protestant nationalist Thomas Davis. Davis sought to achieve the impossible, basing his pleas for combination 'regardless of blood'[9] on the idea that there was no racial purity after centuries of inter-mingling. Boyce (1991:58) summarises the problem facing him:

> Davis wished to apply racial concepts to Anglo-Irish relations but not to relationships within Ireland itself; he wanted to erect linguistic and cultural barriers between Ireland and England, and at the same time use those weapons to break down barriers between the descendants of Englishmen and Irishmen now dwelling in Ireland. What was an obstacle on one context must become an open door in another.

The contradictions of this position were the outcome of historical change and material conditions. As Whelan has argued, it was not a historical inevitability that nationalism should assume such an intimate and exclusive relationship with Catholicism, even as late as the turn of the nineteenth century. The strain of nationalism that favoured inclusiveness toward Protestants came under attack from Moran's Irish Ireland perspective at the turn of the twentieth century, in which it was viewed as indicative of nationalists who were happy to ape their British overlords rather than concentrate on forging something distinctively Irish, and grounded in language and values (O'Callaghan, 1993). Moran's argument that Catholics were the true Irish, culminating in 'If a non-Catholic nationalist Irishman does not wish to live in a Catholic atmosphere let him turn Orangeman',[10] was thus merely one of a set of confident assertions of identity aimed at staking out territory within the broad nationalist terrain of early twentieth-century Ireland. In any case, being open to Protestant contributions in the independence movement (*de facto*, since many of the leading lights in the Gaelic Revival were Protestant scholars) did not mean that this openness was extended to other minorities. Griffith's is the epitome of this non-sectarian yet anti-Semitic and white supremacist nationalism.

'Race' is about essence and nature, resistant to and predatory on the social; the potency of the claims that transcend the social cannot be diluted by arguments derived from the social world. In the world of 'race' and of nations founded on racialised populations that was the doxa of late-nineteenth-century imperialism, the social was an arena in which nature's inequalities found expression. The relationship was always causal and unproblematic. The Irish 'racial' nationalists were of their time: in the last quarter of the nineteenth century and the first decade of the twentieth, the language of national liberation was racial-nationalist. Entitlement to a homeland required the construction of a tradition of homogeneous cultural continuity. Yet Irish activists entered the discourse from a position of relative disempowerment, seeking to instate the Irish or Celtic 'race' at a level at least the equal of Anglo-Saxons. And the project involved compliance with the rules. The Irish saw themselves as unambiguously 'white' in an imperial context in which that meant special bargaining power. In terms of autonomy within empire, as was the case in urban America and the Midwest, this meant creating and sustaining distance from other 'races'. Remember that as late as 1913 Griffith wrote: 'The right of the Irish to political independence never was, is not, and never can be dependent upon the admission of equal right in all other peoples' (Mitchel 1982 [1913]:371).[11] In the same preface he defends Mitchel's pro-slavery line, and states that no Irishman should have to hold 'a negro as his peer'. Yet we should bear in mind that refracting the racialised Irish identity relative to that of the African through intertwined notions of slavery and colour was not brand new to political thought. A century before, O'Connell had referred to British Whigs' ambivalence over Catholic rights in the following terms: 'I did imagine we [Irish Catholics] had ceased to be whitewashed negroes, and had thrown off, for them, all traces of the colour of servitude.'[12]

John Mitchel, maverick though he was, had understood the founding principle of nineteenth-century American democracy, that collective identities were based on a clear binary of civilisation at whose apex was the unhyphenated 'white' man. His contrasting of the natural tendencies of, and due political rights accruing to, the white and the black in his *Southern Citizen*, was combined with serialised polemical pieces such as *The Last Conquest of Ireland (Perhaps)* (1858),[13] in which he asks his American reader: 'Can you picture in your mind a race of white men reduced to this condition? White men! Yes of the highest and purest blood and breed of men.'

Mitchel thus deployed the assumptions of his audience: white men were made to govern; black men to toil; and women were absent from the representation, to bolster his case for an Ireland free of British rule. By contrast, the whiteness of the Irish is rarely stressed in European contexts unless in relation to something that disturbs the narrative of European nationhood. MacDermott's description of nationalist writer Thomas D'Arcy M'Gee (1896) is such an example:

M'Gee's countenance was not pleasing, from its decided African caste and woolly hair [...] This Negro race mark, in Irishmen, I have noticed in two or three other instances; and I can only attribute it to a probable descent from one of those faithful countrymen of ours whom Cromwell and his son Henry sent as slaves to the West Indies, and who may be presumed to have married there ladies of African stock.

Here the racial question mark is erased ambiguously by reference to the narrative of oppression. The 'not pleasing' result is seen as a form of branding in the bloodline.

Anti-Semitism is a strand of nationalist thought that has endured into the contemporary period, as borne out by the findings of Mc Gréil (1996) and the Citizen Traveller (2000) polls. Feeley and O'Riordan (1984) provide documents relating to the 1904–06 attacks on Jews in Limerick that show debates from the 1980s on the meaning of the incidents, and a line of defence that asserts that the actions were not anti-Semitic but aimed by their architects at ending the exploitation of Irish workers and consumers. Feeley and O'Riordan suggest a line of continuity linking the Limerick Redemptorist Order to Griffith and Moran, Davitt's writings on what he termed 'economic anti-Semitism' in Eastern Europe[14] and running through St John Gogarty, Duffy and the Blueshirts and beyond, ending with Sean South in the 1950s. Keogh (1998) adds the Jesuit reformer Thomas Finlay to this pedigree. This judgement is concurred with by O'Drisceoil (1997), expanded by Lentin (1997) in his documentary on refugee policy and the Holocaust, summarised by Fanning (2002) and further analysed by Lentin (2002a). The persistence of notions of deicide identified in Mc Gréil (1996) can partly be attributed to the Catholic Church's teachings, but the strand that combines with these, and posits the Jew as an inassimilable and exploitative fifth columnist, has a European genealogy going back at least to the Middle Ages. It would not be accurate to state that Irish nationalism is *a priori* anti-Semitic. Rather leading nationalists have been anti-Semites, and the racial exclusiveness of the hegemonic version of nationalism has subsumed anti-Semitism and utilised it in particular historical conjunctures.

As noted in the previous chapter, the Home Rule period (c.1885–1914) ushered in a form of mobilisation based on Celtic/Catholic/Gaelic racial identification against a Saxon/Protestant/English oppressor. This discourse was also indulged in by British and Irish Unionists (MacRaild,

1996; Hennessey, 1998) to cast aspersions on the appropriateness of Celts to run their own affairs.

The 'race' card for Irish nationalists was thus a double-edged sword in more than one way. The ideological labour embarked upon by Irish and American-based activists (Jacobson, 1995) bore fruit in the success of the project: the existence of an Irish 'race' is still a core belief in contemporary Ireland. Yet, the politicians seeking to establish Irish equality with other white nations in the imperial family were ultimately hamstrung by the historical weight that racist ideas and practices focussed on the Irish had accumulated. The only way to prove that Celts were fit for self-government was to have self-government, yet in order to do so they had to undo centuries of glacial ideological movement whose racialised sediment lay beneath Victorian culture. The only exit was via ideological aporia: Home Rule political leaders ended up praising the Irish contribution to Empire as a way to endorse their place in the imperial sun yet the cultural nationalist case was based on the non-material, communitarian and rural essence of the Irish 'race' that set them apart from their acquisitive, material, urban-powered colonial masters (Maume, 1999:53). Connolly (1910:5–6) argued that indeed Gaelic culture was ideally suited to socialism because of its 'distinct anti-capitalist culture' and this pedigree was confirmed by the remark that 'the Gael reached the highest point of civilisation and culture in Europe'.

Additionally, 'Celticism', a literary response to 'Anglo-Saxonism' propounded by cultural nationalists such as Hyde, is equally problematic. Conjuring the nation-in-waiting through a positing of its cultural continuity was a project endorsed by nationalists in terms of literary achievements and sport (see below), yet, as Morash (1998) points out, 'race' theory as a basis of putative continuity was actually the site of great instability, particularly when used to examine the divisions within the 'white race', which is what Celticism was engaged in. Moreover, as an emancipatory instrument, Celticism defeated its own object; making a case for Irish specificity. The leading nineteenth-century European philologists and anthropologists saw the Celtic contribution to European civilisation as a source of mystery and genius for their own particular local branches of the race in Switzerland, France and Germany (ibid:211–12).[15]

Matthew Arnold's attempt to incorporate the Celtic into the Anglo-Saxon in British culture should thus be interpreted in this context. Hyde's claims then, for a Celtic civilisation coeval with Christianity, which had dominated most of Europe, when filtered through the prism of nineteenth-century 'race' theory, emerged as part of an Aryan heritage, whose ownership had been ideologically prised away from the Irish. Morash's summary is that: 'The spatial and temporal sweep of the Celtic race, properly understood, makes the business of real politics in Ireland mundane, parochial and diminished' (1998:212). Thus paradoxically again, focus on 'race' leads away from the distinctiveness of Ireland and its people's demands for independence within the family of racialised white European nations, and into a situation where the Irish have more to link them with the British than to separate them. In terms of empire, the Irish input into the business of coercion and administration (implicitly shared values of loyalty, industriousness and vicarious racial superiority) had to be highlighted in the Home Rule debate. In cultural nationalism, the narrow racialised path to the Celtic particular ended up diverted to the thoroughfare of the Aryan universal.

Noting that sport has been largely neglected in critical assessments of Irish nationalism such as that of Brown (1985), which claims to be a 'cultural and social history', Cronin (1999) contends that Gaelic games and the Gaelic Athletics Association (GAA) constitute major sites of nationalist ideology, a significant segment of which relates to the theme of racialisation. In parallel with the cultural nationalists' project of positing continuity of cultural (that is, national) cohesion in the literary and linguistic domains, a similar role was assigned to sport. Running from the foundation of the GAA in 1884 through to the present day, a body of writing has sought to make Gaelic games a privileged depository of racialised Irishness, of the values that comprise that which makes the Irish distinct from the English. Linking Gaelic games to medieval ball games in an unbroken genealogy, as nationalist writers have done, Cronin maintains, was an ideological project, and one that ignored the paradox that the GAA's business principles, that is, the codification of rules and regulations under a governing body, were actually an embodiment of (Anglo-Saxon) late Victorian culture (ibid.:75). He quotes a number of writers, both contemporary and post-independence who raise the 'race' question.

GAA founder-member Maurice Davin's letter from October 1884 calls Gaelic games 'the characteristic sports and pastimes of the Gaelic race' (ibid.:103), while Cronin questions whether the ball games referred to differed from those played all over Europe since medieval times. *United Ireland* stated firmly in an editorial from the same month that:

The strength and energy of a race are largely dependent on national pastimes for the development of a spirit of courage and endurance. A warlike race is ever fond of games requiring skill, strength and staying power. The best games of such a race are never free from danger.[16]

Cronin claims that these are fundamentally British public school values adapted for a different audience's consumption (ibid:109).[17] The 'martial spirit of the race' (Mehigan, 1946:112) is a recurrent theme, not just in writing on Gaelic games but in nationalist construction of Irish attributes (as noted in Chapter 4). The 'fightin' Irish' strand of national identity still resurfaces in the most mundane of scenarios. American golfer Jerry Kelly, lying second to Tiger Woods in the 2002 American Express World Championship in Ireland, told his interviewer: 'I'm from a Kelly clan in Cork, and my mother's side is McCann, so I'm 100% Irish [...] There's no bad blood in me.' The journalist ran with the ball: 'and he intends to use those battling qualities heading onto the biggest weekend of his career'.[18] No such qualities had been mentioned, but the unsullied bloodline generates the common-sense inferral of 'fighting Irish' characteristics.

Yet it was not merely the worship of muscular Christianity and manliness, the rejection of urbanisation and a celebration of the purity of rural life (with the organisation of clubs by parish like the Catholic Church) that emerged as the ideological justifications of the GAA. The link between Church, parish, GAA and identity is referred to as an important late-nineteenth-century construction by Gillespie and Moran (1987) in their work on local history in Mayo. More importantly, the retention of racial purity emerged as one of these justifications. Devlin (1934:76) concludes that 'the grip of the native ash fortifies [the players] against national submission and racial perversion', while McLua (1967) argues that GAA Rule 21 (banning members of the security forces from playing Gaelic games) was central to the very existence of the GAA as it 'constantly reinforced the purity not only of the actual games, but also of the Irish race' (Cronin, 1999:98).

The construction of the GAA, as analysed by Cronin, developed the idea that Gaelic games were 'racially' specific, and that national purity was embodied in their playing. The sports, particularly hurling, remained untainted by the English presence,[19] and expressed core Irish values. The sport's organisation also articulated a vision of the nation as a family, a set of parishes united in commitment to, and appreciation of, an overarching 'imaginative possession'.

All this emphasis on the external frontier of Irishness should not, however, obscure equally important internal exclusions. The intention of the argument is in no way to suggest that class and gender were of minor significance in the founding definitions of Irishness at the base of the Irish Republic, merely to claim that racialisation is a key and hitherto almost invisible element of the process of nation-building.[20] It is also important to acknowledge Lloyd's point in *Nationalisms Against the State* (1999) that the trajectories of various liberation movements (women, labour, etc.) did not necessarily coincide with the nationalist one, although some of the personnel of revolutionary nationalism, socialism and feminism may have overlapped. My point is that, by the 1990s, racialised Others in Southern Irish society, like Travellers, Jews and occasionally Protestants, had already experienced exclusion, if not just from particular parts of the nation's territory, then from the imaginative space of Irishness, or – like the working class and women of all classes – had had particular restrictions placed on their participation.

## THE 'COLOUR LINE' IN CONTEMPORARY IRELAND

The racialisation of the Irish resident population along colour lines long predated the mid 1990s (Nic Suibhne, 1998; Paulin, 2000; Mullin, 2001; Murphy, 2001; Lentin and McVeigh, 2002; McCarthy, 2001) and has intensified in a period of growing net prosperity that distinguishes its context from earlier ones.[21]

One outcome of the racialisation of Ireland has been to underscore the line in the imaginary between national and non-national based on somatic difference. While anti-Semitism, anti-Traveller racism and hostility toward minorities in general in the Republic have far longer histories (McLoughlin, 1994:85–6; Brown, 1985; Fanning, 2002), the new forms of discrimination have amalgamated black nationals, migrants, asylum-seekers, refugees, students and tourists (Boucher, 1998). In January 2002, a Chinese student learning English was killed in a racist attack.

Indeed, the process in which the national becomes suspected of 'non-nationality' has shifted dimension. This has occurred against a backdrop of the state's response to its fears of illegal immigration, which determined its border-policing stance from spring 1997 (Cullen, 1997b; Tynan, 1997). The practice of immigration officials and police at points of entry involved selecting non-white passengers (and staff) for questioning (Cusack, 1997; *Irish Times*, 1998a). Small-scale research reports (Pilgrim House Foundation, 1998, 1999; African Refugee Network, 1999) had also identified blacks (with Roma and Travellers) as the groups most likely to experience verbal and physical abuse.

By summer 2000, Amnesty International was using a radio advert for its anti-racism campaign in which a black Irishman complains of a significant negative change in attitude towards him over recent years. Moreover, in that organisation's study of the experiences of minorities (Amnesty International, 2001b) the minority group expressing the highest rate of discrimination suffered was 'Black Irish' (88.6 per cent). Recent erroneous arrests of asylum-seekers in Dublin under the 1935 Aliens Act for failure to provide proof of identity to Gardai, combine with passengers' reports of black people being taken off the Belfast–Dublin train and obliged to show ID, while their foreign white counterparts were left alone. Hysterical responses to non-whites include the temporary jailing of some Pakistani businessmen in 2000 (*Irish Times*, 2000b) and of a British-based Nigerian woman making an enquiry in a social welfare office in Cork in January 2003.[22] These practices indicate that the 1997–98 policy of victimising 'non-white' individuals has been continued into the twenty-first century in an unchanged form.[23]

Although equality legislation has been enacted to deal with discrimination on a number of grounds, including 'race' in 1998 and 2000,[24] a landmark prosecution passed almost unnoticed before this had come into force. In October 1998, a Dublin pub was refused its licence after a case taken against it by a black Dubliner who claimed she had been refused service when the pub had changed hands earlier that year. This was the first prosecution of a defendant accused of discrimination on the basis of colour to take place in the state. The telling element of the story is the woman's comment that despite experiencing racism all her life, 'things had got much worse since asylum-seekers started arriving in larger numbers over the past few years' (*Irish Independent*, 1998; Cullen, 1998).

Indeed, in a small-scale 1998 survey (Pilgrim House Foundation, 1998) 70 per cent of those polled stated that they had formed opinions about asylum-seekers 'based on what they saw', implying that without speaking to a member of that group (only 2 per cent said that they had spoken to an asylum-seeker) they had categorised individuals as 'asylum-seekers'. Those individuals might have belonged to any one of a number of categories, including that of Irish nationals. The act of equating colour with legal status is a primary indication of racist attitudes, and it is clear that the process of assimilating all non-white people in Ireland to the status of asylum-seeker, with all the negative connotations and symbolic powers the term has accrued, was already well advanced by summer 1998. In view of this, outbursts by public officials in more recent times are signs of continuity and the point of contact between underlying racist thinking and official discourse rather than isolated blips.[25] Cork North Central TD Noel O'Flynn claimed that Cork's Northside was home to many 'illegal immigrants' in January 2002, a supposition questioning the legal legitimacy of the presence of black people *per se*. How could their illegal status be determined on sight, if the implicit point were not the blanket supposition that all asylum-seekers are bogus and therefore illegal? Local media[26] was supportive of O'Flynn's supposedly courageous stance, which went unsanctioned by his party leader, the Taoiseach. Compare this at least to the Labour Party's expulsion of Cllr Joe O'Callaghan, a former lord mayor who had spoken in similar terms the previous year, and ran as an unsuccessful independent candidate at the May 2002 general election, in which O'Flynn topped the poll.

On 20 February 2003, two District Court judges made official apologies to women they had recently sentenced. Judge Harvey Kenny's remarks in Castlebar on 14 January 2003 centred on his opinion that Ms Bukky Abejano, found guilty of driving without insurance, should be imprisoned to send out a message to all Nigerians that they need insurance to drive. Judge John Neilan had told two women who had shoplifted that shopping centres in Longford would soon be banning 'coloured people' if this behaviour didn't stop (Haughey, 2003a). It is hard to imagine the judges telling a defendant that local shopping centres would introduce a policy of banning people on low incomes, or suggesting that an Irish national driving without insurance should be imprisoned to send the message out 'to that community' that insurance was necessary. Aside from the inappropriateness of the remarks, and the probability that they found favour with a proportion of locals, the important element of these stories is that they are based on the most basic racist connection between appearance (natural) and behaviour (social–cultural), tarring (or whitewashing, let's be inventive with our language) every 'coloured' person with the same brush, and even suggesting sanctions from civil parties. This reasoning is also at the root of the stop-and-interrogate policies described above, and results in a reduction of all non-whites in Ireland to the catch-all 'asylum-seeker' category, fundamental to which is the strong suspicion of illegality.

The reassessment of Irishness I am interested in examining thus revolves around, but is not exclusively based on, its intrinsic whiteness; a specific version of whiteness: sedentariness, Catholicism and Gaelic culture. Hart (2003) shows that there were relatively large numbers of black people in Ireland in the eighteenth century, and that they were treated in a less hostile fashion than their contemporary counterparts, an impression endorsed by the positive experiences of illustrious visitors such as Equiano in the 1790s, and Lenox Remond and Douglass in the 1840s.[27] Moreover, as referred to in Chapter 3, the fundamental somatic traits of Irishness are being questioned in contexts as banal as the search of labour abroad and traditional beauty pageants.

## IRELAND AS 'DIASPORA SPACE'

The previous sections have sketched some of the parameters of the ideological space of racism in contemporary Ireland with reference to its historical development. While Ireland also 'happens elsewhere' (O'Toole, 1994:13), and the Irish diaspora is a theme of growing academic and political interest, recent demographic shifts mean that other people's diasporas have now extended to encompass Ireland as part of the prosperous West.[28]

Yet what happens when *other people's diasporas* converge on the homeland of a diasporic people? Brah (1996) coins the term 'diaspora space' to alter the focus and the questions asked. She argues that viewing diaspora as one-dimensional (that is, from the perspective of a homeland and representatives of that homeland relocated) neglects to problematise the involvement of the inhabitants of the countries in which the diasporic nationals live. The area of inquiry is thus extended by 'diaspora space' to embrace the relationship between the host nationals and the migrants within a polity dominated by the former. This is a brave attempt to reconceptualise the rather over-theorised but under-researched and unsociological concept that 'diaspora' has become, yet it remains a little vague. What it gains is dynamism and implicit interrogation of the notion that host cultures play no part in diaspora formation. It is also embedded in Brah's four-part dissection of the concept of 'difference' (1996:95–127). Yet, as Anthias (2002) remarks in a concise and perceptive summary, the resurgent work on diasporas has involved rich theorising based on little empirical research and few substantive elements. Moreover, diaspora is constructed as overwhelmingly positive in outcomes, encouraging mixture, hybridity and openness, while the overall understanding is of a concentration on origins rather than on the 'in-place' relations. The call for more localised studies is timely. Where these have been undertaken, what emerges is far greater ambivalence about the value of the ethnic culture of 'homeland' and its desirability in the specific arenas in which migrants live out their diaspora existence. Gray's study of Irish women's experiences in the UK (2000) shows estrangement from values seen partially as restrictive and disempowering, while Corcoran's (2002) survey of Irish workers in the USA points to differential attachment to, and necessary investment in, 'Irishness'. The line of reasoning that posits a direct line into and out of the diasporic community binding it to the homeland seems likely to snap under the pressures of what Brah refers to as 'multi-locationality' (1996:194). In other words, the relationships of migrants to their home culture and to that of their new home are likely to be fraught with tensions about degrees of belonging, and thus unstable and constantly recreating themselves in particular contexts around specific combinations of identities. Moreover, in the process of attaching meaning to 'race', citizenship, and so forth, a key actor is the state, which is in fact absent from Brah's 'diaspora space' discussion. Additionally, the media is another vital institution playing a complex role, generating representations that fuel racism and reflect and inflect debates.

The primary line of anti-racist argument to have developed in Ireland, which draws a parallel between Irish and other people's diasporas, unites secular and non-secular lobbies. The humanist version sees asylum-seekers for example as the economically and politically-persecuted Irish of other times. This is what we might term the 'historical duty' argument. It runs as follows: Irish people have been (and still are) immigrants elsewhere. Therefore today they should empathise, and treat others in that position with respect and welcome. This liberal postulate is expressed across the NGOs, political opposition parties, trade unions, interested church bodies and more radical anti-racist organisations. A succinct example of this is from a speech by Labour Deputy Liz McManus in a 1998 parliamentary debate:

For this global celebration of Irishness [St Patrick's Day], this focus of investment, this tourism opportunity, we have to thank the generations of Irish asylum-seekers who were driven out to seek refuge among strangers. They were often poor, hungry, sick and homeless people. Sometimes they died in flight, sometimes they were political outcasts and convicted criminals. They were the kind of undesirables that the Ireland of IDA promotions likes to disavow. I refuse to accept that our past has no bearing on this debate. *Our history requires us to be generous and just.* (My emphasis)[29]

Thus, in this logic, a moral obligation is derived from a national collective experience. The obligation has ramifications that lie within the political, economic and social spheres, but are not touched on. Its pertinence lies in the equation of experiences of location and identity. Irish emigration stretched the notion of Ireland to include parts of the diaspora, and tacitly recognises other people's diasporas as legitimate spaces to be incorporated within that system.

Similar, but deriving its potency from scripture and moral imperatives incumbent on Christians, is the argument put forward by religious groups both lay (Pilgrim House Foundation, 1998) and clerical (ICJP, 1997). This appeal underlines Christians' duty to extend solidarity to strangers. Moreover, there is a particular element of this argument that binds the universal message to the particular Irish 'space' of migrant experience.[30] The Irish Commission for Justice and Peace's (ICJP) call for solidarity refers to God's instructions to Moses in the Old Testament: 'If a stranger lives with you in your own land, do not molest him. You must count him as one of your own countrymen and love him as yourself – for you were once strangers yourselves in Egypt' (Leviticus 19:33–4). The Israelites had experienced slavery and forced migration to Egypt, and this enjoinment had particular resonance for them. The parallels with the Irish experience are clear. The view of Irish anti-racism envisaged here then is one in which a historical debt is being called in.

However, an alternative discourse stresses the profane over the sacred. The idea that migrants are consuming taxpayers' money is articulated in relation to diasporas in Ireland, and in terms of a finite pot (that might be better spent on more deserving cases). A letter from an American-based emigrant, published in the *Irish Times* in 1998, encapsulates an opposing discourse that posits the exceptional nature of the Irish experience as an antidote to the liberal excess of the 'historical duty' argument:

we come prepared to work hard and make a go of it. We would not be allowed to claim unemployment benefits or otherwise scrounge off the state [...] taxes in Ireland are appallingly high – they will remain so if we keep subsidising the economically challenged from abroad [...] I suggest that many of the recent influx of foreigners have come to Ireland, not for the love of the country either, but because the word is out that we are suckers for a sob story.[31]

This argument of Irish exceptionality then takes broadly the following form. When the Irish went to find work abroad it was different. They had no option but to work hard and didn't get social security. Today's immigrants are spongers. Here, economics takes precedence over the moralistic reading of immigrant experience. Moreover, an implicit distinction is made between the qualities of those seeking work in America and the qualities of their counterparts in Ireland. The former, industrious Irish emigrants, made a positive contribution to the economy of the host country, while the foreigners in Ireland subtract from it and absorb without contributing. This strand of anti-immigrant response relies on an anachronistic argument, since there was no social security in nineteenth-century America or Britain comparable to that existing today, nor were there international treaties on refugees. Moreover, it demonstrates a misunderstanding of legal realities that helps explain a certain degree of the resentment of asylum-seekers widely held in Ireland. The main point is that before July 1999, no asylum-seeker was allowed to work for payment in Ireland. In the legislation passed in that month it became legal for those who had entered the state up to the date of the law's enactment, and who were awaiting the outcome of their application for refugee status, to work once they had obtained a work permit. So, at the time of the letter quoted above, an asylum-seeker would not legally have been able to work even if (s)he were willing to.

Upon these two baseline contentions, a moral duty versus an economic imperative, are constructed all the other related arguments in the discourse on immigration into Ireland. Although the historical duty argument is stridently moral, it has no economic dimension, whereas the anti-immigrant economic one also has a moral grounding: the hardworking are defensible, whilst the inactive are repugnant. This distinction between 'deserving' and 'undeserving' poor has a long lineage, traced back in Ireland to the Middle Ages (O Ciosáin, 1998). In the poll carried out by the lay Catholic organisation Pilgrim House in July 1998, 81 per cent of those polled stated that they felt that asylum-seekers should be allowed to work while they awaited their decision (Pilgrim House Foundation, 1998). By the time of an

*Irish Times*/MRBI poll 18 months later (*Irish Times*/MRBI, 2000a), the result was almost identical (77 per cent). What strikes about the latter (larger) survey are the levels of uniformity, with virtually all the variables being more or less within the statistical margin of error. Higher levels of agreement were expressed by ABC1s (81 per cent) and those with third-level education (83 per cent), and slightly lower ones by C2DEs (73 per cent). These results might be interpreted as a desire to see people earn their keep rather than any expression of support for the freedom of movement of labour.

However, there are other more critical viewpoints expressed on the resources question, even if they are in a minority. One of these, which labels the Irish illiberal response as hypocritical, is represented by a cartoon published in the magazine *Phoenix* in June 1997 (Figure 5). Two young working-class men are sitting at a bar, where one is holding a newspaper called 'The Sindostar', an amalgam of three tabloids: the *Irish Independent* (the 'Indo'), the *Sun* and the *Star*. The front page reads 'Johnny Foreigner Invades Ireland – Racism Increases'. The man reading it says 'Jayz. Them bleedin' immigrants are taking over the country!!', and his companion, dole card protruding from his top pocket, retorts 'Yea. When I was signing on in London, the place was full of the bleedin' parasites.'

*Figure 5*   A Laconic View of 1990s Discourse on Immigration and Irish Racism. 'Parasites', Dog Sharkey. © Dog Sharkey.

## THE IRISH STATE

Both the competing logics, 'moral duty' and 'Irish exceptionality', collapse asylum-seekers, refugees and immigrants into the same category. The state's most identifiable ideological response has been a combination of the neo-liberal, labour market perspective, and a bureaucratic construction of asylum. In Chapter 2, the work permit and work visa schemes were referred to. The Department of Enterprise, Trade and Employment, headed by the Tánaiste, Mary Harney, since 1997, has developed *ad hoc* regulations (sometimes in conjunction with the Department of Justice, Equality and Law Reform) in place of an immigration policy. There is no immigration policy *per se* produced by the government, and only the Labour Party has drafted a policy on immigration (Labour Party, 2002). Harney's party, the Progressive Democrats, which has been part of the governing coalition since July 1997, is ideologically neo-liberal, and Harney herself has gone on record as locating Ireland economically as closer to 'Boston than Berlin'. It is not surprising to see her ministry framing the issue of immigration in purely labour market terms. The work permit and visa regulations are very flexible and ambiguous, in that on the one hand permits can be renewed with relative facility, but on the other, the worker is in a permanent 'gastarbeiter' situation, paying taxes yet excluded from accessing benefits on an ongoing basis. While this is all quite new in the context of Irish labour regulations, it should be pointed out that this enduring limbo status is not conducive to integration and likely to be a target for demands for reform among workers in the future.[32] The sporadic raising of the price of work permits, coupled with obligations to advertise employment within Ireland before a permit can be issued, interventions considered unhelpful by the business community, underscore the ideological element of this 'policy'. No other dimension of immigration is dealt with or referred to by this ministry.

The Department of Justice, Equality and Law Reform has constructed the issue of asylum primarily, and again, unsurprisingly, as a set of bureaucratic procedures to minimise criminality. Its focus in terms of policy has been on illegal immigration, while the way in which it addressed the increasing numbers of asylum-seekers under Minister John O'Donoghue (1997–2002) was labelled a 'shambles' by Cabinet colleague Liz O'Donnell and the civil servants' newspaper *Public Affairs News* (2000:8).

A few years previously, the poor handling of the small numbers of programme refugees from the former Yugoslavia (around 1,000) gave rise to an inter-departmental report which explicitly warned against complacency:

> The Committee would emphasise that many European Governments have found that the absence of appropriate resources in this area has led to significant backlogs, which have resulted in an increase in the number of applications and an even greater expenditure in maintaining asylum applicants over long periods. (Government of Ireland, 1993:12)

While the sudden rise in numbers of asylum applications must account for some of the administrative problems, the construction of the issue as a crisis in which 'floods' and 'influxes' of asylum-seekers overwhelm the system (Cullen, 2000; Hennessy, 1999; Guerin, 2002) is thus attributable to inadequate planning (in that this report was ignored). On the one hand the 1997–99 period was characterised by selective use of legislation: the decision to implement only the negative parts of the 1996 Refugee Act, the unilateral suspension of the Common Travel Area, the 1999 Illegal Immigration Act (focussing on trafficking rather than defining an immigration policy), and a failure to apply international procedures correctly that provoked criticism from the UNHCR in 1997 (Cullen, 1997). These elements stress the security-related aspects of the issue. On the other hand, a focus on the financial costs of the new strategies for dealing with asylum applications by civil servants and the media cast asylum as an illegitimate use of public money. The themes of security and overloaded systems are focussed on by the media throughout the period (Hennessy, 1999; Cullen, 2000; Guerin, 2002). The effect of this is to frame discussion of asylum principally in terms of numbers and money, positing these as neutral and indisputable facts around which a debate is constructed, whereas the parameters of debate are themselves the result of classification systems and government priorities.

Take the 'numbers game' around asylum as an example. The Department of Justice puts forward figures on the authenticity or otherwise of asylum-seekers, derived from its own hearings process. The proportion of what are labelled 'bogus' applicants (that is, those who are not granted 'refugee' or associated statuses) increased as the quality of the hearings fell in 1997 and 1998, while the number of those granted status on appeal rose, indicating that the initial applications were not being dealt with correctly. The proportion of successfully appealed cases rose steadily from 4.75 per cent in 1994 to 35.6 per cent in 1998[33] and reached 40 per cent in late 1999 (*Public Affairs News*, 2000). Indeed, in January 2000, Senior Counsel Peter Finlay, one of the Department's barristers responsible for overseeing the appeals procedure, resigned in protest over the scheme in place, having labelled it 'a total and complete travesty' weeks previously (Haughey, 2000). Finlay's argument was backed up by research published by the Irish Refugee Council (IRC, 2000). Thus the apparent increase in the number of 'bogus' asylum-seekers was partially explained by the Department's own faulty procedures. Extra staffing, a dedicated unit with a number of interpreters, and more effective methods since 2000 have reduced the scope for that line of criticism. Nevertheless the idea persists that most asylum-seekers in Ireland are there under false pretences, thus feeding hostility towards them, as measured in opinion surveys relating to perceptions of Others as criminal and a burden on resources, and unmeasured in the daily acts of attrition, verbal and physical abuse.

Stepping back to a further level of abstraction, we might consider how the official categories used in bureaucratic procedures become constructed as having moral value that maps onto older ideas in popular culture. The grounds for asylum, for example, are political rather than economic, as if a distinction can always be made between the two. From this perspective, can Irish people fleeing the Famine be categorised as 'refugees' by today's standard? If the message is that economic oppression does not constitute grounds for refugee status then no, but could an argument that the specific form taken by the Famine was not the result of political actions (and inaction) over the long and short terms be sustained? This artificial dichotomy (evidently not limited to Ireland) leads onto labelling those who are able to prove a 'well-founded fear of persecution' as 'genuine' refugees. Those who cannot prove this or simply do not fit the criteria are stigmatised as 'bogus', and become fair game for media and politicians to castigate as 'illegal'. The categories are administrative and not moral ones, yet the judgement when it reaches the terrain of the debate, assumes a moral tone. The logical conclusion is that 'bogus' asylum-seekers are actually economic migrants. Over the past few years, even that term has become one verging on abusive, as if economic migration was somehow illegal or damaging. Moreover, it is particularly amnesiac in the Irish context to attribute negative connotations to economic migrants.[34]

The wording of the Geneva Convention, however, cannot be the basis of a critique of the Irish state's handling of the asylum issue, any more than the EU's ideological border between EU national and 'non-EU national', now also part of Irish administrative assumptions, can be. These are general points about the way in which bureaucratic distinctions develop autonomy.

However, the 1997 Dublin Convention indicates a much more active attempt to use administrative technical regulations to justify exclusionary policy. According to the Dublin Convention, asylum-seekers are obliged to make their claim for asylum in the first EU country in which they arrive. If an asylum-seeker applies to Ireland after having travelled through France or the UK, for example, the Irish government would be within its rights to return that person to the country of first contact. The ramifications of this are important: in theory, no asylum-seeker should currently be granted refugee status in Ireland, because they have all set foot in another EU country before travelling on to Ireland. As of April 2003, there are no *direct* flights to Ireland from the five countries at the top of the 'league table' of asylum applications in 2002 (Table 13, Chapter 2). This point is not widely referred to, yet it sends a crystal clear message that Ireland would like to minimise its intake of asylum-seekers. We might speculate that the reason the Dublin Convention is not enforced to the letter has more to do with the potential response of Ireland's EU partners, than a desire to accept the responsibilities commensurate with the status of a wealthy nation. In any case, the dominant technical and bureaucratic framing of asylum has led to an impoverished debate focussing on one or two elements of a multi-faceted phenomenon.

## CONCLUSION

While work on the Irish diaspora is a flourishing addition to the academy, empirical studies of how migrants construct their diaspora space in Ireland are minimal. There are nascent minority communities developing throughout Ireland and interacting with various agencies, local community organisations and creating spaces for themselves that so far have attracted little attention from academia. These communities are situated politically and economically, while the multiple and 'multi-axial' social locations from which people live out their diasporic existences are mediated by the governance of the space in which they are physically located.

The island of Ireland has been a 'diaspora space' in the sense attributed to it by Brah for centuries; with invaders and colonisers settling there sporadically, forming what has been referred to as the 'Irish race'. The concept of diaspora space, as a mixture of diaspora spaces within a given territory, starts to become more difficult to manage when it involves the 'homeland' of a diasporic people, as is the case of Ireland, since the Irish diaspora space therefore includes many other territories, and a key point is the governance of a particular space by a dominant culture. The one on which I focus in this book is governed by the Irish state and saturated in historical experiences, not just 'cultures'. The asylum issue in Ireland has been 'bureaucratised' in the Weberian sense of the term: the humanistic dimensions of the problem have been minimised by the state in favour of a number of processes appealing to technical and legal instruments, so that it appears that these are the only compelling source of parameters. Weber argued that bureaucracy could become 'amoral' in that it is set up to perform any rationalised task asked of it in the most efficient form possible, a point that Bauman (1991) applies to the Holocaust. State bureaucracies dealing with asylum tend organisationally toward this 'amoral', technocratic approach. Beyond the ministries dealing with the technical side of these matters, debates have grown up that place emphasis on differing readings of Irish diaspora history, running from empathetic to resistant, seeing the reflection of Irish experience either as compelling or unwanted and distorted.

# 7
# 'New Racism', Old Racisms and the Role of Migratory Experience

In this chapter I shall examine the issue of racialisation from a European perspective, indicating the relationship of the Irish case to the 'new racism' and asking to what extent that paradigm is relevant. Then, given that the new racism is located in a framework that posits post-war migration as the key formative process, I shall sketch out a research agenda around the articulation of collective migrant experiences in European countries of emigration and the impact they have on racist discourse, particularly in respect of working-class responses to difference. This will involve indicating some of the changes involved in the transition from a country of emigration to one of immigration, a situation shared with Ireland by a number of countries. The comparison drawn will be with Italy.

The lineage of the paradigms developed in the Anglo-American literature to deal with racialisation runs through 'race relations', and they focus principally on racism based on skin colour (see Chapter 1). While this focus is shared to a certain extent in continental Europe, immigration and culture hold a more influential place in work done around the same issue there, of which Noiriel's (1988) contribution is exemplary. The strong points of this type of approach are that it *de facto* strikes a balance between the materialist and differentialist lines, and that it more readily takes into account the racialisation of 'white' European migrants who historically have formed a larger proportion of immigrants. This is not an attempt to take the focus away from the dominant racialised groups' constructions of alterity, but to stress continuity and change in the way the Other is represented and dealt with.[1] This in itself constitutes a welcome antidote to political projects which maintain that contemporary or post-war immigration represents a new problem, or the get-out clause that posits an absence of racism due to the absence of racialised groups (until recently). However, the danger of immigration monopolising our attention is that responses to indigenous minorities are sidelined.

Despite some promising and lucid attempts to rethink racialised power relations and dissect whiteness (Miles, 1984, 1993; Brah, 1996;

Brah et al., 1999; Mac an Ghaill 1996; Sivanandan, 2001, 2002), the
focus in the emerging European canon remains fixed on migration,
particularly, in the fin de siècle climate, on asylum-seeking. This
ideologically prioritises the response to the foreign, that is to say, it
postulates xenophobia as a dominant element of racism. Ideas about
differential access to power and the more complex models encapsulating the often contradictory ideologies expressed by working-class
subjects identified by Cohen (1997), Back (1996) and Cole (1997)
could theoretically be extended to cover internal minorities. There
is still a gap to be filled. This perspective informs the following critique
of the 'new racism'.

## WHAT IS THE 'NEW RACISM'?

The dominant paradigm for the last two decades in terms of analysing
racist manifestations in Europe has been that of 'new racism' (Barker,
1981; Taguieff, 1990a, 1990b; Cole, 1997). It is worth drawing out
the threads of this particular paradigm because of its implicit reliance
on xenophobia as a means of conceptualising racism in late
capitalism, before looking at the Irish experience, in order to identify
conceptual problems.

The new racism is seen as a response to post-war immigration by
former colonial subjects. It takes shape through the 1960s (or even
the 1950s (Brown, 1999)), becoming a dominant discourse in the
second half of the 1970s in the UK and France for example. The
principal features of this mode of racism are the use of 'culture' as a
stalking horse for 'race', and the expression of hostility to outsiders
perceived as threatening both the cultural fabric of the nation and
its resources, typically welfare and employment. Coded references to
racialised difference, whether Margaret Thatcher's image of neighbourhoods being 'swamped' by 'alien' cultures (1978), or Herrnstein
and Murray's indictment of educationally 'different' minorities in
the USA (1994), even dominate anti-racist responses, which are articulated principally through multiculturalism in policy and educational
strategies reliant on essentialised notions of difference (Gilroy, 1990).

The perception of culture in new racist discourse is a popular essentialised one. Culture is conceptualised as a national (where the
'national' is defined by bloodlines) expression of difference, that is,
bounded, static and 'unmeltable'. So prominent is culture in the
lexicon of the far Right, that even the culture of immigrant groups
is presented as a valuable asset that should not be endangered by

mixing with that of the host country. Examples offered by Taguieff for France in the mid 1980s (1990a) demonstrate this strategy, as expressed by Alain de Benoît, chief theoretician of the Front national and head of the think tank GRECE: 'the truth is that people must preserve and cultivate their differences [...] Immigration merits condemnation because it strikes a blow at the identity of the host culture as well as the immigrants' identity.'[2]

This discourse emerges as ultimately reasonable in its own terms, constructed on common-sense ideas about culture, which is left as vague as possible to maximise support. In this view, cultures are monolithic and static entities, whose innate mutual incompatibility leads inexorably to conflict, and no reference is made to other sources of conflict, such as class, gender, and so on. However, cultures have long been theorised as dynamic continuums, whose natural state is one of flux. A girl who grows up in Ireland, for example, whose parents are from China, will undoubtedly have a big input from them in a number of ways. Yet she will learn English and in all probability some Irish at school, she will speak with her friends' regional accent, learn how to *céilidh* dance, maybe play camogie. Children of immigrant parents across the world have gone through a process whereby they learn the cultures of their parents simultaneously with those of their host country. It is only by bestowing a mystical irrational essence on culture as accessible only by the initiated that such platforms of thought as those articulated by Alain de Benoît, *inter alia*, can be justified. Culture, *per se*, is never an unbridgeable terrain.

As a counterpoint to the features picked out from national cultures as bestowing continuity, such as the monarchy, the English language, or parliamentary democracy in the UK for example, a rigorous sociological view of culture sees the finite historical contexts for the emergence and development of these ideas, institutions and practices. It thus identifies discrepancies in the signified over time, regardless of the signifier's continuity.[3] Yet the idea of a bounded and defensible culture is easy to grasp for voters because, like 'race', it appears to link the natural to the social, and provide answers. 'Third world' or 'backward' cultures explain immigrants' perceived effects on the areas where they settle (physical degradation of townscape), failure to communicate with advanced cultures, and the unremitting otherness of their religion (particularly Islam). However, how does this account for young Muslims who see themselves as equally French as their Catholic and secular compatriots, yet are referred to as 'beurs' or 'immigrés': indicators of segregation.[4] Or how does it account for the hostility of sections of Irish society to Catholic, anglophone Africans, surely closer culturally than a secular Czech computer technician? At the end of the aporia of cultural defensiveness upon which unbridgeable cultural difference is premised is the cul-de-sac of racism.

## NEW RACISM AND INTERNAL 'OTHERS'

Jews, other religious (and linguistic) minorities and Travellers/Sinti/ Roma constitute long-standing objects of racist representations and practices all over Europe. Jews and Gypsies were of course the two groups that suffered most appallingly under the Nazis.[5] The 'new' racism glosses over their experiences, since its focus is outwards to the external 'outsider'. Even Sivanandan's concept of 'xeno-racism' (2002, 2001) focusses exclusively on the logic of external threat, and treats xenophobia as a distinct autonomous phenomenon on the same conceptual level as racism.

The Irish experience, as I have argued throughout, is one that might help bridge these conceptual gaps with empirical material. Both in Ireland and as immigrants elsewhere, the Irish have been made the subjects of discourses seeking to establish their inferiority in terms of 'civilisational' development since the Anglo-Norman conquest, a process that came to a head in the 1570s (Canny, 1976; Quinn, 1966) with Plantations being justified on the basis of bringing civilisation to the country and making the land fruitful (*vis-à-vis* the unproductive barbarian practices of transhumance and collective landowning). What is striking from sixteenth-century accounts is the absence of physical difference between the Irish and the English: revealing differences are cultural, and include clothing and language. A central problem for dominant groups in the UK, North America and Australasia has been how to depict the Irish lack of civilisation in somatic form. The solutions have included darkening the skin, simianising the facial structure (particularly from the 1860s) and contrasting Irish characters with the 'normal', that is, civilised, figures, such as Britannia, Hibernia and the 'good Celt'. Even these strategies, however, have been selective: they focussed mainly on men, distinguished between the 'good' and the 'bad' Celt, and emerged principally in the post-'Origin of Species' period (Curtis, 1997).[6]

Culture, from the Enlightenment onward, was thought to express itself in the bodies of people: a racist construct developed to high point in the work of Linnaeus, Hume and de Buffon, among others (Eze, 1997). In relation to the Irish, degraded images of inferiority were internalised famously by Carlyle, and even otherwise radical nineteenth-century thinkers such as Engels (1969 [1844]). Indeed, Robert Young (1995) contends that culture was from the outset an inextricable component of the idea of 'race'. Irish nationalists themselves have made productive use of culture as a racialising instrument, particularly in the Gaelic Revival, where a key discourse sought to wrap Irish identity with Catholicism, the use of the Gaelic language, the playing of particular sports, and to express particular non-capitalist values. This mobilising strategy also enabled unflattering comparisons to be made with Jews around the notion of inassimilable difference. Griffith's ideas on Jewish immigration in 1904, for example, are prototypical 'new racist' ones:

> No thoughtful Irishman or woman can view without apprehension the continuous influx of Jews into Ireland and the continuous efflux of the native population. The stalwart men and bright-eyed women of our race pass from our land in a never-ending stream, and in their place we are getting strange people, alien to us in thought, alien to us in sympathy, from Russia, Poland, Germany and Austria [...] people who come to live amongst us, but who never become of us.[7]

Similarly, exclusionary ideas about Travellers in contemporary Ireland are culturally-charged interpretations of normality (settled living, property-ownership) and morality (order) juxtaposed with mobility and perceived disorder and untidiness. Indeed, the same themes are present here as in English discourse about the sixteenth-century Irish, prompting Ní Shuínéar (1994) to argue that the transference onto Travellers of narratives of displacement constructed originally by the coloniser is part of a pathology aimed at distinguishing them from the settled population. The opposition of wandering, migratory Celt and settled Anglo-Saxon was also a well-used trope in nineteenth-century discourse on the Irish (Mac Laughlin, 1998:53). In the Irish context, cultural themes then have been deployed to articulate racialised difference within power relationships going back centuries.

### NEW RACIST DISCOURSE IN IRELAND: DEFENDING MONEY AND PLACE

Although the putative newness of the 'new racism' should be questioned, there is no doubt that the type of discourse it embraces is a dominant one, and that it has specific characteristics that might assist us in theorising racism in contemporary Europe. The following four areas might be identified as the pillars of new racist discourse: welfare, employment, health and sex.

## Welfare

Welfare in its current form of state-directed benefit and insurance systems dates back only to the turn of the twentieth century, if not later in many European countries. It represents a victory for working-class movements that extracted concessions from liberal and not-so-liberal states in the form of redistribution of wealth, that is, the embodiment of an anti-capitalist value in institutional form at the heart of the state, whose task is to create the best conditions for capitalism. Initially, the welfare state was based on universal access, but rapidly and progressively became selective, under the influence of dominant neo-liberal ideas recycled from the nineteenth century about the deserving and undeserving poor in the late 1970s. Somewhere over the next decade, welfare became transformed from a symbolic and material badge of society's solidarity into one of stigma, quite likely self-induced by the idle poor: single mothers, invalids and minorities (disproportionately caught in the lower reaches of the class structure of advanced economies). Those in employment foot the bill for welfare, and the idea that closer supervision of its recipients should be a priority caught on. Conditions for receipt of unemployment benefits for example altered so that a 'job-seeker' now has to prove that he/she is 'actively' seeking employment. Yet this view of the complicated twentieth-century welfare state neglects the fact that even the most minimal versions still provided a site for anti-immigrant grumblings. Nineteenth-century indignation was expressed about Irish vagrants attempting to access poor relief in areas of high concentration of immigrants (see Chapter 5), a set of attitudes that O'Connor (1972) finds evidence of even in the thirteenth century. If welfare has been a key arena for the expression of racist ideas, it is therefore because the values encapsulated in it are coming under challenge from a refreshed ideological assault.

Moreover, the key expressions of anti-asylum-seeking discourse in relation to welfare focus on establishing invalid claims to public money based on nationality. Calls for restrictions on asylum (because it costs so much) are framed in the same breath as calls for more deserving use of funds, such as dealing with homelessness. This symbolic hierarchy places the most disempowered group of insiders in Irish society, without even an address, and not through choice, in direct competition with non-nationals. A letter to the *Irish Times*, from early 2003, spells out this frequently made connection, arguing that 'illegal immigrants are competing with the poorest in society for the available space', and that the '€300 million spent on people who should not be here' would be better given to charities for the homeless and to fund the building of social housing.[8] The constant challenging of asylum-seekers' right to be in Ireland and their peremptory labelling as 'illegal immigrants' is as characteristic of this reasoning as the focus on money wasted.

Furthermore, claims that asylum-seekers were accessing housing and child benefits and even food were presented as a scoop in the free newspaper *Inside Cork* in January 2002 for example, under sub-headlines such as 'Irish significantly worse off'. The food is part of 'direct provision',[9] yet the presentation of a menu made it appear that this was privileged treatment. Indeed, the story would have no purchase if there were not an assumed hierarchy, in which foreign nationals, regardless of status, should either not receive anything from the state, or wait until all other groups viewed as having more legitimate claims are satisfied.

## Employment

While excoriated for their absorption of public money, migrants are also viewed with suspicion in terms of their capacity to compete for employment and access it ahead of Irish nationals. This janus-faced response to immigration is far from specific to twenty-first-century Ireland. As we have seen, an essential component of anti-Irish racism in nineteenth-century Britain saw Irish migrants as both recipients of poor relief and strikebreaking, wage-lowering reserve labour. Moreover, immigrants have been characterised as stealing the bread from the mouths of indigenous workers in numerous situations up to and including post-war Europe, where the simple equation of migrants with unemployment has even formed the basis of immi-gration policy in contexts as different as nineteenth-century France and post-war West Germany. Yet it is also proven that generally immi-gration falls in response to job losses, particularly when those jobs are lost from the primary and secondary sectors of economies, in which immigrants are traditionally over-represented. The SOPEMI 1988 report, for example, shows a virtually identical pattern in different post-war European economies: high levels of migration in the 1950s and early 1960s gives way to a dramatic decline from the mid 1970s in the wake of the oil crisis, and migration rises and falls roughly in parallel with higher and lower employment levels respectively. Indeed, some of the most compelling treatments of post-war and contemporary immigration (Castles and Kosack, 1985; Phizacklea, 1990; Wrench et al., 1999; Kaufman et al., 2000; Andall, 2000; Mendoza, 2000) argue that there is a *de facto* dual labour market. In the 1950s and 1960s, migrants worked principally in low-paid and/or difficult positions in industry, public services (transport and health) and domestic service. At the turn of the twenty-first century, agricultural, service sector and catering jobs are more likely to be the destination, with the added condition that, in an increasingly fragile labour market, migrants are more likely to be concentrated in insecure temporary contract or non-contract work. The actual amount of competition between indigenous and immigrant workers is difficult to discern, but in a number of ways there are structural impediments to this in the first place: the reservation of areas of work for nationals only; the requirement of particular specific qualifications that cannot be accessed by non-nationals; the construction of visa and permit systems based on the principle of protected national labour markets (first preference to nationals, and/or targeted recruitment into areas of job shortage).

The German *gastarbeiter* schemes of the 1960s and 1970s represented the embodiment of national protection: envisaging a tightly-controlled workforce that could be managed to fit existing shortages and removed from the national territory in times of downturn. These proved to be a failure of imagination and an ineffective policy, with thousands of foreign nationals settling in Germany despite the restrictions of 'gastarbeiterdom'. Overall, Irish work permit and visa schemes exhibit the same aims: work permits can only be obtained by employers with proof that positions cannot be filled from domestic labour, while fast-track visas can be procured by immigrants with specific skills that are in demand at a particular moment. Changes in the facility with which these can be obtained (conditions, price, and so on) are introduced in response to economic forecasts and job losses. In August 2001, the first signs of downturn in the computer industry were met with comments from the Tánaiste, Mary Harney (also Minister for Enterprise, Trade and Employment), who stated that the number of work permits granted might be reviewed in the light of job losses (*Irish Times*, 2001). She followed this up with price increases for work permits in late 2001 and January 2003. In April 2003, a new quarterly re-appraisal of the particular types of position eligible for work permit applications (applicable even when the necessary criteria of seeking local applicants first have been documented)[10] was introduced.

As the Irish economy has expanded since the early 1990s, the groups previously particularly excluded from participation (the long-term unemployed and married women) have begun to filter back into the active population at rates approaching the EU15 average. Female labour force participation reached a peak of 50.2 per cent in summer 2002, and was slightly above the EU average of 47 per cent by the end of the year. ILO-defined long-term unemployment fell to 1.3 per cent in quarter 3 of 2003, down from 10.4 per cent in April 1988. As this process continues, the labour supply has shrunk correspondingly, decreasing to between 5 per cent (S1) and 8.4 per cent (S3), as of the last quarter of 2002 (CSO, 2003a).[11] On the ground, employers in the tourist trade, the IT sector, and the health service have been filling vacancies with applicants from abroad since the end of the 1990s (Smyth, 2000).

Moreover, a March 2000 poll of employers by *Decision* magazine showed that 82 per cent of them wanted immigration laws relaxed. However, 34 per cent wanted to see only targeted immigration for high-skilled jobs, and 33 per cent wanted an annual quota system, something consistently argued for by editorials in the populist *Irish Independent*. In the same survey, one in three senior executives forecast potential social tension as a result of relaxing the immigration laws. The perception that foreign workers will edge locals out of employment is thus considered real by important actors. Policy on work permits and visas appears to be as strict (that is, tied to actual labour shortages) as could possibly be conceived. Yet while perhaps appeasing the perceived need for the government to appear 'tough' on abuses of such schemes, the politicians' view is neither necessarily shared by employers nor based on statistical evidence that these specific jobs could otherwise be filled from the Irish and EEA workforce. Moreover, the business experience of even the recent relatively small rise in unemployment begun in the last quarter of 2002 does not tally with the view that competition exists. Pat Delaney, Director of the Irish Small Firms Association commented that the 25 per cent increase in the cost of work permits announced by Harney in January 2003, due to 'a downturn in the economy', 'won't do anything to reduce unemployment because immigrant labour is not responsible for higher unemployment. Ireland is still gripped by an endemic skills shortage' (Humphreys, 2003).

Without further research on this apparent mismatch of solutions to problems it is difficult to conclude anything more detailed than that there is a divergence of opinion between the state and the business community about the nature of the current Irish labour market. If, as I suspect, the latter have the clearer picture, then the consequences for immigration are important: the number of specialist skilled workers will continue to grow, granting them a relatively privileged place in Ireland's class system, and numbers of those located in the unskilled and semi-skilled labour markets will also continue to grow, more slowly as a result of the new obstacles to participation, while criticisms of the state's failure to remedy unemployment will increasingly be heard. An equation will be established between foreigners and unemployment of Irish workers, and migrant workers who are not in competition with Irish workers may well be the victims of any further policy at that point.

## Health

Immigrants fleeing poor socio-economic conditions have sometimes arrived in their countries of destination with illnesses. The Famine-driven flight to North America and Britain involved weakened people embarking on arduous, long voyages in cramped and unsanitary conditions. It is not altogether surprising that they reached their destinations 'with pestilence on their backs and famine in their stomachs' (Mac Laughlin, 1999a). The result for the host society was expenditure, anxiety over contagion, and the characterisation of the immigrants as bearers of threat and impurity. While the basic premise has not changed, the context into which immigrants arrive in Ireland is one in which the nature of the threat carries additional moral overtones. Ireland became a country of immigration in the AIDS era, and the sexual and moral overtones of that disease have bubbled under the surface of elements of the debate. The Immigration Control Platform (ICP) had first called for compulsory AIDS testing of asylum-seekers in 1998, a demand contained in letters to the press and leaflets distributed in a few constituencies in the Cork and Dublin areas. This type of tactic is not without precedent. Mario Borghezio, the Italian Lega Nord's director of anti-immigrant mobilisation repeatedly called for AIDS tests for migrants throughout the 1990s, for example (Gomez, 2002:118). Within four years, the ICP's demand had migrated through Health Board policy (non-mandatory testing) into Fine Gael's 2002 election manifesto. Immigrants and asylum-seekers from particular regions in the world would be compulsorily tested by a future Fine

Gael government, in an attempt to control the disease, and other tropical illnesses that risked having devastating effects on Irish society and entailing heavy spending.

However, this ostensibly security-driven agenda concealed a more ideological one. Public health policies on AIDS normally prioritise high-risk groups: drug-users, young people with multiple partners, gay men, plus those who have spent time in areas where the disease is prevalent. Yet there was no mention of checks on visitors to these countries returning to Ireland, merely a focus on asylum-seekers. The message was that foreign bodies *per se* constitute a risk for Irish health. This in a year in which the Lindsay Tribunal on infected blood in the health service was reaching its concluding phase. Moreover, a dramatisation of the role of the victim support group for women infected through an inoculation in the 1980s (Positive Action), the events that gave rise to the Lindsay tribunal, appeared on state television. The then Minister for Health who had haggled the victims down to the minimum compensation was Michael Noonan, short-lived Fine Gael leader 2001–02, whose manifesto included the AIDS testing pledge.

The theme of defending blood from infection and the dire consequences of not doing so was given further resonance by a public campaign to prevent foot and mouth disease originating in the UK from infected livestock. Thus protection of borders, with its overtones of defending the nation from imported impurities, provided the backdrop to the racialisation of immigration in Ireland in which disease is seen as a key theme.

In addition to issues of dangerous blood are those of reproduction. The services provided by maternity hospitals and wards were being stretched over the late 1990s and early twenty-first century, allegedly by foreign women who usurped locals from beds in order to have children, and avail themselves of the Irish-born children 'loophole' that allowed them residence as a result until the January 2003 Supreme Court ruled that this practice should no longer be automatic (Sheehan, 1998; O'Connor, 2001). The presentation of these stories and their link with 'non-national women' who 'sometimes arrived in labour straight from the airport or boat' (O'Connor, ibid.) places the emphasis on implied illegitimate use of funds, when the birth rate for Irish nationals has been rising through the late 1990s. The inter-censual population increase is in the order of 8 per cent (from 3.6 million (1996) to 3.9 million (2002)), with 2002 showing the highest excess of births over deaths since 1984 (CSO, 2002b).[12] Sheehan's *Sunday Tribune* article is a masterpiece of innuendo and sloppy fact-checking.[13]

Master of the Rotunda, Dr Peter McKenna, is quoted as saying that 'with 5,000 asylum-seekers in the country, the number of non-nationals having babies in Dublin "just doesn't add up, it is quite disproportionate"'. Yet he quotes a figure of 250 non EU-nationals having children in his hospital, and cites their countries of origin as 'Nigeria, Zaire, former Soviet Russia, the Middle East and Eastern Europe'. At the time in question, around 90 per cent of asylum-seekers were concentrated in Dublin, and especially in certain sections, and the majority of them came from exactly those places. Thus it would be unsurprising to see a rise in the number of births from mothers from those places in Dublin public hospitals in 1997 and 1998. Moreover, the link between Irish-born children and obtaining 'nationality' (as opposed to 'residence') is, taken in isolation, baseless. 'Nationality' and 'residence' are vastly different statuses, but, as with the distinction between asylum-seekers and refugees, separated by a gulf in terms of rights, the press generally fails to use the appropriate term or contribute to its readership's understanding of the social realities it represents.

Fears of demographic imbalance brought about by immigrants have been around since at least biblical times. Egyptians complained that the Israelites were too fecund in Exodus (1:9–22) and concerns that they would ally with potential enemies resulted in the Pharaoh's decision to have every boy child killed. Anglophone Americans have viewed their Spanish-speaking compatriots with suspicion in the south-western states since the 1980s, as the implications of bilingual south-western states in which Hispanics were the majority started to be discussed. Similarly, Loyalists in Northern Ireland have been keen observers of Catholic demography, seeing their higher birth rates as proof of immoral popish practices and of imminent swamping. In the Republic of Ireland, the balance of populations is far from having reached this level of sensitivity, but the symbolic role of maternity and family in the Irish nation and constitution, the relationship of 'Irish-born children' and access to residence rights, plus the actual overcrowding in inner-city Dublin hospitals make a heady mixture.

In this context, Minster Martin's blaming of foreign women in August 2001 for placing increased burdens on the health services' midwifery capacity is hard to see as anything other than an attempt to distract attention from the government's faulty management of resources. The failure to keep up with the birth rate in terms of maternity facilities coupled with the foreign input into staffing public hospitals might be mitigating factors in a more balanced discussion of the overall problems of the Irish health service. Moreover, the debate ought to be placed within broader parameters taking into account the burdens generated by indigenous alcohol abuse (an estimated €2.4 billion per annum) (Donnellan, 2003), for example, and the fact that birth rates have risen over the last decade, while maternity hospitals have not increased their bed capacity by the same levels over the same period. Moreover, there is great stress placed on the number of foreign women patients in maternity hospitals, but little mention of the numbers of foreigners staffing Ireland's hospitals. A government document, 'Report on Cultural Diversity in the Healthcare Sector', published in March 2002, stated that as of November 2001, 1,500 of 3,500 non-consultant doctors (including 60 per cent of registrars) and over 3,000 nursing staff in the public health service were from outside the EU, a proportion described as 'significant' (Snuggs, 2002). The result of the Minister's comments is a one-dimensional and misleading portrait of the use of national resources.

### Sex

On the one hand, the sexuality of immigrant men, particularly but not exclusively black men, has long been represented as exotic, taboo and dangerous. On the other, the outcome of sex, reproduction, threatens the very border of racialised communities, breaking down the logic of biological exclusivity on which the idea of 'race' is constructed. Given that rape has assumed the status of a weapon in recent genocides, the symbolism of unbridled black sexuality menacing the population is lurid to say the least. The notorious *Irish Sun* headline 'Somali Rapist on the Loose' in summer 1997 indicates the potency of this image at a local level.[14] The use of mass rape as a military tactic (aimed at domination, impregnation and/or the spread of disease) during the war in the former Yugoslavia in the early 1990s, and the Rwandan genocide in 1994, prompted the United Nations to incorporate rape as a 'crime constitutive of genocide' in 1996.

In summer 1998, a group of Romanians claimed asylum and were temporarily housed in Wexford. In early August, an editorial in the *Wexford People* expressed a number of criticisms of the authorities and the Romanians, one of which was of the threat posed by young men hanging around a girls' school in the town. This editorial argued that 'some young asylum-seekers were intent on striking up relationships with impressionable young girls, fully aware that a baby would ensure permanent residence in this country' (Newman, 1998). Ger Walsh, the article's author, said the situation was 'causing serious concern for parents' (ibid.). Inextricable from this point are the other financial-based critiques: perceived preferential access to housing, and men 'flaunting' their cash handouts in the street. The symbolic space of exclusion had been apparently usurped by the Roma.

Moreover, foreign women have also been represented as exotic and objectified as a result of the West's relationship with the colonised world. Not only are they viewed as available and sexual, but in the context of *ius soli*, in Ireland, as the Trojan horses of alien penetration into Ireland. 'Pregnant black women are routinely physically assaulted upon exiting maternity hospitals – the assumption is that they are having babies merely to be allowed to remain in Ireland' (Lentin, 2001).

## NEW RACISM AND OLD RACISMS IN IRELAND?

Discourse in Ireland is dominated by the 'new racist' ideology, particularly in terms of threats to the nation's resources, but in this does not exclude two other things: first that forms of discrimination based on physical appearance co-exist with these welfare-based articulations of illegitimacy, and second that formulating exclusionary ideologies not based on skin colour is part of an old process, going back to the twelfth and sixteenth centuries. In the context of Ireland, domination on the basis of culture, mobility and rootlessness rather than appearance is a recurring theme. Irish racism, while often being articulated around the 'new' racist themes of defence of territory and resources in political discourse, is anchored in a centuries-old set of ideas about belonging as expressed through community, settlement, civilisation/barbarity, and so forth, to which the Irish have been exposed, principally as victims, but sometimes as perpetrators, in various geographical and social locations.

Thus the contours of difference constituting Irish discourse lean toward the distinction between rootedness and rootlessness. Asylum-seekers fall principally into the second category and are in some cases prevented (by direct provision) from accessing paths to rootedness. Not only are they rootless (like Jews and Travellers before them), but they are compulsorily unproductive (because banned from paid employment), where productivity is a prized normative value. Asylum-seekers even fall into two groups, the 'bogus' and the 'genuine', to be sorted like wheat and chaff. Paradoxically, 'bogus' asylum-seekers are castigated for simultaneously being a drain on resources and as *de facto* economic (that is, productive) migrants.

Understanding this about Irish racism relies on links with the racial-isation of Travellers and Jews in the nineteenth and twentieth centuries, and bears out Balibar's (1991a) contention that racism is constantly reconfiguring itself.

The 'new' forms of racism experienced in contemporary Ireland are influenced by the development of an Irish nation state, the rela-tionship between mass migration and immigration, the nature of economic development at the turn of the twenty-first century and the access to diasporic models of dealing with difference (examined in previous chapters). Moreover, the paradigms deployed to research these issues can have an impact upon the success and failure of political resistance to racism. Research has shown that focussing on immigration, even to defend immigrants, is a strategy that fuels the electoral strength of anti-immigration groups (Hargreaves, 2002). Analyses based so heavily on the logic of xenophobia, even if with the intention of deconstructing it, start the clock in the post-war migration period and, by operating a set of erasures inherent in the new racism of nationalist parties and their ideological fellow-travellers, place the responsibility for the more or less comprehensible if disap-pointingly racist 'response' (as if there were none before) at the feet of the immigrants themselves.

While the concept of the 'new' racism is indicative of particular trends in late capitalism, it tends to advance from an ahistorical departure point and ignore the salience of experiences of earlier times and internal minorities. Moreover, it helps reify concepts of 'culture' and 'nation' that actually bolster racist ideologies and grant legitimacy to the division into ethnos and demos. The political project of xenophobic movements aims, *inter alia*, to make it an assumption that there is a cut-off point after which immigration became quali-tatively different, foreigners became too alien and integration became impossible. Approaches which fail to compare post-war migration with previous migrations and internal minorities are bound to reflect that project, and enable ahistorical political arguments the space to develop. French Front national deputy, and now leader of the breakaway Mouvement National Républicain, Bruno Mégret (Front national, 1997:91), for example, argues that France's stock was formed 6,000 years ago:

Thus the people of France were formed in the distant past. The contributions brought since then have been minimal, and from the end of the first millennium to the end of the last century, there was practically nothing added to it. Those people it took in before and after this period belong to the same ethnic group. The contemporary period marks a break with four thousand years of continuity.

An alternative is to look more closely at the range of racist expressions, conceptualising them as embracing both internal minorities and external migrants, and working on the power differentials within the host community to gain greater insight. Work which has begun to question the assumption of monolithic 'communities', both 'minority' and 'majority' ones, has itself been a minority discourse (Brah, 1996; Mac an Ghaill, 1999, 2001). The 'new racist' ideas have now taken root in Ireland. These ideas use defence of territory, nation and culture, rather than any precise mention of 'race', as a mobilising platform for a discourse that seeks to exclude the Other from symbolic and actual space, typically arguing that developed and underdeveloped cultures do not and should not mix, and that incomers pose economic, sexual, health-related and cultural threats to the host nation. The pattern will be drawn out and examined in relation to their development as key elements of European political debate.

## THE SOUTHERN AND WESTERN PERIPHERY: SOME POINTS OF COMPARISON

From the point of view of migration, the countries with which Ireland has most in common are not English-speaking or outside Europe, but the states on the southern and western periphery (SWP) of Europe: Italy, Spain, Portugal and Greece. The term periphery is used here in its geographical sense, rather than to denote a pole in the core–periphery model. Mac Laughlin (1997) correctly points out that there is no fixed place that is a core or periphery, rather a combination of economic and political factors changes the relationships between the economies of different parts of the world, continent, or country. The nations listed above share with Ireland the experience of having been providers of labour in the post-war period for the larger economies in Europe and providers of labour to other continents, North America in particular. At various points in the last two decades, these nations have become net importers of people.

The national myths of these countries have come under tension from changes stemming from the dual requirements of the Schengen Agreements and individual historical ties with former colonies. They are all experiencing serious changes in their national self-image as a result of demographic shifts.

There is a historical contestation between opposing metanarratives of the Spanish nation. The first, based on the *reconquista*, sees the history of modern Spain beginning in 1492 with the expulsion of the Moors and the Jews (Peres, 1999). This Christian core identity is therefore more susceptible to threats from the Islamic world, and its assumed whiteness under attack from African immigrants. This is part of the ideology that has fed into Spain's diverse and sizeable far Right since the Franco era (CERA, 1998). The contrasting account is a democratic and pluralist (and federalist) modernising nation-myth that sees Spain as a 'mosaic of cultures' (Mercadé, 1986) with Moorish and Jewish origins alongside the Christian ones (Cáchon Rodriguez, 1995). This view appears as decidedly abstract or minority when the extent of hostility toward Moroccan workers in Spain is revealed, in the virtual pogrom at El Ejido in 1999 for example. The debate over identity is complicated by the Franquist heritage in which the role of the Catholic Church is identified with repression and dictatorship, hence the eagerness to re-incorporate pluralism into the idea of modern Spain.

Portugal has seen its colonial past come into direct conflict with its modern European present, precisely over the issue of immigration (Dupraz and Vieira, 1999). In post-revolutionary Portugal (1974) after the abandonment of overseas colonies, significant numbers of former colonial settlers and natives of the Portuguese colonies immigrated to Portugal. By the 1980s immigration exceeded migration, yet the classification in terms of status did not correspond to what was found in countries with longer experiences of immigration. According to Lopes (1992), former colonials, or PALOP (for example, Chinese from Macao, Indians from Goa, and Portuguese-speaking Africans), were not categorised as different from Portuguese nationals. Brettell (1993) even sees the emigrant as having been subsumed into the Portuguese narrative of exploration, part of a 'pilgrim people' that is the bearer of culture. Indeed it is only when the security imperatives of Schengen became overriding that terminology and policy altered. Portugal has aimed to retain a privileged position for subjects of former colonies *vis-à-vis* other non-EU nationals. This has created tension between the attempt to maintain sovereignty over immigration and the necessity of complying with Schengen's provisions for border control (Dupraz and Vieira, 1999) in which the principal dividing line is

EU/non-EU. Yet for Portugal, immigration in official discourse has been deemed a welcome symbol of modernity.

This is not the case in Italy, where anti-immigrant politics has assumed the most considerable space of any SWP country. Ritaine (1999) argues that immigration is an issue that highlights the political restructuring of the late 1980s and early 1990s, and mirrors Italy's crisis of modernisation. It was only in 1998 that Italy was allowed to join Schengen. Hesitation on the part of the centre and the Left allowed the Right to colonise the theme of immigration: 'a long period of inconsistency in state action having left a symbolic space available for xenophobic exploitation in which a security-based interpretation was imposed on immigration' (1999:63). National insecurity over the values of modern Italy, Ritaine asserts, has created three ideal-types that haunt representations of political life: the corrupt politician, the potentially Mafia-linked Southerner and the delinquent immigrant.

In all three of these countries then, even from this briefest of readings, the issue of immigration has attached itself to long-term political processes in a specific way. While it is important to restate that internal minorities (particularly Gypsies and Jews) have still suffered discrimination and are to differing degrees included and excluded from the imagined nation, the transition from a country of emigration into one of immigration has produced collective responses ranging from racism through amnesia to solidarity and combinations of all things in between.

Indeed the interplay of migratory experience (particularly its recent and contemporary varieties) with responses to immigration represents a potentially fruitful line of enquiry for social scientists interested in exploring the dynamics of racism in contemporary Europe. The testing beds of the former countries of emigration on Europe's southern and western periphery may reveal more complex relationships than seem to be assumed in models that use the 'new racism' as a given. In the previous chapter, it was argued that one of the two broad lines of argument on positive treatment for incoming minorities (the other being the labour market one) was based on a historical duty derived from Ireland's experience as a country of emigration. The question is to explore the degree to which the migratory experience enables the complexity and contradiction of attitudes to minorities to emerge. I shall now turn to Italy, for an explorative study of this kind.

## THE ROLE OF MIGRANT EXPERIENCE IN CONTEMPORARY RACIST ATTITUDES: THE EXAMPLE OF ITALY

In the course of seeking perspectives on the Irish transition to immigration, the SWP countries suggest themselves. While it is important not to attach too much importance to national rather than regional experiences of emigration – some areas within countries of traditional emigration have relatively little – the theme of migration in collective consciousness is the focal point for this argument.

Yet, we should ask what do we mean by 'Italian' or 'Irish' migrant experiences? This consciousness is mediated by gender and class, and shaped by the destination and the timing. Even when people arrive in the same place at the same time they may have differential experiences based on their multiple identities and the economic and political structural factors pertaining to the diaspora spaces in which they are located (Corcoran, 2002; Gray, 2000, 2003; Lennon et al., 1988). With these issues in mind, the object of the following analysis is to tease out the question of how collective migrant experiences of the host population, which do not have to be first hand, inform, influence and shape responses to immigrant Others.

### Attitudinal surveys

It is received wisdom that working-class people are 'more racist' than other groups, and attitudinal surveys are seen to bear out this assumption. One of the contributions made by attitudinal surveys to knowledge about racism is to profile particular categories of people who are more likely to express hostility. In European surveys, the analysis shows that factors such as lower educational attainment, experience of unemployment, occupation of lower levels of socio-economic categories, age and location influence attitudes expressed in opinion polls. In Chapter 2 it was observed that opinion polls in Ireland had led to profiling of older people living in more rural areas and from socio-economic groups C2 downwards who expressed the most hostile attitudes towards minorities. Yet there are relatively few critical questions being asked about such polls and the way knowledge is constructed. A variety of factors qualify such material: sample size, phrasing of questions, timing in relation to events of national and international relevance, proportion of missing values.[15] Moreover, explanations that use attitudinal surveys to explain action are moving into treacherous terrain: attitudinal polls measure what people say they think, not what they actually do. Explaining racism through attitudinal surveys alone is methodologically misleading. Important factors such as institutional racism and structural economic and political elements are completely absent from the equation.

This methodological inadequacy obfuscates the crucial framing influence of structural factors such as power relations between classes. The relationship between the dominant ideas in a particular period and the vast majority of people who are not involved in decision-making activities is not unimpeded one-way traffic, but neither is it the jousting of equal partners. We ought to shy away from the notion that the working classes are the victims of a ruling-class plot to transfer their antagonism over class to one involving immigrants and minorities. Yet the other extreme, that is, the liberal model of equal citizenship, in which every individual is seen as rational, self-serving and detached from their social location, and thus starting from the same position, is also to be treated critically. Opinions are made on the basis of information available, life experiences and aspirations, and are contingent to a large extent on people's social locations. Moreover, there is no automatic relationship between working-class respondents and hostile response to questions about minorities. In any case, the distinction identified is relative rather than absolute.

Cole (1997:64), for example, points to the difference between discourses on immigration engaged in by his Italian working-class and middle-class respondents. Those from working-class areas generally used Sicilian dialect and terminology in their often contradictory explanations. Their discourse was usually 'everyday' rather than 'specialised' (Reeves:1983), and served to express opinions. Official political discourse was in Italian, used phrases derived from legislation and European directives, and its functions were to persuade, justify and describe.

Decision-making on institutional issues such as legislation, court rulings, policy implementation and guidelines is carried out principally by middle-class managerial-level employees and those above them. Within this framework, attitudes are important indicators of collective response to difference on the ideological level but as measurements of racism they are hardly scientific and cannot be used as tools of analysis. Rather they are a component of the problem to be analysed. Although the focus in this section is on working-class respondents, the key elements of the analysis are qualitative rather than quantitative. With notable exceptions (Cohen, 1997; Back, 1996; Mac an Ghaill, 1996), few attempts are being made to look closely at the power relationships inside the dominant ethnic groups held to be monolithic and wielders of relative power in all situations. Indeed, working-class racism in current work appears to have passed into the area of taken-for-granted knowledge, borne out by sporadic relatively high voting for anti-immigration parties in white working-class wards and constituencies in the UK, Holland, Belgium and France for example over the last decade or so.

The idea of Irish empathy with other migrant groups arising from the specifics of the Irish experience of emigration, needs to be tested properly in the field, and what follows is more of an attempt to frame the questions effectively than to arrive at any concrete conclusions. The research questions are: (to what extent) do migratory experiences play a role in contemporary expressions of racism, and if so what does this role consist of? The following is aimed at constituting a starting point for examining these questions, and is grounded in three methodological assumptions.

First, racism serves to *express class struggle* and *internally fragment the working class* (Hall, 1980). This is not the same as saying that racism is a plot concocted by the bourgeoisie to bamboozle workers, or that class is the only struggle. Moreover, not only black workers, or men, or the employed are involved in it. Second, different forms of racism over time should not be treated as the same phenomena (Miles, 1984; Noiriel, 1988; Balibar, 1991a; Hickman, 1995a), but as distinct yet closely associated configurations containing similar elements. Lastly, in these configurations contemporary factors are articulated to the global and the local in the form of, *inter alia*, labour markets, imagined communities and representations. The most valuable material from attitudinal surveys is that which enables us to grasp how these artic-ulations are being made.

### Parallels in historical experience

Both Italian and Irish emigrants shared similar experiences of racial-isation in the USA. Famine immigrants and Southern Italians found themselves categorised as not quite white, or 'inbetween people' to use Orsi's phrase (1992), at different moments: the Irish in the middle and the Italians at the end of the nineteenth century. Yet they also left environments in which they had already been racialised by dominant cultures: the Irish by the British and the Southern Italians by the Northerners (Richards, 1999: 107–8). Richards refers to Alfredo Niceforo's *Contemporary Barbarian Italy* (1898) as an indicator of the idea that Southerners were more primitive and less developed culturally and socially than the Northerners. Both Irish Catholics and Italians in America thus had to negotiate their identities in the framework of a black–white binary that bore elements of the civil-isation–barbarity tropes they had already encountered at home (see Chapter 3). In the USA, whiteness held social capital and advantages, even for working-class members. Italians arrived in the largest numbers during a period of resurgent political racism from the 1890s through to the 1920s, and their initial failure to distance themselves as required from black people, areas and jobs led to their categorisation as closer to black than white (and exposed them to lynching). At the end of the nineteenth century this meant anything from being housed separately from other white employees of a Louisiana lumber company in 'quarters' similar to those for blacks (Barrett and Roediger, 1997:17), to being symbolically banished from the universe of fitness for governance, labelled as 'black as the blackest negro in existence' (Cunningham, 1965:34, cited in ibid.:9). Their relatively radical politics led to their being viewed as anarchists, and their resulting vulnerability in the Palmer raids. Increasing anxieties about 'race' in the form of Anglo-Saxonism and its articulation with whiteness created a paranoia about difference exploited and in part extended by the influential eugenics movement, whose impact on public policy resulted in, *inter alia*, the 1924 Immigration Act and the National Origins Quota System (1924–65). It was a period in which the former president Roosevelt could tell a packed Carnegie Hall in 1915 that: 'There is no room in this country for hyphenated Americans' (Richards, 1999). A black American tried for miscegenation in 1922 walked free because the woman he was accused of having sex with was a Sicilian immigrant, and the judge decided that the evidence was 'in no sense conclusive that she was therefore a white woman' (Jacobson, 1998:4).[16] Orsi (1992) refers to a path away from proximity to non-white Others and the formulation of sometimes contradic-tory exclusionary ideologies drawing the line around Italians as white Americans from the 1920s onwards. The American odyssey then required a redefinition of identity, in the form of ideological attachment to whiteness, an identity unnecessary at home, and which then entered the perceptions of Italians at home through contact with the diaspora.

### Racist attitudes in contemporary Italy

There are also superficial points of comparison between Ireland and Italy in terms of politics. Both are relatively young nation states, whose legitimacy has been the object of contestation and who have experienced difficulties in securing allegiance, although for very different reasons. There is also in both a strong strain of internal othering, not only in relation to minorities, but between communities that view themselves as intrinsically different: Northern Protestants and Northern Italians in their self-definition *vis-à-vis* Catholics and Southern Italians respectively, and vice versa.

Indeed, the surveys conducted by Sniderman et al. (2000) showed that Northern Italians generally expressed greater hostility toward Southerners (*meridionali*) than immigrants. This is echoed by the respondents interviewed by Cole (1997) in Palermo, who complained that Southerners were victims of racism in Northern Italy, a contempt expressed in terminology such as *'terroni'* (peasants), and *'africani'*, in the period prior to mass immigration of real Africans. Comparison of attitudes toward three different types of immigrant – Northern African, Eastern European and Central African – by Sniderman revealed the foci of hostility (see Table 19). Notions of direct racial superiority appear to reflect a minority attitude, but where they do appear, they are concentrated more on Central (that is, black) Africans than the others. Yet Eastern Europeans score poorly in areas where the others score highly. All in all, these figures give a qualified, complex and ambivalent picture of how Italians make sense of 'racialised' difference, with both negative and positive characteristics attributed to the immigrant groups mentioned. The authors confess that the results were surprising in that they expected black immigrants to emerge the least popular across the board (Sniderman et al., 2000:30). They did not, and even Southern Italians appeared less favoured than immigrants *per se*. Yet this particular conclusion: 'Hostility to blacks by virtue of their being black is overshadowed by hostility to immigrants whatever their race' (ibid.:128), is based on an understanding that 'race' is an attribute of physical appearance only. This assumption has already been identified as something to be investigated rather than to be used as an analytical tool (Chapter 1). My understanding of racism is that it embraces elements that can and often do include skin colour, yet does not do so exclusively. The attitudes to the three groups of immigrants may well show hostility to immigrants *per se*, and to Southern Italians *vis-à-vis* foreign immigrants, but this does not mean that 'race' is a minor factor. All of those populations have been racialised, that is, had a set of characteristics imputed to them as being typical and innate, and occupy varying inferior places on the scale of civilisation from the peak of which Northern Italians look down at their Others.

*Table 19* Italian Attitudes Toward Immigrants and Southerners

| Characteristic | North Africans | Central Africans | East Europeans | All Immigrants (a) | All Immigrants (b) | Southern Italians | SD |
|---|---|---|---|---|---|---|---|
| Honest | 75.1 | 76.5 | 75.8 | 76 | 73 | 68 | –5 |
| Selfish | 31.7 | 27.7 | 35.2 | 32.4 | 33 | 36 | No |
| Law-abiding | 51.1 | 63.3 | 56.7 | 56.9 | 51 | 35 | –16 |
| Intrusive | 55.9 | 49.7 | 41.8 | 49 | 55 | 61 | +6 |
| Slackers | 33.1 | 36.6 | 36.3 | 35.4 | 37 | 57 | +20 |
| Violent | 31.7 | 30.7 | 36.9 | 34 | 34 | 41 | +7 |
| Complainers | 60.7 | 55.5 | 56.6 | 57.3 | 56 | 67 | +11 |
| Naturally inferior | 18.4 | 17.8 | 13.2 | 15.7 | – | – | – |

Source: Sniderman et al. (2000), Tables 2.1 (p. 28), 2.2 (p. 30) and 3.6 (p. 86)

All figures are percentages of responses to questions about the characteristics of the group specified.
(a)   Figures refer to average for the three immigrant groups specified in one poll.
(b)   Figures refer to separate poll of Northern Italians only, *vis-à-vis* Southerners and immigrants in general.
(SD)  *Significant Difference:* in these datasets, 5 per cent is a significant difference. It is expressed in relation to the responses from Northerners about immigrants and Southerners. The latter emerge as less sympathetic in every case. The question on natural inferiority was not asked in that poll.

One interesting trend to emerge then is the partial dissociation of colour from systematic negativity of representation. Both Sniderman's and Cole's surveys demonstrate that, to a certain extent, the signifier–signified relationship of blackness and low status is undergoing tension. Yet in certain arenas in Italy, such as soccer, the opposite seems to be the case, with terms such as 'dirty', 'black' and 'Jew' used by sections of supporters to denigrate people other than immigrants such as opposing supporters (Carroll, 2001).[17] The behaviour of particular clubs' supporters toward black players has been the subject of criticism even over the last couple of seasons.

Cole's qualitative study of attitudes in the Palermo area (1997) based on 1990 fieldwork throws up some interesting pointers as to the construction of racist attitudes. He deals with both working- and middle-class attitudes in different chapters, but here I focus on the former. While the historical importance of migration out of Italy had become a key theme in the debate on immigration by the late 1980s, Cole found that this core collective reality was processed very differently by his working-class and middle-class respondents. Fear of competition in the labour market, and to a lesser extent the housing one, expressed itself alongside the idea that immigrants and Sicilians principally did different types of work, the former occupying niches abandoned by or felt to be demeaning by locals. Moreover, very few people saw immigrants as the source of any problems they encountered in terms of labour, poverty and political disempowerment, with local, regional and central government and the Mafia cited as sources instead. Empathy with immigrants was articulated through acknowledgement of parallel experiences particularly in Northern Italy, and less so in the USA, yet the parallel lines of narratives did not quite touch. Cole notes this point at which shared experiences were not allowed to fuse and respondents avoided making the final connection. The immigrants are exploited like us, but not like us; the contexts for migration are similar but vitally and inexplicably different. The denial of shared positions points to the idea that representations of immigrants are informed by self-hate. The degraded position of immigrants in Italy reminds Italians of what they used to be or might become again – even more powerless – and instead of inspiring desire to change that situation, provokes the need to banish the image, because the political and economic basis is too flimsy to use as a springboard for activism.

## MIGRATION AND IRISH RACISM

No research has yet been conducted into the relationship between Irish migrant experience and racist discourse among the Irish in Ireland. This section is therefore an attempt to highlight a potentially fruitful research question that would enable the particular versions of racism there to be more fully comprehended. Does the experience of being a migrant nation (even if it is second-hand collective experience) mediate the construction of racist discourse? Wieviorka (1993) suggests this might be the case, and Cole's work certainly highlights a number of ambivalences. In the Irish context, we might look at the response to an opinion poll question posed in January 2000 (*Irish Times*/MRBI, 2000a) as indicative of similar ambivalence. The wording used the term 'refugee', which, in view of the haze of incomprehension around migration into Ireland, can be made equivalent to 'immigrants' in Italy (where discourse on asylum-seekers and refugees is relatively minimal). Respondents had to state their level of agreement with the following statement: 'We should take a more generous approach to refugees in view of our history.'[18] The inclusion of Irish history in a question on minorities is not replicated elsewhere, and its results proved interesting in that the level of positive feedback was high compared with other questions on minorities (see Chapter 2). The following points summarise the response to the statement:

1. The mean score for the 'more generous view of refugees' was a positive 3.38 out of 5.
2. 27 per cent 'strongly agreed' and 33 per cent 'somewhat agreed' (that is, 60 per cent positive).
3. 14 per cent 'strongly disagreed' and 16 per cent 'somewhat disagreed' (30 per cent negative).
4. A significant result was in the strong agreement among ABC1s and double income families (the latter being a variable only used in these polls).
5. Only 5 per cent of Fs (people employed in agriculture) strongly disagreed, qualifying somewhat the picture of above average hostility among people employed in this sector.
6. Equally pertinent is the fact that even those 'with no paid employment' gave responses not significantly different from the average (26 per cent 'strongly' agreeing and 32 per cent 'somewhat'

agreeing), again pointing to a higher level of empathy than is usually identified.

Indeed, the role of migration appears to underpin the way Irish racism and anti-racism are configured. It was noted in the previous chapter that two lines of argument saw immigrants as reflections of the Irish, while another promoted the idea that the Irish were exceptional in that they worked hard and did not absorb public funding in the countries where they worked. Two cartoons illustrate these two conflicting visions. The first was published in the Cork *Examiner* in October 1997.[19] Printed above the headline of an opinion column entitled 'More Free Rides on the Tiger's Back' (Brosnan, 1997), it shows checkouts at Rosslare Port labelled 'Customs', 'Dole', 'Passports' and 'Asylum'. The customs checkout is unmanned, indicating freedom of passage into Ireland. The 'Dole' and 'Passports' checkouts are busy, and the last is manned by a smoking civil servant. Four non-white figures (an Iranian Muslim, a black woman and two dark-skinned and bearded men, one of whom has a child in his rucksack) are in the Rosslare arrivals hall taking advantage of the benefits provided. All are entering the country rapaciously with their hands on Irish resources, as implied in the headline.

There are two things to observe from this, it must be said, uncharacteristic cartoon in that particular publication. First, the stereotypical bestiality of the figures recalls images of Jews in Europe of the 1930s and simianised Irish figures from *Punch* to the Jak's *Evening Standard* (Curtis, 1984). The message from this type of image is clearly that foreigners are here to take from us, and their deceit is mirrored in their physical Otherness.

Second, the story above which the cartoon appears has nothing to do with non-Europeans and is instead about Romanians who had stowed away in a container lorry. Even in that column, the case of five people who have already been granted asylum elsewhere is conflated with 'thousands of illegal immigrants' (a groundless figure). It is concluded, on no basis whatsoever, that of the 4,000 'immigrants' who have presented themselves for asylum, 'the bulk of them are just trying to leech off the Celtic Tiger' (Brosnan, 1997). At first glance, the cartoon might appear to be a representation of the story, as it does provide an image to fit the caption. However, none of the figures in the cartoon could be seen as stereotypical Romanians. As the distinctions between asylum-seekers, refugees and immigrants (legal or illegal) are progressively blurred by imprecise use of the terms as synonyms, so in this cartoon are the biographies of those in each category swapped round: black people are synonyms for Romanians, and the social security payments to which they are entitled under law are undermined by an image positing them as gaining them under false pretences. This cartoon, juxtaposed with the article on the page on which it is printed, raises the spectre of illegal and unjustified access to resources (a 'free ride') which should, it is assumed, be targeted on those who have first claim to the 'Tiger's back'.

The second cartoon, (Martyn Turner in the *Irish Times*, June 2000) follows the logic of the Immigration Control Platform's call for all non-EU foreigners to be repatriated if applied to the Irish diaspora (Figure 6). ICP spokeswoman Áine Ní Chonaill speaks at a rally over the slogan 'Everyone Go Home', while the returning migrants huddle on a crowded island on which there is standing room only.

The issue of migratory experience therefore seems to play a role of some kind, which further research should aim to pinpoint more precisely. In the work of McVeigh (1992, 1996) and Rolston and Shannon (2002), the idea that migrants return with racist ideas and/or import them through communication is assumed but important. The evidence from the poll question cited above indicates that the relationship may well be worth exploring further. It flags up ambivalence around people's collective location in global power hierarchies, and refers to collective experience of trauma, displacement and loss. Lentin (2001) points to the centrality of migration in Irish racialisation, calling it 'the return of the national repressed'. Certainly, migrant experience provides a 'specular' mediation because the place and

*Figure 6*   The Logical Conclusion of the Immigration Control Platform. 'Everyone Go Home', Martyn Turner, 2000. © Martyn Turner.

function of immigrants is understood as in part a reflection and distortion of one's own precarious attachment to an ever-more insecure employment and welfare base. From an orthodox Marxist perspective then, migration functions as both a structural factor (part of the economic base) and a superstructural one (an ideological relationship of person to labour to social hierarchy), generating ideas about self-worth. Yet the rigid distinction between base and superstructure is not supported in application to an example such as migrant experience, which continuously merges these two virtual arenas.

## CONCLUSIONS

'Working-class racism', a term used here to denote a difference of emphasis only, appears to have coalesced around welfare and employment and perceived illegitimate competition between nationals and foreigners. In this process of making sense of change, there is an articulation of the local with the global, and with new employment conditions (more casualisation, greater precariousness), that focusses on an implicit critique of the state, seen as privileging the Other over the national.

In terms of the collective national imaginary, there is a reinvestment of old images with new content; memories of migration mitigate hostility but generate painful ambivalence and contradiction. The fact that the immigrant Other is 'us', exploited and mauled by market forces, thwarts the process of racialisation, which places 'them' and 'us' irrevocably on distinct sides of a boundary. For those experiencing the most insecure conditions, and in the midst of rising prices, this re-emphasises the precariousness they experience (hence the near-obsessive focus on welfare and employment) despite evidence of dual labour markets and the non-existence of financial privilege for foreign nationals.

The hypothesis to be tested then is that in terms of racist discourse there is *heightened ambivalence due to experience of migration*. Migration is specular and blurs some of the connections made between 'race' and nation. It is continually disrupting the narrative of nation as essentialised community (from which racism draws ideological sustenance). Indeed, the effort to re-imagine an idealised community is one of the motors both of resistance to globalisation (seen as faceless omnipresence) as well as of right-wing populist parties' electoral success in Western Europe. Yet permanent full-time work in an industrial sector with union backing is increasingly a minority experience, and the family values and work ethics of migrant groups are frequently seen as desirable yet alienating representations of 'our' communities in the past (White, 2002).[20] Indeed, Hall (2000:229) pinpoints this as a danger area, arguing that 'the temptation to essentialise community' is 'a fantasy of plenitude in circumstances of imagined loss'. In racialisation, a process that derives its potency from decomposing the collective into the personal and then recomposing racialised fractions of a class, the shared experience of migration acts as a brake on the facile adversarial alignment of 'us' and 'them'; rather it sketches a fragile bridge binding 'us' to 'them'.

Yet the trauma of separation and alienation, and the debilitating blow to self-worth sustained by most participants in the migratory process and transmitted in the collective consciousness that is 'Irishness' or 'Sicilianness', for example, cannot be worked out without conflict. The desire to bridge this separation is coupled with desire to repress it. Working-class racism is a balancing act involving contradictory impulses that spur people to re-imagine themselves as others. Around the bodies of migrants emerges a force field of anxieties and tensions engaging both the 'national' and the 'migrant'. Perhaps this is also one way to conceptualise Brah's 'diaspora space': as a zone of counterbalancing tensions in which the actors attempt not to lose sight of who they are not.

# 8
# 'Remember Blanqui?': Nation State, Community and Some Paradoxes of Irish Anti-Racism

By the early 1990s anti-racism projects in Europe were in crisis over objectives and frameworks (Gilroy, 1990; Taguieff, 1990a, 1990b). The populist Right had long since captured the agenda, advocating national preference in employment and welfare in the face of new migrations in the post-war period. This ended up influencing the platforms of mainstream parties, both traditional conservative and social democrat, which now speak in terms of 'getting tough' on asylum-seekers and thresholds of tolerance.

Moreover, the ideologies of both anti-racist and racist organisations have shared an attachment to the trope of difference (Taguieff, 1990a, 1990b; Gilroy, 1990, 1998). Anti-racist practice values difference, placing respect for 'cultural difference' at the centre of its project since the mid 1970s. The anti-immigration lobbies had treated racial (that is, phenotypical) difference as the primary focus of opposition until the late 1960s, when they transformed their political discourse to refocus on culture and reappropriate difference as a mobilising instrument. The French Front national for example hijacked the radical slogan 'droit à la différence' (the right to be different) from the Left and used it to sanction rights to segregation. Mixing between alien and national cultures, they argued, would ultimately dilute both (Taguieff, 1990a, 1990b). Gilroy (1990) notes that much anti-racist theorising in the 1970s and 1980s drew from the same well as racism, taking as its founding assumption that 'races' were real biological entities whose members should have equal rights.

Indeed, seen from this perspective, not only have anti-racists differed only in interpretation from racists, but anti-racist political projects have sometimes done the latter's work for them. What might be labelled 'municipal anti-racism' among Labour-led councils in 1980s UK used the equation: prejudice + power = racism. The surrounding logic, argues Gilroy (1987, 1990), reinforced stereotypes of minorities as victims (always powerless) having things done to them while offering no resistance, and relying on white people (as the empowered agents of change) to re-adjust their attitudes. Focussing on individuals altering their attitudes and behaviour, as embodied in racism awareness training or 'RAT' (Sivanandan, 1985), served not to liberate but further disempower racialised minorities. Apart from reifying the 'black–white' paradigm (by assuming homogeneity of power among the 'white' group), against which I argue throughout this book, this formulation also ignored the institutional element of racism which has been recognised since the late 1960s in North America and since the 1970s in European legislation.

By the beginning of the twenty-first century, the politics of anti-racism has been led into cul-de-sacs. Even tackling the Right or social democratic governments directly on the issues of immigration and asylum has fuelled the development of a new racist consensus (between Left and Right in government) that limiting numbers and being 'tough' on 'bogus' asylum-seekers is the only reasonable policy option. This has been clearly evident in the UK and Italy, where immigration is the principal arena in which racism is debated (Ritaine, 1999; Andall, 2000) and attention is focussed onto this at the expense of human rights themes. Moreover, Hargreaves (2002) argues that media attention granted to the issue of immigration *per se*, from whatever perspective, actually boosted the Front national's vote more than its own activities managed to do. Indeed, not only is there a consensus that immigration represents a threat for the European Union, but also the first signs of a political willingness to challenge the acquis of the post-war period. The Danish presidency of the EU (July–December 2002) saw the floating of the idea that refugee status should no longer be permanent but subject to frequent review based on the political situation in the refugee's country of origin (Statewatch, 2002).

Working from the French republican paradigm, Cathie Lloyd (1998) has highlighted the continuing struggle between the universal and the particular over meanings in anti-racist struggle. The universal is viewed as a creation of the Enlightenment that has since come to assume hegemonic status; it is the basis of the notion of equality within the liberal nation state. Yet this value comes to demonstrate its own particularity when confronted with collectively-oriented cultural values derived from non-Western traditions. This topic has exercised writers on multiculturalism and citizenship such as Parekh (2000) and is key to thinking through the relationships between social movements and the state, since it is by assuming the terrain of the universal that the state places itself in a position to delineate areas of struggle as particular (that is, sectional and detrimental to its claim to just governance).

Against the backdrop of the broad debates outlined above, this chapter focusses on some of the crucial framing issues of the nation state impinging on the anti-racist vision, from an Irish perspective. Its objective is to clarify some relationships between the hegemonic ideology of the nation state and anti-racist struggle, and some structural limits that these impose. The assumption on which this analysis is constructed is that anti-racism is caught in a self-defeating trap if it reifies either 'race', or nation, or both and ignores the articulation of racism, class domination and sexism. This is especially true of Ireland, where the development of feminism and the working-class movement has been subsumed, reconfigured and retarded by the political energies devoted to resolving the 'national question' and the ensuing flourishing of sectarianism in the post-1922 period, Connolly's famous 'carnival of reaction'.

Yet it is the form of the nation state rather than nationalism itself, which constitutes the largest ideological obstacle to the development of a holistic politics of liberation. Nationalisms are plural and multifaceted, but the nation state in twentieth-century Ireland (Lee, 1989; Mac Laughlin, 1997, 1999b, 2001) assumed the bourgeois form that had been predictable from the elite formation process of the second half of the nineteenth century. In Chapters 5 and 6, some of the ideological streams within nineteenth- and early-twentieth-century nationalism were identified as placing emphasis on 'race' as national essence. These streams stressed lines of closure and inclusion around the Gaelic, Catholic, sedentary and rural. This, despite the increasingly secular nature of contemporary Ireland, remains the 'default setting' of nationalism as represented by the Constitution (Lentin, 1998, 1999), populist nationalist and republican parties and the institutional creations of the state. The challenge facing anti-racism in this context is thinking beyond the ideological confines of the nation state.[1] The political imperatives of formulating vernacular anti-racist strategies and 'inventing' a tradition of open rather than closed 'fictive ethnicity' (Balibar, 1991b) thus have to be balanced against the necessity of deconstructing the very framework within which the initial process is put into action. By this I mean that the notion of Irish anti-racism supposes work within a nation state, around a network recognising itself to be distinctively national. Yet qualifying anti-racism as a project *with borders* detracts from the overriding transversal dynamic required to reconceptualise 'race' (as well as class and gender) as both contained within, and extending beyond, the nation, that is, inhabiting a space other than the nation state alone.

## REMEMBERING AND FORGETTING

One of the major ideological functions of the nation is to suppress inequalities, which is accomplished through erasures and denial and an ideological position representing the nation state as the modern destination of civilisation, while portraying all other struggles (class, feminism, ethnic minorities, and so on) as 'sectional', 'tribal' and backward. A secondary function is thus an intentional suppression of memory such as that referred to by Renan, one of the first theorists of the nation state. Renan remarked laconically that regarding the development of national feeling: 'Forgetting, and I would go so far as to say even error, are essential factors in nation-building, and this explains why progress in historical studies is often a threat for nationalist feeling' (1992 [1885]:41).[2]

Lloyd (1999) states that in nationalist (that is, mainstream) historiography, social movements are addressed only in so far as they can be seen to contribute to the victory of nationalism in capturing the state. Other than that, they become 'history's incommensurables' (ibid.:26), viewed merely as pre-rational splinters of the nation state trunk. Walter Benjamin (1969:260) identifies this type of suppression as a form of repression, a symbolic violence enacted against movements whose trajectories exceed nationalism in its nation state form and yet are articulated with it. The French radical tradition's affirmation of memory over forgetting, 'Remember Blanqui!', served to keep open one interpretation of the revolution that had not been appropriated. This rallying cry, argues Benjamin, was erased by social democracy.[3]

The problem then is to keep open lines of contestation of the nation state's appropriation of other movements, be they ecology, feminism, equality or anti-racism. More precisely, in terms of the latter, there is a requirement to find an internationalist source of inspiration from within a national (and in Ireland's case, largely nationalist) tradition, a 'Blanqui' to remember as life-reaffirming force, as protection against the deadening handshake of the state. The snag for Irish anti-racism is that the political tradition available for trawling is one peopled principally with characters whose historical mission was to unite or represent a vision of the Irish people (or 'race') in its struggle not to be a political subsidiary of the English people (or 'race') and British state. There was no dynamic of internationalism available that could take root in the Irish situation after the failure of the United Irishmen movement, with its toes dipped in French revolutionary-style activity and support for abolition of slavery.

Indeed it is another irony that the most internationalist Irish leader, Daniel O'Connell, active in the struggle for emancipation from slavery and anti-imperialism in India (Riach, 1976; Allen, 1994b; Rolston and Shannon, 2002),[4] was also the one who focussed his efforts most exclusively on representing the nation 'properly so called', and, most importantly, on opening the doors of professional life to its most-educated strata. 'Remember Connolly' may be the closest we can get, although 'Remember Ryan' would have slightly more purchase in emancipatory critical politics, while 'Remember Casement' is too shrouded in controversy to rally anyone other than a handful of academics to a seminar. Maverick internationalists like Margaret Cousins, Hubert Butler and Edward Despard[5] were thrown up and their contributions are worthy of incorporation into an anti-racist tradition, but no indelible collective path from Irish struggle to that of other oppressed peoples was trodden until very recently, despite the largely ignored tracks heading in the other direction (Rolston and Shannon, 2002:44–8) involving activists such as Claude McKay and Marcus Garvey. Even when the hands of solidarity were held out, it was usually within the framework of nations or nations-in-waiting attempting to remove colonial masters (the Indian National Congress and the Boers), rather than anything more sophisticated, and, as was noted in Chapter 6, care was usually taken to leave clear blue water between the Irish claims for independence and those of other colonised people.

It is by this narrowing of the framework in which progressive politics are viewed, that the nation state represents a considerable hurdle. The nation state is our doxa, limiting the spectrum of possibilities without us being aware of it. It is the 'natural' unit, the territory within which social action is to take place. Moreover, the state itself enacts an active policy, according to Balibar (1991b:93), of 'producing the people'. This degree of dominance in terms of organisational possibilities is particularly damaging when the issue is one of counteracting social forms justified by appeals to 'nature', as is the case of anti-racism, since the nation state itself is one of these forms. Balibar writes: 'It is the characteristic feature of states of all types to represent the order they represent as eternal, though practice shows that more or less the opposite is the case' (ibid.:88).

The corollary of this representation is that alternatives have to be neutralised, by sapping them of their sustenance. In 'Nationalisms against the State', David Lloyd argues that:

> without doubt the desire of nationalism is to saturate the field of subject formation so that for every individual, the idea of nationality of political citizenship, becomes the central organising term, in relation to which other possible modes of subjectification – class or gender, to cite only the most evident instances – are differentiated and subordinated. (1999:27)[6]

His thesis includes the idea that the nation state posits itself as the bearer of modernity and rationality, implicitly opposing this to the regressive and irrational 'transversal' social movements: class politics, feminism, minority rights, and so on. From this perspective, 'the people' are viewed always as potentially 'excessive' in their capacity to disturb the narrative of the nation state as work completed. Moreover, the state develops 'ideological or repressive state apparatuses' to 'expunge' 'cultural or social forms which are in excess of its own rationality and whose own rationale is other than its own' (ibid.:36). The experience of trade unions and community organisations in Ireland conveys some of the tension between the two poles of rationality and irrationality raised by Lloyd, and I shall examine this before engaging with a theoretical model put forward to explain the relatively small democratic space available for the advance and consolidation of anti-racist, counter-hegemonic ideas in Ireland in the early twenty-first century.

## WORKERS AND COMMUNITY GROUPS IN THE STIFLING EMBRACE OF PARTNERSHIP

The 'social partnership model' involves corporate involvement of interest groups in negotiating medium-term national agreements on the management of the economy. The model was developed in Ireland in the late 1980s, with the Programme for National Recovery (1987–90). Partnership 2000 (1997–2000) and the Programme for Prosperity and Fairness (PPF) (2000–02) cover most of the period investigated in this book, while Sustaining Progress (2003–05) was being negotiated in spring 2003.[7] There are four 'pillars' (Trade Unions, Employer and Business, the Farming Pillar and the Community and Voluntary Pillar (included for the first time in negotiations on

Partnership 2000)). In his critique of partnership, Allen (2000) contends that class politics become represented as 'sectional', 'selfish', and anti-national because they would be 'bad for the economy'. The interests of the dominant classes, assisted by what he refers to as 'business unionism', which helps the state and the business community to manage the labour force and thereby benefit the higher wage-earners and shareholders disproportionately (see Chapter 2), are depicted as 'national' (that is, rational and modern). An opposing view to Allen's, arguing that wage restraint and active involvement from other pillars have enabled a greater distribution of wealth than would otherwise have been possible can be found in Sweeney (1998). Allen's argument is based on the idea that the labour movement in Ireland has been subservient to the interests of the nation state since its post-Connolly inception, and to the interests of capital under the partnerships agreements, which are negotiated by groups of professional unionists whose lives and outlooks are far closer to those of their counterparts in government and employers' associations than to those of their membership. He cites union leader Tom Johnson claiming in 1925 to be a 'community-ist and a nation-ist before I am a trade unionist'. Sounding like Griffith, Johnson stated: 'We must preach the gospel of faithful service – for the uplifting of the nation – materially and spiritually.'[8]

Mergers of unions, actively encouraged by state subsidy, argues Allen (2000.:115), citing the creation of the Communications Workers Union (1989) and the Services, Industrial, Professional and Technical Union (SIPTU) in 1990, decreased the probability of breakaway unions engaging in strike action. Moreover, the Department of Enterprise brought in regulations that made the issuing of a licence to a union contingent upon having 1,000 members. This has had the effect of *de facto* reducing the number of participants in the trade union arena, and making it easier to find consensus.

After fraught discussion, the largest unions recommended the new partnership agreement to their members in March 2003. The Community Pillar, however, refused to sign up, and is poised to begin campaigning for greater public spending and anti-exclusion initiatives. This is not surprising given the experiences of community sector delegates (Galway Community Workers' Co-operative, 2000; Murphy 2002). Partnership is a model based on the concept of sectional representation, with 'pillars' comprising various sectors of the nation, a microcosm of the national family. The power relations within partnership, however, are not only visible in the material disparities

ensuing from the agreements, but in the experiences of new participants. Invited to take part in negotiations in 2000, community
organisations expressed dissatisfaction with the arrangements, sensing
that they were seen as being there 'on sufferance', or 'by invitation
only' (Murphy, 2000), while the more powerful pillars had made their
demands the core of partnership and consensus, that is, 'common
sense' interests, dictating the 'rational' way to proceed, to use Lloyd's
framework for the ideological work of the nation state. In the wake
of early rejection of the 2003 agreement by both Farming and
Community pillars, Green Party spokesman Dan Boyle TD criticised
the parameters of the partnership process:

> Of course the exclusion of opposition party input has long been
> a flaw of the social partnership process, but this now seems to have
> been extended to exclude some of the social partners themselves.
> The non-involvement of the community and voluntary and the
> farming sectors, underlines the extent to which social partner-
> ship is now a partnership where some 'partners' are more equal
> than others [...] by discussing, and seeming to agree on items of
> a social nature, the Government and 'superior' social partners are
> undermining the prospect of including other social areas in a wider
> national agreement. (Green Party, 2003)

Under the PPF, the eponymous notion of fairness was questioned by
community representatives, as budget surplus was used to pay off
national debt rather than invested in revitalisation programmes.
Moreover, community organisations in partnership also had to
negotiate hard to retain any ownership over their projects derived
from the PPF, such as the RAPID initiative aimed at urban areas of
high unemployment (O'Donoghue, 2000). The rationale for rejecting
the 2003–05 partnership agreement is exactly this deprioritisation of
social exclusion relative to macro-economic development, of which,
as evidenced by patterns of income distribution and types of wealth
created over the 1990s (Chapter 2), for example, the wealthier groups
are disproportionately the beneficiaries. In this 'solidarity without
equality', in the ESRI's words, 'one's "fairness quotient" is broadly
dependent on one's class of origin' (O'Keeffe, 2001:15). However,
while it is clear that the Community and Voluntary Pillar is critical
of the spending priorities, it is less obvious to what extent criticism
takes the structural element of power relationships into account.
Partnership is posited as above all serving the national interest through

the creation of a consensus that has laid the foundations for Ireland's dramatic economic growth over the last decade, yet it appears to be based on a profoundly undemocratic practice, in that it is dominated by a very small number of interests and key actors. Given the ambiguous relationship between state and community outlined here, what is the link between notions of 'race' and community and how does it impact upon the Irish anti-racist struggle?

## 'RACE', 'FICTIVE ETHNICITY' AND COMMUNITY

It has been stressed throughout that although 'race' has no biological basis, it is perceived, in a myriad of incoherent and only sporadically articulated forms, as a way of making sense of phenotypical and cultural differences. The classic form of the nation state, expressed in its nineteenth-century model, is a people with a historical claim on a territory who share a culture and, by extension, bloodlines. The political effort to make people coterminous with territory was one of the objectives of nineteenth- and twentieth-century nation-builders, and failure to do so is cited as a principal cause of instability in a paradigm of timeless ethnic conflict of which Rwanda and the former Yugoslavia, *inter alia*, are given as examples. Since the model referred to above is an ideal, the reality is that borders usually do not coincide with ethnic groups' own ideas of where 'their' territory begins and ends, and the exclusive and possessive attachment to contested territory is often one element of conflict. The social reality for nation-builders is that shoehorning people into places is messier, and more contradictory and open to question than they would like, and a dominant idea of who is a member of the nation emerges in a dominant national myth, in which opposing narratives are elided or minimised. Balibar (1991b:93) writes:

> No modern nation possesses a given 'ethnic' basis, even when it arises out of a national independence struggle. And moreover, no modern nation, no matter how 'egalitarian' it may be, corresponds to the extinction of class conflicts. The fundamental problem is therefore to produce the people. More exactly, it is to make the people produce itself continually as national community.

What he terms 'fictive ethnicity' is produced by the nationalist movement and/or the state to make it appear as though each generation transfers some national 'essence' to the next. This is achieved through language and/or 'race' (ibid.:95).

Yet language alone is not enough. It can be learned perfectly by those outside the ethno-national 'we': children of immigrants and excluded minorities for example. Membership of a linguistic community then is not in itself a reliable gauge of membership of the nation properly so called. The biological essentialising element of 'fictive ethnicity' is 'race', which provides a marker of closure: and 'race' is family on a larger scale.

From this angle, the Irish case generates some interesting points. The Gaelic League, which promoted the Irish language as the vehicle of national values and identity from the end of the nineteenth century, was to a disproportionate extent the work of Protestant scholars. Linguistic community (read as Irish ethnicity) enabled them to posit equal claims on membership of a nationalist tradition whose space had narrowed for them since they had dominated the movement a century before. The ideological work of Irish Ireland nationalists in this respect was successful in that mastery of Irish, while still retaining a symbolic power[9] was not the dividing line between genuine (Catholic) and bogus (Protestant) national, but between exceptional and common Irish people. The idea of 'racial' closure, that is, the key component of Irish 'fictive ethnicity' from the inception of the state, was focussed on the English intervention. I have referred to comments about the composition of the Irish racial stock by Charles Haughey (Chapter 2), George Sigerson, Sean O'Faoláin, and Micheál Martin (Chapter 3). They all envisage a formative period in which Normans, Danes and Celts are absorbed into a Gaelic culture, which then becomes the essence of the Irish 'race'. As Moran famously stated, the 'Gael must be the element that absorbs'.[10]

From the arrival of the English, all immigration is alien and unassimilable. The political reasons for this portrayal are complex and comprehensible within the logic of Irish nationalism: it would have made no political sense to argue in the late nineteenth century or early twentieth that the gene pool of coloniser and colonised was virtually identical (Saxons, Normans, Danes, Celts). The point to note, however, is that this cut-off point in Irish lineage is a political not genetic one. It is not necessarily an anti-racist argument *per se* to advance a nation's capacity for absorbing various 'races' into its own, since it presupposes both the existence of 'races' beyond the social, and power relations inimical to the absorbed groups. What the argument does invite, however, is logical consistency: migration and inter-marriage (regardless of the structural relationships governing the individuals) have meant that, genetically, the Irish, like other Europeans, have no absolute racial boundary, any more than any other nation. This is not to say that Irish culture is no different from any other, merely to underscore the separation of the ideological from the biological.

Given the particular spin put on the Irish nation, that is, that it was naturally Gaelic, rural, Catholic and sedentary, what effect does this have on the development of racism and anti-racism? After all McVeigh (1992) cites the particular emphasis given to community as one of the 'specificities of Irish racism'. A clear and concise argument is put forward by O'Carroll (2002). He critically models the various forms of representation of Irish society by the state (see Table 20). Setting the development of the state in Ireland against the corresponding underdevelopment of civil society, he argues that the early Free State's 'essential task' was 'legitimation and identity formation' (ibid.:13). This placed limits on voluntary activity and local government and immediately limited the potential growth of civil society. The 'small community' was what he terms the 'modal identity' of Irish life, and 'community' implied 'unity, wholeness and belonging; it imparted a strong sense of place and a hierarchy of entitlements' (ibid.:126). Indeed, the rural communal ideal was increasingly deployed as an image of the nation by the reactionary state throughout the 1930s and 1940s. Gibbons (1996:103) comments:

> the rhetoric of the 'nation', based on ideals of organic, small community, continued to be pressed into service to conceal the gap between the periphery and the centre, the parish and the state, in republican politics. The idealisation of an agrarian order of small-holders increased in proportion as its practical implementation receded from view.

Distinctive features of this community were that it was thus open to clientelism, dominated by face-to-face relations, and that the boundary between similarity and difference became primordial. As a result, Irish identity became deeply embedded in the idea of the normal. Referring to Brow (1990), Gibbons argues that its power lay not in rational persuasion but in remaining unspoken (1996:127).

The modern format for representation based on social partnership, is corporatism, which conflates economy and society, and evokes constant uses of 'we' to describe the country. In this model, the

*Table 20*   Representations of Irish Society by the State

| Society as: | Implications for society | Political consequences |
| --- | --- | --- |
| Nation | Elites in direct contact with 'the people' | Aim is political integration |
| | Attribution of common culture | Loyalty and partnership emphasised |
| | Society itself becomes less visible | Intermediate structures excluded |
| | | Local government and voluntary activity suspect |
| Community writ large | Over-emphasis on harmony, consensus and reconciliation | Validity of dissent questioned |
| | Society misrepresented as face-to-face interaction and tacit understandings | Little concept of citizenship or public sphere |
| | | Cronyism and clientelism |
| | 'Deviant' or stranger easily stigmatised | Tendency toward xenophobia |
| Corporation | State-directed organisation of economy | Agenda limited and agency denied, particularly to unorganised |
| | Participation licensed by state: self-organisation hindered | Major difficulty instigating new policies or raising issues identified by communities |
| | Focus on economy de-emphasises society, culture and public space | |

Source: O'Carroll, 2002

emphasis is on consensus and co-optation, which deprive communal organisations of the capacity to raise and mobilise around the defence of difference. As a result, the public sphere is fragile and underdeveloped. There is difficulty finding space for articulating difference and arguments. Community organisations are seen by the state not as bodies for articulating difference but sameness. This is combined with the neo-liberal philosophy that views affluence as a panacea, and O'Carroll maintains that the model thus arrived at has debilitated Irish society in that it has made it virtually incapable of dealing with social change, particularly that involving socially-constructed difference, for instance, immigration. Thus the understanding of 'community' as inherently small-scale, closed and ethnic militates against more pluralist interpretations involving mobility.[11] Perhaps it should not be so surprising, in this light, that the most vehement opposition to the Department of Justice's dispersal programme in spring 2000 came from villages and small towns such as Clogheen (Co. Tipperary), Myshall (Co. Carlow) and Rosslare (Co. Wexford).[12] Moreover, O'Carroll's model matches that of community organisations' experiences accrued in social partnership over the last few years. This constriction of public space in which to operate 'at home' is mirrored in the contradictory processes occurring in terms of civil society in the EU and beyond. The trend toward dismantling borders (if only to rebuild them elsewhere) is taking place parallel to one in which the social gains accrued over a century or so are also being taken apart, more surreptitiously.

## NO FRONTIERS?

In her discussion of Germany since unification, Räthzel (2002) points out that racism cannot be fought adequately within the nation state. She gives the example of the limits acting on potentially progressive social actors, such as the trade union movement, which grounds its calls for equality in national preference. Retaining wage levels for German construction workers involves foreigners losing their (less well-paid) jobs, yet the lower wages accepted by them means that there is a level of constant unemployment among their German counterparts. 'It seems as if fighting for social justice on a national level is bound to (re)produce social injustice between nationals and non-nationals. Or to put it more sharply, it seems as if the fight for social justice is based on racism' (ibid.:81). This same response is shared by Irish protagonists. In response to the passage of the Employment Act 2003, which allows workers from the ten 'accession states' to enter and work in Ireland without visas (O'Brien, 2003) as of 1 January 2004, the President of the Irish Congress of Trade Unions (ICTU), (Senator) Joe O'Toole, 'welcomed the Government's decision, but warned our first priority must be the labour needs of our own citizens'. The qualifying statement was to assert that 'it was important that foreign workers were not exploited, and that employers must respect their rights'. The ideological contradiction that such nationalising logic and class aporia represent has been naturalised to the point where it appears reasonable for a workers' solidarity organisation to defend 'national' labour markets from foreign competition, even in the face of evidence that there are still labour shortages. Moreover, workers from 'third countries' have not been allowed to compete directly, and, unless they collectively and dramatically change professions, will not be in positions to do so for years. The line of national defence places foreign workers structurally into a permanent temporary position, with all the attendant insecurity, inability to plan and enjoy one's home life, and impediments to social equity (they pay taxes but cannot vote, do not have company pensions, and so on).

Indeed, the national labour movements are trapped within this differential logic in a way that capital is not and has scarcely ever been. It is not for nothing that the relatively underdeveloped role and position of EU-level trade unions (ETUC) and European Works Councils have been identified with concern by proponents of a 'Social Europe' with greater balance between employers and workforces, such as Bourdieu (1998:71).[13] The ability of organised labour to operate beyond national boundaries (albeit within the supranational ones of the European Union) will be a key check on, or ally of, neo-liberal forces in the decades ahead.

For Irish workers, there is a confusing set of historical echoes in all of this. Ireland is diasporic and, on one level, an international idea. It has experienced vast and ongoing emigration. The charges of foreign workers potentially lowering wages recall the same accusations levelled at the Irish in nineteenth-century Britain and America, while the option of going illegal in the USA is open principally because of Irish immigrants' 'possessive investment' (Lipsitz, 1995, 1998; Luibhéid, 1997a) in whiteness. Moreover, they underwent the transition from strike-breaker to unionist in both those destinations, playing progressive and radical roles in the Chartists, the syndicalist unions of the last decade of the nineteenth century, and becoming labour martyrs like the Molly Maguires in the Pennsylvania coalfields in 1877. Grounded within a tradition in which mobility and solidarity are key features of the landscape, Irish labour is now coming face to face with its reflection: in the growing Irish-based diasporas of Eastern Europe, Asia and to a lesser extent Africa.

It has been noted in previous chapters that opposing lines of discourse seek to establish a duty to treat immigrants with respect and solidarity on one hand, and on the other to mark them as more threatening and less willing to work than Irish emigrants. The Irish trade union movement has so far been an active and progressive element in the institutionalised anti-racist effort of the past few years. The real test of its membership's resolve may well be in 15 to 20 years' time, when the children of today's immigrants enter the job market as hyphenated Irish, thus bringing the issues of belonging, citizenship and eligibility to the fore in a new arena. That arena will be a European labour market, access to which is governed by contemporary legislation on migration, asylum, equality, and so forth, derived from the European Union.

In the post-11 September order, global security agendas have usurped civil society's claims on defining and addressing risk. Civil liberties, and among those the right to equal and fair treatment for minority groups, have suffered greatly from the fallout of the attacks on the USA. The outburst of opposition to the dispersal of asylum-seekers in Britain in winter 2003 is indicative of the results of state policies that criminalise immigrants *en masse* as part of measures concerned with tightening up security.

We should, however, be wary of the notion that a clampdown on immigration and focus on the movement of particular groups began in late 2001. Ireland's anti-dispersal rebellions occurred in spring 2000 for example. Within the European Union, unaccountable executive bodies such as Trevi and the Rhodes Group have been acting to limit the movement of EU and non-EU citizens alike, in contravention of the Union's founding charter, the Treaty of Rome. Moreover, the process of formalising hitherto informal security arrangements together with the practice of the USA sitting in on EU preparatory working groups means that the United States' input into the European Union on these matters is at least as important as any EU member-state government, which leads Bunyan (2002:7) to the conclusion that 'the USA is in effect the 16th member of the EU'.

The process formally begun by the Schengen Accords in the early 1990s, of constructing a *de facto* common EU immigration policy, was accelerated, rather than generated by, the events of 11 September. Whilst theoretically allowing greater freedom of movement within the Schengen Zone for EU nationals, its parallel aim of bolstering external borders has enabled the immigration agenda to be dominated not by questions of integration and citizenship (a secondary issue left to DG V (Social Affairs)) but those of security, policing, and the obtaining and holding of data in extra-legal contexts. Indeed the ever-broadening scope of powers accumulated by security forces within the EU, much of which is occurring beyond the reach of elected representatives (Mac Éinri, 2002),[14] makes arguments about losing national sovereignty to Brussels academic. In the meantime, moves are under way to roll back the gains derived from implementation of the 1951 Geneva Convention and the 1967 New York Protocol. I noted earlier that the question of refugee status became a priority when Denmark took over the EU presidency. The idea that status would require periodical re-assessment was debated (Statewatch, 2003, 2002).[15] In late March 2003, the UK Home Secretary, David Blunkett, revealed plans for a strategy of militarising Europe's borders and pressurising non-EU neighbours such as Turkey, Tunisia and Russia to take responsibility for holding asylum-seekers (IRR, 2003).

Clearly, the EU's immigration policy is moving to a new period in which the social gains of the post-war period are being jettisoned. This is why the distinction made between European Economic Area (EEA) nationals[16] and non-EEA (or 'third country') nationals is increasingly important and becoming a new racialised border. For Irish activists, this has to be a principal structural feature of any analysis seeking to understand the pertinent distinction between Irish national and non-national, and its ramifications. Calls for fingerprinting of all non-EEA nationals from the head of the Garda National Immigration Bureau in the wake of the Supreme Court's January 2003 decision on rights of residence (Collins, 2003) only make sense in a context of intersecting lines of demarcation classifying people into EEA (that is, unproblematic migrants) and non-EEA nationals (problematic migrants), where the precedent of fingerprinting asylum-seekers *per se* (that is, suspected of no crime) after the 1999 Tampere Meeting of EU Ministers, had already been established.

'Third country' nationals, those unfortunate enough to enjoy citizenship of countries outside Europe, require visas for travel into and within the EU. Additionally there are 'white lists' of countries whose nationals do not require Schengen, or Irish visas[17] although they do for employment and residence. For these individuals, the process of obtaining a tourist visa is complicated, time-consuming and demanding, since they have to satisfy not only the requirement to show financial support but also prove that they are not going to overstay the visa and work illegally. There is obviously no way to prove that a future action will not take place, and it is the right of the official processing the application to refuse a visa. The onus then is on applicants to prove they have no criminal intent. The mere fact of having citizenship of a nation not listed as 'clean' places the applicant in a position of suspicion.[18] One example is indicative. In 2002, a colleague who is an Irish citizen applied for a member of his immediate family (from a 'third country') to stay during the summer on a three-month tourist visa. The family member is a single man in his 20s who speaks little English. The application was refused on the basis that the man fitted a profile of someone who was likely to overstay. In the context of citizenship thrown up by the 2003 Supreme Court ruling referred to below, this incident appears to fit into a framework of institutionalised selectivity about which citizens enjoy which rights. That particular Irish citizen was *de facto* prevented from receiving a family member as a guest in his home, let alone family reunification (another right guaranteed by citizenship).

Yet in a way the ambivalence exhibited by successive Irish admin-istrations is an echo of similar contradictions at EU level. Equality and social justice directives are introduced and implemented against a backdrop of liberalisation and the emphasis on security, which means there is a permanent contradiction in welcoming and excluding, seeking a workforce, restricting access to European labour markets, and so on. Having said this, Ireland has a record of procras-tination in the area of transcribing EU directives on equality into national law, and even though it is not a Schengen state, the Common Travel Area was a proto-Schengen Zone (Mac Éinri, 2002). It is impossible to talk of Irish state responses to asylum-seeking without acknowledging that, territorially, Ireland and the UK are enmeshed in one another, with all the repercussions that has for the border-policing activities of the two states. With an entire continent's immigration policy predicated on a Manichean distinction between potentially good and potentially bad aliens, and a framework based on Europe's colonial past, the space for anti-racist activity appears narrow, contested and shrinking.

## TOWARDS THE CONSTRUCTION OF AN IRISH ANTI-RACIST TRADITION

Just as nations require metanarratives, so do radical movements. The slim strands of Irish anti-racism remain relatively isolated, geograph-ically, ideologically and culturally, and this a speculative attempt to help construct (or invent!) a tradition. What follows is necessarily sketchy, and is intended to begin rather than close a discussion.

A general point to make is that while Irish nationalists have made a very good job of creating a narrative of continuity in the Irish nation, as people, 'race' and territory, this should not be seen as the blueprint for projects other than nationalism. As demonstrated in the preceding chapters, not all resistance to imperialism takes an anti-racist form, any more than it does a 'nationalist' one. The type of narrative that will be produced is certain to be non-linear, contradictory and incoherent: there is no grand storyline, no culmination of historical forces towards the great victory. In an Irish tradition of storytelling, it is likely to be along the lines of *Finnegan's Wake* or even *At Swim Two Birds*.

So let's begin in the middle. In Ireland, the structures associated with anti-racism in countries of immigration in the post-war period, that is, those derived from defence groups for immigrant workers and indigenous national and regional support groups, are largely missing. Anti-racism has instead been the province of Traveller groups, overseas development workers and isolated community activists. McVeigh (2002b) cites the Dublin Travellers' Education and Development Group (DTEDG)[19] in the early 1990s as the first Irish organisation built on the principle of anti-racism. He also cites one-off campaigns such as the Dunnes Stores anti-apartheid strike in 1986, and the East Timor Solidarity Group in the 1990s as examples of grass-roots action. Tannam (2002) additionally argues that her group, 'Harmony', 1986–99, was the first specifically anti-racist organisation in Ireland. Her overview suggests that anti-racism is fragmented and has been in a 'transitional' phase since the late 1990s. She raises the question as to whether new minorities can feel part of the new community-based alliances developed as a response to increasing numbers of migrants and a shifting legislative and attitudinal base. The question of representation, as we have seen with reference to the partnership process above, is vital. Operating in a restricted civil society space in the Republic, where genuine debate (that is, involving conflicting opinions that cannot always be fully resolved) is not fostered, anti-racist organisations have to address the issue of having their voices heard, and making sure that the voice actually speaks for minorities rather than their spokespeople. O'Carroll's theorisation of community points to this being a difficult objective to attain.

Small-scale grass-roots initiatives such as the Anti-Racism Campaign, Residents Against Racism and Immigrant Solidarity have operated in Ireland and folded since the late 1990s.[20] Alanna Lentin (2002) points to the domination of grass-roots Irish anti-racism by the Socialist Worker Party. The result of this is the dominance of one particular perspective, in which an innocent working class is force-fed racism by leaders, bent on divide and rule: racism for the Socialist Worker Party is largely reduced to a function of capitalism. In this view, immigration policies are criticised in a critique of borders *per se*. The favouring of direct action and support groups is also typical of the

Party, and while tactically suited to the form of struggles that arise in uncoordinated and reactive phases that might constitute adjustment to Ireland's new and changing immigration patterns, the space for minority activists to determine their own agendas and priorities that do not necessarily rely on an orthodox Marxist reading appears questionable. They may well be squeezed at that end just as they are squeezed out by steering committee corporate approaches at the other.[21]

Organisations set up by former asylum-seekers, refugees and racialised minorities, notably the Association of Refugees and Asylum-Seekers in Ireland (ARASI)[22] have also been appearing on the political landscape in recent years. The durability of small voluntary organisations is fragile at best, and these are no exception. It is too early to tell which direction the networks will follow, whether organisational pressures will force nationality-based groups to adopt coalition strategies, whether the Dublin-based groups will prosper while provincial ones suffer from lack of critical mass, whether government-level partnership-style initiatives will co-opt the activist leadership from them, or whether all of these or none will occur. Moreover, the extent to which their work, like that of Traveller organisations and Community Development Projects (CDPs), is solely anti-racist (Gilroy, 1987) and the way they network with sister organisations outside Ireland do not currently figure on research agendas. The contemporary situation then is 'transitional', and in many ways potentially progressive, but the key actors, the minorities themselves, are currently working more informally at local rather than national level. There are some interesting exceptions, such as the Nigerian-run newspaper *Metro Eireann*, operating since 2000.[23]

Historically, the problem is one of focus. Irish historiography has primarily concentrated on narrating the struggle for Irish nationhood. In terms of constructing an anti-racist tradition, the important dialogue between 'nationalists' and 'revisionists' is interesting in as far as the assumptions of participants on both sides are highlighted, and a degree of reflexivity on the construction of the nation has been incorporated into 'revisionist' studies. The relationship between nation and racism has been tackled implicitly and explicitly throughout this book. From this we should emerge with the knowledge that nations are constructed on a set of exclusions and inclusions that impinge in a fundamental way on anti-racist work. The argument is that anti-racism is by definition internationalist, and seeks to understand the relationships between different forms of oppression, not just racism. With this in mind, the following is a brief review of some potentially fruitful avenues.

It was noted that on the Caribbean plantations a tiny number of revolts took place in the seventeenth century that involved Irish bond-labourers and African slaves. Although Linebaugh and Rediker (2000) have overplayed this trend, it does not mean that the revolts were not radical. They temporarily displaced the certainties of the racialised hierarchy and focussed on abolishing property in man and land.

No slave-trading was allowed to occur at Irish ports due to the strong Presbyterian support for abolition in the eighteenth century, and according to Hart (2003), eighteenth-century Ireland was a good deal more ambivalent toward the institution of slavery and its justifications than England. He cites the *Belfast News-Letter* (5–8 September 1786):

> That the Africans are an inferior link in the grand chain of nature is a prejudice, which has been indulged and propagated by Europeans, especially in modern times, from considerations peculiarly sordid and contemptible; the fact is, that the mental faculties of the negroes are by no means of a subordinate description to those of any other men.

In addition to the relatively sympathetic atmosphere described by Hart, the political scene was also open to influence. Linebaugh and Rediker (2000:43) refer to a speech given by Equiano in Belfast in 1791 where a number of United Irishmen were present and signed his abolitionist petition.

The late eighteenth and early nineteenth centuries were periods in which revolutionary ideas were circulating alongside those of reaction. While the British Empire was employing Irishmen as loyal leaders, cannon-fodder, and administrators, and fixers such as Michael Keane (see Chapter 3) were helping to forge a transatlantic nexus of power involving Irish landowners in the enterprise of Caribbean colonisation, there were also figures whose experiences turned them toward more radical positions. Edward Marcus Despard (1751–1803), born in Queen's County, was a British navy officer who became governor of the Mosquito Shore and the Bay of Honduras. In 1782 he commanded a successful expedition against the Spanish posses-sions in neighbouring areas and in 1784 he took over the administration of Yucatan. Despard married a Jamaican woman and came to adopt a critical position on Britain's role in Central America. He was ousted from his office and returned to England, where after being imprisoned in the Tower, he eventually hatched a plot with other London radicals to take over the Bank of England and assassinate the King. He and six other conspirators were the last men to be hung, drawn and quartered in Britain in 1803, the year of Robert Emmet's failed uprising, and Thomas Russell's sister plot in the North.[24]

There is little to engage us until the 1840s, when O'Connell, the inheritor of a nationalist space from which non-sectarian politics had been expunged, began to pick up on a unifying theme: the strident affirmation of anti-slavery. The structures of the Repeal Association were used to produce anti-slavery material and support visiting black American activists such as Charles Lenox Remond, his daughter Sarah and Frederick Douglass, all of whom toured Ireland on the abolitionist platform, lecturing in the major towns. Their reception was warm and, on a personal level, refreshingly devoid of antagonism. Douglass stated:

> I can truly say, I have spent some of the happiest moments of my life since landing in this country [...] I meet nothing in return to remind me of my complexion. I find myself regarded and treated at every turn with the kindness and deference paid to white people. (Foner, 1999:18–19)[25]

O'Connell's position illuminates a specifically Irish location, locked into racialised logic as inferiors, yet fully aware of the gradations within the nineteenth-century racial hierarchy and the political and economic links between the power of slave-owners and empire. Unfortunately, the loss of O'Connell's influence to that of the Young Ireland movement in the mid 1840s spelled an end to mass backing for abolition in Ireland. Indeed, although O'Connell is known primarily for his espousal of Catholic causes and his leadership of an Irish nation fundamentally based on appeals to Catholicism as an overarching source of identity, his political campaigning was, in comparison to key figures within the later cultural nationalist movement, far more pluralist and sensitive to echoes of oppression in other places. Moreover, as Rolston and Shannon (2002) demonstrate, the relationship of black activists and resisters of imperialism with Irish nationalists frequently consisted of a one-way traffic particularly from black American sympathisers.

The episode of the San Patricios (see Chapter 4) illustrates a counter-argument to the one which postulates the inevitable acceptance of dominant ideas of nationalism and racism in America. A group of mainly Irish and marginalised soldiers serving in the US army joined the Mexican forces in revolt against their treatment by Protestant officers, and in solidarity with a non-white Catholic nation.

Against an intellectual backdrop of white supremacy, mediated through eugenics and social Darwinism, Irish nationalism in its cultural form embodied a specific version of 'race'-based politics. The Irish were racially defined against their various Others: Anglo-Saxon oppressors, Jews, Travellers, fellow colonials. Yet prominent nationalists such as Thomas McDonagh,[26] Frederick Ryan,[27] and Eoin MacNeill (1919)[28] all developed an alternative perspective on 'race', critiquing emphasis on racialised membership of the nation. Roger Casement's work in Africa politicised him into adopting an internationalist stance, in which he linked all anti-imperial struggles. The current controversy over the so-called 'Black Diaries' should not prevent his political thinking from being analysed for its contribution, and neither should the sparse but important activism of the labour movement, the Irish Communist Party and the radical elements of the IRA in the 1925–35 period (Hanley, 2003) be written off *a priori*. Here, Gibbons' recuperation and re-narration of the Jim Gralton affair (1996) is exemplary.[29] Gralton was a political activist seeking to organise along class rather than nationalist lines in Roscommon and Leitrim in the early 1930s. He was finally deported in August 1933 after five months on the run. Gibbons ties in a critique of Griffith's version of racist nationalism, and sees in it a parallel of the abolition of difference inherent in forms of imperialism and some strands of socialism. His observation of the destructive edge of the 'universal' is echoed by Bourdieu's analysis of the 'imperialism of the universal' (1992, 1998), flowing from the United States' cultural, economic and military hegemony, especially that of neo-liberal ideas enshrined in international organisations such as the IMF and the World Bank.[30]

Aside from this case, there was also an alternative Ireland of activists whose political work did not solely repose on the establishment of Home Rule, or even of a United Ireland, but was part of a socialist and/or feminist critique, and involved commitment to internationalist ideas. Margaret Cousins (Kapur, 1997:27–8) has already been referred to, as has Hubert Butler, while the contribution of Annie Besant to British and Indian radical politics is slightly better known (Rolston and Shannon, 2002:63; Kapur, 1997:21–3). There is a daunting task of digging up the alternative Ireland from its resting place in libraries and other archival sources, referred to in relation to the life of Quaker activist and novelist Rosemary Jacob (Ingman, 2003). A couple of generations' worth of activists whose commitment extended to international struggle may well have passed beneath the radar of nationalist historiography, and now is as good a time as any to begin reclaiming their contribution.

The links made between Irish people employed as aid workers and anti-racist action (McVeigh, 1996) is another more contemporary source of activism, as evidenced by Comhlámh (the returned development workers' organisation)[31], its publications, awareness-raising projects such as the artists against racism programme, Chéile (2001), and its role in facilitating anti-racist organisation. Indeed, the NGO sector is ideologically vibrant in Ireland, with Trocaire, Concern and Amnesty having input into awareness-raising work. Moreover, there is a particularly interesting ideological circle being completed, with Sinn Féin's late conversion to internationalism and multiculturalism. Beyond the rhetoric of murals proclaiming parallel international struggles with the Palestinians and black Americans, there has been support for an anti-racist nationalism from a quarter that, according to the logic of this chapter, we might least expect to see it (Adams, 2000). With Sinn Féin's growing influence in the Republic since the May 2002 elections[32] it will become a key player in the development of social issues, as its appeal is based partly on the articulation of radical grass-roots political activism with a national network, and its impact in the current parliamentary term is structurally tied in with that of the Labour Party and the Greens.

Finally, the Equality Authority and the National Consultative Committee on Racism and Interculturalism are recent additions to this submerged tradition, though as semi-state agencies dependent on the Department of Justice, they are thus structurally limited in what they can achieve. The former particularly, plays an influential role in the cultural transition toward a climate of equality to be fostered through efficient implementation of the Employment Equality Act (1998) and the Equal Status Act (2000). It is a bridge-building institution with the ear of government and is a key player in contemporary policy-making. However, it should also be borne in mind that the framing of its mission dictates particular, primarily labour-market oriented, pro-equality strategies. Neither the Equality Authority nor the NCCRI can be expected to engage in radical and/or grass-roots activism, yet they ought also to be the allies within the state, of those types of movement.

## CONCLUSION

One of the major pitfalls for Irish anti-racists then is the danger of being sucked into nationalist quicksand. If 'republicanism' is to mean anything progressive on the island of Ireland, it needs refreshed content, an organic intelligentsia and a framework of participative civil society, to turn itself into a socially transformative movement that interrogates unequal power relations and makes that issue central not marginal to its project. This argument does not make you a bad nationalist, rather a good republican.

Social movements, argues Lloyd (1999:25–6), can be fragmented, incoherent and interrupted, and are treated as 'history's incommensurables' by historiography seeking to explain the rise of nationalism to take over the state. Moreover, the set of exclusions operated by the dominant (that is, victorious) version of republican ideas in Ireland serves to promulgate the notion of class politics, or feminism, for example, as sectional. This is expressed not simply in the relative poverty of anti-racist organisation, but also in the difficulty of putting together a tradition, as much activity in this field has been ignored or sidelined.

The pulse of an anti-racist tradition in Ireland is weak but present. The process of elaborately constructing such a tradition may involve a re-evaluation of historical and contemporary contributions toward human rights and against the existing status quo. Anti-racism's trajectory is discontinuous and underdeveloped.

The most fruitful strategies are likely to be combinations of *human rights* (universal, comprehensible and relevant) and *empathy* (with a focus on migration and parallels). Yet the form of universalism should not be 'imperial', but one that attempts to embrace the particular, rather than impose Western norms as universal ones. Indeed, Ireland's long experience of colonialism, and anti-colonial organisation, its positive links with the developing world, and potential empathy with emigrants and the migrant experience are as yet untapped resources. One crucial aspect of the work of anti-racist organisations is to draw parallels that clearly link Ireland to its international context and place people in positions to confront their disempowerment by drawing on knowledge of shared experiences. Anti-racism's role in Ireland might be to link struggles of community activists, trade unions, the unemployed, and Travellers with the narratives of disempowerment recounted in immigrant biographies. The first objective is to find common ground, and develop a structural analysis involving and explaining status (migrant worker, refugee, asylum-seeker, Irish national, and so forth) and articulating it with the grass-roots experiences of individuals.

The third strand is tying these ideas up into a broader analysis that links the forms of exclusion and tries to understand how they articulate. This would involve, for example, the recognition that equality discourse and practice have in-built limits. They do not seek to confront power structures, either organisationally or analytically, and leave the question of social class oppression, the most widespread and transversal form of exclusion, untouched. Moreover, there is an inherent ideological contradiction, in that capitalism both generates and relies on structural inequalities. Individual states can reduce or increase the disparities through pro-active fiscal, social and employment policies, but cannot and have no desire to eradicate them altogether. The logical conclusion of equality of opportunity is an ever-broadening middle class, but not a challenge to class domination (in whatever form). The logical conclusion of full citizen participation, which should be part of anti-racism's organising principles, supposes a shift in the basis of governance toward the local, and a radical state willing to abandon its position as systematic champion of big international business.

Even at the basic level of social partnership negotiations, the idea of community participation is breaking down, so there seems little scope for action within that model. This organisational form is intrinsically conservative, and a reason why government-led initiatives on racism, *inter alia*, are generally ineffective. Steering committees are set up through word-of-mouth and nomination takes place in a top-down dynamic that could be unproblematically placed in O'Carroll's diagram (where face-to-face interaction replaces genuine openness and dialogue). While individual members may well be extremely competent and progressive, this cannot compensate for the structural flaw, and, in any case, some co-optees have no expertise in or experience of the issues the particular steering committee is investigating. The partnership model may be death by committee for durable and radical anti-racist initiatives.

Lloyd's synthesis of nationalisms (1999) argues that the state has monopolised or hegemonised modernity and rationality, and delegitimised social movements by depicting them as traditional and sectional. The predominant place of neo-liberal economics within this problematic at the turn of the twenty-first century begs further thought. Bourdieu (2002:349) argues that the 'conservative revolution' effected by neo-liberalism

> has taken a brand new form. It no longer invokes an idealised past, as it did in other times, by exalting blood and soil, agrarian and archaic themes. This new style conservative revolution identifies itself with progress, reason, science (economics in this case) to justify the restoration, and thus attempts to banish progressive thought and action to the realm of archaism.[33]

Can neo-liberalism be construed as a constitutive element of modern European state nationalisms, or as a separate but overarching layer of ideology? It appears to have itself appropriated the language of modernity and may in some ways be sustaining itself with a critique of the nation state as irrational, as it galvanises not only transnational flows of capital and labour, insinuates itself at the core of transnational projects such as NAFTA and the EU, and fuels itself in the staged destruction and reconstruction of 'third countries' through warfare. It drains the 'social' from social security, and tips the balance of wealth distribution ever further into a more concentrated circle of interests. It is clear that any anti-racism worthy of the name must operate from within this context and its imperatives are simultaneously national and international, global and local. There cannot be 'anti-racism in one country', any more than there could have been 'socialism in one country', to borrow from Lenin, because those projects involve shifting expectations and frameworks for reflection and action beyond the parameters of the naturalised social world of common sense we inhabit (which includes the nation state as the natural building block of world organisation). Consequently, discourses (even defensive ones) focussing on employment and/or immigration are potentially self-defeating. They are functionalist and neo-liberal: treating people as people only to the extent that they satisfy 'national' labour demands. Surely anti-racism should involve more than appearing reasonable at all times.

Anti-racism is a transformative vision of what social relations might be, or it is nothing. It is utopian and informed by notions of freedom, equality and solidarity. It cannot simply open the doors of the nation wider, without developing a critique of 'race', an understanding of racism and the disfiguring collective and individual relationships it generates.

Twin intertwined dominant discourses should be the target of this counter-hegemonic project: the nation state and 'race'. The primary questions (that of course lead on to more detailed ones) are: who is represented by the state? What is the nation, where are its borders (in all the senses of the word) and why? The analytical framework within which these could be answered must be one that categorically rejects essentialism, including nationalist metanarratives that postulate transcendental essences. Anti-racists have to be rigorous and candid in their methods and in the questions they ask.

# 9
# Beyond the New Socio-Economic 'Pale': Racialisation and Belonging in Contemporary Ireland

It was argued in the introduction that one of the most fruitful perspectives for studying racialisation was to situate oneself within the tension created between two broad approaches: the differentialist (seeking to make specific and perceived cultural difference the focus of study) and the materialist (seeking to locate social identities within a framework of long-term, wide-scale change in the economic and political realms). A differentialist approach would prioritise differences in culture between migrants and elements of the host nation as a point of departure, while a materialist one would look to macro-level economic change and the workings of late capitalism for inspiration. In this section, a constructive balance will be sought between these two in synthesising the arguments developed over the previous chapters so that the theory is applied to the case of Ireland, yet without claiming exceptionalism.

## HOW DOES RACISM 'WORK'?

How does racism accomplish its ideological labours? In relation to 'race', one of the principal architects of theory, integrating class as a cultural and material phenomenon, has been Stuart Hall (1980). His attempt to define the linking of 'race' to class in ideology under the term 'articulation' throws up a particular line of enquiry and starting point for making sense of the configuration adopted by racism in Europe at the turn of the twenty-first century. Hall's work on 'articulation' serves here as the basis for attempting to link the cultural to the material, with the proviso that in approaching the issue through economics there is an alternative risk: 'one cannot explain racism in abstraction from other social relations – even if, alternatively, one cannot explain it by reducing it to those relations' (ibid.:337).

As a body of ideas, racism 'articulates other ideologies to itself', most evidently the 'us/them' distinction of social class. It also

225

de-historicises through collapsing everything into the category of the 'natural' as opposed to the 'social', where the latter opens possibility of change closed off by the former. It finally decomposes classes into individuals and re-composes them into reconstructed unities as 'races'. Racism then is a particularly deep and powerful force because 'in such racial characteristics as colour, ethnic origin, geographical position, etc., racism discovers what other ideologies have to construct: an apparently "natural" and universal basis in nature itself' (ibid.:342).

In Gramsci, contends Hall, 'ideologies are not simply "in the head", but are material relations – what Lenin called "ideological social relations" – which shape social actions, function through concrete institutions and apparatuses, and are materialized through practices' (1980:334). So 'material relations' might be focussed on perceived and actual positions; that is, class structure experienced as labour market, housing market, welfare, urban space. 'Encroachment' by others upon this space diminishes already-dwindling resources (Keohane, 2001; Humphreys, 2001). The structural background in the developed world is comprised of elements such as the economic transition from permanent to temporary employment in different sectors; greater levels of migration into countries of emigration, the relative insecurity of the job market, illegal work, temporary and part-time contracts (casualisation) and the specific deficits between classes, regions, genders, and so on. There is no unequivocal answer to the question 'what is the relationship between class and racism?' Yet some of the contingent factors can be analysed and explained, and part of the process of producing provisional answers involves clarifying the contours of the current conjuncture.

## ECONOMIC ELEMENTS OF RACISM IN IRELAND

Ireland has been part of an international movement toward relocating particular sectors of employment close to markets where profit and workforce are available. Undoubtedly, the UK's failure to join the Euro zone has boosted Ireland's credentials as the sole English-speaking Euroland member. The type of rapid development dominated by FDI has been flagged up as potentially fragile by O'Hearn (1998) *inter alia*. Apart from this critique, Ireland's economic growth has seen a specific combination of variables: labour shortage in particular sectors, rising standard of living; and constants: proximity to the UK and mainland Europe, strong links with North America. As indicators of wealth have risen, and economic growth appeared durable, there have been critiques (Allen, 2000; Kirby, 2002) focussing on the distribution of this wealth.

The relevant consequence of this growing income inequality is that the diversification of the Irish population is running in parallel with *de facto* denial of access to full and active citizenship, (in Bottomore and Marshall's (1992) sense of comprising economic, social and political rights), particularly in the economic domain. Moreover, anxieties focussing upon structural problems such as welfare (in the broadest sense) and pensions, can easily be attributed to the kinds of changes represented by (although not generated by) the arrival of racialised Others. Those groups then become identified with unfavourable change, and are transformed into agents of injustice and privileged recipients of diminishing funds. When those foreigners are identifiable as non-productive, in any society whose values are those in which the productive is quantified in terms of work (cf. the 'deserving poor') then particular groups such as asylum-seekers ('bogus' or otherwise) will be more open to these roles. Travellers fall within this 'unproductive' domain, seen as dependent on the public purse for the provision of halting sites, among other things. At the same time, at the other end of the spectrum, Jews are seen by many as having too much economic influence, and the question of productiveness begins to define a normative middle ground bounded by 'spongers' and racketeers, that is to say, virtually criminal Others.

This form of anxiety can be read as projection of the host society's conflict between stated and actual values: if asylum-seekers are 'spongers' because they (are forced to) live off welfare, what does that say about the thousands of Irish nationals who do so without the same constraint? In a period in which tribunals have been set up to examine tax evasion, property price-fixing and speculation among the state's political and financial elite, for example, the influential 'racketeers' appear to be Catholic Irish nationalists. There is a frustration derived from the failure of wealth to trickle down to the bottom layers and the revelation of fraud on a massive scale. A kind of anomie in which accelerated social change has raised pertinent questions about values but not yet provided answers emerges from this process. This frustration is finding an outlet in forms of aggression, with higher recorded levels of crimes against the person, which easily finds a focus in visible difference whilst other types of crime fall relatively.[1] What might be termed 'the new racial geography' of Ireland is partly a corollary of the mismatch of expectations and reality in a period of intense economic and social change.

What is important then is to situate the precise combination of ideological and economic processes that have given rise to what I have termed the 'current configuration' of Irish racism from the mid 1990s. There could be no 'refugee issue' without the economic boom and its ensuing cleavages because racialisation (in the sense in which Miles uses it) is a process that emerges from capitalism's generation of ever-adjusting inequalities. Its structural parameters are those of specific locations, under specific economic conditions, and particular conjunctures in the world economy.

The rise of racism in a boom period in Ireland has passed without comment. Resource competition theories (summarised and applied by Scheepers et al., 2002 for example) are based on the assumption that perceived threat to resources increases only when unemployment rises. This is demonstrably false in the case of Ireland since the mid 1990s and indicates the authors' greater familiarity with the copious material on surveys, psychology and ethnicity than with the founding thinkers in sociology. It was one of Durkheim's findings that suicides rose in periods of boom and bust, not just the latter, while Weber attributed the intensification in inter-group hostility to rapid social change *per se* (in whichever direction). In short, the message from the Irish case is that just as there can be 'blackness without blacks' (Gilman, 1982), and anti-semitism without Jews (Goldhagen, 1996), there can also be perceived economic threat during expansion. It might be more fruitful to look at indicators other than those of unemployment and increasing per capita income, such as discrepancies between incomes, the type of new job being created (proportion of temporary and/or part time), and the average level of income in relation to inflation and the price of housing for example, as departure points for theorising, as attempted in Chapter 2. Allen (2000) uses some of these as well as the proportion of tax provided by PAYE and businesses, the long-term impacts of tax breaks, and argues that a significant element to be included in any such evaluation is the negative impact of low tax levels and high tax evasion on public services available to PAYE workers.

Relative impoverishment, as a process, is one key factor in explaining a rise in racist attitudes among working-class Irish people charted in the opinion polls taken over the past few years. Yet this should be qualified by the proposition that racist ideas, as I have attempted to emphasise, are not merely generated in the economic realm, and that the attitudes are identifiable throughout social classes and differ only by degree. It cannot be an explanation for attitudes among the middle classes. Indeed, while the economic background is an influential factor in the frameworks in which people construct ideas about identity, there can be no automatic causal link between belonging to a group experiencing economic difficulties and expressing racist ideas. If this link existed, then how could the positive attitudes to minorities expressed by occupational groups C2-F (albeit slightly lower than that for A-C1s) be explained? The relatively small class-based variations in degrees of hostility expressed in opinion polls should be treated with particular caution because they are statistically unrepresentative sub-samples. The polls from which analysis is carried out contain a minimal sample of just over 1,000. Once this is split into groups by class, gender, age, and so on, the sample drops below the representative point. There we enter the realm of qualitative rather than quantitative research.

## TERRITORY

Intrinsic to conceptions of geographical space and territory are Articles 2 and 3 of the Constitution which, prior to their amendment in the Citizenship Act, 2001 following the 1998 Good Friday/Belfast Agreement, claimed sovereignty over Northern Ireland ('the whole island of Ireland'), pending 'the re-integration of the national territory'. The 2001 version of Article 3 refers to 'all the people who share the territory of the island of Ireland'. Yet in everyday speech and the media Northern Ireland is referred to as 'the North' (that is, of Ireland the nation), and the UK government minister as the 'Northern Secretary', and so forth. It is difficult to predict whether this usage will cease. Although this seems trivial, it is a symbolic twitch on the stump of the nationalist psyche: both Sinn Féin and Fianna Fáil have now *de facto* renounced the objective of a united Ireland in favour of greater participation in regional government and cross-border bodies. Since a significant element of political heritage in the Republic derives from the nationalist agenda, it permeates political assumptions about the physical and imagined parameters of the Irish state. Dissident republican organisations such as the Real IRA and Continuity IRA are still pledged to a united Ireland, for example, while a variety of organisational structures (the Royal Irish Academy, the Irish Rugby Football Union, the GAA, RTE) construct the country explicitly or implicitly as one unit.[2] Importantly, people born in Northern Ireland since 1921 are now entitled to citizenship of the Republic of Ireland as of right, rather than having to qualify through parents or grandparents. In the post-Agreement era, ambiguity still characterises the nature of the 'provisional' border of 1921.

Whilst the population increases and the labour market is expanding, geographical space appears to be shrinking. CSO estimates in 2000 put the population back above that of the 1881 census for the first time, the visibility of 'racialised' groups in certain areas of the capital is rising swiftly, and overall demographic concentration in the Greater Dublin area is increasing. The issue of housing is particularly sensitive given the current crisis in which demand is outstripping supply to such an extent that prices more than doubled in the 1996–2002 period (Chapter 2). The locally-expressed defensive antipathy towards second home-owners in the South and West of Ireland has led to some planning authorities bringing in residential qualifications for planning permission. What definition is used for 'local' must be seen as crucial, but it is clear that some unofficial discrimination is likely if such systems are actually operational. Clare County Council's approval of such a plan, for example, sparked a controversy debated in the national press.[3]

There is a link here with some of the reactions expressed over the government's purchase in spring 2000 (especially in Rosslare, and Clogheen, Co. Tipperary) or renting (for example, Wexford) of accommodation on behalf of asylum-seekers perceived as prioritising that group over needy locals. Editor of the *Wexford People*, Ger Walsh, in an editorial on the Romanian asylum-seekers staying in Wexford in July and August 1998 (Newman, 1998), argued that responsibility for housing the Romanians fell to the Health Board, which rented 'good quality' accommodation for them, a fact considered favouritism by some locals, and reflected in Walsh's column. He defended himself from criticism on this line by stating: 'it's not too good for them but it's better than what is available to people in Wexford themselves. Wexford natives would not get that type of accommodation from the health board if they saw themselves in difficulty.'

In the case of Rosslare, local disapprobation was so intense that plans were abandoned, and the premises set aside for housing asylum-seekers in Clogheen, Co. Tipperary were twice the object of arson attack. The professional middle classes deployed less desperate measures, using the planning process to oppose the development of a hostel in Dublin 4 in April 2000.[4] Links between anxiety over property and exclusionary practices are just beginning to be made and are a contextual factor feeding exclusionary ideologies. Moreover, legislation, introduced in March 2002 and aimed at halting Traveller encroachment onto privately-owned land, made trespass a criminal rather than civil offence. Here not only is the state shrinking legitimate space for Travellers to stop in, but there are implications also for mobility. Traveller culture is founded on mobility and, pending the construction of halting sites by local authorities, it is only feasible if there are stopping places.

Another site of contested meanings is that of local space as attractive to tourists (that is, income-generating) based on notions of unspoilt landscape. Comments made in response to the dispersal of asylum-seekers to provincial sites around Ireland in April–May 2000 produced a series of intertwined discourses, elements of which point directly to asylum-seekers 'spoiling' the areas for tourists. Kenmare, Tramore, and Mosney are towns in which this connection has been made. The presence of particular outsiders (that is, unproductive ones) is thus viewed as a physical blot on the landscape, another reference to the ubiquitous historical theme of a pure Ireland defending itself against infection (moral, physical)[5] and/or against invasion[6] or both, as witnessed in the campaign to protect Ireland from foot and mouth disease in 2001 and the government's peremptory ban on athletes from particular SARS-affected countries attending the Special Olympics in 2003. Fanning (2002) charts Clare County Council's protracted institutionalised failure to provide accommodation for Travellers from the 1960s to the 1990s. He notes the role of councillors as both power-wielders and activists leading opposition; the attempts to redefine eligibility in terms of 'the local' as opposed to the 'transient'; the depiction of Travellers as threatening and their supporters as unreasonable; and the unwillingness of the Council to impose any solution on settled residents who organised into lobby groups. Local communities, businesspeople, the authorities, Travellers and now asylum-seekers, in direct provision, are thus increasingly engaged in 'frontier wars' over control of and access to territory (Quinn, 2002), in which the latter groups are disadvantaged protagonists, particularly since Travellers have low turnout and asylum-seekers cannot vote: there are therefore very few votes in supporting such platforms. Ireland's political geography of exclusion is thus in a way self-aggravating.

## INTERROGATING WHITENESS: ROOTLESSNESS AND INVISIBILITY

Jacobson's analysis of the debates on citizenship in the US senate in 1870 (1998: 73–85) led him to conclude that 'whiteness' referred to four overlapping factors: colour, degree of freedom, level of civilisation and devotion to Christianity.

It might thus be argued that neither Jews nor Travellers in the Irish context are really 'white' if this implies not skin colour but degree of freedom, level of civilisation and devotion to Christianity, that is, fitness or unfitness for democratic government. However, we might amend this list of criteria to include (provisionally), in the Irish context, sedentary lifestyle, commitment to values of modernity, Christian culture, and the holding of decision-making power in some public context. It is partly the lack of this power that makes Travellers clearly not 'white' by any accepted use of the term other than the purely phenotypical, and Jews borderline.

The most disturbing form of Otherness is that which cannot immediately be perceived. One limit of the whiteness theory emerges in the discrepancy between the degree to which Jews and Travellers are invisible and can thus move freely. I suggest this is the last criterion to be added to Jacobson's checklist. Westernised Jews are to all intents and purposes unidentifiable in the crowd. They therefore generate more suspicion in the aporia of anti-Semitism: they are both everywhere and nowhere. The lengths that the Nazis went to in order to prove that Jews were biologically different (Burleigh and Wippermann, 1991; Burleigh, 2000) demonstrate insecurity over inability to identify them otherwise. To use an American term, Jews can 'pass for white', while Travellers have less facility to do so.

What links Irish Jews and Travellers is their perceived lack of rootedness in a society where community is such a potent idea (McVeigh, 1992; O'Carroll, 2002). The key element of being a Traveller is belonging to a mobile community with non-capitalist values, while Jews are diasporic people, linked in anti-Semitic ideology both to international (that is, not rooted in particularity) communism and capitalism. Jews were regarded by influential Irish nationalists well into the twentieth century as rootless and cosmopolitan (Maume, 1999:53; Keogh, 1998:22–5, 54–6, 92–102) and thus a threat to cohesion. This theme is still evident in French far-Right politics (McMaster, 2001:211). Both Jews and Travellers are thus simultaneously everywhere and nowhere: they are perceived as irrepressibly mobile and unfixed to place and nation, in cultures that place a premium on fixity and patriotism.[7] Bloom's attempt to encompass his dual Irish and Jewish identities by defining a nation as: 'the same people living in the same place [...] Or also living in different places' (Joyce, 1922), neither placates his tormentor, Citizen, nor does it sit comfortably in the Irish context of community.[8] Indeed, the Constitution makes it explicit that non-Catholics are not full members of the national family (Lentin, 1998, 1999).

Yet Leopold Bloom's definition of a diasporic nation, as articulated above, would apply equally to Ireland, and in one of the Traveller-origin stories, their rupture with landholding parallels the consequences of British imperial policy in Ireland, such as the Cromwellian settlement of 1654, and the aftermath of the Famine. Ní Shuínéar (1994) argues that the transference onto Travellers of narratives of displacement is part of a pathology distinguishing them from the settled population. It is hard not to take this assertion seriously when contemplating the irony of using ideas about root-lessness as the basis for exclusion in contemporary Ireland. Originally justifying the murder of Catholics and their removal from their land in the sixteenth century, this serves the dominant white Catholic majority as a means of both *de facto* excluding Travellers from citizenship, and underpins popular anti-Semitism. The very cultural perspective that justified the Irish being removed from their land is reworked to underpin the assimilation of Travellers in the twenty-first century.[9]

Could this displacement of anxieties onto 'Others' be conceived of as the return of the 'national' repressed that Lentin (2001) refers to? She argues that the experience of emigration has not properly been dealt with and that this collective trauma means that the Irish see asylum-seekers and refugees as degraded images of self. Emigration in the contemporary period is not confined to highly-skilled graduates, nor is it solely the province of those whose opportunities for work are seen as non-existent. It is a national, not class-based phenomenon. Although Corcoran (1997, 2002) suggests that the reasons for it, and the experiences of it are somewhat conditioned by class. Like Luibhéid (1997a), she concludes that in the USA, emigrants' life chances and work experiences require differing degrees of attachment to ethnic Irishness. Illegals, who benefit from Irish networks inserted into an ethnic hierarchy, reap the greatest reward for being Irish *per se*, while white-collar workers find themselves in occupations where nationality is less important.

## CLASS, RACISM AND 'ARTICULATION':
## A POST-GRAMSCIAN SUPPLEMENT TO HALL'S THEORY

The relationship between social class and expressions of racism is therefore less obvious than it may at first seem. There are a number of reasons for this. First, the limits of attitudinal surveys should be recognised. They cannot account for structural features of racism. The management and perpetuation of institutional racism and the barrage of racist ideas disseminated in the media are primarily the work of educated middle-class people. This is a far cry from claiming that only the elites are racist and they deploy racism as a divide-and-rule strategy. If ideology were transmitted and swallowed as fully and unproblematically as that there would be no anti-globalisation, no civil rights marches, no Suffragettes, no Gandhi and no French revolution. Second, the ideologies that people construct to make sense of their social world are never one-dimensional but frequently contradictory. The examination of the way that ideas are contested and differentially digested was begun in Gramsci (1971) and has been unevenly pursued since then. We have started to think through the 'ensemble of relations' as Hall calls it, of subordination along the lines of, *inter alia*, class, gender and racialised identities, by reference to an economic base. The ideological framework of othering already maps onto the 'us' and 'them' divide of social class. One dimension of racism, as it articulates with class, is the transformation of the racialised Other[10] into 'embodiments' of the mobility of capital rather than of labour. The question is, what particular conditions give rise to the forms of racism now prevalent? And what is particular about the precise moment we are experiencing in Ireland? Five broad areas for further reflection follow:

1. Foreign nationals have differing statuses, each of which grants differential access to resources; these range from refugees, EU nationals and their spouses (who have the same rights as Irish nationals) through students, workers on work visas, workers on work permits, people with humanitarian leave to remain, down to asylum-seekers. There is thus a structured differential social hierarchy in terms of actual life chances that is crystallising around the one already in place: deficits in power between various groups of Irish nationals is meshing with one that is being constructed in response to increasing numbers of migrants.

2. The variety in the countries of origin of migrants is now matching that experienced in other developed countries over the past decade (Brah, 1996). Over a hundred nations are now represented amongst applicants for asylum in Ireland at any point, and work permits were granted to nationals of over 130 countries in 2002. Ireland is currently part of that nexus of modern economies that attracts people with no historical ties to individual locations.

3. The turnaround in the Irish economy since the early 1990s and the growth spurt in sectors related to Information and Communications Technology (ICT) were indicated in Chapter 2. This has given rise to particular patterns of consumption, employment growth and reduction: the basic framework in which migrants are located (economic ones primarily in the labour market and asylum-seekers as welfare recipients).

4. Economic migrants do not comprise homogeneous groups in terms of their skills levels. They occupy qualitatively different locations in market economies to do with the economic niche that they are in; work visa holders, already slightly privileged in terms of rights, enter at a professional level, enjoy higher salaries and thus command broader consumption options in housing, and so forth, than work-permit workers. The largest proportion of permit workers in Ireland are employed in services and catering.

5. At least two phenomena, fear of competition for welfare resources and competition for jobs, compound each other to reduce racialised populations to one problematic status. Racially-motivated attacks have taken place against residents, students, holiday-makers, asylum-seekers, and others. On one level at least, the crudest indicator of 'difference', non-white appearance, is focussed on. We might suppose that factors such as insecurity and precariousness of employment, relative income, depoliticisation and lack of legitimacy of the state compound the vulnerability of visible minorities/non-white people in Ireland. However, it could be difficult to draw a line at which 'white' begins, running as it does through Irish Jews, Travellers, and Muslim converts, all of whom are the targets of types of abuse.

So it is important to restate the idea that although Hall's summary and synthesis of ideas into a new perspective ('articulation') is a detailed and lucid analysis, the project it began is still a work in progress. From studying the Irish case, it seems critical to add here the role of old ideas (anti-Semitism, anti-nomadism) that have outlived their economic moment of birth and been re-articulated with the contemporary. In the opening chapter I pointed to a compelling image of 'race' proposed by Jacobson (1998), that of a palimpsest. Using his concept, the multiple simultaneous representations of racialised groups can be comprehended as constitutive of racism, rather than an aberrant process that has to be explained away. Moreover, the 'palimpsest' itself is an outcome rather than a process. It is therefore the process producing the 'palimpsest' that needs examining in any attempt to understand the articulations of Irish racism.

Moore (1981) argues, for example, in his study of anti-Semitism in Ireland, that negative attitudes to financial irregularities have a long history. Money-lending, in which Jews were over-represented *vis-à-vis* their proportion of the population in the 1880–1905 period, is a profession described as 'racketeering' *per se* (even when it is carried out legally), and was one of the few available niches into which Jews could obtain entry on a self-employed basis. Even with Jewish tradition there is ambivalence toward money-lending (Leventhal, 1945), so it is inaccurate to blithely describe it as 'part of Jewish culture'. Moore's treatment of the economic aspects of anti-Semitism exemplifies one indispensable element of the approach we are advocating here: it focusses on the local outcomes of broader economic forces in terms of the content imparted to racism in the Irish context. If we move on a century from the period he covers, we find similar ideas about Jews uncovered by Mc Gréil and Citizen Traveller. Yet this time they are expressed in a period in which Jews are neither immigrants nor harbingers of new forms of consumption or undercutting economic competitors. We can abstract elements of the anti-Semitism of the late nineteenth century and re-apply them to the twenty-first: cultural differences defying assimilation, unequal competition, values construed as threatening, for example. In various ways these points apply to Travellers, asylum-seekers and labour migrants.

Making sense of the social world through its economic hierarchy, its relations of production, posits the asylum-seeker and Traveller as unproductive spongers, migrants ('non-nationals') as less deserving of employment than a 'national', and all as bearers of cultural norms that diverge from those of secular Catholicism.

## GREEN, WHITE AND BLACK ALL OVER?

There is, alongside the hostility outlined elsewhere, a stream of positive work (see Chapter 8) and, moreover, of mainstream normalisation of difference, particularly in the field of popular culture, the two key areas being music and sport. Music has provided Ireland's black population with two key representatives, Phil Lynott and Samantha Mumba, each encapsulating something of their time. Thin Lizzy's rock'n'roll lifestyle and posturing were perfectly in keeping with the 1970s and 1980s dominant themes of excess, both in terms of trouser material and loudness of music and behaviour. Lynott's awareness of his uniqueness in a band that leant on its ethnic roots for its fan base, and his comfort in the unusual combined identity of black rock singer–Irishman marks him out as distinctive, even apart from his considerable song-writing skills and vocals. 'Black Boys on the Corner' (1972) the first single, and 'Ode to a Black Man' (1980), indicate his willingness also to make political statements.

Samantha Mumba on the other hand is a teenage pop star in the age of manufactured and homogenised pop. She states that what is distinctive about her is her 'attitude' and that she is unlike her blonde-haired blue-eyed cohort.[11] However, this is really yet to demonstrate itself, and her musical output is transatlantic, utterly contemporary in its statelessness and lack of specificity. Mumba has included a song about racism on her second album. What is positive is the way she is unproblematically absorbed into Irishness; her very lack of distinctiveness (apart from physical appearance) is intrinsically modern in an increasingly featureless form of expression. More than half the students asked as an exercise to identify her in 2003 did so as 'Irish' (37 per cent) and 'Irish African' (16 per cent).[12] Additionally, black Irish singers distinguished themselves in popular television competitions in 2002, reaching the finals of UK *Pop Idol* and *Popstars the Rivals*, and winning *Stars in their Eyes*.

Sport is also an arena where traditionally identity comes under scrutiny and new possibilities emerge. Traveller boxer, Francie Barret, and GAA players Jason Sherlock (Dublin) and Sean og O'hAilpin (Cork) are nationally-known figures whose prowess has raised the question of difference in terms of representation. As noted in Chapter 6, the GAA is one of the most zealously guarded of Irish Ireland's domains. As with Mumba, the non-Irish elements of Sherlock's and O'hAilpin's identities have been more or less glossed over. Humphries' chapter on Sherlock (1996) makes one reference to him bearing the 'looks of a long-vanished father' (ibid.:146), and then focusses on the tussle between North Cork and Dublin as his 'home'. Sherlock himself has gone on record as having suffered racist abuse, but while playing soccer not Gaelic games.

The relationship of soccer to Irish identity has been looked at by journalists, academics (Cronin, 1999) and artists (Bolger, 1992, 2002). While it is an embodiment on the one hand of the ambivalence of the Anglo-Irish relationship, with the foreign game an anathema to the architects of cultural nationalism and generations of diehard GAA enthusiasts, its attraction as the biggest media profile international sport means that it receives critical attention in excess of its Irish playing and fan base. Ironically, coverage is geared toward England (particularly Manchester United) and Celtic. No surprise then that the contribution to Irish identity identified by playwright Dermot Bolger is of crystallising diasporic awareness of a form of accessible and authentic Irishness for contemporaries, located beyond the fixity of old certainties of place and whiteness. Black defender Chris Hughton (now a member of the national team's coaching staff), claims the narrator in the monologue *In High Germany* (about the 1988 European Championships), 'could have been first cousin to any of us'. In Bolger, Hughton's Afro-Caribbean London background makes him no less Irish than any of the others, in a squad containing players with regional English and Scots accents who qualified through their grandparents' birthplaces (and in Tony Cascarino's case, falsely). While Terry Phelan and Phil Babb played lesser roles in the high-achieving Irish teams of the Charlton era, the key figure is Paul Mc Grath, the 'black pearl of Inchicore'. Mc Grath's is an epic tale. Born in London and adopted by Irish parents, he grew up (like Lynott and Mumba) in working-class Dublin and was snapped up from the semi-professional Irish league. His career with Manchester United, Aston Villa and Ireland was undermined by alcoholism, a battle from which he emerged to become a businessman and frequent contributor to the national media and fund-raising events, notably SARI (Sport Against Racism in Ireland), and a role in the government's 'Euro changeover' press campaign in 2000. Clearly, on one level, the acknowledgement of Lynott, McGrath, Hughton et al. as Irish has contributed to the lack of comment about Samantha Mumba. Even after Lynott it would have no longer have been possible to state that the identities of 'black' and 'Irish' were mutually exclusive.

Yet the experiences of not-so-famous black Irish people have been of lifelong rejection and marginalisation (McCarthy, 2001; Murphy, 2001; Mullin, 2001). Moreover, the minority group reporting the highest experience of racism in the 2001 Amnesty survey was 'Black Irish', 88 per cent of whom claimed to have experienced discrimination. Colour lines are emerging then, as argued in Chapter 6, with nationals being lumped together with non-nationals by phenotype. Yet, on another level, the representation of Irishness on sports fields and television is increasingly diverse.

## POST-FAJUJONU CITIZENSHIP:
## A RACIAL–LEGAL GEOGRAPHY OF IRISHNESS

The state's attempt to grasp the nettle in managing the perceived problem of asylum resulted in a significant change in interpretation of citizenship. The Minister of Justice brought his case against two asylum-seeking families who had appealed a decision to deport them on the basis of having Irish-born children. A 1989 Supreme Court ruling (Fajujonu) had granted foreign parents of three Irish-born children (that is, Irish citizens) the right to remain resident in Ireland due to the Constitution's Articles 41 and 42, enshrining the family as the basic unit of society and giving children the right to enjoy the company, society and protection of their family. This right was seen to take precedence over the Minister of Justice's rights to remove foreign nationals from Irish territory, granted under the 1935 Aliens Act and the 1946 Aliens Order.

In January 2003, the Supreme Court ruled by 5–2 to uphold the Department of Justice's decision that Fajujonu could not be applied in every similar case. This means that thousands of children who are Irish nationals can, potentially, be deported from Ireland with their parents.

Any children born in Ireland acquire citizenship as of right (Citizenship Acts 1956, 1986, 2001). Prior to the new judgement, a few thousand foreign nationals with Irish-born children (between 7,000 and 10,000, depending on the source) had been granted residency on the basis of the Fajujonu ruling. Around 10,200 more applications were already in the system as of January 2003. The arguments advanced by the Minister of Justice included those of legislative and social context: there were fewer than 50 asylum applications annually in 1990, and the Refugee Act was years away from introduction. Due process, it was argued, had been applied, and granting residence to every foreign parent of Irish-born children would lead to people abusing the asylum and immigration systems, thus threatening the integrity of these latter two. Indeed, some women in advanced stages of pregnancy arrive in the queue for asylum applications, and given the waiting time for decisions on asylum, the original ruling may well have encouraged many asylum-seekers with

Irish-born children to drop their asylum applications and use this alternative route to residency.

However, the interpretation made by the Supreme Court brings out the possibility of an implicitly racialised imaginative geography of Irish nationality. The legal arguments of the case revolved principally around the question of whose rights should take precedence: the child's right to unqualified citizenship and family protection in his/her country of birth, or the state's right to control the movement of aliens across and within its borders, including the maintenance of the integrity of its asylum and immigration policies. Yet as the two dissenting judges, Fennelly J and McGuiness J, pointed out in their rulings, the Minister of Justice had focussed on the rights of the parents rather than those of the child under the Constitution. Neither judge felt that the Minister's rights should usurp those of the child, which was in effect the substance of the majority ruling.

This ruling still has to be legislated on and tested in the courts, but it opens a revealing line of reasoning, underlying the development of a *de facto* two-tier Irish citizenship along the lines of UK citizenship since the 1960s, where *ius sanguinis* replaced *ius soli* as the governing principle (Garner, 1998). Another constitutional principle, recognising Ireland's heritage as a diaspora nation, is that proof of only one grandparent born in Ireland suffices for citizenship. So people whose bloodlines run through Boston, Sydney or London for example, can obtain the full array of rights open to citizens and bring family to settle permanently in Ireland with no questions asked. Yet children born in Ireland but whose direct ancestry is 'non-EU', the new dividing line between civilisation and barbarity, must have their constitutional right weighed on a case-by-case basis.[13] Moreover, the term 'Irish-born child' even points to a distinction being made between full and marginal citizens. When is a child 'Irish' and when is he or she 'Irish-born'? The latter appears to be applied only in the case of parents who are not nationals, yet the vision of citizenship and membership explicit in the Citizenship Act, 2001 states the opposite: birth in the island of Ireland confers Irish citizenship (regardless of parentage).

Since, in the short term, this ruling will impact solely on Central and Eastern European, African and Asian parents (represented among asylum-seekers), it cannot be described as anything other than institutional or indirect racism.[14] The fact that the victims can also be racialised separately (as white Eastern Europeans, Africans, Asians, and so forth), rather than belonging to one commonly racialised group, is immaterial. The criterion for unequal access to citizens' rights is to have ancestry outside of the Anglo-Celtic settled world.

## THE 'ANOMALOUS STATE' OF IRISH RACIST LOGIC

The anomaly in the state of Ireland, is that categorisation in terms of colonial and contemporary frameworks produces confusion, or at least fascinating ambiguity. Yet, perhaps the kind of smouldering polemical conflict problematised by Kiberd (1997) and Waters (1997), which assumes the guise of 'modernisers' vs. 'traditionalists' at every juncture (reflected in split decisions ensuing from the referenda on abortion, divorce and the Nice treaty, for instance), is ultimately the reddest of herrings. 'Ireland: Postcolonial or European?' is a journalistic device for conferring the status of an organising principle on a set of historical and political positions. It is not an adequate attempt to embrace the shape-changing entity that is Irish identity at the beginning of the twenty-first century. The anomaly consists of a country whose people have long spilled beyond its territory, with the consequence that 'Ireland' goes on simultaneously in more than one place (O'Toole, 1994), and which is at once colonial, postcolonial and European.

In terms of literature syllabi, Ireland has every right to be considered 'postcolonial', perhaps more so than Canada or Australia, yet this is not its overriding and defining national identity. Parallels are frequently drawn between Irish struggles for liberation from the imperial yoke and those waged by Africans, West Indians, Asians, and African Americans (Dooley, 1998). Another parallel, with Said's 'orientalism' is drawn by Kiberd (1995). He argues that much as the West invented the 'Orient', the British invented 'Ireland' and some Irish people bought into it. This line of argument can be illuminating, drawing our attention to the assumptions that 'white' countries cannot be colonised or othered in the same ways as 'black' ones. Yet the specificity of Irish people's experience is that they were colonised, but also had access to positions in which they took part in colonisation, particularly from the eighteenth century onwards in the British Empire, and a little earlier in the Hapsburg one. However, with the orientalist stream of argument, that important element is neglected to the point where the silence surrounding it becomes oppressive. And this need not be the case.

Studying the development of Irish racism cannot logically conclude in a historical equivalence being made between the contemporary situation in Ireland, and European imperialism in the Third World. Nor does it produce a justification of colonialism, or of the British state's partition of Ireland. Neither should it be a means of reinstating a hierarchy of oppression. Pointing out why Ireland's state is anomalous focusses thoughts on contemporary liberation struggles linking migrants, workers, women, the working poor, and the myriad oppressed people in various positions across the globe. To note that Ireland occupies a different space in British imperialism from India, Kenya, Singapore or Guyana is not to argue that it was not colonised, or colonised any less brutally. Comparing the scale of violence used against various peoples, however, as Howe (2000:270) does in his argument about the proportion of coercion to consent, strikes me as a perilous one. The comparison covers recent times, and draws out the idea that white Europeans could not be dealt with by blanket bombing and mass murder as were the unfortunate Iraqi civilians in the 1920s and Mau Mau guerrillas in the 1950s. Yet this does not take into account the earlier massacres in the sixteenth and seventeenth centuries, before the Irish became 'white' and that term meant something concrete in terms of global social positioning. Moreover, those killed in the 'Bloody Sunday' incident were brought down by troops firing machine guns in a residential area of a city in the UK. The complicity of authorities in this is only now beginning to be officially proven in the Saville Enquiry. Finally, the assassination of key republican activists and sympathisers by people acting with the support of, or at least with information supplied by, state sources until the very recent past makes the thesis that the Irish cannot be compared with Third World colonised peoples, at least in this respect, unconvincing.

Yet the British civil service and armed forces in Ireland were not staffed by Indians, Kenyans, Singaporeans or Guyanese, for example, and this is a significant fact because it shows us that there are finite limits to our theorising about parallels, and that every theory must have these so that their valuable parts can be retained and used. Whiteness and Europeanness are identity factors that meant that Ireland has been treated differently from other colonies and post-colonial states, and that Irish people can occupy positions of relative power over those not racialised as 'white'.

A focus on this contradiction on the part of historians would be termed 'revisionist' in certain quarters. Yet there is nothing inherently reactionary about locating social relationships in their precise contexts. Explaining 'whiteness' as a collective identity for example requires looking at power differentials between groups of people who consider themselves 'white' rather than assuming that whiteness equates with a monolithically dominant position. In the same way, Brah (1996:169) indicates that Irish identity is problematic from a European perspective: 'the Irish represent a subordinate racialised category within anti-Irish racism in Britain, but as "Europeans" they occupy a discursive space of dominance via a racism that constructs all non-Europeans as the "Other"'.

All nationalist discourses, all constructions of the nation, function through a series of erasures, or denials. This is one of the principal assertions made by Hobsbawm and Ranger (1983) in their theory of the 'invention of tradition'. Without offering a rigorous critique, Howe (2000) labels this term a cliché of historical studies. While the expression may be, the idea it expresses is nonetheless salient to the theme of racialisation. The nation is not based on historical record but on a selective reading of it, with parts actively contested and dis-remembered. It would, however, be a cliché to suggest that nowhere was this more true than Ireland. There I would be setting foot on the swampy terrain of racist stereotyping. What is relevant to my argument is that, in the Irish case, there are a number of historical erasures effected in nationalist discourse ranging from the Irish dead of the two world wars, women going to the UK for abortions, institutionalised child abuse, and continuing emigration of the economically marginal. Against this background it should not be difficult to see why the erasure from the narrative of Irish history of the Irish role in oppressive practices and positions of dominance overseas, and of Irish racism, particularly anti-Semitism and anti-Traveller racism from the nineteenth century onwards, has been desirable, or why these themes have been of little interest to Irish academia.

Contributors to *Reinventing Ireland: Culture and the Celtic Tiger*[15] for example, make minimal references to asylum-seekers, while examining almost every other aspect of identity that could be construed as important in contemporary Ireland. 'Race' apparently is not important to cutting-edge sociologists and thinkers from other disciplines, unless it is in the nationalist project of consolidating the metanarrative of unbroken and unchanging discrimination across time (cf. Gibbons, 1996) (700 years of oppression by a foreign power, and so on). The 'whiteness' of the Irish as a factor enabling them to rise up the social scale in North America and Australasia formed a vital collective resource from which was generated imperialist-derived ideas about superiority, and more contemporary notions of defence of territory against identifiable Others. Just as whiteness, the racialisation of Others and racist practices are erased and invisible themes for the diaspora, so they are in Irish academia. Morrison (1993) asks how the practitioners of the entire discipline of literary criticism in the USA can function with no acknowledgement or knowledge of the African presence in America, while blackness is an important trope in American literature. She argues that the resulting criticism lacks edge and integrity. We might pose a similar question about Irish academia and 'race'. The work is still relatively restrictive and has not yet reached the mainstream (if work of this type can ever be really mainstreamed into the sociological canon). This book is part of this intellectual enterprise, attempting to analyse the current of hostility toward minorities that only now has somewhere to flow, in the climate created by a complex interaction of media messages, political (in)activity and changing perceptions of Ireland's place in the world.

Analytical, rather than descriptive and empirical work on Irish racism is at a nascent stage, but it is already clear that the problem of 'race' in Irish history has been approached only from one direction. The issue is not simply the historical racialisation of the Irish *per se*, but the differing trajectories and meanings generated by the racialisation of various groups at different moments in history. 'White' Irish communities (with all their internal distinctions) are agents in the process of racialising other groups in Ireland.

The current situation must not be seen as having been generated only in the past few years. The references made by those on both pro- and anti- sides of the debate extend for centuries. Contemporary discourse is more the acting out of a complex set of ambivalences about Irishness that had previously found neither a catalyst nor a historical moment in which to express themselves. Ongoing anxieties about prosperity and property within the context of a rapidly expanding economy have induced divergent interpretations of Irish migration history, and these are deployed implicitly and explicitly in the debates over refugees and asylum-seekers. Yet these inter-related concerns about 'race' (blood) and place (soil) and are bursting their banks under the protracted deluge, not of foreign bodies into Irish space, but of traumatic recollections being acted out and generating their own autonomous sets of logic and aporia about what it means to be Irish at the beginning of the twenty-first century.

In practice, Travellers and non-white groups, whether Irish or not, find themselves clearly mapped on the far side of the border: beyond the new Pale in a new racialised geography of Ireland. Rootlessness has been the fulcrum around which the racist ideologies examined in this book have been developed. In the Irish experience of 'race', Travellers, Native Americans, Australian Aborigines, Jews and the 'wild' or 'mere' Irish of the fifteenth century onwards have all been negatively constructed within this framework. A colonial, proto-racist logic re-emerges as the blueprint of contemporary ones, and has now turned full circle. It has justified land seizure, mass clearance, transportation, massacre, imprisonment, and genocide. It is a weapon of the powerful, swung by foot soldiers at the heads of the disempowered, and has now been internalised and used against the racialised Other in Ireland.

Contemporary analysts such as Kiberd (1995) and Lloyd (1993, 1999) have sought inspiration in the work of Fanon to explain the colonial–colonised relationship. Fanon is a better place to start than most, and his reading of the postcolonial is agonisingly authentic. Yet applying Fanon to imaginative literature, and attributing the same status to all types of text raises the hackles of historians, while sociologists have steered clear in general of the postcolonial paradigm partly because of this tendency. I have a sense of frustration reading such texts, with their absolute Foucauldian focus on discourse and analytical divorce from the material conditions of oppression,[16] even when they are as rich in references and as beautifully written as David Lloyd's. There is a point at which, in the context of critical analysis, understanding should empower the reader and generate action. In the face of the phenomenon of racism in contemporary Ireland there seems to be a bridge waiting to be constructed between the concerns of this stream of literature and those of activists seeking to combat racism, and while there is much work to do in Ireland, there is also a latent energy.

For sociologists, whose task lies neither with remembering nor forgetting, but is concentrated on the perpetual interrogation of the unquestionable, these gaps indicate collective trauma, forms of managing loss. This makes migration (movement between and within states) such a crucial departure point for studying racism and building anti-racism. Not because only migrants are racialised, but because they are rootless, mobile people, modern and timeless, everywhere and nowhere, dis-located and unlocatable, and so many Irish people have also been and will continue to be migrants. The presence of Ireland's 'Others', emerging from a church in Cork, a school in Dublin, their comely daughters *céilidh* dancing, or sons gazing out over the Atlantic from the Cliffs of Moher, reminds the Irish 'us' of its own continuing flight, unheals the wounds of alienation, recalls the hope of finding familiar faces in a foreign street and the humiliation of accepting much less than you are worth because there is nothing better on offer in an inhospitable place.

If any Europeans should be equipped to understand the destructive capacity and impact of the logic of racism on people's lives, it is the Irish. Being a full citizen of an 'anomalous state' allows for deviation from accepted ideas on order and resistance, and it would not be surprising to find in such a set of people the seeds of new orders; below the surface and requiring Heaneyesque unearthing maybe, but capable ultimately of assuming the burden of at least some branches of a new tree of liberty.

# 10
# Conclusions

The argument propounded in this analysis has sought to stress the fluidity, ambiguity and complexity of the phenomena of 'race' and racism in some parts of the Irish experience. In doing so, some elements have been neglected and others prioritised ahead of what could also be argued as essential. At all times, the objective has been to open lines of enquiry rather than propose definitive answers.

Moreover, as I contended at the outset, the stories of racism and vicissitudes of the idea of 'race' are linked to class, gender and nation, but cannot be reduced to them. More urgently, racism should not be allowed to be subsumed by other metanarrative-generating academic and political projects such as Marxism, postcolonial studies, neo-liberalism and nationalisms.

The definition of racism used stresses unequal power relations and the idea of constant change in the way 'race' is understood and the forms in which processes of racialisation function at different times within differing social contexts. This was looked at in terms of colonial Ireland, and one part of the British Empire, the USA and Great Britain, with emphasis being placed on the nineteenth and early twentieth centuries. The notion that racism exclusively involves a black–white paradigm, or even a white–Other paradigm, has been comprehensively disproved by reference to the experience of the Irish, racialised at home and in their diaspora spaces of the Americas and Britain.

Indeed, in analytical terms, the racialisation of the Irish and their racialisation of the Other are parallel and constantly-related processes. The forming and reforming of notions of civilisation only emerge in definition from their opposite, and the same is then true of racialised collective identities based sometimes explicitly, sometimes implicitly on the civilisation–barbarism binary. The lines separating the two may be more blurred at some times, and what lies on one side may differ, but the perception of superiority always underpins racist power relations. This produces constantly changing configurations of belonging and exclusion. In the scope of this book, these have covered *inter alia*, the borders between Gaelic Irish/New English, Irish

American/black American, Protestant English/Catholic Irish, settled Irish/Traveller, Irish/Asylum-seeker and EU national/non-EU national.

Moreover, part of the argument is that 'race' has been a dominant not minor theme framing the development of Irish nationhood, just as it has framed the development of British and American nation-hoods (in which the Irish and the dominant cultures' perceptions of them have played significant roles). Hopefully, some of the ambiva-lence of the structural position of the Irish will have appeared clearly in this study. Ireland has never been a colonising country except by proxy, yet it has been a colonised one (and some will argue that it still is). Contemporary Ireland, moreover, is an open space for transna-tional movements of capital and labour, but the ambivalence has merely assumed new forms. The white Catholic and secular Irish at home find themselves in positions of relative power *vis-à-vis* incoming migrants, just as they do in their relations with Travellers and Irish Jews for example. Hickman and Walter (2002) maintain that the Irish in Britain continue to face discrimination, but, apart from that durable site of conflict, it cannot really be supposed that most Irish are anything but white Europeans, with all the social privilege that entails.[1] That is not a natural and inevitable outcome, but the social resting place of many strategies involving self-defence and the attainment of independence.

The 'whiteness' of the Irish has been a factor enabling them to rise up the social scale in the Americas, Australasia and the UK. It constitutes a critical collective resource from which is generated imperialist-derived ideas (whether second-hand or not) about supe-riority, and more contemporary notions of defence of territory against identifiable Others. The question of whiteness thus emerges as a research priority because it shows how factors other than skin colour have shaped the historical experiences of a racialised nation, invites readjustment of theories focussed on the black–white paradigm, and stresses the dissection of power relations within dominant 'white' nations. To some extent some of these power differentials have been alluded to throughout the book. In Chapter 7 I suggested that whiteness was a hallucination of solidarity induced by the narcotic discourse of the 'national': the unmasked immigrant Other revealing herself as ourselves, distorted. 'Whiten' is an active verb, and it covers a process of seeking social agency, a factor left out of accounts that stress Catholic, Gaelic, rural norms of Irishness as if they were natural and uncontested.

Whiteness[2] is so buried under norms that it is invisible. Over the last four years of personal experience, two examples of this will suffice. A worker visiting my workplace from an organisation collaborating on an EU project told a joke involving a maternity hospital in Limerick. A Limerick man, a Tipperary man and a Nigerian man are waiting to see their new-born children. The nurse takes the two Irishmen to one side and informs them there has been a mix up and the hospital is no longer sure whose baby belongs to whom. The Limerick man immediately picks up the Nigerian child and heads for the exit shouting 'I'd rather this than rear a Tipp child.' The weight of the joke relies on in-depth knowledge of rivalry between those two counties, and the assumption that the measure of the distaste for all things Tipperary is to prefer even a black child to a white one that may be inherently alien. The second incident, also meant as a joke, was a mass email containing an attachment entitled 'Anne Frank's Diary'. This contained the inside of a week planner. The single activity recorded on every day was 'Hid'. Both jokes were told without the slightest fear that they might offend, so monolithically unconnected to anything or anyone Jewish or black was the assumed audience. Two relatively trivial occurrences yet profoundly revealing about what people think is normal and acceptable.

From the vantage point of Ireland, an EU member-state at the beginning of the twenty-first century, it is clear that one of the functions of racism is the control of bodies, moving into and within territory and the imaginary space of the nation. Most asylum-seekers are fixed by 'direct provision' and prevented *de facto* from travelling long distances by withdrawal of papers and minimal benefit (€19.10 per adult per week as of April 2003). Travellers are now faced with criminal law procedures for trespass, which limit the space they can access to enact their culture, based on mobility. Non-white passengers of trains, aeroplanes and boats entering the Republic of Ireland are customarily checked for ID ahead of white foreigners. Half a millennium after the period in which the Gaelic Irish were cast as Scythians on the lowest level of civilisation because of their migratory farming patterns, control of movement is a central aspect of the Irish state's racialising practices: this is one colonial value that has been internalised.

Underlying these strategies is the assumption that all these people are potentially criminal, based simply on racist notions now referred to as 'racial profiling'. Indeed the confluence of security-driven agendas from the late 1990s with the racialisation of the EU/non-EU border has led to a situation in which bureaucratic measures undo decades of civil liberties struggles. The state fingerprints and AIDS-tests people who have never committed, or been accused of, a crime, while in response to trafficking and fraud committed by foreigners, absurdly draconian measures are suggested. In January 2003, Detective Chief Superintendent Martin Donnellan, the head of the Garda National Immigration Bureau (GNIB), proposed that:

> All asylum-seekers, refugees and foreign nationals entering Ireland should be finger-printed at the point of entry to end fraud by a cross-section of foreigners using multiple identities [...] Finger printing would conclusively establish who they were, that is one way of doing it. It is not racist and it is not intended to be. (Collins, 2003)

Yet this type of blasé dismissal of institutional racism and the assumption underlying flagrantly differential treatment for one group of people based on passport-holding, is uncomfortably linked in with a hegemonic idea, Bourdieu's (1998) 'imperialism of the universal', and the state's ongoing monopoly of the rational *vis-à-vis* the irrational people. This relationship is mediated by amoral Weberian bureau-cracy[3] (an administrative machinery and process devoid of moral contextualisation), with a resulting nonchalance about consigning decades of civil liberties struggle to the paper-shredder. This is the kind of ad hoc unravelling of civil society implicit in the types of projects embarked upon by governments of developed countries since the mid 1980s in terms of infrastructure, pensions and other social welfare rights,[4] which is exacerbating polarisation. It is also at the heart of the new American manifest destiny mission in the Middle East.

The false binary of modern/rational v. traditional/irrational in the discourse promulgated as a corollary of contemporary neo-liberal governance is reflected both within societies,[5] and between developed and developing countries. Maybe the battle has now shifted also to the area of contest between super-state and nation state (with little 'irredentisms' like Ireland and Denmark's 'no' votes to the Nice Treaty as manifestations of this irrational).

Within this broad framework, the ideological weight of the dis-tinction between civilised (i.e. rational) and uncivilised (i.e. irrational) as brought to bear in the Irish experience gains explanatory power. In turn, the Gaelic Irish, the Catholic Irish, Native Americans, the

Catholic Irish in America and Britain, and black Americans have found themselves on the wrong side of this equation. The experience of minorities in Ireland since the nineteenth century can be viewed from the same perspective, with mobility and rootlessness as key characteristics that enable Travellers and Jews, for example to be made scapegoats and excluded from the imagined and actual space of the nation.

In contemporary Ireland then, a focus on immigrants and non-nationals as harbingers of disease, criminality and poverty overlooks the fact that similar discourses have been applied to the Irish themselves as well as internal minorities in Ireland. These ideas displace responsibility from nationals to non-nationals, and hold the racialised responsible for kinds of activities that undermine the position of the most vulnerable in Ireland. The extent to which this type of attitude had taken hold by 2000, was revealed in the 'Eurobarometer 2000' exercise, which found 56 per cent of respondents agreeing that minority groups abused social welfare, with only 22 per cent (the lowest in the EU) in disagreement (European Union Monitoring Centre on Racism and Xenophobia, 2001). Connected to this was Ireland's highest score in the EU for those who felt that minorities were afforded preferential treatment (48 per cent, cf. EU average of 33 per cent).

Yet a cursory glance through the newspapers reveals all kinds of financial irregularities and imbalances of power that have nothing whatsoever to do with 'non-nationals'. In the same week as the Supreme Court ruling on Irish-born children, stories were printed about a variety of drains on resources. A Kinsale-based oil company, Marathon, signed an agreement with the state in 1959 which in practice means that it avoids paying any tax (Moloney, 2003). The Committee of Public Accounts heard evidence that Marathon would normally have paid €150m over the previous twelve years. An inquiry into price-fixing by the Competitions Authority met with stonewalling from various professional associations (Williams, 2003). As a matter of policy, fees are not made public, which militates against competition, and helps maintain artificially high prices for particular services. The two stories occupied a quarter of a page in the *Irish Independent*, which devoted four pages and eight stories to the Supreme Court ruling (of which seven were sympathetic to the decision). Implicitly then, the issue of draining public finances and raising the cost of living is more compelling when it involves temporarily resident non-nationals with no decision-making power than it is when the collective actors are entrenched interests such as American multinationals and the indigenous professional classes.

Indeed massive and unremitting over-burdening of PAYE workers parallel to an equally unremitting freedom for business and private landowners emerge as characteristics of the 1990s and the early twenty-first century. House prices rise at a rate that outstrips the costs of building by around 40 per cent, and the current status quo favours landowners holding onto land so that this process reaches a point where money-lending institutions develop programmes to enable parents to borrow money to lend their children against their own property, jeopardising their own future capacity to raise money in retirement. Amid a steady haemorrhage of tax money and artificial inflation fuelled by a minority's absolute detachment from the values of civil society, there is a compartmentalisation of discourses and unwillingness among politicians to link them. The issues of immigration and asylum appear in relation to this occluded structural one. Neo-liberal perspectives that frame discourse on welfare and managed immigration, and question the value of asylum also postulate the trickle-down theory of economics first promulgated by Adam Smith in the eighteenth century. Smith's 'hand of God' distributing prosperity throughout society evoked a natural structuring of a man-made economic system, in the same way as the 'natural' inequalities of class, gender and nationality are the assumptions of the 'real world' of economic decision-making. Yet the 'hand of God' experienced by most people is closer to Maradona's: bending the rules with impunity. People apprehend the choices of the state as either paying for asylum or for education or housing or welfare. The choice of constructing a more equitable tax policy is scarcely broached.

Indeed the most depressing factor of this type of poverty of choice is the degree to which civil society colludes in its own ideological straitjacketing. The responses of the Labour Party and the Irish Refugee Council to the Supreme Court ruling were to ask for clarification and amnesty rather than to argue on a constitutional or human rights basis. On this specific issue, there is nowhere left to run that does not further implicate these types of arguments in the circular closure of racist logic.

The question is not really one of specific detail, that is, who is ripping off who and by how much? Rather 'what are the conditions in which this can happen, on such a scale, and with impunity?' The whole process of imputing responsibility for frittering vital money on the vulnerable groups in society has become a doxa: so far across the line into unquestionable knowledge has this strayed, that retrieving it for interrogation involves a lengthy process, of which this book aims to be a tiny step. It might seem as if I have wandered a long way from the topic of racism, but one of the major lessons to be drawn from this narration of Irish racialisation is that racism remains abstract unless it is placed in its historical, economic, political and social contexts. Doing so begs many questions, some of which have been raised in this book, not least the question of how to construct a tradition of anti-racism for ourselves. Indeed, the questioning process is crucial to re-assessing who and what constitutes the Irish 'we' at the beginning of the twenty-first century. And the questions do not throw up the easy answers the 'we' would like.

# Glossary

**GDP**

Gross Domestic Product (GDP) at market prices represents total expenditure on the output of final goods and services produced in the country ('final' means not for further processing within the country) and valued at the prices at which the expenditure is incurred.

**GNP**

Gross National Product (GNP) is equal to GDP plus net factor income from the rest of the world and represents the total of all payments for productive services accruing to the permanent residents of the country.

**GVA**

Gross Value Added (GVA) at basic prices is a measure of the value of goods and services produced priced at the value received by the producer minus product taxes payable and plus subsidies on products receivable. Total GVA at market prices is equivalent to GDP at market prices.

The following definitions are from Callan et al., 1999.

**Poverty**

'People are living in poverty, if their income and resources (material, cultural and social) are so inadequate as to preclude them from having a standard of living which is regarded as acceptable by Irish society generally. As a result of inadequate income and resources, people may be excluded and marginalised from participating in activities which are considered the norm for other people in society.' (Irish government, National Anti-Poverty Strategy (NAPS))

**Income Poverty**

Households earning less than 50 per cent of the average income. Income lines for this study were set at 40 per cent, 50 per cent and 60 per cent of average household income. The 50 per cent and 60 per cent lines are more commonly accepted as reflecting the reality of poverty, while the 40 per cent line is mainly used for comparative purposes.

## Basic Deprivation

Deprivation refers to the extent to which someone is denied the opportunity to have or do something that is considered the norm in society. A basic index of eight deprivation indicators has been developed by the ESRI to assess basic deprivation levels. The index includes indicators such as not having adequate heating, a day without a substantial meal, arrears on mortgage, rent, electricity or gas, and the lack of a warm winter coat.

## Consistent Poverty

Using deprivation indicators in conjunction with income lines provides a measure of consistent poverty. This shows that those with the lowest incomes are not always those with the lowest standards of living, nor do all those with higher levels of current income necessarily enjoy a higher standard of living. Those who experience both low income and deprivation are identified as being consistently poor, and therefore subject to long-term poverty.

# Appendices

## Appendix 1. Surveys on attitudes towards minorities and minorities' experiences of racism–discrimination in the Republic of Ireland, 1972–2001

| Date | Author(s) | Title | Respondent Group | Sample |
|---|---|---|---|---|
| 1972* | Mc Gréil, Fr. M. | *Prejudice in Ireland* | General Public (Dublin) | 2,017 |
| 1989* | Mc Gréil, Fr. M. | *Prejudice in Ireland Revisited* | General Public | 1,005 |
| 1997 | European Commission | Eurobarometer | General Public | 1,000+ |
| 1998 | Boucher, G. | *The Irish are Friendly but ...: A Report on Racism and International Students in Ireland* | Overseas Students | 48 |
| 1998 | Pilgrim House Foundation | *Asylum Seekers and Prejudice Study* | General Public | 199 |
| 1999 | Pilgrim House Foundation | *Characteristics and Experience of Asylum-seekers in Ireland* | Asylum-seekers | 157 |
| 2000 | African Refugee Network | *African Refugees: A Needs Analysis* | African Refugees and Asylum-seekers | 40 |
| 2000 (January) | *Irish Times*/MRBI | *Irish Times* /MRBI poll, *Political Issues* | General Public | 1,001 |
| 2000 | *Sunday Independent*/IMS | *Survey on Refugees* | General Public | 1,102 |
| 2000 | Citizen Traveller/Behaviour and Attitudes | *Attitudes to Travellers and Minority Groups* | General Public | 1,002 |
| 2000 | *Star*/Lansdowne Market Research | *Racism in Ireland: Special Survey* | General Public | 1,123 |
| 2000 (April) | *Irish Times*/MRBI | *Irish Times*/MRBI poll, *Political Issues* | General Public | 1,000 |
| 2000 | Faughnan, P. and Woods, M. Social Science Research Centre, UCD | *Lives on Hold: Seeking Asylum in Ireland* | Asylum-seekers | 85 |
| 2000 | Citizen Traveller/ Behaviour and Attitudes | *Survey of Travellers* | Travellers | 513 |

| 2000 | Casey and O'Connell[**] | 'Pain and Prejudice' | Minorities | 146 |
|---|---|---|---|---|
| 2000 | Horgan[**] | 'Seeking Refuge' | Migrants | 72 |
| 2000 | Keogh[**] | 'Talking About the Other' | Irish Schoolchildren | ? |
| 2000 | Curry[**] | '...She Never Let Them In' | Refugees and Asylum-seekers | 419 |
| 2001 | Citizen Traveller/Behaviour and Attitudes | A Barometer Study | General Public | 1,200 |
| 2001 | SORA[***] | 'Attitudes Towards Minority Groups in the European Union: A Special Analysis of the Eurobarometer 2000 Survey' | General Public | 1,000 + |
| 2001 | Amnesty International/ Lansdowne Market Research | Attitudes to Minorities | General Public | 1,200 |
| 2001 | Amnesty International/ FAQs | Racism in Ireland: The views of Black and Ethnic Minorities | Minorities | 622 |

[*]   Date indicates when survey was carried out. Mc Greíl published the results from both of the surveys cited in *Prejudice in Ireland Revisited* (1996).
[**]   Published in Mac Lachlan and O'Connell (2000).
[***]   SORA produced the report from the collated figures. It did not carry out the research for Eurobarometer in Ireland.

## Appendix 2. Address from the people of Ireland to their countrymen and countrywomen in America, 1842

You are at a great distance from your native land! A wide expanse of water separates you from the beloved country of your birth – from us and from your kindred whom you love, and who love you, and pray for your happiness and prosperity in the land of your adoption. We regard America with feelings of admiration: we do not look upon her as a strange land, nor upon her people as aliens from our affections. The power of steam has brought us nearer together; it will increase the intercourse between us, so that the character of the Irish people and of the American people must in future be acted upon by the feelings and disposition of each.

The object of this address is to call your attention to the subject of slavery in America – that foul blot upon the noble institutions and the fair fame of your adopted country. But for this one stain, America would, indeed, be a land worthy of your adoption; but she will never be the glorious country that her free constitution designed her to be, so long as her soil is polluted by the footprint of a single slave.

Slavery is the most tremendous invasion of the natural, inalienable rights of man, and some of the noblest gifts of God, 'life, liberty and the pursuit of happiness'. What a spectacle does America present to the people of the Earth! A land of professing Christian republicans, uniting their energies for the oppression and degradation of three millions of innocent human beings, the children of one common Father, who suffer the most grievous wrongs and the utmost degradation for no crime of their ancestors or of their own!

Slavery is a sin against God and man. All who are not for it, must be against it. None can be neutral! We entreat you to take the part of justice, religion and liberty.

It is in vain that American citizens attempt to conceal their own and their country's degradation under this withering curse. America is cursed by slavery! We call upon you to unite with the abolitionists, and never to cease your efforts, until perfect liberty be granted to every one of her inhabitants, the black man as well as the white man. We are all children of the same gracious God; all equally entitled to life, liberty and the pursuit of happiness.

We are told that you possess great power, both moral and political, in America. We entreat you to exercise that power and that influence for the sake of humanity.

You will not witness the horrors of slavery in all the states of America. Thirteen of them are free, and thirteen are still slave states. But in all, the pro-slavery feeling, though rapidly decreasing, is still strong. Do not unite with it: on the contrary, oppose it with all the peaceful means in your power. Join with the abolitionists everywhere. They are the only consistent advocates of liberty. Tell every man that you do not understand liberty for the white man and slavery for the black man: that you are for the liberty of all, of every color, creed and country.

The American citizen proudly points to the national declaration of independence, which declares that 'All mankind are born free and equal, and are alike entitled to life, liberty and the pursuit of happiness.' Aid him to carry out this noble declaration, by obtaining freedom for the slave.

Irishmen and Irishwomen! Treat the colored people as your equals, as brethren. By all your memories of Ireland, continue to love liberty – hate slavery – cling by the abolitionists – and in America, *you will do honor to the name of Ireland.*

(Published in the abolitionist newspaper the *Liberator*, 25.3.1842)

# Notes

## INTRODUCTION

1. TG4 is the Irish-language state broadcaster's television station, and *súil eile* means 'a fresh perspective'.

## 1 SOCIOLOGICAL FRAMEWORKS FOR UNDERSTANDING RACISM

1. For example, Carl Schultz, director of the Federal Department of Health, Education and Welfare's Population Affairs Office estimated that in 1972 alone his office had paid for 100,000–200,000 sterilisations. Moreover, Choctaw physician Dr Connie Uri told the Senate Committee hearing that by 1972 around 24 per cent of Native American women of child-bearing age had been sterilised under government programmes (Davis, 2001:215–18).
2. See Barker's contribution to Goldberg D. and Essed, P. (2001).
3. For an account of 'race relations' as a paradigm in the US see Jacobson (1998).
4. In any case, Raymond Williams (1961:260), referring to correspondence between Engels and Bloch (1890), suggests that even Marx and Engels did not consider the distinction between base and superstructure absolute and unequivocal: 'According to the materialist conception of history, the determining element in history is *ultimately* the production and repro-duction in real life. More than this neither Marx nor myself have ever asserted. If therefore somebody twists this into the statement that the economic element is the *only* determining one, then he transforms it into a meaningless, abstract and absurd phrase.'
5. Logically, to deny someone access to something, the denier must exert a form of power within the specific arena that this denial occurs. A landlord refusing to let to foreigners has the power to dispose of the housing resource he owns, although that same person may well feel politically disempowered in many other areas of his life.
6. It is from misunderstandings of the structural that statements along the lines of 'European societies are inherently racist' are criticised for imposing a mechanistic interpretation of racism as original sin, when it is clear that some individuals are racists and others are not. The salient point is that the structural level is virtually divorced from individual agency; it constrains the actions of individuals and places parameters on them. While the impact of structural factors does not systematically prevent people from exceeding these parameters, organisational and ideological work must be accomplished for the parameters to be crossed.
7. Gramsci distinguished between middle-class intellectuals who championed working-class causes and theorised social change, and

working-class activists and intellectuals (the 'organic intelligentsia') who worked from first-hand experience of class oppression.

8. The ICP won only a few hundred votes in Cork South Central and Dublin South Central. The US-based neo-Nazi movements behind the 'nsrus' web site, and other sites such as 'Atlantic Island' and the 'Irish Nationalist Network' have published racist material.

9. The Tánaiste (Deputy Prime Minister), Mary Harney, stated that the number of work permits might be reviewed in the light of job losses (*Irish Times*, 2001).

## 2 MONEY, MIGRATIONS AND ATTITUDES

1. Figures given in euro equivalent of £IR 11,525 to £IR 21,518 and £IR 10,224 to £IR 18,118 for the sums respectively.

2. S1, S2 and S3. S1 represents unemployed plus discouraged workers *as a percentage of* the Labour Force plus discouraged workers; S2 represents unemployed plus marginally attached plus others not in education who want work *as a percentage of* the Labour Force plus marginally attached plus others not in education who want work; S3 represents unemployed plus marginally attached plus others not in education who want work plus underemployed part-time workers *as a percentage of* the Labour Force plus marginally attached plus others not in education who want work. 'Discouraged workers' are those who are not looking for work as they believe they are not qualified or that no work is available.

3. The figures begin in 1997 because the measurements changed in that year, which saw the introduction of the Quarterly National Household Survey to replace the Labour Force Survey.

4. From 1997 onwards, the parameters for the concept of 'part-time working' were slightly different as the QNHS replaced the Labour Force Survey, and International Labour Organisation definitions were adopted.

5. cf. the USA and Canada with 25 per cent and 24 per cent of their workforces on low pay.

6. In 2001, suicide was the largest cause of death for males aged 15–24 (CSO, 2002d).

7. In the twelve months from 23 February 2002 to 2 March 2003, there were 9,270 assaults, 3,000 of which resulted in serious harm. In the same period, public order offences almost doubled, up from 17,805 in 2001 to 33,792. There were also 22,404 incidents of threatening behaviour in 2002, compared with 15,718 in 2001; 10,027 cases of failing to comply with a Garda direction in 2002, compared with 4,502 in 2001; and 4,993 cases of disorderly conduct in 2002, compared with 2,924 in 2001 (O'Keeffe, 2003).

8. Operation Encounter was launched on 23 February 2002, and ran until 2 March 2003. It was set up to deal with drink-related crime, focussing on pubs, nightclubs and fast-food restaurants. The operation highlighted an alarming increase in street crime since the previous year, 2001.

9. Moreover, in the 2000 USA census, many people who might otherwise be categorised as 'Hispanic' opted to classify themselves as 'white' or

'other race' demonstrating the fluidity of the concept among the public, and how categories provided by official bodies do not necessarily tally with people's own views of themselves.

10. Throughout this chapter there is a sustained critique of the ideological framing of statistics. This does not imply a critique of the CSO staff. As a CSO employee in 1999, I became aware that the power to define topics for study, categories for use in surveys, and the uses to which figures are put lies beyond the area of that agency's responsibility. Indeed there is a high level of professionalism and attempts to intervene judiciously in social debates against a background of understaffing and underfunding.

11. More detailed analysis is due in the publication of data related to migration and nationality in October 2003.

12. The only categories used by the Central Statistics Office in its data collection on migration are: Irish, UK, USA, EU and Rest of the World. The CSO recognised that it was underestimating the number of non-nationals because it excluded institutional residents (i.e. most asylum-seekers) from its surveys. It is therefore likely that estimates prior to 2001 are on the low side.

13. In all the tables relating to percentages of work permits, the totals may add up to slightly less than 100 per cent because of the exclusion of group permits in this breakdown.

14. Czech Republic, Estonia, Latvia, Lithuania, Hungary, Poland, Slovenia, Slovakia, Malta and Cyprus.

15. E-mail from Office of the Refugee Applications Commissioner, 24 January 2003.

16. 120 from Chile (1973); 582 from Vietnam (1979–98); 25 from Iran (1985); and 1,089 from Bosnia (1991–99).

17. The full detailed version of this section is in Garner and White, 2002.

18. Mc Gréil's work is pioneering in many ways and, despite the sometimes unorthodox interpretations and occasionally flawed methodology, merits closer inspection than it has yet received from those interested in racism in Ireland.

19. Social distance surveys date back to a method pioneered by American social scientist Emory Bogardus in the late 1920s. They involve the use of questions that ask the respondent for a degree of acceptance of a member of a given group. These questions refer to whether the member of that group would be accepted as a friend, neighbour, fellow citizen, workmate, spouse of the respondent's child, and so on. Answers are given as numbers from one to five, with the lowest score representing the highest degree of acceptance. The total score is divided by the number of respondents to give a 'mean social distance' lying between one to five. The lower the score, the less the 'social distance', that is the greater the extent of acceptance. Scores of over 3.25 generally mark the group in question as particularly distant.

20. That the ethnic categoristion model proved unsatisfactory is not a fault of the survey design as such, but a problem caused by the overlapping and multiple nature of identities, as alluded to in Chapter 1.

21. 622 returned questionnaires out of 625.

## 3 RACING THE IRISH IN THE SIXTEENTH
## AND SEVENTEENTH CENTURIES

1. Micheál Martin, TD, Minster for Health, opening address to conference on 'Multiculturalism after September 11th', University College, Cork, 2.3.02. Martin's use of the term echoes that of Douglas Hyde (1892).
2. Keating's book, written in Irish, was not published for around a century.
3. Leersen (1988) traces the development of this dialogue from the twelfth to the seventeenth century.
4. Queenan mentions Leonardo Di Caprio, Paul Newman and Tom Hanks as examples, before generalising his argument to other perceived ethnic casting mismatches. His frame of reference is nuanced with American sensitivity to the somatic aspect of ethnic (i.e. racial) phenotypes. The kind of homogeneity Queenan assumes is simply not borne out by the current population of Ireland. Oddly, several Irish people have told me that they have come across individuals abroad whom they thought 'looked Irish' and who indeed turned out to be. I have never heard any other national group make such adamant claims.
5. Thomas Hariot, *A Briefe and True Report of the New Found Land of Virginia.*
6. Bruce and Perowne, 1833. The time lapse is not adequately explained however, either by Canny or Quinn, both of whom study the period after this comment was made. Parker's comment predates the shifts described by them by a decade or two.
7. I am indebted to Allen White for this line of thought.
8. See as a well-known example, Patrick Pearse's retreat in Connemara, where he went regularly to imbibe Irishness.
9. In a letter by Sir Thomas Smith. The Irish are also likened to the Scythians and Tartars in Spenser's *View* and more boldly linked *racially* with the Scythians by Fynes Morison in *An Itynerary*, 1617. (All quoted in Canny, 1976:126–7.)
10. Smith (1947) and Silke (1976) talk of the Puritan Mathew Cradock who shipped people from Kinsale to the New World from 1636, and who also engaged in trade in pork and grain.
11. Even Argentinian Che Guevara's maternal grandmother was a Lynch from the west of Ireland. The linguistic barrier must explain part of this academic inactivity, as well as difficulty in accessing sources. There is, however, a long bibliography on this subject compiled by Brian McGinn available at <www.irishdiaspora.net>.
12. Silke lists missionaries: Fr Achilles Holden, Santo Domingo, 1525; Thomas Field (SJ) in Paraguay at the same time; Fr Richard Arthur in St Augustine, 1597, for example.
13. See Dunn, 1972:127.
14. The argument that Africans were fit for physical labour in the tropics gained ground in the eighteenth century and is found in many justifications of slavery (often alongside contradictory complaints of laziness among them). It was conferred with spurious scientific validation by the work of craniologists and phrenologists working in Europe and America (Fryer, 1984).

15. Beckles (1990a) attributes the arrest of the Irish in this case to paranoia on the part of the authorities. O'Callaghan, who refers to the same incident (2000:128) described a quite different conclusion: with fewer people executed and Irish among them. He quotes no source and does not include Beckles' article in his bibliography. The episode is also referred to in RTE's 1999 *Irish Empire* TV documentary series. Beckles' work (see bibliography) comprises by far the most comprehensive account of seventeenth-century white labour in the anglophone West Indies and his references are replete with primary sources.

16. Dicks, W. (1815) 'Mitigation of Slavery' London, cited by Beckles (1990:509–10).

17. Willoughby to Privy Council, 16 December 1667, C.O 1/21, no. 162 cited by Beckles (1990:509–10).

18. Willoughby to King, 16 September 1667, Stowe MS 735, folio 19, British Library, cited by Beckles (1990:508).

19. These terms indicate varying degrees of whiteness/blackness that make sense only in the context of New World social hierarchies. *Pardo* is closer to white than *moreno* which is somewhere in the middle.

20. Brereton (1998:48) notes that the French thought of the Irish priests who usurped them as 'uncultivated peasants'.

## 4 THE 'FILTHY ARISTOCRACY OF SKIN': BECOMING WHITE IN THE USA

1. Rolston and Shannon (2002:74), quote 60,000, while Allen (1994a:172) states that 60,000 signed in 1841 and a further 10,000 in 1842.

2. Cincinnati Repeal Association letter, 28.8.1843.

3. Allen (1994a:174–6) addresses O'Connell's response to the Cincinnati Repeal Association in detail, and covers the implications for the Repeal Association.

4. The context of these issues is one in which closure on the idea of who was really 'white' (defined in US terms as not black) was not reached until the paradigm shifted in the 1940s. Jacobson (1998) traces a series of court cases in which Southern Europeans, Arabs and Indians contested the definition of 'white' through the 1920s and '30s.

5. Flick, A. (1935) *History of the State of New York*, vol. 7, p. 56, cited by Miller (1969), p. 11.

6. This scholarship in turn owes a debt to historians such as Handlin (1941), Man (1951), Fox (1917).

7. One well-known image is that of stereotypical Irish and black characters sitting in scales, entitled 'The Ignorant Vote – Honours Are Easy', *Harper's Weekly* 9 December 1876. This cartoon can be viewed, *inter alia*, on the website of Yale University's Gilder Lehrman Center, at <http://www.yale.edu/glc/archive/971.htm>.

8. October 1864, p. 517. Quoted by Jacobson, 1998:55.

9. *The North Star*, 5.12.1850.

10. 'Even his views on negro-slavery have been deprecatingly excused, as if excuse were needed for an Irish nationalist declining to hold the negro his peer in right.' Preface to the 1913 edition of Mitchel (1982:370).
11. Quoted by Gibson (1951:90).
12. Allen uses figures from Ernst, 1949.
13. Some details of specifically Irish regiments' contributions are covered by Keneally (1998), Chapters 18–22.
14. Brown cites Garretson, M. (1938:128); and Hornaday, W.T. (1889:496–501).
15. *Irish World*, 12.3.1898.
16. *Irish World*, 11.6.1898.
17. *Catholic Citizen*, 30.7.1898.
18. 'Why We Don't Want the Philippines' *Catholic Citizen*, 10.12.1898.
19. *Pilot*, 4.2.1899 (cited by Jacobson, 1995:190).
20. 'The Wearing of the Green: Irishness as Promotional Discourse in the Career of Colleen Moore', in Negra, 1995:25–53. Moore was of English and German origin, as much as Irish. For the promotion of her film *Sally* (1925) in Dublin, eight men walked around the streets in blackface holding up a placard reading: 'No wonder I look black. I can't see Colleen Moore in *Sally* at the La Scala this week.'

## 5 IN THE BELLY OF THE BEAST: NINETEENTH-CENTURY BRITAIN, EMPIRE AND THE ROLE OF 'RACE' IN HOME RULE

1. Irish settlement in Britain was seen as a social problem before the Famine. A parliamentary report, *The Report on the State of the Irish Poor in Great Britain* (Parliamentary Papers XXXIV), was published in 1836. James Shuttleworth's study of the cotton industry in Manchester, *The Moral and Physical Condition of the Working Classes Employed in the Cotton Manufacture in Manchester* (1832), contained sections on its Irish workers, and Carlyle's vituperative *Chartism* (1839) contains his characteristic verbal bludgeoning of the 'miserable Irish'.
2. Miles (1984) in his sections dealing with Irish immigration attempts to do just this, while Hickman (1995a, 1995b, 1998) and Mac an Ghaill (2001) quite rightly critique the failure of sociologists working in the post-war 'race' paradigms in Britain to acknowledge the historical Irish dimension to racism.
3. Paz (1992) asserts that according to his historical sources, it was the Maynooth Grant affair of 1845 that *de facto* split the Tories rather than the repeal of the Corn Laws.
4. The problem with these figures is that, on the one hand, children of Irish-born parents were not counted but still members of the Irish community, and so census figures in this respect underestimated the size of that entity nationwide. On the other hand, although Protestants comprised a certain proportion of the Irish-born population counted, they tended to identify themselves as other than 'Irish'. For this reason it is not possible to come up with precise figures on the numbers of Irish and Irish-descended Catholics in Britain.
5. Primary source documents relating to agricultural and industrial occupations can be found in Swift, 2002:47–70.

6. This will ring a loud bell for anyone familiar with studies of urban disorder in Britain in the early and mid 1980s.

7. He also studies support for anti-Catholic petitions and concludes that this derived primarily from the 'respectable' orders of society (pp. 280–96).

8. Beddoe (1885) explained the index thus: 'A ready means of comparing the colours of two peoples or localities is found in the Index of Nigrescence. The gross index is gotten by subtracting the number of red and fair-haired persons from that of the dark-haired, together with twice the black-haired. I double the black in order to give its proper value to the greater tendency to melanosity shown thereby [...] From the gross index, the net, or percentage index, is of course readily obtained.' Strikingly, Beddoe could arrive at no conclusion as to the blackness of the Irish as a group.

9. Butler-Cullingford (2001) discusses the Irish attempts to reappropriate the Milesian and Phoenician origin stories in the early twentieth century and infuse them with positivity.

10. Quoted by Kestner, in West, 1996, p. 126. The reference for Huxley is 'The Forefathers and Forerunners of the English People' *Pall Mall Gazette* 10.1.1870: 8–9.

11. *Waterford News*, 6.2.1874, cited by Boyce (1991:197).

12. Maurice Healy, *Cork Daily Herald*, 24.11.1885, cited by Boyce, ibid., p. 215.

13. Cf. Boyce (1986).

14. Curtis 1968:102, cited in McCraild, 1996:137.

15. Letter to Perceval, dated 23.0.1803.

16. In my local sub-post office prior to its closure in 2003, there were five missionary collecting tins, three of which bore pictures of black children and white priests.

17. Waters (1997: 165–6) makes a similar point, and focusses on internalised racism towards all things Irish. This forms part of his argument about tradition and modernity, according to which traditional forms of Irish social organisation are belittled 'racially'.

18. In any case we shall observe in the next chapter that there can be both anti-black racism without blacks and anti-Semitism without Jews.

19. Yet Morash (1998) argues that Sigerson is arguing from within a view that accepts 'race' uncritically, a point with which I concur.

20. Since there were no attitudinal surveys in the nineteenth and early twentieth centuries to gauge popular feelings on 'race', debate has to be confined to discussions of the output of nationalists in terms of speeches, newspapers, pamphlets, and so forth.

21. Foster (2001), always cited as the arch revisionist, looks at the narration of the nation in the essays 'The Story of Ireland', pp. 1–22, and 'Colliding Cultures: Leland Lyons and the Reinterpretation of Irish History', pp. 23–36.

22. Cf. the different dynamic in the USA where the non-white Other was constitutive of the space of whiteness to be filled.

23. *House of Commons Debates* Vol. LIII (*Hansard*, 10.6.1913) Col.1514.

24. *Belfast News-Letter*, 17.4.1912.

25. *House of Commons Debates* Vol. XXXVI (*Hansard*, 11.4.1912) Col. 1490.

26. The cross-border analysis is for another day. It is currently the basis for funding applications.

## 6 OTHER PEOPLE'S DIASPORAS:
## THE 'RACIALISATION' OF THE ASYLUM ISSUE

1. Cf. Butler-Cullingford's (2001) chapter 'Phoenician Genealogies and Oriental Geographies: Language and Race in Joyce and his Successors', pp. 132–60, for a review of the debates on this question.
2. The title of Robbie McVeigh's contribution to Hainsworth's collection (1998).
3. The argument is used for Germany, Central and Eastern Europe, and requires testing against the Irish case.
4. Directed by Louis Lentin and researched by Katrina Goldstone. Broadcast on RTE, 13.10.97.
5. 44 per cent of Travellers reported living in fear of attack and persecution on the roadside (Citizen Traveller: 2000b).
6. For example, Chair of the Southern Health Board and Kerry County Councillor Michael Cahill told Radio Kerry in March 2000 that Travellers were, by nature, thieves.
7. His analysis is of a pamphlet entitled *The Ethics of Sinn Féin*, Dublin, September 1917.
8. In which he sought to unite Catholic and Dissenter under the common name of Irishman.
9. Davis, T. (1890:281).
10. The *Leader*, 27.7.01.
11. Howe (2000:44–9) lists more comments in this direction from such notable figures as Frank Hugh O'Donnell, Hyde and Childers. They operate from the assumption that the Irish are cultured Europeans denigrated by comparison with non-whites. The concept of self-government is posited as a whites-only affair.
12. Speech to meeting of the Catholic Board, Shakespeare Gallery, Exchequer St, Dublin, 8.1.1814. Cited by Allen (1994a).
13. The articles were collected in a book of the same name published in 1861. Sections are reproduced in Deane 1991:177–84.
14. *Within the Pale: The True Story of Anti-Semitic Persecution in Russia* New York: Barnes, 1903.
15. Morash refers to the Swiss Adolphe Pictet, who wrote *Indo-European Origins, or the Primitive Aryans: An Essay in Linguistic Palaeontology* in 1859, and more generally to Bopp, Zeuss, Hermann Ebel, Henri Martin, d'Arbois Jubainville and Camille Jullian, all of whom were writing in the 1850s and 1860s.
16. *United Ireland*, 11.10.1884, cited by Cronin, 1999:109.
17. This author attended an English comprehensive school with a grammar school ethos in the late 1970s and early 1980s. These themes, of the easy overlap between sport and war, and sport as a test of manliness, ring particularly clear bells.
18. Reid (2002).
19. Cf. soccer, the 'foreign game', played primarily in garrison towns.
20. See as exemplary work Lentin (1998) on ethnicity and gender in the 1937 constitution.

21. This in itself is an interesting counter-case: the usual explanation of resource-competition based arguments states that hostility intensifies in economic downturns. One modifier would be that it is rapid social change *per se*, rather than boom or bust, that exacerbates feelings of insecurity that are expressed as racist. Another point is that writers such as Kieran Allen (2000) and Peadar Kirby (2002), *inter alia*, posit a polarisation of income parallel to a net increase. This might suggest that those feeling themselves left behind in Irish society's material advances would be most likely to exhibit racist tendencies. However, although the surveys and opinion polls conducted on attitudes to minorities shed some light on this, it should not be forgotten that institutional racism, more the province of the educated middle classes, cannot be measured in opinion polls.
22. Kelleher (2003).
23. 'Asylum-Seekers Plagued by Legally Questionable ID Arrests' *Irish Examiner* 4.1.02; 'Letters to the Editor' *Irish Times*, 11.5.02.
24. The Employment Equality Act, 1998 and the Equal Status Act, 2000 both list race (sic) as one of the nine grounds for discrimination.
25. The twin problems were articulated by various elected representatives such as Liam Lawlor (Fianna Fáil), Ivor Callely (Fianna Fáil), and Helen Keogh (Progressive Democrat) in the run-up to the 1997 general election and after, with Callely referring to 'a culture that is not akin to Irish culture', and 'the bleeding of lambs in back gardens' ('Callely Targets "Rogue" Asylum-Seekers' *Irish Times* 26.11.97) in the context of an attack on refugees receiving social benefits. Keogh labelled asylum-seekers 'professional beggars', in her election campaign in Dublin.
26. Particularly radio station 96FM, and local free newspaper, *Inside Cork*, which ran a series of 'exposés' on the conditions for asylum-seekers, e.g. 'Shock Government Disclosure on Asylum Welfare Benefits: Irish significantly worse off', *Inside Cork* front page headline, 31.1.02.
27. Equiano (Rolston and Shannon, 2002:3); Lenox Remond in 1841 (Allen, 1994b:172); Douglass in 1845–46 (Allen, 1994b:179).
28. In the documentary series showing the impact of migration on rural Romanian communities, *The Last Peasants*, Channel 4, screened in March 2003, Dublin is referred to by some of the protagonists in the same terms as London and Paris, as a magical Western space in which the migrant can be transformed into a modern wealthy individual.
29. *Dáil Debates*, 10.3.98.
30. This relationship will be explored in depth in Chapter 7.
31. 'Letters to the Editor' *Irish Times* 27.5.98.
32. The 'sans papiers' of the Eglise St Bernard church in Paris, stormed by police in winter 1996, whose case sparked off 'rights for undocumented immigrants' campaigns in neighbouring countries, were principally people in exactly this position, that is, obliged to renew working papers and excluded from state benefits, while paying PAYE taxes.
33. Figures extrapolated from those provided on request by the Refugee Applications Centre, 30.11.99.
34. In any case, there is nothing morally reprehensible about being an economic migrant. I am one, and some of my best friends are also.

## 7 'NEW RACISM', OLD RACISMS AND
## THE ROLE OF MIGRATORY EXPERIENCE

1. As indicated in the chapters dealing with the racialisation of the Irish, in which particular themes and points of similarity emerged in very different socio-political and economic contexts.

2. De Benoît's real name is Robert de Herté, and GRECE stands for Groupe de Recherche et d'Études pour les Civilisations Européennes. This extract is taken from (1983) 'Avec les immigrés contre le nouvel esclavage' *Eléments pour la civilisation européenne* Spring 45:2.

3. The English language is a living thing, adding words and nuances and shedding others; the monarchy has been marked by discontinuity, as various families dispute its ownership, and its relationship to the governed alters; Parliament develops new solutions, such as devolution, and alters the relative weight of its components.

4. Or even more linguistically improbable, 'second generation immigrants', which encases subjects in the transitory legal status of their parents, and marks their otherness through a civil genealogy. For an absorbing assessment of Islam in contemporary France from the inside, see Bencheick (1998).

5. For information on the Gypsy holocaust, 'O parrajmos', see <http://www.geocities.com/Paris/5121/holcaust.htm>.

6. Excellent sources of visual material are: 'The Raced Celt' <http://wsrv.clas.virginia.edu/~dnp5c/Victorian/index.html> and the 'Eugenics Archive': <http://www.eugenicsarchive.org>.

7. *United Irishman*, 23.04. 1904, cited by Keogh (1998:42).

8. 'Coping with Refugees', Fachtna O'Reilly, Cork, in 'Letters to the Editor' *Irish Times*, 4.1.03.

9. Which is part of a package including accommodation and a benefit worth €19.10 per adult per week.

10. This is done by advertising the vacancy on website of the state training agency (FAS) for four weeks and obtaining documentation of the people referred to the vacancy by FAS officials.

11. See Figure 1, Chapter 2.

12. The natural increase (that is, births less deaths) of 29,300 is the largest since 1984 (31,986) (CSO, 2002b).

13. 'Immigrants Exploit "Irish" Baby Loophole', 24.5.98. The article argues that there is apparently a scheme to bring extra-EU women to have their children in Dublin, thus draining the health service of resources and also providing future ammunition for those women's claims to Irish nationality through being the parent of an Irish citizen. However, a stringent analysis of the content finds that this allegation is virtually baseless, and the headline vastly misleading (additionally, people read headlines before they read articles, and in many cases may read headlines only). The first section of the article does not even deal with the hospitals issue, instead focussing on 'a ring of Romanian racketeers, suspected of selling false identification papers to newly arrived illegal immigrants', and another 'French crime gang' thought to be involved in human trafficking. The article contains unsubstantiated suspicions expressed by the

masters of three Dublin hospitals that women were coming to Ireland to give birth, and makes the assumption that this unproven practice is geared to getting rights to a passport through having an Irish-born child. The assumption is then presented as fact in the headline.

14. The article was sourced from a single garda acting in an unofficial capacity, and later denied by the Garda Press Office.

15. Missing values are either 'don't knows' or people who refuse to answer questions. Too high a proportion of missing values tends to reduce the representative character of the sample, as well as raising questions about the motives for failing to give an answer, possibly concealing more extreme views in an effort at self-censorship.

16. *Rollins* v. *Alabama* (1922). The stake for Italian Americans of *not being black* in the USA is still colossal, if the characterisations in Spike Lee's *Do the Right Thing* (1989) and *Jungle Fever* (1992) are accurate.

17. Dutch international Aron Winter, for example, was greeted at his new club's training camp by the slogan 'Welcome to Italy Winter, you dirty Jew!' daubed on a wall. Winter was baffled because it is well known that he is a Muslim (and black). Although Fabio Liverani became Italy's first black international in 2001, the situation on the terraces has hardly improved, as was evident in Newcastle United's match against Inter Milan in the 2003 Champions League for example.

18. The poll also asked for response to the statements: 'Only refugees qualified to do specific jobs should be allowed in' and 'The number of refugees should be limited', which are obviously ridiculous given the clear distinction between refugee and labour migration policies. This backs up the point that the signifiers 'refugee', 'asylum-seeker' and 'immigrant' share a signified. Indeed, on the question on limiting the number of refugees 74 per cent either strongly (42 per cent) or somewhat (32 per cent) agreed with the statement, with only 17 per cent strongly (7 per cent) or somewhat (10 per cent) disagreeing with it. The ambivalence of the respondents is manifest.

19. It is not possible to print this cartoon as permission was denied by the cartoonist in relation to a short article by this author on the media and racism, published in the Comhlámh journal *Focus* (2001).

20. The cover picture and headline for White's (2002) long article on Oldham after the riots are particularly interesting, not to say provocative. A young Asian man holds the arm of an elderly white woman. The headline reads: 'Britain's New Ethnic Minority: It's the Citizen on the Right' (that is, the woman). At the end of the article a man who voted for the British National Party at the general election argues that whites have something to learn from Asian values, sticking together and looking after 'our own'.

## 8 'REMEMBER BLANQUI?': NATION STATE, COMMUNITY AND SOME PARADOXES OF IRISH ANTI-RACISM

1. Faulks (2000) sees an identical problem in terms of citizenship's relationship to the nation state. He terms his solution 'postmodern citizenship'.

2. *'L'oubli, et je dirai même l'erreur historique, est un facteur essentiel de la création d'une nation, et c'est ainsi que le progrès des études historiques est souvent pour la nationalité un danger.'*

3. I am working from Lloyd's (1999) summary of Benjamin's work, and indebted to the insight granted by a philosopher in whom I would not otherwise have been interested.

4. His involvement in anti-slavery is covered amply by the references given. He was also a founder member of the British India Society (1839).

5. In 1908 Margaret Cousins, her husband and the Sheehy-Skeffingtons founded the Irish Women's Franchise League. In 1910 Cousins campaigned for women's suffrage in London and was imprisoned in Holloway Prison. In January 1913 Cousins was imprisoned in Mountjoy and Tullamore Jails for suffragette activities where she went on a hunger strike to secure her release. Cousins supported Irish independence but distrusted John Redmond's Irish Party which had failed to support women's suffrage in the British Parliament. In June 1913 James and Margaret Cousins emigrated to India where, in 1917, she founded the Indian Women's Association. In 1922 Cousins was appointed the first woman magistrate in India and in 1928 she founded the first All-India Women's Conference. In December 1932 Cousins, while still a magistrate, was sentenced to one year in prison for protesting at the introduction of legislation which curtailed free speech in India. While in Vellore Women's Jail she went on hunger strike in support of Mahatma Gandhi, then also imprisoned. After her release in October 1933 Cousins continued to campaign for women's rights and in 1938 she was elected President of the All-India Women's Conference. Hubert Butler (1900–90) was a writer on Irish and European affairs who took part in operations to smuggle Jews out of Nazi-occupied Austria. He developed a critical line on the Free State and this outspokenness resulted in him becoming *persona non grata* in his native Kilkenny.

6. A small but telling point: 'race' is not cited as belonging to this 'most evident' category.

7. Sustaining Progress – Social Partnership Agreement 2003–2005; Programme for Prosperity and Fairness (1 April 2000 to 21 December 2002); Partnership 2000 (1 January 1997 to 31 March 2000); Programme for Competitiveness and Work (1 January 1994 to 31 December 1996); Programme for Economic and Social Progress (1 January 1991 to 31 December 1993); Programme for National Recovery (1 January 1987 to 31 December 1990).

8. Johnson to Irish Trade Union Congress Executive, 5.7.1925. 'Tom Johnson Collection' in National Library of Ireland, Ms 17230, cited by Allen (2000), p. 111.

9. Cf. Goldring's remarks on Sinn Féin's ideas for the civil service, Chapter 6.

10. 'The Pale and the Gael' *New Ireland Review* 1905.

11. An interesting encapsulation of this was the television advert run by the Allied Irish Bank (AIB) in 2001. The AIB sponsors the national gaelic football championship, and the advert showed a small boy being led to the pitch by a man we assume is a grandfather. The GAA operates on a parish basis, like the Church. The slogan ran 'you don't choose your team, you inherit it'. The anchoring of commitment to locality (*vis-à-vis* the international mobility of soccer for example) emerges as a defining value

of gaelic games, and implicitly grants differential access to ownership and access to the symbolic capital of community membership.

12. Clogheen saw protests against the siting of 40 asylum-seekers in 2000, and the premises earmarked for them were the subjects of arson attacks. The villagers finally voted to accept 15 people in May 2000 (McCormack, 2000). For Myshall see Murphy, S. (2000); Rosslare was widely covered in all the national newspapers throughout the April–June period. Ultimately the building purchased there by the Department of Justice was not used to house asylum-seekers. The Mosney holiday camp in Co. Meath was another controversial site for housing asylum-seekers, a controversy that developed later in 2000 (Byrne, 2000; Cassidy, 2000).

13. 'Pour un nouvel internationalisme' Paper given in Frankfurt, 7.6.97, pp. 66–75.

14. There is a large amount of information on this issue contained in the Statewatch News Online journal. See Bibliography.

15. See <http://www.statewatch.org/news/2002/dec/05refugee.htm>.

16. The EU15 plus Norway, Iceland and Switzerland.

17. The lists are laid out in the Aliens (Visas) (No. 2) Order, 2002 S.I. No. 509 of 2002, revoking The Aliens (Visas) Order, 2002 S.I No. 178 of 2002, which had first done so.

18. An entire monograph could be readily compiled on the stories I have heard on this issue.

19. The approach is encapsulated in DTEDG (1992) Travellers: New Analysis and New Initiatives.

20. Anti-Racism Campaign: <http://flag.blackened.net/revolt/arc.html>; Immigrant Solidarity: <http://flag.blackened.net/revolt/is.html>; Residents Against Racism's website seems to have been removed.

21. While the strength of the Socialist Worker Party in Ireland is hardly comparable to that of Militant in 1980s Britain, black community organisations' experience of Liverpool City Council control may be indicative of the types of power and priority problems that emerge (Liverpool Black Caucus, 1986).

22. ARASI: <http://indigo.ie/~arasi/>; African Refugee Network: <http://www.refugee.150m.com/home.shtml>.

23. <www.metroeireann.com>.

24. See Linebaugh and Rediker's chapter on Despard (2000), as well as Bolland (1977), Conner (1999) and Linebaugh (ed.) (forthcoming).

25. Letter to William Lloyd Garrison, 1.1.1846.

26. Poet (Songs of Myself (1910); Lyrical Poems (1913)) and participant in the Easter Rising.

27. Sinn Féiner and first leader of the Irish Socialist Party.

28. Co-founder of the Gaelic League, scholar and minister in the First Dáil (1919–21) and in the Irish Free State (1922–25).

29. 'Labour and Local History: The Case of Jim Gralton, 1886–1945' in Gibbons, 1996:94–106, first appeared in Saothar: The Journal of the Irish Labour History Society (14), 1989.

30. For 1992 reference, see bibliography. The 1998 one is to a speech called 'Les abus de pouvoir qui s'arment ou s'autorisent de la raison' Frankfurt, 15.10.95 in Contre Feux 1:25–6.

31. <www.comhlamh.com>.

32. Sinn Féin emerged with six TDs, gaining five since the previous elections in 1997.
33. Acceptance speech for the Ernst Bloch Prize, Ludwigshafen, Germany, 1997.

## 9 BEYOND THE NEW SOCIO-ECONOMIC 'PALE': RACIALISATION AND BELONGING IN CONTEMPORARY IRELAND

1. Indeed gardai in Dublin went so far as to warn asylum-seekers to keep away from public places at night in 1998. See also Lentin (2002b).
2. Contestants from Northern Ireland also enjoy the potentially lucrative privilege of being eligible to play in *Who Wants to be a Millionaire?* both in the UK and the Republic of Ireland.
3. This issue arose over the refusal of planning permission to a German woman in Co. Clare. 'Clare County Council Accused of Racism as Housing Plan Enforced' *The Examiner* 17.2.00. However, moves toward this policy had already been made, and had been criticised by former Clare TD Mosajee Bhamjee. 'Clare Plan is "Institutional Racism"'' *Irish Times*, 5.11.99. Cf. also 'Review of Plan on "Non-Locals" Welcomed' *Irish Times* 24.5.00.
4. This was ostensibly an issue of planning permission. Local residents led by a solicitor quashed the government's attempt to turn a group of buildings into a hostel for asylum-seekers: 'Department of Justice's Emergency Reception Centre Unlawful' *Irish Examiner* 18.4.00. However, a letter in the *Sunday Tribune* (16.4.00), from someone purporting to be a member of Pembroke Road Residents' Association, declared that the area was 'becoming saturated with unwanted elements who are a threat to the settled community'.
5. Kearney discusses this in reference to the 1930s and 1940s: 'the former *political* threat to our national identity was now replaced by a *moral* threat. And since it was continually asserted in these rather insular years that this threat to our "faith and morals" came principally from abroad [...] the presumption could be sustained that the root cause of our evils came once again from *without*' (original emphasis) (1988:245).
6. Walter Lorenz, Jean Monnet Professor of European Integration at University College Cork, argued in March 1998 that: 'It isn't a question of the numbers of people coming here, but has more to do with the image of ourselves as a society that traditionally has had to defend itself against foreign interests' (*Irish Times*, 1998b).
7. It is no accident either that these were the two groups that suffered most appallingly under the Nazis: both represented degenerate stock and differing forms of threat to the march of the Aryan 'race'.
8. Bloom had converted to Protestantism, thus making himself a double outsider in Ireland (Lentin, 2002a).
9. Roma refugees, who headed the league table of minorities whose presence was felt to be most disturbing by Irish respondents to the two opinion polls in 2000 that posed that question, must surely then also qualify as part of the 'national repressed'.
10. Whether stereotypically feckless, like the Irish in nineteenth-century Britain or Afro-Caribbeans a century later, or too clever and clannish like Jews at the turn of the twentieth century and Asians in post-war Britain.

11. <www.samanthamumbausa.com.biog/index/html.> (in 2001; the interview has been updated since then). Any rough edges seem to have been sandpapered off in the effort to package her as a bland product. The 2000 single 'Body to Body', based note for note and in part lyrically on David Bowie's 'Ashes to Ashes', certainly doesn't rhyme 'funky' with 'junkie'. The track's use in a road safety advertisement, however, is more ironic.

12. UCC, first- and third-year Politics and Social Policy courses 2002–03.

13. Foreign nationals seeking naturalisation must wait five years before entering the process, which currently lasts around 18 months, meaning that *de facto* six and a half years' residency and taxpaying is required to grant eligibility for citizenship, whereas someone who has never set foot in Ireland or paid into its economy can pick up a passport through his or her parents' or grandparents' nationality.

14. Moreover, many of the Eastern bloc countries are candidate states as of April 2003 and will enter the EU on 1.1.04. Ireland has already agreed to grant nationals of those countries free access and residency. None of their nationals will require residence rights through the 'Irish-born child' route, leaving only non-European nationals affected by the ruling.

15. This book is identified because it represents radical thinking on other areas, and the authors are cited approvingly in this book elsewhere. Having seen the names of the editors, I picked it up expecting at least a cursory treatment of the issue of identity seen from the perspective of 'race'.

16. The citing of Foucault a*d nauseam* in contexts of the serious and important debates by writers on the postcolonial ignores both the fact that he was virtually silent on racism, and that a key message from Foucault's writing is not only that words play the determining role in generating and mediating oppression, but that ultimately all metanarratives, even those constructed to develop progressive agendas, are baseless, mere 'effects' of discourse.

## 10 CONCLUSIONS

1. In 20 years this sentence will self-destruct! (I hope).

2. Here I refer to the concept that the world is divided up into races, one of which is 'white', an identity that encloses cultural and social characteristics shared by its members.

3. Strict Weberians will probably berate my redundant use of 'amoral' in this sentence. My defence is that it is a rhetorical device to assist non-specialists.

4. Cf. Bourdieu on the 1995 strikes in the French civil service around alterations to pension rights in '*Contre la destruction d'une civilisation*' (1998:30–3).

5. Maybe even within political families. The ideological blue water placed between 'New Labour' and 'Old Labour' in the Blairite project in the UK since 1996 seems to reflect this justification of the jettisoning of core values as irrational.

# Bibliography

Adams, G. (2000) 'Fighting Racism in Ireland' *Star* 25.8.00

African Refugee Network (1999) *African Refugees: A Needs Analysis* Dublin: ARN

Akenson, D. (1997) *If the Irish Ran the World: Montserrat, 1630–1730* Montreal: McGill, Queens University Press

—— (2000) 'Irish Migration to North America 1800–1920' in Bielenberg (ed.), pp. 111–38

Allen, K. (2000) *The Celtic Tiger: The Myth of Social Partnership in Ireland* Manchester: Manchester University Press

Allen, T. (1994a) *The Invention of the White Race (Vol. 1)* London: Verso

—— (1994b) *The Invention of the White Race (Vol. 2)* London: Verso

Almaguer, T. (1994) *Racial Fault Lines: The Origins of White Supremacy in California* Berkeley: University of California Press

Amnesty International/Lansdowne Market Research (2001a) *Attitudes to Minorities* Dublin: AI, April 2001

—— (2001b) Amnesty International/FAQs *Racism in Ireland: The Views of Black and Ethnic Minorities* Dublin: AI, September 2001

Andall, J. (2000) *Gender, Migration and Domestic Service: The Politics of Black Women in Italy* Aldershot: Ashgate

Andersen, J. (2000) 'The Danish People's Party, Democracy and Foreigners' Paper given at conference on 'The Extreme Right in Europe', Berlin: Hann Siedel Foundation, 2.11.00

Anderson, B. (1983) *Imagined Communities* London: Verso

Aniagolu, C. (1997) 'Being Black in Ireland' in Crowley and Mac Laughlin (eds), pp. 43–52

Anthias, F. (2002) 'Diasporic Hybridity and Transcending Racisms: Problems and Potentials' in Anthias and Lloyd (eds), pp. 22–45

Anthias, F. and Lazaridis, G. (eds) (1999) *Into the Margins: Migration and Exclusion in Southern Europe* Aldershot: Ashgate

Anthias, F. and Lloyd, C. (eds) (2002) *Rethinking Anti-racisms* London: Routledge

Back, L. (1996) *New Ethnicities and Urban Culture: Social Identity and Racism in the Lives of Young People* London: UCL Press

Balibar, E. (1991a) 'Racism and Nationalism' in Balibar, E. and Wallerstein, I. *Race, Class and Nation: Ambiguous Identities* London: Verso, pp. 37–67

—— (1991b) 'The Nation Form' in Balibar, E. and Wallerstein, I., pp. 86–106

Banton, M. (1977) *The Idea of Race* London: Tavistock

—— (1987) *Racial Theories* Cambridge: Cambridge University Press

Barcroft, P. (1995) 'Immigration and Asylum Law in the Republic of Ireland' *International Journal of Refugee Law* 7(1):84–99

Barker, M. (1981) *The New Racism* London: Junction Books

Barnard, T. (1975) *Cromwellian Ireland* Oxford: Oxford University Press

—— (1994) 'The Hartlib Circle and the Cult of Improvement in Ireland' in Greengrass et al. (eds), pp. 281–97

Barrett, J.R. and Roediger, D.R. (1997) 'Inbetween Peoples: Race, Nationality and the "New Immigrant" Working Class' *Journal of American Ethnic History* Spring 1997:3–44

—— (2002) 'Irish Everywhere: The Irish and the "Americanization" of the "New Immigrants" in the United States, 1900–1930' paper presented at conference on Irish History, London: UCL, April 2002

Barrett, A., FitzGerald, J. and Nolan, B. (2000) 'Earnings Inequality, Returns to Education and Low Pay' in Nolan et al. (eds), pp. 127–46

Barrett, A. and Trace, F. (1998) 'Who is Coming Back? The Educational Profile of Returning Migrants in the 1990s' *Irish Banking Review* Summer

Barry, J., Herrity, B. and Solan, S. (1989) *The Travellers' Health Status Study* Dublin: Health Research Board

Bauman, Z. (1990) *Modernity and Ambivalence* Cambridge: Polity Press

—— (1991) *Modernity and the Holocaust* Cambridge: Polity Press

Beckles, H. (1989) *White Servitude and Black Slavery in Barbados, 1627–1715* Knoxville: University of Tennessee Press

—— (1990a) '"A Riotous and Unruly Lot": Irish Indentured Servants and Freemen in the English West Indies, 1644–1713' *William and Mary Quarterly* 47(1):3–22

—— (1990b) *A History of Barbados from Amerindian Society to Nation State* Cambridge: Cambridge University Press

Beddoe, J. (1885) *The Races of Britain*

Belchem, J. (1985) 'English Working-Class Radicalism and the Irish, 1815–50' in Swift and Gilley (eds), pp. 85–97

Bencheick, S. (1998) *Marianne et le prophète: L'Islam dans la France laïque* Paris: Grasset

Benjamin, W. (1969) 'Theses on the Philosophy of History' in Arendt, H. (ed.) *Illuminations* New York: Schocken

Bernstein, I. (1990) *The New York Draft Riots of 1863: Their Significance for American Society in the Civil War Period* Oxford: Oxford University Press

Best, G.F.A. (1967) 'Popular Protestantism in Victorian Britain' in Robson, R. (ed.) *Ideas and Institutions of Victorian Britain* London: G. Bell and Son, pp. 114–42

Bielenberg, A. (ed.) (2000a) *The Irish Diaspora* London: Longman

—— (2000b) 'Irish Emigration to the British Empire, 1700–1914' in Bielenberg (ed.), pp. 215–30

Binchy, W. (2003) 'Thousands of Families at Risk after Court Decision' *Irish Times* 1.2.03

Boate, G. (1652) *Ireland's Naturall History* London

Boemus, J. (1520) 'The Manners, Laws and Customs of all People'

Bolger, D. (1992) 'In High Germany' in his *A Dublin Quartet* London: Penguin

—— (2002) 'Team Spirit' *Irish Times Supplement* 1.6.02

Bolland, N. (1977) *The Formation of a Colonial Society: Belize, From Conquest to Crown Colony* Baltimore: Johns Hopkins University Press

Bonnett, A. (2000) *White Identities: International and Historical Perspectives* New York: Prentice Hall

Boucher, G. (1998) *The Irish are Friendly but ... A Report on Racism and International Students in Ireland* Dublin: Irish Council for International Students

Bourdieu, P. (1977) *Outline of a Theory of Practice* Cambridge: Cambridge University Press

—— (1992) 'Deux impérialismes de l'universel' in Fauré, C. and Bishop, T. (eds) *L'Amérique des Français* Paris: François Bourin, pp. 149–55

—— (1998) *Contre feux, tome 1: Propos pour servir à la résistance contre l'invasion néo-libérale* Paris: Liber

—— (2002) *Interventions, 1961–2001: science sociale et action politique* Marseille: Agone

Boyce, D.G. (1986) 'The Marginal Britons: The Irish' in Colls, R. and Dodd, P. (eds) *Englishness: Culture and Politics 1880–1920* London: Routledge

—— 1991 [1982] *Nationalism in Ireland* London: Routledge

Brah, A. (1996) *Cartographies of Diaspora: Contesting Identities* London: Routledge

Brah, A., Hickman, M. and Mac an Ghaill, M. (eds) (1999) *Global Futures: Migration, Environment, and Globalisation* New York: St Martin's Press

Brereton, B. (1998) 'The White Elite of Trinidad, 1838–1950' in Johnson and Watson (eds) pp. 32–70

Brettell, C. (1993) 'The Emigrant, the Nation and the State in 19th and 20th Century Portugal' *Portuguese Studies Review* 2(2):51–65

Bridges, A. (1984) *A City in the Republic: Antebellum New York and the Origins of Machine Politics* New York: Cornell University Press

Brodkin, K. (1998) *How Jews Became White Folks: And What that Says about Race in America* New Brunswick, NJ: Rutgers University Press

Brosnan, P. (1997) 'More Free Rides on the Tigers Back' *Examiner* 17.10.97

Brow, J. (1990) 'Notes on Community, Hegemony and Uses of the Past' *Anthropological Quarterly* 63(1): 3

Brown, A. (1999) '"The Other Day I Met a Constituent of Mine": A Theory of Anecdotal Racism' *Ethnic and Racial Studies* 22(1):23–55

Brown, D. (1970) *Bury my Heart at Wounded Knee: An Indian History of the American West* New York: Bantam Books

Brown, P. (2001) 'Belfast more Segregated since Process Began' *Irish Times* 4.1.01

Brown, T. (1985) *Ireland: A Social and Cultural History 1922–1985* London: Fontana

Bruce, J. and Perowne, T.T. (eds) (1833) *Matthew Parker's Correspondence* Cambridge

Bryce, J. (1902) 'The Relations of the Advanced and Backward Races of Mankind' University of Oxford, Romanes Lecture

Bunyan, T. (2002) 'The "War on Freedom and Democracy": An Analysis of the Effects on Civil Liberties and Democratic Culture in the EU' Statewatch online, September. Available at: <http://statewatch.org/news/2002/sep/04freedom.htm>

Burleigh, M. (2000) *The Third Reich: A New History* London: Macmillan

Burleigh, M. and Wippermann, W. (1991) *The Racial State: Germany 1933–45* Cambridge: Cambridge University Press

Butler-Cullingford, E. (2001) *Ireland's Others: Gender and Ethnicity in Irish Literature and Popular Culture* Cork: Cork University Press/Field Day

Butt, I. (1866) *Land Tenure in Ireland: A Plea for the Celtic Race* Dublin: John Heywood

Byrne, A. (2000) 'Local Fears over Asylum-Seeker Plan' *Irish Times* 14.12.00

Cáchon Rodriguez, L. (1995) 'Marco institucional de la discriminacion y tipos de inmigrantes en el mercado de trabajo de Espana' *Reis* (69):105–24

Cairns, D. and Richards, S. (1988) *Writing Ireland: Colonialism, Nationalism and Culture* Manchester: Manchester University Press

Callan, R., Layte, B., Nolan, D., Watson, C.T., Whelan, J., Williams and B. Maître (1999) *Monitoring Poverty Trends: Data from the 1997 Living in Ireland Survey* Dublin: Stationery Office/Combat Poverty Agency

Callan, T., Keeney, M. and Walsh, J. (2002) 'The Distributive Impact of Budgetary Policy: A Medium-Term View' in *Budgetary Perspectives, 2003* Dublin: ESRI

Campion, E. (1571) *A historie of Ireland: Written in the Year 1571*

Canny, N. (1976) *The Elizabethan Conquest of Ireland* Brighton: Harvester Press

—— (2001) *Making Ireland British 1580–1650* Oxford: Clarendon Press

Carby, H. (1982) 'White Woman Listen! Black Feminism and the Boundaries of Sisterhood' in CCCS, pp. 212–35

Carmichael, S. and Hamilton, C. (1967) *Black Power: The Politics of Liberation* New York: Random House

Caro de Delgado, Aída R. (1969) *Ramón Power y Giralt: diputado puertorriqueño a las Cortes Generales y Extraordinarias de Espana 1810–1812: compilación de documentos* San Juan de Puerto Rico: [s.n.]

Carroll, R. (2001) 'Racist, Violent, Corrupt: Welcome to Serie A' *Guardian* 6.5.2001

Casey, S. and O'Connell, M. (2000) 'Pain and Prejudice' in Mac Lachlan and O'Connell pp.19–48

Cassidy, C. (2000) 'Mosney Refugee Plan Opposed' *Irish Times* 28.11.00

Castles, S. (2000) *Ethnicity and Globalisation: From Migrant Worker to Transnational Citizen* London: Sage

Castles, S. and Kosack, G. (1985) *Immigrant Workers and Class Structure in Western Europe* Oxford: Oxford University Press

Castles, S. and Miller, M. (1993) *The Age of Migration: International Population Movements in the Modern World* London: Macmillan

CCCS (Centre for Contemporary Cultural Studies) (1978) *On Ideology* London: Hutchinson

—— (1982) *The Empire Strikes Back* London: Hutchinson

*Centre pour l'égalité des chances et la lutte contre le racisme* (2001) Annual Report 2000: Brussels

CERA (1998) *Extremism in Europe: 1998 Survey* Paris: CERA/Editions de l'Aube

Citizen Traveller/Behaviour and Attitudes (2000a) *Attitudes to Travellers and Minority Groups* Dublin: Citizen Traveller

—— (2000b) *A Survey of Travellers* Dublin: Citizen Traveller

—— (2001) *A Barometer Survey*, June 2001

CNCDH (Commission Nationale Consultative des Droits de l'Homme) (2001) *2000. Lutte contre le racisme et la xénophobie: rapport d'activité* Paris: La Documentation Française

Cockcroft, W. (1974) 'The Liverpool Police Force, 1836–1902' in Bell, S.P. (ed.) *Victorian Lancashire* Newton Abbott: David and Charles, pp. 150–6

Cohen, P. (1997) *Rethinking the Youth Question: Education, Labour and Cultural Studies* London: Palgrave

Cole, J. (1997) *The New Racism in Europe: A Sicilian Ethnography* Cambridge: Cambridge University Press

Colley, L. (1992) *Britons: Forging the Nation 1707–1837* New Haven: Yale University Press

Collins, L. (2003) 'All Change Now for our Asylum-Seekers' *Sunday Independent* 26.1.03

—— (2002) 'Travellers Get Preferential Treatment from State: paper' *Sunday Independent* 3.11.02

Commission on Itinerancy (1963) *Report of the Commission on Itinerancy* Dublin: Government Publications

Conner, C. (1999) *Colonel Despard: The Life and Death of an English/Irish Jacobin* Conshohocken: Combined Publishing

Connolly, J. (1910) *Labour in Irish History* Dublin: Maunsel

Coogan, T.P. (2000) *Wherever is Green is Worn: The Story of the Irish Diaspora* London: Hutchinson-Arrow

Corcoran, M. (1997) 'Clandestine Destinies: The Informal Economic Sector and Irish Immigrant Incorporation' in Mac Laughlin (ed.) pp. 236–52

—— (2002) 'The Process of Migration and the Reinvention of Self: The Experiences of Returning Irish Emigrants' *Eire-Ireland* Spring–Summer 37(1–2):175–91

Corkill, D. (1996) 'Multiple National Identities, Immigration and Racism in Spain and Portugal' in Jenkins, B. and Sofos, S. (eds) *Nation and Identity in Contemporary Europe* London: Routledge, pp. 155–70

Coughlan, P. (1989a) (ed.) *Spenser and Ireland: An Interdisciplinary Perspective* Cork: Cork University Press

—— (1989b) '"Some Secret Scourge which Shall by Her Come unto England": Ireland and Incivility in Spenser' in Coughlan (ed.), pp. 46–74

—— (1990) '"Cheap and Common Animals": The English anatomy of Ireland in the Seventeenth Century' in Healy, T. and Sawday, J. (eds) *Literature and the English Civil War* Cambridge: Cambridge University Press, pp. 205–26

—— (1994) 'Natural History and Historical Nature: The Project for a Natural History of Ireland' in Greengrass, M., Leslie, M. and Raylor, T. (eds) *Samuel Hartlib and Universal Reformation* Cambridge: Cambridge University Press, pp. 298–317

—— (2000) 'Counter-Currents in Colonial Discourse: The Political Thought of Vincent and Daniel Gookin' in Ohlmeyer, J. (ed.) *Political Thought in Seventeenth-Century Ireland: Kingdom or Colony* Cambridge: Cambridge University Press, pp. 56–82

Coulter, C. and Coleman, S. (2003) *The End of Irish History?* Manchester: Manchester University Press

Courtney, D. (2000) 'A Quantification of Irish Migration with Particular Emphasis on the 1980s and 1990s' in Bielenberg (ed.) pp. 287–316

Craton, M. (1997) *Empire, Enslavement and Freedom in the Caribbean* Kingston/London: IRP/James Currey

CRE (Commission for Racial Equality) (1991) *A Measure of Equality: Monitoring and Achieving Racial Equality in Employment* London: CRE

Cronin, M. (1999) *Sport and Nationalism in Ireland: Gaelic Games, Soccer and Irish Identity since 1884* Dublin: Four Courts Press

Cronin, M., Gibbons, L., Kirby, P. and Peillon, M. (eds) (2002) *Reinventing Ireland: Culture and the Celtic Tiger* London: Pluto Press

Crowley, E. and Mac Laughlin, J. (eds) (1997) *Under the Belly of the Tiger: Class, Race, Identity and Culture in the Global Ireland* Dublin: Irish Reporter Publications

CSO (Central Statistics Office) (1998) *The Demographic Situation of the Traveller Community in April 1996* Dublin: CSO

—— (2001) *Length and Pattern of Working Time* Cork: CSO

—— (2002a) *2002 Statistical Yearbook* Cork: CSO

—— (2002b) *Population and Migration Estimates – April 2002* (September 2002) Dublin: CSO

—— (2002c) *National Accounts and Expenditure, 2002* Cork: CSO

—— (2002d) *Vital Statistics (Annual Summary)* Cork: CSO

—— (2003a) *Quarterly National Household Survey, Quarter 4, 2002* Cork: CSO

—— (2003b) *Census 2002: Principal Demographic Results* Dublin, Stationery Office

Cullen, P. (1997a) 'The 1997 Border Campaign: Refugees, Asylum and Race on the Borders', in Crowley and Mac Laughlin (eds), pp. 101–7

—— (1997b) 'Increased Surveillance to Stem Flow of Immigrants' *Irish Times* 18.4.97

—— (1998) 'Owners of Pub Deny Racism in Licence Appeal' *Irish Times* 24.10.98

—— (2000) *Refugees and Asylum Seekers in Ireland* Undercurrents series, Cork University Press: Cork

Cunningham, G. (1965) 'The Italian: A Hindrance to White Solidarity in Louisiana, 1890–98' *Journal of Negro History* 50, January

Curry, P. (2000) 'She Never Let Them In' in Mac Lachlan and O'Connell, pp. 137–52

Curtis, L. (1984) *Nothing but the Same Old Story: The Roots of Anti-Irish Racism* London: GLC

Curtis, L.P. (1997 – revised edition) *Apes and Angels: The Irishman in Victorian Caricature* Washington DC: Smithsonian Institution Press

Cusack, J. (1997) 'Officers Accused of Targeting Black Passengers' *Irish Times* 18.10.97

Cusack, M. (1881) *The Present Case of Ireland Plainly Stated: A Plea for My People and My Race* New York: P.J. Kennedy

Davies, J. (1612) *Discoverie of the State of Ireland: With the True Causes Why that Kingdom Was Never Entirely Subdued* London

Davis, A. (2001 [1981]) *Women, Race and Class* London: The Women's Press

Davis, R. (1974) *Arthur Griffith and Non-Violent Sinn Féin* Dublin: Anvil Press

Davis, T. (1890) *Prose Writings* London

Dean, S. (ed.) (1991) *A Field Day Anthology of Irish Writing* Derry: Field Day

Deegan, G. (2002) 'Celtic Tiger Did Not Improve Quality of Life, Study Finds' *Irish Times*, 9.11.02

Delanty, G. and O'Mahony, P. (1998) *Rethinking Irish History: Nationalism, Identity and Ideology* London: Macmillan

Department of the Environment and Local Government (2000) *Housing Statistics Bulletin* Dublin: Department of the Environment and Local Government

—— (2002) *Housing Statistics Bulletin* Dublin: Department of the Environment and Local Government

Department of Justice, Equality and Law Reform (2000) *The First Progress Report of the Committee to Monitor and Co-Ordinate the Implementation of the Recommendations of the Task Force on the Travelling Community* Dublin: Government Publications

De Verteuil, A. (1986) *Devenish and the Irish in Nineteenth-Century Trinidad* Port of Spain: Paria

Devlin, P. (1934) *Our Native Games* Dublin

Dickie, J. (1997) 'Stereotypes of the Italian South 1860–1900' in Lumley and Morris (eds), pp. 114–47

Dicks, W. (1815) *Mitigation of Slavery* London

Dominguez, V. (1986) *White by Definition: Social Classification in Creole Louisiana* New Brunswick, NJ: Rutgers University Press

Donnellan, E. (2003) 'New Approach to Hospital Drink-Related Admissions' *Irish Times* 1.2.03

Donoghue, D. (1998) 'Ireland: Race, Nation', State: Parnell lecture 1997–98, Oxford: Magdalene College, Occasional Paper no. 18

Dooley, B. (1998) *Black and Green: The Fight for Civil Rights in Northern Ireland and Black America* London: Pluto Press

Douglas, R.M. (2002) 'Anglo-Saxons and Attacotti: The Racialisation of Irishness in Britain Between the World Wars' *Ethnic and Racial Studies* 25(1):40–63

Drudy, S. and Lynch, K. (1993) *Schools and Society in Ireland* Dublin: Gill and Macmillan

Dunn, R. (1972) *Sugar and Slaves: The Rise of the Planter Class in the British West Indies 1624–1713* Chapel Hill: University of North Carolina Press

Dupraz, P. and Vieira, F. (1999) '"Immigration et 'modernité": le Portugal entre héritage colonial et intégration européenne' *Pole Sud* (11):38–54

Dyer, R. (1997) *White* London: Routledge

EIRO (2002a) *Comparative Survey: Non-Permanent Employment, Quality of Work and Industrial Relations* July 2002 <www.eurofound.ie/eiro>

—— (2002b) *Comparative Study on Low-Wage Workers and the Working Poor – The case of Ireland* September 2002 <www.eurofound.ie/eiro>

Eisenstadt, S. and Giesen (1995) 'The Construction of Collective Identity' *European Journal of Sociology* 36:72–102

Elchardus, M. (1996) 'Class, Cultural Re-Alignment and the Rise of the Populist Right' in Erskine, A. (ed.) *Changing Europe: Some Aspects of Identity, Conflict and Social Justice* Aldershot: Avebury, pp. 41–63

Engels, F. (1969 [1844]) *The Condition of the Working Class in England: From Personal Observation and Authentic Sources* St Albans, Herts.: Panther

Equality Authority (2000) *Anti-Racism in the Workplace: Resource Pack* Dublin: Equality Authority

—— (2002) *Annual Report 2001* Dublin: Equality Authority

—— (2003) *Annual Report 2002* Dublin: Equality Authority

Ernst, R. (1949) *Immigrant Life in New York 1825–1863* New York: King's Crown Press

ESRI (Economic and Social Research Institute) (1997) *Living in Ireland Survey* Dublin: ESRI

European Union Monitoring Centre on Racism and Xenophobia (2000) *Annual Report 1999* Vienna: EUMC

—— (2001) *Annual Report 2000* Vienna: EUMC

—— (2002) *Annual Report 2001* Vienna: EUMC

Evans, E. (1992) *The Personality of Ireland: Habitat, Heritage and History* Dublin: Lilliput Press

Eze, E. (ed.) (1997) *Race and the Enlightenment: A Reader* Cambridge, MA: Blackwell

Fanning, B. (2002) *Racism and Social Change in the Republic of Ireland* Manchester: Manchester University Press

Farren, S. (1995) *The Politics of Irish Education 1920–65* Belfast: Institute of Irish Studies, The Queen's University of Belfast

Faughnan, P. (1999) *Refugees and Asylum-Seekers in Ireland: Social Policy Dimensions* Dublin: UCD, Social Science Research Centre

Faughnan, P. and Woods, M. (2000) *Lives on Hold: Seeking Asylum in Ireland* Dublin: UCD, Social Science Research Centre

Faulks, K. (2000) *Citizenship* London: Routledge

Feeley, P. and O'Riordan, M. (1984) *The Rise and Fall of Irish Anti-Semitism* Dublin: Labour History Workshop

Fielding, S. (1992) *Class and Ethnicity: Irish Catholics in England, 1880–1939* Buckingham: Open University Press

Finerty, J. (1961) *Warpath and Bivouac: Or the Conquest of the Sioux, 1890* Norman, OK: University of Oklahoma Press

FitzGerald, G. (1992) *Repulsing Racism: Reflections on Racism and the Irish* Dublin: Attic Press

FitzGerald W.G. (1923) *The Voice of Ireland: A Survey of the Race and Nation from all Angles by the Foremost Leaders at Home and Abroad* Dublin: John Heywood

Foley, T. and Ryder, S. (eds) (1998) *Ideology and Ireland in the Nineteenth Century* Dublin: Four Courts Press

Foner, P. (ed.) (1999) *Frederick Douglass: Selected Speeches and Writing* Chicago: Lawrence Hill Books

Foster, R. (1993) *Paddy and Mr. Punch: Connections in Irish and English History* London: Allen Lane

—— (2001) *The Irish Story: Telling Tales and Making it up in Ireland* London/New York: Allen Lane

Fox, D.F. (1917) 'The Negro Vote in Old New York' *Political Science Quarterly* 32:252–75

Frankenberg, R. (1994) *White Women, Race Matters* Madison: University of Wisconsin Press

—— (1997) *Displacing Whiteness: Essays in Social and Cultural Criticism* Durham, NC: Duke University Press

Front national (1997) *Les Origines de la France* Paris: Editions Nationales

Fryer, P. (1984) *Staying Power: A History of Black People in Britain from Roman Times* London: Pluto Press

Gallagher, T. (1985) 'A Tale of Two Cities: Communal Strife in Liverpool and Glasgow Before 1919' in Swift and Gilley (eds), pp. 106–29

—— (1987) *Glasgow – The Uneasy Peace: Religious Tension in Modern Scotland* Manchester: Manchester University Press

Galton, F. (1883) *Inquiries into Human Faculty and its Development* London: J.M. Dent & Sons

Galway Community Workers' Co-Operative (2000) *Strategies for Social Partnerships* Galway: Community Workers' Co-Operative

Garner, S. (1998) 'Playing the Numbers Game: Immigration and "Race" in Wilsonian Britain' in Frison, D. (ed.) *Les Années Wilson* Paris: Ellipses, pp. 62–70

Garner, S. and White, A. (2002) *Racism in Ireland: A Baseline Report on Attitudinal Surveys for the 'Know Racism' Campaign* Dublin: Department of Justice

Garretson, M. (1938) *The American Bison* New York: New York Zoological Society

Garvin, T. (1981) *The Evolution of Irish Nationalist Politics* Dublin: Gill and Macmillan

Gibbons, L. (1996) *Transformations in Irish Culture* Cork: UCC/Field Day

Gibson, F. (1951) *Attitudes of the New York Irish Towards State and National Affairs 1848–1892* New York: Columbia University Press

Giddings, P. (1984) *When and Where I Enter: The Impact of Black Women on Race and Sex in America* New York: Harper Collins

Gillespie, R. and Moran, G. (eds) (1987) *A Various Country: Essays in Mayo History* Westport: Foilseacháin Náisiunta Teoranta

Gilley, S. (1978) 'English Attitudes to the Irish in England, 1780–1900' in Holmes, C. (ed.) *Immigrants and Minorities in British Society* London: George Allen & Unwin, pp. 81–110

—— (1980) 'Catholics and Socialists in Glasgow, 1906–1912' in Lunn, K. (ed.), pp. 160–200

Gilman, S. (1982) *On Blackness without Blacks: Essays on the Image of the Black in Western Popular Culture* Boston: G.K. Hall

Gilroy, P. (1987) *There Ain't No Black in the Union Jack* London: Hutchinson

—— (1990) 'The End of Anti-Racism' in Ball, W. and Solomos, J. (eds) *Race and Local Politics* London: Macmillan, pp. 192–209

—— (1998) 'Race Ends Here' *Ethnic and Racial Studies* 21(5):838–45

Gleeson, D. (2001) *The Irish in the South, 1815–1877* Chapel Hill: University of North Carolina Press

Gobineau, A. (1853) *Essai sur l'inégalité des races humaines* Paris

Goldberg, D. and Essed, P. (2001) *Critical Race Theory* Boston: Basil Blackwell

Goldhagen, D. (1996) *Hitler's Willing Executioners: Ordinary Germans and the Holocaust* London: Abacus

Goldring, M. (1993) *Pleasant the Scholar's Life: Irish Intellectuals and the Construction of the Nation-State* London: Serif

Goldstone, K. (2000a) '"Benevolent Helpfulness?" Ireland and the International Reaction to Jewish Refugees, 1933–9' in Kennedy, M. and Skelly, J.M. (eds) *Irish Foreign Policy 1919–1966: From Independence to Internationalism* Dublin: Four Courts Press

—— (2000b) 'Re-writing You: Writing and Researching Ethnic Minorities' in Mac Lachlan and O'Connell (eds)

—— (2002) 'Christianity, Conversion and the Tricky Business of Names: Images of Jews and Blacks in Nationalist Irish Catholic Discourse' in Lentin and McVeigh (eds) pp. 167–76.

Gomez-Reino Cachafeiro, M. (2002) *Ethnicity and Nationalism in Italian Politics: Inventing the Padania: Lega Nord and the Northern Question* Aldershot: Ashgate

Government of Ireland (1993) *Report of Interdepartmental Committee on Non-Irish Nationals* Dublin: Stationery Office

—— (2003) *Sustaining Progress: Social Partnership Agreement, 2003–2005* Dublin: Stationery Office

Graham, B. (1994) 'Heritage Conservation and Revisionist Nationalism in Ireland' in Ashworth, G. and Larkham, P. (eds) *Tourism, Culture and Identity in the New Europe* London: Routledge, pp. 135–58

—— (1998) 'Contested Images of Place among Protestants in Northern Ireland' *Political Geography* 17(2): 129–44

Graham, B. and Proudfoot, L. (1993) 'Introduction: A Perspective on the Nature of Irish Historical Geography' in Graham, B. and Proudfoot, L. (eds) *An Historical Geography of Ireland* London: Academic Press

Graham, C. and Kirkland, R. (eds) (1999) *Ireland and Cultural Theory: The Mechanics of Authenticity* London: Macmillan

Gramsci, A. (1971) *Selections from the Prison Notebooks of Antonio Gramsci* (edited and translated by Hoare, Q. and Nowell-Smith, G.) New York: International Books

Gray, B. (2000) 'From "Ethnicity" to "Diaspora": 1980s Emigration and "Multicultural" London' in Bielenberg (ed.), pp. 65–88

—— (2003) *Women and the Irish Diaspora* London: Routledge, pp. 135–58

Green Party (2003) 'Greens Question Cynicism of Social Partnership Process', Press release, Dan Boyle TD 13.1.03.

Greene, D.H. and Lawrence, D.H. (eds) (1962) *The Matter with Ireland/Bernard Shaw* London: Rupert Hart-Davis

Greengrass, M., Leslie, M. and Raylor, T. (1994) *Samuel Hartlib and Universal Reformation: Studies in Intellectual Communication* Cambridge: Cambridge University Press

Gribaudi, G. (1997) 'The Images of the South: The *Mezzogiorno* as Seen by Insiders and Outsiders' in Lumley and Morris (eds), pp. 83–113

Griffin, P. (2001) *The People with No Name: Ireland's Ulster Scots, America's Scots Irish, and the Creation of a British Atlantic World, 1689–1764* Princeton: Princeton University Press

Griffith, A. (2003 [1911]) 'Pitt's Policy' in *The Resurrection of Hungary* Dublin: University College Dublin Press, pp. 96–138

Guerin, P. (2002) ''Racism and the Media in Ireland: Setting the Anti-Immigration Agenda' in Lentin and McVeigh pp. 91–101

Gwynn, A. (1932) *Documents Relating to the Irish in the West Indies* Analecta Hibernica, Irish Manuscripts Commission, No. 4. Dublin

Habermas, J. (1976) *Legitimation Crisis* London: Heinemann

—— (1992) 'Citizenship and National Identity: Some Reflections on the Future of Europe' *Praxis International* 12(1):1–19

Hainsworth, P. (ed.) (1998) *Divided Society: Ethnic Minorities and Racism in Northern Ireland* London: Pluto Press

Hall, S. (1978) *Policing the Crisis: Mugging, the State and Law and Order* London: Macmillan

—— (1980) 'Race, Articulation and Societies Structured in Dominance' in *Sociological Theories: Race and Colonialism* Paris: UNESCO pp. 305–47

—— (2000) 'Conclusion: The Multi-cultural Question' in Hesse (ed.), pp. 209–41

Hall, S., Critcher, C., Jefferson, T., Clarke, J. and Roberts, B. (1978) *Policing the Crisis: Mugging, the State, and Law and Order* London: Macmillan

Handley, J. (1943) *The Irish in Scotland, 1798–1845* Cork: Cork University Press

Handlin, O. (1941) *Boston's Immigrants: A Study in Acculturation* New York: Atheneum

Hanley, B. (2003) *The IRA, 1926–35* Dublin: Four Courts Press

Hargreaves, A. (2002) 'France' in ter Wal, J. (ed.) (2002) *Racism and Cultural Diversity in the Mass Media: An Overview of Research and Examples of Good Practice in the EU Member States, 1995–2000* Vienna: European Union Monitoring Centre on Racism and Xenophobia, pp. 208–23

Hart, W. (2003) 'Africans in 18th Century Ireland' *Irish Historical Studies* XXXIII (129): 19–32

Hartigan, J. (1997) 'Locating White Detroit' in Frankenberg (ed.), pp. 180–213

Haughey, N. (2000) 'Refugee Adjudicator Resigns over the System' *Irish Times* 18.1.00

—— (2003a) 'Mixed Reaction to Neilan's Remarks' *Irish Times* 21.2.03

—— (2003b) 'Residents of Limbo' *Irish Times* 'Weekend' section, 7.6.03

Hennessy, B. (1999) 'Refugees and Immigrants in the Irish Media' in *Media Studies Reader* Cork: Dept. of Adult Education, UCC

Hennessey, T. (1998) *Dividing Ireland: World War I and Partition* London: Routledge

Herrnstein, R. and Murray, C. (1994) *The Bell Curve: Intelligence and Class Structure in American Life* New York: Free Press

Hesse, B. (ed.) (2000a) *Un/Settled Multiculturalisms: Diasporas, Entanglements, Transruptions* London: Zed Books

—— (2000b) 'Introduction: Un/Settled Multiculturalism' in Hesse (ed.) pp. 1–30

Hickman, M. (1995a) *Religion, Class and Identity: The State, the Catholic Church and the Education of the Irish in Britain* Aldershot: Avebury

—— (1995b) 'The Irish in Britain: Racism, Incorporation and Identity' *Irish Studies Review* 10:16–20

—— (1998) 'Reconstructing Deconstructing "Race": British Political Discourses about the Irish in Britain' *Ethnic and Racial Studies* 21(2):288–307

Hickman, M. and Walter, B. (2002) *The Irish in Contemporary Britain* London: Longman

Hobsbawm, E. and Ranger, T. (eds.) (1983) *The Invention of Tradition* Cambridge: Cambridge University Press

Hoggart, K. and Mendoza, C. (2000) 'African Immigrant Workers in Spanish Agriculture' Center for Comparative Immigration Studies Working Paper no. 2, La Jolla, CA: UCSD

Holmes, M. (2000) 'The Irish and India: Imperialism, Nationalism, and Internationalism' in Bielenberg (ed.) pp. 235–50

Home Office (2000) *Statistics on Race and the Criminal Justice System* London: HMSO

hooks, b. (1982) *Ain't I a Woman: Black Women and Feminism* London/Boston: Pluto Press/South End Press

Horgan, O. (2000) 'Seeking Refuge' in Mac Lachlan and O'Connell, pp. 49–74

Hornaday, W.T. (1889) *The Extermination of the American Bison* Washington DC: Smithsonian Institute

Horsman, R. (1981) *Race and Manifest Destiny: the Origins of American Anglo-Saxonism* Cambridge: Cambridge University Press

Howe, S. (2000) *Ireland and Empire: Colonial Legacies in Irish History and Culture,* Oxford, Oxford University Press

Humphreys, J. (2001) 'Not Even the Ants are Safe' *Irish Times* 21.4.01

—— (2002) 'An Irishman's Diary' *Irish Times* 6.4.02

—— (2003) 'New Limits on Work Visas for Immigrants are Criticised' *Irish Times* 1.2.03

Humphries, T. (1996) *Green Fields: Gaelic Sport in Ireland* London: Weidenfeld and Nicolson

Hutchinson, J. (1987) *The Dynamics of Cultural Nationalism: The Gaelic Revival and the Creation of the Irish Nation State* London: Allen and Unwin

Hyde, D. (1982) 'The Necessity for De-Anglicising Ireland' in Dean (ed.), pp. 528–9

Hyland, P. (1997) 'Portugal, so Great so Small: Colonial Obesity and Post-Revolutionary Anorexia' in Murray (ed.), pp. 101–14

Hyman, L. (1972) *The Jews of Ireland: From Earliest Times to the Year 1910* Shannon: Irish U.P.

ICJP (Irish Commission for Justice and Peace) (1997) *Refugees and Asylum-seekers: A Challenge to Solidarity* Dublin: ICJP/Trocaire

IDA (Industrial Development Agency Ireland) (2002) *Tax Brochure 2002* Available at the ida.ie website

Ignatiev, N. (1995) *How the Irish Became White,* London: Routledge

Ingman, H. (2003) 'An Englishwoman's Diary' *Irish Times* 29.3.03

Ingolsby, B. (2002) 'Regular Migration to Ireland' Paper delivered at the Incorporated Law Society Seminar: Rights to Reside in Ireland on 14 May 2002 in Dublin

Interdepartmental Committee on Non-Irish Nationals (1993) *Interim Report on Applications for Refugee Status* Dublin: Stationery Office

IRC (Irish Refugee Council) (2000) *Asylum in Ireland: A Report on the Fairness and Sustainability of Asylum Determinations at First Instance* Dublin: IRC

*Irish Examiner* (2000a) 'No céad mile fáilte for foreign workers' 4.2.00

—— (2000b) 'Influx of Canadians set to start work in tourist sector' 14.3.00

—— (2000c) 'Emir's Irishness is questioned during Chicago parade' 17.3.00

*Irish Independent* (1998) 'Pub Loses Licence for Racist Ban on Woman', 23.10.98

*Irish Times* (1998a) 'Dealing with Immigration' 17.1.98

—— (1998b) 'Irish urged to Accept Diversity' 10.3.98

—— (1999) 'Lawyer Calls the Asylum Process a Travesty' 4.12.99

—— (2000a) 'Refugee Adjudicator Resigns over the System' 18.1.00

—— (2000b) 'Court Orders Release of Detained Pakistanis' 27.11.00

—— (2001) '900 Jobs Lost at Gateway as Company Closes Base' 9.8.01

—— (2003) 'Judge Kenny Apologises to Nigerian woman' 21.2.03

*Irish Times*/MRBI (2000a) *Political Issues* January 2000

*Irish Times*/MRBI (2000b) *Political Issues* April 2000

IRR (Institute of Race Relations) (2001) *European Race Bulletin* no. 37, June

—— (2003) 'Summary – the EU's New Border Control Programme' *IRR News* 27.3.03

Jackson, J.A. (1963) *The Irish in Britain* London: Routledge

Jacobson, M. (1995) *Special Sorrows: The Diasporic Imagination of Irish, Polish and Jewish Immigrants in the United States* Cambridge, MA: Harvard University Press

—— (1998) *Whiteness of a Different Colour: European Immigrants and the Alchemy of Race* Cambridge, MA: Harvard University Press

Jeffery, K. (ed.) (1996a) *An Irish Empire?: Aspects of Ireland in the British Empire*, Manchester: Manchester University Press

—— (1996b) 'Irish Military Tradition and the British Empire' in Jeffery (ed.), pp. 94–122

Jenkins, R. (1997) *Rethinking Ethnicity: Arguments and Explorations* London: Sage

Jensen, R. (2002) '"No Irish Need Apply": A Myth of Victimization' *Journal of Social History* 36(2):405–29

Johnson, H. and Watson, K. (eds) (1998) *The White Minority in the Caribbean* Kingston/London: IRP/James Currey

Johnson, N. (1996) 'Where Geography and History Meet: Heritage Tourism and the Big House in Ireland' *Annals of the Association of American Geographers* 86(3):551–66

Jones, D. (1982) *Crime, Protest, Community and Police in 19th Century Britain* London: Routledge

Joyce, J. (1937 [1922]) *Ulysses* London: Bodley Head

Kapur, N. (1997) *The Irish Raj: Illustrated Stories about Irish in India and Indians in Ireland* Antrim: Greystone Press

Kaufman, E., Raguram, P., Phizacklea, A. and Sales, R. (2000) *Gender and International Migration in Europe (Gender, Racism, Ethnicity)* London: Routledge

Kearney, R. (1988) *Transitions: Narratives in Modern Irish Culture* Dublin: Wolfhound

—— (1990) *Migrations: The Irish at Home and Abroad* Dublin: Wolfhound

Kelleher, O. (2003) 'Nigerian Woman May Sue State Over Five Nights in Jail' *Irish Times* 8.2.03

Keneally, T. (1998) *The Great Shame: The Story of the Irish in the Old World and the New* London: BCA

Kenny, Mairín (1997) 'Who are They? Who are We? Education and Travellers' in Crowley and Mac Laughlin (eds), pp. 61–70

Kenny, Mary (2000) 'Opposition to Strangers is Only Natural' *Sunday Independent* 30.4.00

Keogh, A. (2000) 'Talking about the Other: A View of how Secondary School Pupils Construct Opinions about Refugees and Asylum Seekers' in Mac Lachlan and O'Connell (eds), pp. 123–36

Keogh, D. (1998) *Jews in 20th Century Ireland: Refugees, Anti-Semitism and the Holocaust* Cork: Cork University Press

Keohane, K. (2001) 'The Celtic Tiger as Totemic Animal and Collective Representation' Paper presented at the 'Identity Project' international conference, University College Cork, 6–7.4.01

Kestner, J. (1996) 'The Colonised in the Colonies: Representation of Celts in Victorian Battle Painting' in West (ed.) pp. 112–27

Kiberd, D. (1995) *Inventing Ireland: The Literature of the Modern Nation* London: Jonathan Cape

—— (1997) 'Modern Ireland: Postcolonial or European?' in Murray (ed.), pp. 81–100

Kiely, G. (ed.) (1999) *Irish Social Policy in Context* Dublin: University College Dublin Press

Kirby, P. (2002) *The Celtic Tiger in Distress: Growth with Inequality in Ireland* London: Palgrave

Kirk, N. (1980) 'Ethnicity, Class and Popular Toryism' in Lunn, K. (ed.) *Hosts, Immigrants and Minorities: Historical Responses to Newcomers in British Society, 1870–1914* Folkestone: Dawson, pp. 64–106

Knobel, D. (1986) *Paddy and the Republic: Ethnicity and Nationality in Antebellum America* Middletown, MA: Wesleyan University Press

Knox, R. (1850) *The Races of Man* London: Henry Renshaw

Komin, B. et al. (1991) *Research Report: The National Survey of Religious Identification 1989–90* New York: CUNY Graduate Center

Kropotkin, P. (1902) *Mutual Aid: A Factor of Evolution* Bromley, Kent: James Knowles. Available at <http://marxists.anu.edu.am/reference/archive/kropotkin-peter/1990s/1902/>

Kuethe, A. (1986) *Cuba, 1753–1815: Crown, Military and Society* Knoxville: University of Tennessee Press

Labour Party *Ending the Chaos: A Rational Approach to Asylum and Immigration* Dublin: Labour Party 2002

Layte, R., Nolan, B. and Whelan, C. (2000) 'Trends in Poverty' in Nolan et al. (eds) pp. 163–78

Lebow, N. (1976) *White Britain and Black Ireland: The Influences of Stereotypes on Colonial Policy* Philadelphia: Institute for the Study of Human Issues

Lee, J. (1989) *Ireland, 1912–1985: Politics and Society* Cambridge: Cambridge University Press

Leersen, J. (1986) *Mere Irish and Fíor-Ghael: Studies in the Idea of Irish Nationality, its Development and Literary Expression Prior to the Nineteenth Century* Amsterdam: Benjamins

Lennon, M., McAdam, M. and O'Brien, J. (1988) *Across the Water: Irish Women's Lives in Britain* London: Virago

Lentin, A. (2002) 'Wherever it Rears its Ugly Head: Anti-Racism in the European Union' PhD thesis Florence: European Institute

Lentin, L. (1997) (dir.) *No More Blooms* Documentary broadcast on RTE1, October 1997

Lentin, R. (1998) '"Irishness", the 1937 Constitution and Citizenship: A Gender and Ethnicity View' *Irish Journal of Sociology* 8:5–24

—— (1999) 'Constitutionally Excluded: Citizenship and (Some) Irish Women', in Yuval-Davis N. and Werbner P. (eds) *Women, Citizenship and Difference* London: Zed Books, pp. 130–44

—— (2001) 'Responding to the Racialisation of Irishness: Disavowed Multiculturalism and its Discontents' *Sociological Research Online* 5 (4)

—— (2002a) '"Whoever heard of an Irish Jew?" The Intersection of "Irishness" and "Jewishness"' in Lentin and McVeigh (eds) pp. 153–66

—— (2002b) 'At the Heart of the Hibernian Post-Metropolis: Spatial Narratives of Ethnic Minorities and Diasporic Communities in a Changing City' *City* 6(2): 229–50

Lentin, R. and McVeigh, R. (eds) (2002) *Racism and Anti-racism in Ireland* Belfast: Beyond the Pale

Lerner, M. (1993) 'Jews are not White' *Village Voice* 38(18.5): 33–4

Leventhal, A.J. (1945) 'What it Means to be a Jew in Ireland' *Bell* 10(3):207–16 (June)

Ligon, J. (1673) *A True and Exact History of the Island of Barbados* London

Linebaugh, P. (ed.) (forthcoming) *Edward Despard: Radical Irish Lives* Cork: Cork University Press

Linebaugh, P. and Rediker, M. (2000) *The Many-Headed Hydra: The Hidden History of the Revolutionary Atlantic* London: Verso

Lipsitz, G. (1995) 'The Possessive Investment in Whiteness: Racialized Social Democracy and the "White" Problem in American Studies' *American Quarterly* 47(3):369–87

—— (1998) *The Possessive Investment in Whiteness: How White People Profit from Identity Politics* Philadelphia: Temple University Press

Liverpool Black Caucus (1986) *The Racial Politics of Militant in Liverpool: The Black Community's Struggle for Participation in Local Politics, 1980–86* Merseyside Area Profile Group/Runnymede Trust

Lloyd, C. (1998) *Discourse of Anti-Racism in France* Aldershot: Ashgate

Lloyd, D. (1993) *Anomalous States: Irish Writing and the Postcolonial Moment* Dublin: Lilliput Press

—— (1999) *Ireland After History* Cork: Cork University Press /Field Day

Longley, E. and Kiberd, D. (2001) *Multi-Culturalism: The View from the Two Irelands*, Cork: Cork University Press

Lopes, S. (1992) 'Le Portugal et ses immigrés' *Migrations Sociétés*, Centre d'Informations et d'Études sur les Migrations Internationales 19(4) January–February 1992, pp. 69–76

Lorimer, D. (1978) *Colour, Class and the Victorians: English Attitudes to the Negro in the Mid-Nineteenth Century* Leicester: Leicester University Press

—— (1996) 'Race, Science and Culture: Historical Continuities and Discontinuities, 1850–1914' in West (ed.), pp. 12–33

Luibhéid, E. (1997a) 'Irish Immigrants in the United States' Racial System' in Mac Laughlin (ed.) pp. 253–73

—— (1997b) 'The Nod and the Wink: White Solidarity within Irish Immigrants in the USA' in Crowley and Mac Laughlin (eds), pp. 79–88

Lumley, R. and Morris, J. (eds) (1997) *The New History of the Italian South: The Mezzogiorno Revisited* Exeter: Exeter University Press

Lunn, K. (ed.) (1980) *Hosts, Immigrants and Minorities: Historical Responses to Newcomers in British Society 1870–1914* Folkestone: Dawson

Lyons, S. (2003) 'Historian Challenges the "No Irish" Myth' *Boston Globe*, 16.3.03

Marshall, T.H. and Bottomore, P. (1992) *Citizenship and Social Class* London: Pluto Press

Mayer, N. and Michelat, G. (2001) 'Sondages, mode d'emploi: xénophobie, racisme et antiracisme en France: attitudes et perceptions' in CNCDH, pp. 87–102

Mac an Ghaill, M. (1996) (ed.) *Understanding Masculinities: Social Relations and Cultural Arenas* Buckingham: Open University Press

—— (1999) *Contemporary Racism and Ethnicities: Social and Cultural Transformations* Buckingham: Open University Press

—— (2001) 'British Critical Theorists: The Production of the Conceptual Invisibility of the Irish Diaspora' *Social Identities* 7(2):178–202

McCaffrey, L. (1976) *The Irish Diaspora in America* Washington DC: Catholic University of America Press

McCann, M., O Siocháin, S. and Ruane, J. (eds) (1994) *Irish Travellers: Culture and Ethnicity* Belfast: Queen's University Press

McCarthy, M. (2001) *My Eyes Only Look Out* Dingle: Brandon Press

McCormack, C. (2000) 'Clogheen Votes for Hotel Plan' *Irish Times* 19.5.00

McCraild, D. (1996) '"Principle, Party and Protest": The Language of Victorian Orangeism in the North of England' in West (ed.) pp. 128–40

MacDermott, M. (1896) *Songs and Ballads of Young Ireland with Critical Notes* London: Downey

Mac Éinri, P. (2001) *Immigration into Ireland: Trends, Policy Responses, Outlook,* Cork: Irish Centre for Migration Studies

—— (2002) *The Schengen Zone and the Common Travel Area* Cork: Irish Centre for Migration Studies

Mc Gréil, Fr. M. (1996) *Prejudice in Ireland Revisited* St Patrick's College, Maynooth

McKenna, P. (2000) 'Irish Emigration to Argentina: A Different Model' in Bielenberg (ed.) pp. 195–212

Mac Lachlan, M. and O'Connell, M. (2000) *Cultivating Pluralism: Psychological, Social and Cultural Perspectives on a Changing Ireland* Dublin: Oak Tree Press

Mac Laughlin, J. (1995) *Travellers and Ireland: Whose Country? Whose History?* Cork: Cork University Press

—— (1996) 'Anti-Traveller Racism in Ireland' *Race and Class* 37(3):47–64

—— (1997) (ed.) *Location and Dislocation in Contemporary Irish Society: Emigration and Irish Identities* Cork: Cork University Press

—— (1998) 'Racism, Ethnicity and Multiculturalism in Contemporary Europe: A Review Essay' *Political Geography* 17(8):1013–26

—— (1999a) '"Pestilence on their Backs, Famine in their Stomachs": the racial construction of Irishness in Victorian Britain' in Graham and Kirkland (eds), pp. 50–76

—— (1999b) 'Nation-Building, Social Closure and Anti-Traveller Racism in Ireland' *Sociology* 33(1):129–51

—— (2001) *Reimagining the Nation-State: The Contested Terrains of Nation-Building* London: Pluto Press

McLoughlin, D. (1994) 'Ethnicity and the Irish Travellers: Reflections on Ní Shuínéar' in McCann et al. (eds), pp. 78–94

McLua, B. (1967) *The Steadfast Rule: A History of the GAA Ban,* Dublin

Mac Manus, S. (1990) *The Story of the Irish Race* New York: Random House Value

McMaster, N. (2001) *Racism in Europe, 1870–2000* London: Palgrave

MacPherson, W. (1999) *Report of the Stephen Lawrence Inquiry,* London: HMSO

MacRaild, D. (1996) '"Principle, Party and Protest": The Language of Victorian Orangeism in the North of England' in West (ed.), pp. 128–40

McSharry, R. and White, P. (2000) *The Making of the Celtic Tiger: The Inside Story of Ireland's Boom Economy* Cork: Mercier Press

McVeigh, R. (1992) 'The Specificity of Irish Racism' *Race and Class* 33(4):31–45

—— (1996) *The Racialization of Irishness: Racism and Anti-Racism in Ireland* Belfast: CRD

—— (1998a) '"There's No Racism Because There's No Black People Here": Racism and Anti-Racism in Northern Ireland' in Hainsworth (ed.), pp. 11–32

—— (1998b) 'Irish Travellers and the Logic of Genocide' in Peillon, M. and Slater, E. (eds) *Encounters: A Sociological Chronicle of Ireland, 1995–96* Dublin: Institute of Public Administration, pp. 155–62

—— (2002a) 'Nick, Nack, Paddywhack: Anti-Irish Racism and the Racialisation of Irishness' in Lentin and McVeigh (eds), pp. 136–52

—— (2002b) 'Is there an Irish Anti-Racism? Building an Anti-Racist Ireland' in Lentin and McVeigh (eds), pp. 211–25

Maley, W. (1998) 'The British Problem in Three Tracts on Ireland by Spenser, Bacon and Milton' in Bradshaw, B. and Roberts, P. (eds) *British Consciousness and Identity: the Making of Britain, 1533–1707* Cambridge: Cambridge University Press

Man, A.P. (1951) 'Labor Competition and the New York Draft Riots of 1863' *Journal of Negro History* 36(4) October, pp. 375–405

Maume, P. (1999) *The Long Gestation: Irish Nationalist Life, 1891–1918* Dublin: Gill and McMillan

Maxwell, C. (1923) *Irish History from Contemporary Sources, 1509-l610* London: Allen & Unwin

Mehigan, P. (1946) *Hurling: Ireland's National Game* Dublin

Mendoza, C. (2000) 'The Role of the State in Influencing African Labour Outcomes in Spain and Portugal' Center for Comparative Immigration Studies Working Paper no. 3, La Jolla, CA: UCSD

Mercadé, F. (1986) 'España como problema. Reflexiones sobre identidad' in Hernandes, F. and Mercadé, F. (eds), *Estructuras sociales y cuestion nacional in España* Barcelona: Ariel

Miles, R. (1984) *Racism and Migrant Labour* London: Routledge

—— (1989) *Racism* London: Routledge

—— (1993) *Racism After 'Race Relations'* London: Routledge

Miles, R. and Phizacklea, A. (1980) *White Man's Country* London: Routledge

Miller, K. (1969) 'Green Over Black: The Origins of Irish-American Racism, 1800–1863' unpublished paper

—— (1985) *Emigrants and Exiles: Ireland and the Irish Exodus to North America* Oxford: Oxford University Press

Miller, R.R. (1986) *Shamrock and Sword: The Saint Patrick's Battalion in the U.S.–Mexican War* Norman, OK: University of Oklahoma Press

Milward, P. (1985) 'The Stockport Riots of 1852: A Study of Anti-Catholic and Anti-Irish Sentiment' in Swift and Gilley (eds), pp. 207–24

Mitchel, J. (1982 [1913]) *Jail Journal* Dublin: University Press of Ireland

—— (1991[1861]) 'The Last Conquest of Ireland (Perhaps)' in Deane, S. (ed.) *The Field Day Anthology of Irish Writing* Derry: Field Day II: 177–84

Moane, G. (2002) 'Colonialism and the Celtic Tiger: The Legacy of History and the Quest for Vision' in Cronin et al. (eds), pp. 109–23

Moloney, E. (2002) 'McDowell in Move to End Irish Baby Residency "scam"' *Sunday Independent* 21.7.02

—— (2003) 'US Oil Firm Enjoys Huge Tax Savings Here Since 1959' *Irish Independent* 24.1.03

Montagu, A. (1954) *Man's Most Dangerous Myth: The Fallacy of Race* Oxford: Oxford University Press

Moore, G. (1981) 'Socio-Economic Aspects of Anti-Semitism in Ireland, 1880–1905' *Economic and Social Review* 12(3):187–201

Morash, C. (1998) 'Celticism: Between Race and Nation' in Foley and Ryder (eds) pp. 206–13

Morgan, H. (1991) 'Milesians, Ulstermen and Fenians' *Linen Hall Review* December 1991, pp. 14–16

Morrison, T. (1993) *Playing in the Dark: Whiteness and the Literary Imagination* Cambridge MA: Harvard University Press

Morton, S. (1839) *Crania Americana: A Comparative View of the Skulls of Various Aboriginal Natives of North and South America, to which is Prefixed an Essay on the Variety of Human Species* Philadelphia: J. Dobson

Moryson, F. (1617) *An Itynerary* London: John Beale

Mullin, P. (2001) 'Different Words and Words of Difference' *Focus* 64:28

Murphy, A. (1994) *The Irish Economy: Celtic Tiger or Tortoise?* Dublin: Money Markets International

Murphy, M. (2000) 'Is Social Partnership the Only Route to Social Inclusion, and if so, Where is the Voice of the Excluded?' in *Strategies for Social Partnerships* Galway: Community Workers' Co-Operative

—— (2002) 'Social Partnership – is it "the Only Game in Town"?' *Community Development Journal* 37(1): 81–90

Murphy, S. (2000) 'Residents Opposed to Conversion of Centre for Refugees' *Examiner* 18.4.00

Murphy, S. (2001) 'From a Black Irishwoman's Perspective' *Focus* 64:19–20

Murphy, T. (1997) 'Immigrants and Refugees: The Irish Legal Context' in Crowley and Mac Laughlin (eds), pp. 95–100

Murray, S. (ed.) (1997) *Not on Any Map: Essays on Postcoloniality and Cultural Nationalism* Exeter: University of Exeter Press

Myers, K. (1997) 'An Irishman's Diary' *Irish Times* 3.7.97

Nairn, T. (1978) 'The Modern Janus' *New Left Review* 94:3–29

Nash, C. (1993) 'Embodying the Nation: The West of Ireland Landscape and Irish Identity' in Cronin, M. and O'Connor, B. (eds) *Tourism in Ireland: A Critical Analysis* Cork: Cork University Press

—— (1996) 'Men Again: Irish Masculinity, Nature and Nationhood in the Early Twentieth Century' *Ecumene: A Journal of Environment, Culture, Meaning* 3(3): 427–53

Nash, R. (1985) 'Irish Atlantic Trade in the Seventeenth and Eighteenth Centuries' *William and Mary Quarterly* 42(3):329–56

NCRRI (National Co-Ordinating Committee on Racism and Interculturalism) (1998) *Racism in Ireland: North and South* Conference papers for Dublin Castle Conference held on 31 October 1997, Dublin: European Parliament Office in Ireland

—— (2001) *Incidents Relating to Racism Reported to the NCCRI, May–October 2001* Dublin: NCCRI

Neal, F. (1982) 'The Birkenhead Garibaldi Riots of 1862' *Transactions of the Historical Society of Lancashire and Cheshire* 131:87–111

Negra, D. (1995) *Off White Hollywood: American Culture and Ethnic Female Stardom* London: Routledge

Newman, C. (1998) 'Editorial on Asylum Influx not Racist, Says Editor' *Irish Times* 4.8.98

Ní Bhroiméil, U. (2003) *The Gaelic Revival and America, 1870–1915* Dublin: Four Courts Press

Niceforo, A. (1898) *L'Italia barbara contemporanea*

Nic Suibhne, M. (1998) 'Fortress Ireland' *Guardian Weekend* 3.10.98

Ní Shuínéar, S. (1994) 'Irish Travellers, Ethnicity and the Origins Question' in McCann et al. (eds) pp. 54–77

—— (2002) 'Othering the Irish (Travellers)' in Lentin and McVeigh (eds) pp. 177–92

Noiriel, G. (1988) *Le Creuset français. Histoire de l'immigration, XIXe-XXe siècles* Paris: Editions du Seuil

Nolan, B., O'Connell, P. and Whelan, C. (eds) (2000) *Bust to Boom? The Irish Experience of Inequality* Dublin: Institute of Public Administration

O'Brien, C. (2003) 'Ireland Opens Door to EU Accession State Workers' *Examiner* 25.3.03

O'Callaghan, M. (1993) 'Denis Patrick Moran and the "Irish colonial condition", 1891–1921' in Boyce, D.G., Eccleshall, R. and Geoghegan, V. (eds) *Political Thought in Ireland Since the Seventeenth Century* London: Routledge, pp. 146–60

O'Callaghan, S. (2000) *To Hell or Barbados: The Ethnic Cleansing of Ireland* Dingle: Brandon

O'Carroll, J.P. (2002) 'Culture Lag and Democratic Deficit in Ireland: Or, "Dat's Outside de Terms of D'agreement"' *Community Development Journal* 37(1):10–19

—— (2003) 'Aspects of the Changing Political Environment of Applied Social Studies: "You can get there only from here"' in Herrmann, P. (ed.) *Between Politics and Sociology* New York: Nova Science Publishers, pp. 123–9

O Ciosáin, N. (1998) 'Boccoughs and God's Poor: Deserving and Undeserving Poor in Irish Popular Culture' in Foley and Ryder (eds), pp. 93–9

O'Connell, P. (2000) 'The Dynamics of the Irish Labour Market in Comparative Perspective' in Nolan et al. (eds), pp. 58–89

O'Connor, K. (1972) *The Irish in Britain* London: Sidgwick and Jackson

O'Connor, M. (2001) 'Maternity Hospital Warns it May Limit Patient Numbers' *Irish Times* 4.8.01

O'Donoghue, S. (2000) 'Organising for Social Partnership: Difficulties, Dilemmas and Challenges for the Sector' in Galway Community Workers' Co-Operative

O'Drisceoil, D. (1997) 'Jews and Other Undesirables: Anti-Semitism in Ireland During the Second World War' in Crowley and Mac Laughlin (eds), pp. 71–7

O'Faoláin, S. (1947) *The Irish* London: Penguin.

O'Hearn, D. (1995) 'Global Re-Structuring and the Irish Political Economy' in Clancy, P., Drudy, S., Lynch, K. and O'Dowd, L. (eds) *Irish Society: Sociological Perspectives* Dublin: Institute of Public Administration, pp. 90–131

—— (1997) 'The Celtic Tiger: The Role of the Multinationals' in Crowley and Mac Laughlin (eds), pp. 21–34

—— (1998) *Inside the Celtic Tiger: The Irish and the Asian Models* London: Pluto Press

O'Keeffe, C. (2003) 'Alcohol-Fuelled Street Crime Doubled Last Year, Garda Report Shows' *Examiner* 26.3.03

O'Keeffe, M. (2001) 'Citizenship, Social Inclusion and Social Partnership' Unpublished paper

O'Mahony, P. and Delanty, G. (1998) *Rethinking Irish History: Nationalism, Identity and Ideology* London: Macmillan

Omi, M. and Winant, H. (1986) *The Racial State: Racial Formation in the USA from the 1960s to the 1990s* London: Routledge

Orsi, D. (1992) 'The Religious Boundaries of an Inbetween People: Street Feste and the Problem of the Dark-Skinned Other in Italian Harlem, 1920–1990' *American Quarterly* 44(3):313–47

O'Neill, E. (1919) *The Phases of Irish History* Dublin

O'Toole, F. (1994) *Black Hole, Green Card: The Disappearance of Ireland* Dublin: New Island Books

Panayi, P. (ed.) (1996) *Racial Violence in Britain in the Nineteenth and Twentieth Centuries* London: Leicester University Press

Park, R. (1950) *Race and Culture* New York: Free Press

Parmar, P. (1982) 'Gender, Race and Class: Asian Women in Resistance' in CCCS, pp. 236–75

Parekh, B. (2000) *Rethinking Multiculturalism: Cultural Diversity and Political Theory* Basingstoke: Macmillan

Paulin, T. (2000) 'Frozen Out by the Irish' *Guardian* 29.8.00

Paz, D. (1992) *Popular Anti-Catholicism in Mid-Victorian England* Stanford, CA: Stanford University Press

Pearse, P. (1916) *The Collected Works of Pádraic H. Pearse* Dublin: Phoenix

Peres, H. (1999) 'L'Europe commence à Gibraltar: le dilemme espagnole face à l'immigration' *Pole Sud* (11):8–23, November

Petty, Sir W. (1691) *Political Anatomy of Ireland ... To which is Added Verbum sapienti* London

Phizacklea, A. (1990) *Unpacking the Fashion Industry: Gender, Racism and Class in Production* London: Routledge

Pilgrim House Foundation (1998) *Asylum Seekers and Prejudice Study*, Inch, Co. Wexford: Pilgrim House

—— (1999) *Characteristics and Experience of Asylum-seekers in Ireland*, Inch, Co. Wexford: Pilgrim House

Pollak, A. (1999) 'An Invitation to Racism? Irish Daily Newspaper Coverage of the Refugee Issue' in Kiberd D. (ed.) *Media in Ireland: The Search for Ethical Journalism* Dublin: Open Air

Pooley, C. (1977) 'The Residential Segregation of Migrant Communities in Mid-Victorian Liverpool' *Transactions of the Institute of British Geographers* 2(3)

Pred, A. (1997) 'Somebody Else, Somewhere Else: Racisms, Racialized Spaces and the Popular Geographical Imagination in Sweden' *Antipode* 29(4):383–416

—— (1998) 'Memory and the Cultural Reworking of Crisis: Racisms and the Current Moment of Danger in Sweden, or Wanting it Like Before' *Environment and Planning D: Society and Space* 16: 635–64

Preston, M. (1998) 'Discourse and Hegemony: Race and Class in the Language of Charity in Nineteenth-Century Dublin' in Foley and Ryder (eds), pp. 100–12

Proudfoot, L. (2000) 'Hybrid Space? Self and Other in Narratives of Landownership in Nineteenth-Century Ireland' *Journal of Historical Geography* 26(2) 203–21

*Public Affairs News* (2000) 'Refugees' Policy "Shambles"', February 2000

Queenan, J. (2002) 'Acting the Mick' *Irish Times Weekend* 14.9.02

Quillian, L. (1995) '"Prejudice as a Response to Perceived Group Threat": Population Composition and Anti-Immigrant and Racial Prejudice in Europe' *American Sociological Review* 60:586–612

Quinn, D.B. (1966) *The Elizabethans and the Irish* Ithaca: Cornell University Press

Quinn, D. (1999) 'Racial Mix Must be Right to Avoid an Identity Crisis' *Sunday Times* 16.5.99

—— (2002) 'Fighting the Frontier Wars Does Not Make us Racist' *Sunday Times* 29.7.02

Quinn, G. and O Mailán, C. (2001) 'Ireland' in Ter Wal (ed.)

Quintanilla, M. (forthcoming, 2003) 'Planters on the West Indian Frontier: British Settlement of the Ceded Islands, 1763–1779' *The Historian*

Räthzel, N. (2002) 'Germans into Foreigners: How Anti-Nationalism Turns into Racism' in Anthias and Lloyd (eds), pp. 78–99

Reeves, F. (1983) *British Racial Discourse: A Study of British Political Discourse about Race and Race-Related Matters* Cambridge: Cambridge University Press

Reid, P. (2002) 'Tiger Tightens Grip with Another Show of Strength' *Irish Times* 21.9.02

Renan, E. (1992 [1885]) *Qu'est-ce qu'une nation? et d'autres essais politiques* Paris: Presses Agora

Rex, J. (1970) *Race Relations in Sociological Theory* London: Weidenfeld and Nicolson

Rex, J. and Moore, R. (1967) *Race, Community, and Conflict: A Study of Sparkbrook* Oxford: Oxford University Press

Rex, J., Tomlinson, S., Hearnden, D. and Ratcliffe, P. (1969) *Colonial Immigrants in a British City: A Class Analysis* London: Routledge

Riach, D. (1976) 'Daniel O'Connell and American Anti-Slavery' *Irish Historical Studies* 20(77):3–26

Rich, P. (1993) *Race and Empire in British Politics* Cambridge: Cambridge University Press

Richards, D. (1999) *Italian American: The Racializing of an Ethnic Identity* New York: New York University Press

Ritaine, E. (1999) 'L'Enjeu migratoire, miroir de la crise politique italienne' *Pole Sud* (11):55–69

Roediger, D. (1991) *The Wages of Whiteness: Race and the Making of the American Working Class* London: Verso

Rolston, W. and Shannon, M. (2002) *Encounters: How Racism Arrived in Ireland* Belfast: Beyond the Pale

Rossa, J. O'Donovan (1898) *Rossa's Recollections, 1838–1898* Mariner's Harbour, NY: O'Donovan Rossa

Ryan, W. (1971) *Blaming the Victim* New York: Pantheon Books

Saxton, A. (1995) *The Indispensable Enemy: Labor and the Anti-Chinese Movement in California* Berkeley: University of California Press

Scheepers, P., Gijsberts, M. and Coenders, M. (2002) 'Ethnic Exclusionism in European Countries: Public Opposition to Civil Rights for Legal Migrants as a Response to Perceived Ethnic Threat' *European Sociological Review* 18(1):17–34

Schlesinger, A. (1988 [1945]) *The Age of Jackson* Boston: Little Brown

Sheehan, J. (1998) 'Early Viking Age Silver Hoards from Ireland' in Clarke, H.B., Ní Mhaonaigh, M. and O Floinn, R. (eds) *Ireland and Scandinavia in the Early Viking Age* Dublin: Four Courts Press, pp. 166–202

Sheehan, M. (1998) 'Immigrants Exploit "Irish" Baby Loophole', *Sunday Tribune* 24.5.98

Sigerson, G. (1868) *Modern Ireland* Dublin

Silke, J. (1976) 'The Irish Abroad, 1534–1691' in Moody, T.W., Martin, F.X. and Byrne, F.J. (eds) *A New History of Ireland, Vol. 3*: Oxford: Oxford University Press, pp. 591–633

Sivanandan, A. (1982) *A Different Hunger: Writings on Black Resistance* London: Pluto

—— (1985) 'RAT and the Degradation of the Black Struggle' *Race and Class* 26(4): 1–33

—— (1990) *Communities of Resistance* London: Verso

—— (2001) 'Poverty is the New Black' *Guardian* 17.8.01

—— (2002) 'The Contours of Global Racism' Speech delivered at *Crossing Borders: The Legacy of the Commonwealth Immigrants Act 1962*, London Metropolitan University, 15–16.11.02. In *Institute of Race Relations News* 26.11.02

Smith, A.E. (1947) *Colonists in Bondage: With Servitude and Convict Labor in America 1607–1776* New York: Norton

Smith, T. (1583) *De republica Anglorum*

Smyth, J. (2000) 'Tech Sector Lures Thousands of Non-EU Residents' *Irish Times – Business this Week* 8.12.00

Sniderman, P., De Figueiredo, R., Peri, P. and Piazza, T. (2000) *The Outsider: Prejudice and Politics in Italy* Princeton, NJ: Princeton University Press

Snuggs, N. (2002) 'Martin Promotes Medical Cultural Diversity Report' *Irish Times* 25.3.02

Sopemi (1988) *Trends in International Migration. Continuous Reporting System on Migration. Annual Report 1988* Paris: OEDC

SORA (2001a) 'Attitudes Towards Minority Groups in the European Union: A Special Analysis of the Eurobarometer 2000 Survey', Vienna: EUMC

SORA (2001b) 'Attitudes Towards Minority Groups in the European Union: A Special Analysis of the Eurobarometer 2000 Survey, Technical Report', Vienna: EUMC

SORA (2001c) 'Attitudes Towards Minorities in East and West Germany: A Special analysis of the Eurobarometer 2000 Survey', Vienna: EUMC

Spenser, E. (1633) *A View of the Present State of Ireland* Dublin

*Star* Lansdowne Market Research (2000) *Racism in Ireland: Special Survey* Published in *The Star* 19–20.4.00

Statewatch (2002) 'All Refugee Status to be Temporary and Terminated as Soon as Possible' Statewatch Bulletin, Press Release, 11.12.02

—— (2003) 'Asylum in the EU: The Beginning of the End?' *Statewatch News Online* 27.3.03

Stevens, P. (1998) *Rogue's March: John Riley and the St Patrick's Battalion* Dulles, VA: Brassey's

Storch, J. (1975) 'The Plague of the Blue Locusts: Police Reform and Popular Resistance in Northern England, 1840–1957' *International Review of Social History* 20:61–90

*Sunday Independent* (IMS) (2000) Survey on Refugees 30.4.00 (Irish Marketing Surveys, 27.4.00)

Sweeney, P. (1998) *The Celtic Tiger: Ireland's Economic Miracle Explained* Dublin: Oaktree Press

Swift, R. (1984) '"Another Stafford Street Row": Law, Order and the Irish Presence in Mid-Victorian Wolverhampton' *Immigrants and Minorities* 3(1):5–29

—— (2002) *Irish Migrants in Britain 1815–1914: A Documentary History* Cork: Cork University Press

Swift, R. and Gilley, S. (eds) (1985) *The Irish in the Victorian City* London: Croom Helm

—— (eds) (1989) *The Irish in Britain, 1815–1939* Savage MD: Barnes and Noble

Synon, M.-E. (2000) 'Racism Smear Reveals Elitist Press Contempt' *Sunday Independent* 30.4.00

Taguieff, P.-A. (1990a) 'The New Cultural Racism in France' *Telos* (83): 111–22

—— (1990b) *La Force du Préjugé: essais sur le racisme et ses doubles* Paris: Gallimard

Tannam, M. (2002) 'Questioning Irish Anti-Racism' in Lentin and McVeigh, pp. 193–210

Task Force on the Travelling Community (1995) *Report of the Task Force on the Travelling Community* Dublin: Government Publications

Ter Wal, J. (ed.) (2001) *Racism and Cultural Diversity in the Media*, EUMC, Vienna.

Thatcher, M. (1978) BBC interview (as leader of the opposition) 30.1.78

Tinker, H. (1974) *A New System of Slavery: The Export of Indian Labour Overseas, 1830–1920* Oxford: Oxford University Press

Trade Union Congress (1999) *Black and Excluded: Black and Asian Workers in the 1990s* London: TUC

—— (2000a) *Qualifying for Racism* London: TUC

—— (2000b) *Tackling Racism* London: TUC

—— (2000c) *Resisting Racism at Work* London: TUC

Travelling People Review Body (1983) *Report of the Travelling People Review Body* Dublin: Government Publications

Troyna, B. and Hatcher, R. (1992) *Racism in Children's Lives: A Study of Mainly White Primary Schools* London: Routledge

Tynan, M. (1997) 'Immigrants to be Vetted at Entry Points from Britain' *Irish Times* 26.6.97

UNHCR (2002) *Number of Asylum Applications Submitted in 30 Industrialized Countries, 1992–2001*. Available on the UNHCR website

Valarasan-Toomey, M. (1998) *The Celtic Tiger: From the Outside Looking In* Dublin: Blackhall

Wade, P. (1997) *Race and Ethnicity in Latin America* London: Pluto Press

Walter, B. (2000) *Outsiders Inside: Whiteness, Place, and Irish Women* London: Routledge

Ward, T. (2001) *Immigration and Residency in Ireland* Dublin: City of Dublin Vocational Education Committee

Waters, J. (1997) *An Intelligent Person's Guide to Modern Ireland* London: Duckworth

Waters, J. (1998) 'Irish Racism Expresses Collective Sense of Our Own Identity' *Irish Times* 27.1.98

Watt, P. (1998) *Refugees and Asylum Seekers in Ireland – The Potential of Community Development Strategie*s Dublin: Combat Poverty Agency

Weber, M. (1978) *Economy and Society* Vol. I (eds/tr. Roth, G. and Wittich, C.) Berkeley: University of California Press

West, S. (ed.) (1996) *The Victorians and Race* Aldershot: Scholar Press

Westwood, S. and Phizacklea, A. (2000) *Trans-Nationalism and the Politics of Belonging* London: Routledge

Whelan, K. (1996) *The Tree of Liberty: Radicalism, Catholicism and the Construction of Irish Identity, 1760–1830* Cork: Cambridge University Press/Field Day

White, H. (1985) *Tropics of Discourse: Essays in Cultural Criticism* Baltimore: Johns Hopkins University Press

White, L. (2002) 'This Ghetto is the Home of a Racial Minority in Oldham. Its Residents are White People' *Sunday Times Magazine* 13.1.02, pp. 46–54

Wieviorka, M. (1993) 'Tendencies to Racism in Europe: Does France Represent a Unique Case or is it Representative of a Trend?' in Solomos, J. and Wrench, J. (eds) *Migration in Western Europe* Oxford: Berg, pp. 53–66

—— (1995) *The Arena of Racism* London: Sage

—— (1998) 'Is Multiculturalism the Solution?' *Ethnic and Racial Studies* 21(5):881–910

Williams, E. (2003) 'Professionals Refuse to Disclose Earnings' *Sunday Independent* 26.1.03

Williams, J. J. (1932) *Whence the Black Irish of Jamaica?* New York: Dial Press

Williams, R. (1961) *Culture and Society, 1780–1950* London: Penguin

Winant, H. (1994) *Racial Conditions: Politics, Theory, Comparisons* Minneapolis: University of Minnesota Press

Wrench, J., Rea, A. and Ouali, N. (1999) *Migrants, Ethnic Minorities and the Labour Market: Integration and Exclusion in Europe (Migration, Minorities, and Citizenship)* London: Palgrave

Young, R. (1995) *Colonial Desire: Hybridity in Theory, Culture and Race* London: Routledge

Yuval-Davis, N. (1997) *Gender and Nation (Politics and Culture)* London: Sage

# Index

abolitionism, 91, 98 (*see also*
    Appendix 2 (256–7)
Act of Union, 115
Africans, 9, 37, 62, 65, 71, 72, 171,
    184, 244, 262 n
  in Caribbean, 83, 84, 85, 217
  comparison with the Irish, 74,
    83–4, 124–5, 127, 150
  comparison with Southern
    Italians and European
    migrants, 190–2
agency, 132–3
AIDS, 177–8, 250
Akenson, Donald, 88, 92
Aliens Act, 156
Allen, Kieran, 46–7, 49, 204
Allen, Theo, 101, 103
Amnesty International, 60, 64, 144,
    156, 238
Anglo-Saxons, 31, 77, 110, 116,
    119, 127, 135, 150–2, 207, 29
  Anglo-saxonism, 102, 109,
    124–8, 152, 189
Anthias, Floya, 8, 158–9
anthropometry, 11
anti-abolitionism, 95, 98
anti-discrimination legislation,
  European, 20
  Irish, 64, 146, 156, 220
anti-racism, 3, 159–60, 162, 198
  in Ireland, 199–224
  internationalism, 219–20
  minority organisations, 216
  prospects, 221–2
  Socialist Workers' Party, 215
  support groups, 215
Anti-Racism Campaign, 215
anti-Semitism, 24, 25, 59–60, 133,
    142–4, 151, 172, 232–3, 236,
    *see also*, Lentin, Ronit
Antigua, 82, 86
ARASI, 216
Aston Villa, 238

Arnold, Matthew, 126, 128, 152
asylum, 140–1
asylum-seekers, 49, 68, 141, 156,
    159–66, 211, 244
  AIDS testing, 177–8
  appeals, 55, 164–5
  applications, 55–6, 239
  fingerprinting, 213, 250
  link with Travellers and Jews,
    147, 181–2, 227, 233, 245
  media, 164
  mobility, 249
  nationalities, 55–6
  reproduction, 179
  right to work, 161
  spending on, 174, 230, 252
  statistics, 49
*Atlantic Monthly*, 94, 98
attitudinal surveys, 59–68, 141,
    186–8
  disturbing presence of minorities,
    61–2
  minority experiences, 64–5
  political opinions, 67
  *see also* opinion polls, Appendix
    1 (256–7)
Australia, 49, 131, 136, 241
Australian aboriginals, 147

Babb, Phil, 238
Balibar, Etienne, 20, 182, 202, 206
Barbados, 82–6
Barker, Martin, 14
Barret, Francie, 237
Barrett, James, and Roediger, David,
    100, 102, 111
Bauman, Zygmunt, 9, 14, 167
Beckles, Hilary, 84–6
Beddoe, John, 125, 265 n
Belfast, 30, 156, 217
Belgium, 1, 188
Benjamin, Walter, 201
Benoît, Alain de, 170

Besant, Annie, 137, 219
Bewley, Charles, 143
Bhamjee, Moses, 142
Biology
  birth rates, 178–80
  link between appearance and
    culture, 10–16, 71, 93–4, 171,
    198, 232
  relationship with the social,
    8–16, 69, 123, 134–5, 207
  physical and social sciences, 11
black Americans, 91, 189
  comparison with the Irish, 98,
    105
  conflict with the Irish, 91, 95,
    99–103, 132
  support for struggle, 202, 218
  in the workforce, 101–2
  in the army, 104
black feminism, 18
black people in Ireland, 141–2,
  155–8, 237–9
Blanqui, Auguste, 201
'Bloody Sunday', 242
Bloom, Leopold, 232
Blueshirts, 151
Blunkett, David, 213
Boate brothers, 76, 79
Boemus, Johannes, 76, 81
Boers, 137, 202
Bolger, Dermot, 238
Book of Invasions, 69
Borghezio, Mario, 177
Bourdieu, Pierre, 11, 211, 219, 223,
  250
Boyce, George, 72, 127
Boyle, Dan, 205
Brah, Avtar, 3, 58, 141, 158–9, 167,
  197, 243, see also diaspora
  space
Brazil, 58
British Empire, 125
  Dominions, 135–6
  experiences of Irish people,
    129–30, 137, 217, 241
  relationship with Irish
    nationalism, 136–8
  role in generating racism, 31,
    131–9, 242

British Guiana, 86
Bryce, James, 16–17
budgetary policy, 43–4
Butler, Hubert, 202, 219, 270 n
Butler-Cullingford, Elizabeth, 69

Cambrensis, Giraldus, 72, 145
Campion, Edmund, 75, 77
Canny, Nicholas, 75–6
Carlyle, Thomas, 72, 172
Carmichael, Stokely, 22
Carmin, Baron de, 117
Caribbean,
  Irish in the, 81–8, 217
  revolts, 85–6, 217
  and Scots, 82
  statistics, 82
Cascarino, Tony, 238
Casement, Roger, 130, 202, 219
Castlebar, 157
Catholic Citizen, 107, 110
Catholic Emancipation Act, 115,
  116
Catholicism, 80, 158, 172, 200, 218,
  236
  anti-Catholicism, 91–2, 95,
    114–17, 124, 127–8
  as basis for foreign allegiance, 85,
    93–4, 115
Catholics, 73–4, 87–8, 100, 124,
  150, 170, 218, 233, 248
  Church in America, 101, 103–4
  Church in Britain, 117
  Church in Spain, 184
  Church and anti-semitism,
    143–4, 151
  demography, 179
  GAA, 153
  immigrants to America, 91–2, 95,
    109, 189
  immigrants to Britain, 114–17,
  role in nationalism, 148–9
Celtic FC, 238
Celts, 31, 69, 72, 77, 98, 119,
  126–7, 133, 135, 207
Celtic 'race', 79–80, 93–4, 123–8,
  132, 150–2, 171
Celticism, 152–3
Census 2002 (Ireland), 50

Census Amendment Act (UK), 49
Central America, 218
Childers, Erskine, 136
Chinese, 57, 95, 102, 111, 155, 184
Christianity 8, 9, 184
    and anti-racism, 160
    contrast with paganism, 78, 81,
        89
    justification of slavery, 9
    symbolism of colours 8–9, 71, 89
Choctaw Club (New Orleans), 101
Churubusco, Battle of, 104
Cincinnati Repeal Association, 91
citizenship, 187, 212, 213–14,
        229–30, 239–40, 273 n
Citizenship Act, 229, 240
civilisation contrasted with
        barbarity, 14, 75, 77–9, 105–6,
        171, 188–9, 247, 250
Clare County Council (in relation
        to Traveller accommodation),
        25, 54, 145, 231, see also
        Fanning, Bryan
    planning regulations, 230, 271 n
Clogheen (Co. Tipperary), 210, 230,
        271 n
Cole, Jeffrey, 187, 192–3, see also
        racism in Italy
'Colour line', 155–8
Comhlámh, 220
Common Travel Area, 164, 214
Concern, 220
Connaught Rangers, 130, 133
Connaught/Ulster (province), 61–2,
Connolly, James, 152, 200, 202
conquest and colonisation
    of Ireland, 8, 16, 25, 26, 29,
        74–81, 140, 171, 233
    of New World, 9, 77, 78
Conservative Party, 127
Constitution (Irish), 229, 233,
        239–40
Corcoran, Mary, 159, 233
Cork, 156, 157, 177
Coote, Eyre, 130
Coughlan, Patricia, 72, 78, 79
Cousins, Margaret, 137, 202, 220,
        270 n (see also internationalism)
craniology, 11, 93

Craton, Michael, 84–5
Creagh, Fr., 143, see also Limerick
        Redemptorists
Crime, 48, 227, 260 n,
Cronin, Mike, 153–4
Cuba, 82, 87

Danes, 80, 140, 207
D'Arcy M'Gee, Thomas, 150–1
Darwin, Charles, 12, 125
data collection, 48–9
Davies, John, 72
Davin, Maurice, 153
Davis, Thomas, 148–9
Decision magazine, 176
Delaney, Pat, 176
Democratic Party (US) 95, 98, 99,
        100–1, 103
Denmark, 41, 67
    presidency of the EU, 199, 213
Department of Enterprise, Trade
        and Employment, 52–3, 163,
        204, see also work permits,
        work visas)
Department of Justice, 55–7, 163–4,
        220
    'direct provision', 174
    'dispersal' programme, 61, 210
    Minister, 163, 239–40
Desmond, Humphrey, 110
Despard, Edward, 202, 217–18
'diaspora space', 141, 158–67, 197
Dillon, John, 136
Donegal, 79
Douglass, Frederick, 99, 158, 218
DR Congo, 56 (see also Zaire)
Draft Riots (New York, 1863), 30,
        95, 103, 104 (see also New York)
Dublin, 44, 47, 67, 141, 156, 177,
        179, 230, 238
Dublin Convention, 166
Duffy, Eoin, 151
Durkheimian sociology, 48, 228

Economic and Social Research
        Institute (ESRI), 43,
Economy, 35
    basis for racist ideology, 226–9,
        267 n

economic boom, 33–4, 35–48,
    235, 244
growth sectors, 36–8, 45, 176, 235
'hand of God', 252
relationship between GDP and
    GNP, 36, 39, *see also* Glossary
    (254)
relationship of profits to wages, 46
US contribution to, 36, 39
transfer-pricing, 39
El Ejido, 184
Elchardus, Mark, 32
Emmet, Robert, 148, 218
employment
    levels, 36, 38
    men in, 41, 46, 118–19
    migrants in, 174–5, 195, *see also*
        'New racism'
    part-time, 40–3, 46, 58
    precariousness, 195
    temporary, 40–2, 58
    women in, 40–1, 46, 58, 119
    *see also* work permits
Employment Act, 210
Employment Equality Act, 220
Engels, Friedrich, 72, 119, 259 n
England, 218
English,
    in Caribbean, 83–89
    in Ireland, 74–81, 89–90, 100,
        140, 207
    workers, 117–23
Enlightenment, the,
    ideas on 'race' 9, 93, 171
    justification of slavery, 10
Equal Status Act, 64, 146, 220, *see*
    *also* anti-discrimination
    legislation
Equality Authority, 64, 145, 220
Equiano, Olaudah, 158, 217
Esmonde, Sir Thomas, 137
eugenics, 13, 189
European Council directives, 21
European Economic Area (EEA), 52,
    68, 213
European Union, 166, 214
    distinction between EU/EEA and
        non-EU/EEA nationals, 165,
        184–5, 212–3, 240, 250

enlargement, 210
refugee status, 199, 212–13
role of US, 212
security dimension of
    immigration policy, 212–14
unaccountable bodies, 212
'white lists', 213
Evans, Estyn, 140
*Evening Standard*, 194

Fajujonu (ruling), 239
Famine Irish (migrants), 92, 94,
    102, 115, 118, 160, 165, 177
Fanning, Bryan, 25, 64, 145
Fanon, Frantz, 245
far-Right political parties, 14, 15,
    169, 182–4, 188, 198, 232
    absence of in Ireland, 32
FAS, 52
Fenianism, 107, 117, 126
Fennelly J, 240
Fianna Fáil, 32, 229
fictive ethnicity, 206, *see also*
    Balibar
Fine Gael, 33, 177–8
Finlay, Peter, 165
Finlay, Fr. Thomas, 143
France, 12, 32, 33, 41, 55, 169, 174,
    182–3, 188
    Islam, 170
Frank, Anne, 249
French in Caribbean, 86–7
Front national, 182, 198, 199

GAA, 153–4, 229, 237, 270–1 n
Gaels, 69, 71, 76, 140, 207
    cultural dominance, 140, 143,
        147, 158, 200, 207, 248
    Gaelic conquest, 72
    Gaelic customs and culture, 76–7,
        152
    Gaelic League, 207
    Gaelic language, 148, 172, 207
    Gaelic Revival, 149, 172
    physical appearance, 77
    *see also* cultural nationalism
Gaelic games *see* GAA
Galton, Francis, 13
Gardai, 48, 64–6
    Garda National Immigration
        Bureau, 213

Garvey, Marcus, 202
Genesis (Book of), 9
genocides, 180, 206
Germany, 12, 174, 210
    *gastarbeiter* system, 175
Gibbons, Luke, 128–9, 131–4, 208,
    219
Gilley, Sheridan, 128–9
Gilman, Sander, 142
Gilroy, Paul, 5, 6, 19, 198
Glasgow, 116, 119–20
Goldberg, Gerald, 142
Gobineau, Arthur de, 11, 13, 124
Goldhagen, David, 142
Goldring, Maurice, 148
Goldstone, Katrina, 26
Gogarty, St John, 151
Good Friday/Belfast Agreement, 29,
    229
Gralton, Jim, 219
Gramsci, Antonio, 22, 226, 234,
    259–60 n
Gray, Breda, 159
Greece, 28, 41, 183
Greenock, 116, 119
Griffith, Arthur, 99, 136, 143, 148,
    151, 172

Hall, Stuart, 17, 19, 129, 197,
    225–6
    articulation, 17, 225–6, 234–6
Hamilton, Charles, 22
Hargreaves, Alec, 199
Harmony, 215
Harney, Mary, 163, 175, 176, 260 n
*Harper's Weekly*, 98, 125
Hart, Bill, 141, 158, 217
Haughey, Charles, 80, 207
Hickman, Mary, 26, 64 n
historians, 72, 216, 242–3
Hobsbawm (Eric), and Ranger
    (Terence), 243
Home Rule, 126–8, 135–8, 147
house prices, 47–8, 230, 252
    and incomes, 47
Howe, Stephen, 137, 242–3
Hughton, Chris, 238
Huxley, Thomas, 126
Hyde, Douglas, 152

identities
    collective, 8, 20, 186–97, 243
    combination, 7–8, 18–19, 166, 186
Ignatiev, Noel, 103
Illegal Immigration Act, 164
Immigrant Solidarity, 215
Immigration into Ireland, 28, 50–9,
    141, 176, 211
    cartoons on, 162, 194–5
    debates over, 160–7, 244
    illegal, 155, 164, 194–5
Immigration Act, US (1924) 13, 92,
    111, 189
Immigration Control Platform, 32,
    177, 195, 260 n
income disparities, 42–4, 205
    and budgets, 43–4
    and 'poor workers', 45
    regional dimensions, 44–5
indentured labour, 81, 83–5, 88
India, 130, 137, 202
Indian National Congress, 202
Indians, 59, 62, 132, 184
Indian wars, 104–5, *see also* Native
    Americans
Industrial Development Agency
    (IDA) Ireland, 42, 59
Ingolsby, Brian, 57 (*see also*
    Department of Justice)
*Inside Cork*, 174
Iraqis, 242
Irish-born children, 57, 178–9,
    239–40
Irish Commission for Justice and
    Peace, 160
Irish Communist Party, 219
Irish diaspora, 18, 25–6, 28, 138,
    158, 240, 241, 243, 248
    Caribbean, 86–9
    missionaries, 82, 88, 130
    soccer, 238
    soldiers, 104, 130
    USA, 73, 86, 89, 105–13, 138
Irish nationalism, 23–4, 106–7, 112,
    134, 137, 147
    contribution to Irish racism,
    147–55, 200–24, 219
    cultural nationalism, 79–80, 107,
    132, 134, 138, 143, 171

erasures, 243–4
links with Third World nation-
    alisms, 137, 241–2
'Irish 'race'', 2, 69–73, 152
    blood, 71, 178
    borders, 140, 167, 178, 200–1,
        207–9
    community, 208–9
    comparison with British, 109–10,
        171, 201
    construction of by Irish
        Americans, 105–13,
    Irish American response to
        Spanish American War,
        109–10,
    martial prowess, 110, 153
    origins and debates, 140, see also
        Milesians, Phoenicians,
        Normans, Vikings, Danes
    Race Conventions, 95
Irish Refugee Council, 164–5, 252
Irish Republican Army (IRA), 219
    Continuity IRA, 229
    Real IRA, 229
Irish Star, 60, 162
Irish Sun, 180
Irish Times, 4, 174
Irish World, 107, 109
Israelites in Egypt, 160, 179
Italians, 188–92
    attitudes, 187–92
    in US, 189
Italy, 28, 67, 168, 183, 187–92
    racism in, 177, 185–8, 189–92, 199

Jacob, Rosemary, 220
Jacobson, Matthew, 6
    'race' as palimpsest, 6, 111, 236
    definition of whiteness, 92, 127,
        231–2
    popular Irish American culture,
        108–10
Jamaica, 84, 86
Jeffery, Keith, 130
Jensen, Richard, 107, see also 'No
    Irish need apply'
Jews, 59, 62, 107, 142–3, 171, 172,
    184, 194, 219
    economic activities, 236

numbers in Ireland, 142
whiteness, 232–3, 235–7
Johnson, Tom, 125 (see also trade
    unions in Ireland)
judges
    and racist comments, 157
    and Supreme Court, 240
    see also individual entries

Keane, Michael, 87, 217
Keating, Geoffrey, 72
Kenmare, 231
Kenny, J, 157, see also Castlebar
Kenny, Mary, 71
Kiberd, Declan, 241
Know-Nothings, 98, 107, 108
Knox, Robert, 93, 124–5
Kropotkin, Peter, 12

labour force
    control of, 81, 82–8, 118–19,
        175–7, 212, 223
    labour supply, 37, 260 n
labour market, 33, 36, 163, 188,
    210, 212, 220
    dual, 175, 192, 195
    in nineteenth-century Britain,
        114, 118–23
    in nineteenth-century US, 95, 99,
        100–3
    three-tier, 58
Labour Party (Ireland), 33, 163, 252
Lally, Thomas, 130
Lancashire, 117, 119
landholding, 73, 76, 86, 233
Las Casas, 9, 77
Latvia, 54
Leader, 143
Lebow, Ned, 125
Leeward Islands 82, 83, see also
    Caribbean, and individual
    islands
Lega Nord, 177
Lenin, 223, 226
Lentin, Alanna, 215
Lentin, Ronit, 24–6, 144
    Irish attitudes toward migration,
        24, 195, 233
    multiculturalism, 24

Ligon, Jean, 84
Limerick, 249
  attacks on Jews, 130, 151
  Redemptorists, 130, 143
Lindsay Tribunal, 178
Linebaugh (Peter) and Rediker
  (Marcus), 94, 117
Linnaeus, 9
Lithuania, 54
Liverpool, 116, 119–20, 122
Lloyd, David, 131, 155, 201, 203,
  221–2, 245
London, 116, 218
Longford, 157, *see also* Neilan J
Luxembourg, 41
*Lyceum*, 143
Lynott, Philip, 142, 238

Mac an Ghaill, Mairtín, 8, 26, 27
Mac Laughlin, Jim, 24, 79, 145, 183
Mac Neill, Eoin, 134, 219
MacPherson, Sir William, 21–2
Magnus, Olaus, 76
Man, Albon, 101–2, 103
Manchester United, 238
Marathon (oil company), 251
Martin, Micheál, 71, 179–80, 207
Marxism, 7, 18, 195
Massy, Richard Tuthill, 125–6
maternity, 178–81
Mau Mau, 242
McCraild, Don, 126–7
McDonagh, Thomas, 134, 219
McGrath, Paul, 239
Mc Gréil, Fr. Micheál, 59–60, 62, 68,
  143
McGuiness J, 240
McKay, Claude, 202
McKenna, Dr Peter, 179
McManus, Liz, 159
McMaster, Neil, 142
McVeigh, Robbie, 22–3, 112, 195,
  208, 215
Meagher, Thomas, 105
media, 68, 164, 199, 268 n (*see also*
  individual newspapers)
Mégret, Bruno, 182, *see also* far-
  Right parties
*Metro Eireann*, 216
Mexican War, 104

migrant workers, 18, 58
  comparison between Irish and
    Italian emigrants in US, 188–9
  economic migrants, 165, 181, 235
  health, 118, 177–80, 268 n, *see
    also* 'New Racism'
  in Italy, 192
  returning migrants, 51–2
  status in Ireland, 163, 211
  women, 159
migration, 15, 175, 182, 245
  emigration from Ireland, 25,
    51–2, 58, 92, 233, 244, 246
  migration to the US, 92–5, 160–1,
    183, 188–9, 211, 233
  migration to Britain, 114, 116,
    117–18
  waves in history, 15, 235
  *see also* 'diaspora space',
    Immigration into Ireland
Miles, Robert, 5, 6, 7, 19
Milesians, 69, 72, 126, 140
Miller, Kerby, 101
Miss Ireland, 73
Mitchel, John, 99, 112, 150
Moldova, 56
Molly Maguires, 211
Montagu, Ashley, 4
Montserrat, 82, 85, 87
Moors, 184
Moore, Colleen, 111–12,
Moran, D.P., 143, 148, 151, 207
Morash, Chris, 152–3
Morrison, Toni, 106, 244
Morton, Samuel, 11, 94
Moryson, Fynes, 72
Mosney, 231, 271 n
Munster, 62
  massacres in, 76
Mumba, Samantha, 237
Murphy, William, 117, *see also* 'No
  Popery'
Muslims, 61–2, 170, 184, 194
Myers, Kevin, 70–1
Myshall (Co. Carlow) 210, 271 n

National Consultative Committee
  on Racism and
  Interculturalism, 220

Nationalism, 23, 206–7
   as ideology contributing to
      racism, 23–4, 31, 32, 69–73,
      134, 147–55, 200–24
   British, 31, *see also* Empire
   relationship of nationalism to
      other struggles, 155, 200–24
Native Americans, 95, 104–5, 138
   comparison with the Irish, 74–5,
      81, 105, 126, 146
Nazism, 1, 171, 232
Negra, Diana, 111
Neilan J, 157
neo-liberalism, 3, 223, 250, 252
Nevis, 82
New English, 73, 76, 78, *see also*
      Protestantism
'New' Racism, 3, 14–16, 81, 168–83,
      194–7
   culture used as surrogate for
      'race', 14, 169, 183
   link with migration, 168–9
   nationalism, 15
New York, 92, 94–5, 101, 104
   press, 99
   *see also* Draft Riots
Nigerians, 56, 59, 156, 249
Ní Chonaill, Aíne, 195
Ní Shuínéar, Sinéad, 26, 135, 145,
      172, 233 (*see also* Travellers)
'No Irish need apply', 107–8, *see*
      *also* Irish diaspora, Jensen
Noonan, Michael, 178
'No Popery', 117, 123
Normans, 69, 71, 77, 80, 116, 140,
      207
Northern Ireland, 29–30, 49, 80,
      141, 179, 229

O'Brien, J.M., 135
O'Callaghan, Joe, 157
Oceanworld (Dingle), 140
O'Carroll, Paddy, 208–10, 215, 222,
      *see also* Irish 'race' as
      community
O'Connell, Daniel, 91, 148, 150,
      202, 218
O'Donnell, Liz, 163
O'Donoghue, John, 163

O'Donovan Rossa, Jeremiah, 109
O'Faoláin, Sean, 69, 207
O'Flynn, Noel, 157
O'hAilpin, Sean og, 237
O'Higgins, Bernardo, 130
Old English, 73, 76
Omi, Michael, 6
opinion polls,
   European, 15–16, 60, 251
   Irish, 27, 59–68, 141, 156, 162, 193
   methodology, 65–7, 186–7
   *see also* attitudinal surveys,
      Appendix 1 (256–7)
Orange Order, 120, 124, 127
Order of Caucasians, 95, 102
O'Reilly, Alejandro, 87, 130, *see also*
      Spanish Empire, Cuba
Orsi, Daniel, 188, 189
O'Toole, Fintan, 26, 105
O'Toole, Joe, 210

Papal Aggression, 117
Park, Robert, 16–17
Partnership agreements, 203–6
   dates of, 270 n
   Programme for Prosperity and
      Fairness (PPF), 203, 205
   Sustaining Progress, 203–4
   (*see also* Social partnership)
Paz, Donald, 114, 124, 128
Pearse, Pádraic, 134–5
Penal Laws, 80
Pennsylvania, 92, 211
Phelan, Terry, 238
Philadelphia, 103
Philippines, 54, 58, 133, *see also*
      Spanish–American War
Phoenicians, 69, 140
*Phoenix*, 162
phrenology, 11, 93
Pilgrim House, 161
police, 122–3 (*see also* Gardai)
political violence, 29
Pondichery, Battle of, 130
Poor Law, 118
Portugal, 28, 183, 184–5
poverty, 45–7, 228–9, *see also*
      Glossary (254–5)
   and disease, 118

Presbyterians, 92, 115, 217
Progressive Democrats, 163
Protestantism, 75, 77–8, 115,
        116–17, 123
    Calvinism, 76,
    Protestant Associations, 117, 123,
        124, 147
Protestants (Irish), 91–2, 94, 127,
        143, 190, 207
    role in Irish nationalism, 148–9
*Punch*, 125, 194

Quarterly National Household
        Survey (QNHS), 40, 49, 50
Queenan, Joe, 73
Quinn, D.B., 146

'race'
    as a palimpsest *see* Jacobson
    development of idea of 'race', 5–16
    in Irish academia, 22–34, 243–4
    relationship with culture, 10, 11,
        14, 75, 89, 129, 135, 169–70,
        *see also* 'New Racism'
    scientific invalidity of concept, 3–8
'Race' Relations, 14, 16, 168
racialisation, 128, 227
    of the Irish, 2, 27, 71–90, 142,
        147–55, 171, 225–46, 247–8
    of the Irish in America, 91–113
    of the Irish in Britain, 115–29,
    of nomadic groups, 29, 131, 135,
        142, 145–6 , 171–2, 181
    of 'Others', 74, 89, 106, 110–13,
        138, 141–2, 165, 190, 194, 219,
        227, 235, 240, 243, 248
    of Southern Italians, 188–92
    of white migrant workers in
        Europe, 55, 190, 240
racism,
    anti-Irish, 1, 111, 115, 123,
        127–9, 174, 242–3
    anti-Traveller, 23, 24–5, 60, 144–7
    definitions, 16, 19–20, 190, 247
    and difference, 198
    institutional, 20–1, 33, 234, 249
    Irish, 1, 22–34, 59, 100–3, 131,
        133, 138, 141–2, 155–9,
        173–83, 193–7, 225–46, 251

and mobility, 249
    working class, 186–8
rape, 180
Räthzel, Nora, 210
Redesdale, Lord, 127
Redmond, Willie, 137
Refugee Act, 164
refugees, 55–6, 61, 68, 160, 193,
        244
    former Yugoslavia, 164
    Hungarian, 25
    Jewish in World War II, 143
religious divisions, 72, 73 (*see also*
        Old English, New English)
Remond, Lenox, 158, 218
Remond, Sarah, 218
Renan, Ernest, 201
Republican Party (US) 95, 98
Rex, John, 16–17
Riley, John, 104
Residents Against Racism, 215
Ritaine, Evelyne, 185
Roche, James, 110
Rolston, Bill, and Shannon,
        Michael, 25, 26, 112, 137, 195,
        218
Roma, 56, 66, 67, 171, 181
Romanians, 56, 60–1, 180, 194,
        210, 267 n
Roosevelt, Theodore, 189
rootlessness and rootedness, 24, 25,
        80, 119, 143, 181, 232, 245,
        251
Rosslare, 194, 210, 230, 271 n
Russia, 12, 179
Ryan, Frederick, 134, 202, 219

Salisbury, Lord, 127
San Patricios, 104, 132, 219, *see also*
        St Patrick's Battalion
Saville Enquiry, 242
Schengen,
    Agreements, 183–4, 212
    Zone, 212–14
science,
    role in racist ideologies, 10–14,
        92–3
Scotland, 124
    Irish in, 115, 116

Scots, 69, 80, 82, 85, 100, 120, 140
Scythians, 76
Sepulveda, 9
Sexuality see also 'New Racism'
    of minorities, 180–1
Shatter, Alan, 142
Shaw, George Bernard, 69
Sheridan, General Philip, 104–5
Sherlock, Jason, 237
Sicilians, 187–8, 189, 192
Sigerson, George, 134, 207
simianisation
    of the Irish, 98, 125
    of Africans, 98, 125
Sinn Féin, 147, 220, 229
Sivanandan, A., 17, 55, 171
slave holding, 84, 88, 132
slave trade, 9, 10, 82, 98
slavery, 9, 83–8, 98
    contested meanings, 99–100, 138
Smith, Sir Thomas, 72, 75, 78
Sniderman, Paul, 190–2
soccer, 192, 238
    black players in Italy, 192
    Irish identity, 238
Social Darwinism, 12, 109
social distance (surveys), 60, 261 n
Social Partnership, 203–6, 222, see
    also Partnership agreements
    Community (and Voluntary)
        Pillar, 203–5
pillars, 203
social space and racism, 24, 30–1,
    48, 65, 67, 89, 146, 229–31
    residential segregation, 95,
        98–100, 122
Somalia, 56
South Africa, 20, 58, 136
South West region, 44–5
Southern and Western European
    Periphery (SWP), 55, 57, 183–6
Spain, 28, 41, 183, 184
Spanish Empire, 82, 87, 130, 242
Spanish–American Wars, 109–10,
    133, 137, 138, see also Irish
    diaspora
Spencer, Herbert, 12

Spenser, Edmund, 72, 75, 76, 77,
    79, see also View of the Present
    State of Ireland
Stapleton, Governor William
    (Leeward Islands), 82, 87
status
    confusion over status of
        individuals, 67, 155–8, 163,
        179, 193, 194
    consequences for life chances,
        234–5
    Ireland's national status, 135–7,
        241–3
St Christopher (island), 82, see also
    St Kitts
St Kitts, 85, see also St Christopher
St Patrick's Battalion, 104, see also
    San Patricios
St Vincent, 87
Stephen Lawrence Inquiry, 21
Stockport 117, 118
    riot, 117
Sullivan, A.M., 135
Sun, 162
Sunday Tribune, 178
Supreme Court rulings on residency
    rights, 178, 213–14, 239–40,
    251–2
Swift, Roger, 122

Taguieff, Pierre-André 170
Tammany Hall, 95
Tannam, Marian, 215
Tartars, 76, 81
Tax, 46–7, 211, 227–8, 251–2
Taylor, Mervyn, 142
Thatcher, Margaret, 169
Theories of racism,
    general, 16–22, 90, see also 'New
        Racism'
    in Irish context, 22–34, 81, 142,
        181–3, 225–46
    linked to economic growth, 33,
        35–48, 68
    relationship with class, 16–19,
        188, 196–7, 225–9, 234–6
    xeno-racism, 55, 171
Tipperary (County), 249
Tone, Wolfe, 148, see also United
    Irishmen

Trade Unions
  European level, 211
  German, 210
  Irish 203–4, 210–11
  Irish participation in abroad, 102, 211
Tramore, 231
transhumance farming, 76, 80, 171
Travellers, 26, 90
  anti-racist organisations, 215–16
  attacks on, 29–30
  attitudes toward, 59–60, 62–4, 144–5, 147, 172, 244
  Citizen Traveller project, 62, 64
  DTEDG, 215
  ethnicity, 26, 63, 67, 145–6
  fear of attack, 64
  legislation affecting, 146, 230–1
  other nomadic groups, 146
  state intervention, 144–5, 231
  Task Force on, 144
Trinidad, 86–8
Trocaire, 220

Ukraine, 56
Ulster, massacres in, 76
Unionism, 31, 134
Unionists, 69, 136–7, 151, 179
United Ireland, 127, 154
United Irishman, 143, 153
United Irishmen, 116, 148, 202, 217
United Kingdom, 55, 169, 170, 188, 198–9, 226
universalism, 192, 220–2, 250

vagabondage, 74
vagrancy, 74
View of the Present State of Ireland, 77, 79, see also Spenser, Edmund
Vikings, 69, 71, 72, 77, 141
Vintners' Association, 64, 146
Virginia, 82, 92

Wales, 114, 116, 123, 124
Walsh, Ger, 180–1, 230, see also Wexford People

Welfare and minorities, 15, 160–1, 173–4, 235
Weber, Max, 7, 228
  markets, 17
  Weberian sociology, 7, 17, 167, 228, 250
Wexford, 180–1, 230
Wexford People, 180–1, 230
White, Hayden, 77
Whiteness, 18, 23, 98, 242–3
  becoming white, 2, 27, 28–9, 94, 111–13
  division of white 'race' into groups, 11, 81–90, 93, 124, 52
  class, 169, 187–8
  contrast with blackness, 8, 26, 71, 82–90, 100, 106, 112, 142, 189, 198, 241, 244
  of Empire's dominant groups, 135–8, 153, 241–2
  invisibility, 232, 249
  of the Irish, 71–3, 82–90, 98, 103, 107, 136, 150, 202, 232, 242–3, 248
  of migrant workers in the Americas, 82–90, 106, 111–12, 132, 150, 189
  of migrant workers in Europe, 55, 90, 168, 190
  symbolism in Christianity, 8–9,
  US constitution, 92
  use of by trade unions, 102
  voting bloc, 101
Wieviorka, Michel, 193
Wildness
  of people, 77–9, 94, see also barbarity
  of terrain, 78–80
Willoughby, Governor (Jamaica), 86
Winant, Howard, 6
Wolverhampton, 122–3
work permits, 52–3, 57, 58, 163, 175
work visa, 52–3, 163, 175

Young Ireland, 148, 218

Zaire, 179